HEALTH AND FITNESS IN THE WORKPLACE

Health Education in Business Organizations

Edited by
Samuel H. Klarreich

PRAEGER

New York
Westport, Connecticut
London

Library of Congress Cataloging-in-Publication Data

Health and fitness in the workplace

    Includes bibliographies and index.
      1. Industrial hygiene. 2. Health education.
3. Health promotion. I. Klarreich, Samuel H.
[DNLM: 1. Health Education. 2. Health Promotion.
3. Occupational Health Services. 4. Physical Fitness.
WA 412 H4332]
RC969.H43H43 1987   613.6'2   87-18262
ISBN 0-275-92359-2 (alk. paper)

Library of Congress Catalog Card Number: 87-18262
ISBN: 0-275-92359-2

First published in 1987

Praeger Publishers, One Madison Avenue, New York, NY 10010
A division of Greenwood Press, Inc.

Printed in the United States of America

∞™

The paper used in this book complies with the Permanent
Paper Standard issued by the National Information Standards
Organization (Z39.48-1984).

10 9 8 7 6 5 4 3 2 1

This is a tribute to you, Eugene.
You, whose zest for joy and happiness

was surpassed only by your love
for those you cared about.
Your memory glows in the minds
and hearts of all those
you loved, who in turn loved you.

Contents

Introduction — SAMUEL H. KLARREICH   xi

Part I:
History and Development of Health Education Programs

1   **Health Promotion in the Workplace: A Historical Perspective**   5
PENNY R. KLARREICH

2   **Worker Education and Training in Health and Safety in the United States**   13
MICHAEL A. VOJTECKY

Part II:
Implementation of Health Education Programs

3   **Corporate Health and Corporate Culture**   35
JACK SANTA-BARBARA

4   **A Health Education Committee: The Doorway to Health Education for an Employee Assistance Program**   45
SAMUEL H. KLARREICH

5   **Developing an Action Plan for Health Promotion Programs**   59
ANGELICA T. CANTLON and BETTY J. CARTER

6   **Wellness: Make It Happen through Effective Communications**   71
ANNE RAWSON

7   **Effectively Marketing a Wellness Program**   81
PHYLLIS L. FLEMING

8   **You Are Not Alone: Computer Networks Help People Learn from Others**   94
SUSANNA OPPER

Part III:
Health Education Programs in the Workplace

9   StayWell: A Pragmatic Approach to Wellness in the Workplace   113
C. R. JONES

10 HEALTH PLUS: Union Carbide's Health Promotion Program,   124
a Comprehensive Approach to Employee Health
DEBORAH J. LEWIS

11 Tel-Med: Delivering Health Information   140
A. L. MacKEIGAN and KEVIN McCORMACK

12 A Systems Approach to Back Injury Control and Other   148
Wellness Interventions
JEANNETTE M. JACOBSON

13 A Comprehensive People Maintenance Program: Employee   163
Assistance Programs and Rehabilitation
BETTE NEALE

14 Stress Management in the Workplace   172
LOCKIE JAYNE McGEHEE

15 Burnout: A Real Fire or False Alarm?   183
SAMUEL H. KLARREICH

16 In Pursuit of Personal Excellence   200
GERALD D. PULVERMACHER

Part IV:
Research and Evaluation in Health Education Programs

17 Evaluation Tools for Use in Workplace Health Promotion   215
Programs: Practical Applications
LARRY S. CHAPMAN

18 Motivating People to Become Involved and to Stay Involved in Physical Activity   234
JOHN K. YARDLEY

19 A Strategy for Evaluating Occupational Health and Safety Training   258
MICHAEL A. VOJTECKY and EMIL BERKANOVIC

20 Economics and Worksite Health Promotion   270
JONATHAN E. FIELDING

21 Comprehensive Evaluation of a Worksite Health Promotion Program: The StayWell Program at Control Data   284
DAVID R. ANDERSON and WILLIAM S. JOSE II

Part V:
Critical Issues Relevant to Health Education Programs

22 The Difference between Health Education, Fitness, and Wellness Programs and the Importance of Communicating These Differences   305
W. DENNIS DERR

23 Health Promotion: Health Care Cost Containment or Human Resource Development?   319
D. W. EDINGTON

24 How Health Promotion Programs Can Enhance Workplace Creativity   325
THOMAS E. BACKER

25 Implementation of Fitness and Lifestyle Programs: Critical Issues   338
MICHAEL H. COX

26 Workplace Smoking Control in the United States: Economic, Health, Legal, Programmatic and Policy Issues   355
REBECCA S. PARKINSON and MICHAEL P. ERIKSEN

27 Training the Practitioner to Provide Comprehensive   373
   Health Promotion Programs
   RICHARD ROTONDO

28 Selecting a Health Promotion Program   378
   DON R. POWELL

   Conclusion: Will Health Education and Fitness in the Workplace   385
   Remain Healthy and Fit for the Future?
   SAMUEL H. KLARREICH

Bibliography   389
Index   393
About the Contributors   405

Introduction

Samuel H. Klarreich

Is half a glass of orange juice half full or half empty? Specialists in wellness promotion might say that it is half full. Specialists in illness prevention, however, might say that it is half empty. Is there a correct answer? Not really. Specialists in their respective fields of endeavor recognize what is before them, but their particular perspectives might differ.

What is very exciting, however, is that both perspectives exist. Both wellness promotion and illness prevention are flourishing today more than ever before.

This phenomenon, called health education, health promotion, fitness, and, most recently, wellness, has been occurring in the workplace and has been hailed as a boon to industry as well as to society in general. The movement, as it expands in leaps and bounds, has brought together many talented professionals who have the basic goal of bringing primary health care to business and industry.

Industry with its watchful eye has incorporated health programs into its environment for both humanitarian and economic reasons. Corporations increasingly realize that such programs are beneficial to the health and well-being of its employees. Smoking cessation programs are regarded as a vehicle to reduce the risk of various pulmonary and cardiovascular problems. Fitness programs are recognized as a method to augment physical and emotional well-being. Back injury control programs are seen as an approach to reduce serious injuries and to improve safety records. Stress management programs are viewed as a tool to control stress-related disorders.

Corporations increasingly recognize that a healthier and happier workforce has better morale, is more innovative, is more efficient, and is more productive. It also is less absent, is less ill, and experiences fewer accidents. The "bottom line" is that it saves businesses considerable insurance dollars and replacement costs. Government and health officials clearly appreciate that proactive corporations who establish their own health programs in an attempt to create a healthier work force are assisting to ease the burden on the health care system and are helping ultimately to save health care dollars.

Because this field is relatively new and growing rapidly, striving for clarity, definition of purpose, direction, and evaluation becomes especially important. This text, which is truly a unique North American effort presents the essential components of health education and fitness programs in the workplace and addresses the above issues and other issues through the contributions of influential and prominent health care experts, virtually a "Who's Who" of North American health education and fitness programs.

There are five sections to the textbook. The history and development section traces the health education and fitness movement from its early beginnings to its present day status. This prepares the foundation for the implementation section that describes in detail the necessary requirements to set a health education and/or fitness program into motion. Defining, setting objectives, designing, planning, and marketing are but a few of the essential steps that are carefully described and discussed. This further prepares the groundwork for the next section on health education and fitness programs in the workplace. In this section leading practitioners detail, in a thorough and comprehensive fashion, some of the best programs in the country.

The fourth section reviews a pressing concern, research and evaluation. If the movement is to continue to gain credibility and to advance, research efforts regarding data collection, results, benefits, and effectiveness must be pursued vigorously. The articles here shed considerable and valuable light on these and other topics.

Finally, as any emerging field grows and develops, key issues surface. As professionals in the health education and fitness arena, we need to heed these questions and attempt to answer them. In the last section some of our leading thinkers address current critical issues.

This textbook is truly a landmark and offers to academics, practitioners, and students alike a comprehensive and integrated picture of this emerging and significant phenomenon of the 1980s — health education and fitness in the workplace.

I
History and Development of Health Education Programs

Health education has had a very interesting history. It has been influenced by a number of key individuals and a number of significant trends. In order to appreciate fully the health education movement and its effect in the workplace, it is important to examine its roots.

Klarreich in her chapter points out that the 1980s have witnessed a dramatic increase in health promotion programs in the workplace. They have evolved primarily as a remedy for growing health care costs. It is also widely recognized that modern diseases, often termed "diseases of choice," are, to a great extent, preventable if health lifestyles are adopted. She steps back in time to point out that health lifestyles were of concern even to Hippocrates and his medical students.

She indicates that the wellness movement has evolved as a result of the efforts of a number of significant individuals who are regarded as the grandfathers and the fathers of the movement. Their concepts and theories are amply chronicled. They all believed that one should strive to become "more well" even in the absence of disease. She further specifies that this notion has filtered into the workplace, where today it is hoped that wellness programs will lower health care costs, increase staff productivity, and encourage employees to adopt healthier lifestyles.

Vojtecky extensively reviews and illustrates the application of psychological principles that lead to the acquisition of knowledge, attitudes, and behaviors for developing and improving worksite health and safety conditions. Behavioral norms, learning objectives, curriculum, specificity of instruction, practice and transfer of learning, and reinforcement principles are discussed and their roles elucidated. He examines worker education and training as practiced in the United States. Finally, he discusses the developing interest in education and training for job health and safety and its implication for the future.

1 Health Promotion in the Workplace: A Historical Perspective

Penny R. Klarreich

INTRODUCTION

In the last decade and particularly in the 1980s, there has been a growing trend for companies to offer health promotion programs at the worksite. Between 1979 and 1982 the numbers of such programs have increased by 100-fold (Saxl 1984). "Employee wellness programs," "health enhancement programs," "health promotion programs," or "disease prevention programs," as they are commonly referred to, describe a series of activities that advocate adopting healthier lifestyles. Examples might include programs directed toward smoking cessation, physical fitness, stress management, nutrition education, weight management, cardiopulmonary resuscitation, alcohol and drug abuse counseling, employee assistance programs, and others.

The underlying explanation of the movement toward wellness is that corporate health care has become increasingly proactive (Brennan 1983) because corporate health care costs have been increasing at a staggering rate. Companies that sponsor health promotion programs thus operate under two assumptions. First, they recognize that it is far less costly to prevent illness than to cure it and, second, that optimal health can be approached through improved personal lifestyles (Saxl 1984). The benefits for the company include lower health care costs and increased staff productivity while employees learn to change health-threatening behavior patterns and thus avoid becoming ill.

THE HISTORY OF HEALTH PROMOTION

The first proponent of health promotion or wellness may have been Hippocrates himself (Grossman 1983). When he and his medical students encountered an unfamiliar city, he would advise his students to become acquainted with the lifestyles of the local residents by noting their work patterns and eating habits.

The Young Men's Christian Association has been described as one of the oldest wellness organizations (Grossman 1983). The triangular emblem of the Y.M.C.A., which symbolizes its dedication to mind, body, and spirit, was adopted in the early 1880s. Many wellness proponents today subscribe to the idea of the person as an interrelated whole consisting of mind, body, and spirit.

Edward Steiglitz, a Chicago physician and one of the grandfathers of the wellness movement, presented several novel ideas in his book, *The Second Forty Years* (Steiglitz 1952). The human life span, he wrote, was being prolonged due to the control of infectious disease, scientific developments in agriculture, better methods of food storage and transportation that made good foods readily available, and a better understanding of nutrition and its relation to health. Because the proportion of older individuals in the population was increasing, Steiglitz was concerned that they not become a social and economic burden to society. He hoped that senior citizens would continue to render service to society and lead more fulfilling lives in doing so. While he did not deny the gradual impairments that might accompany the aging process, Steiglitz noted that improved hygiene, medical guidance, and "living in accordance with today's understanding of the nature of man" (Steiglitz 1952, p. ix) could delay the onset of these impairments and decrease their severity. Although the prevention of disorders that accompany aging is important, Steiglitz felt that it was not enough.

To understand this point, we must look at the definition of health that was commonly accepted at the time: "that state of being, existing in the absence of disease" (Steiglitz 1952, p. 14). This definition, Steiglitz wrote, was inadequate as well as negative in context. Health, he articulated, was a kinetic as opposed to a static state involving "reserve forces" that were hidden but nevertheless available. He described "perfect health" an an ideal that was probably never attainable; nevertheless, one must strive to attain it by using all available reserve forces.

Steiglitz recognized that it did not suffice to treat disease by reconstructing damaged health. Better health, he elaborated, could be worked toward "even in the absence of florid disease" (Steiglitz 1952, p. 301). The means to achieve better health was coined "constructive medicine," which differed from preventive medicine in that the focus of attention was on the patient and not on the disease itself. Constructive medicine, nonetheless, included the notion of preventive medicine.

Steiglitz elaborated further on the differences between the terms. He viewed preventive medicine as having a negative connotation because prevention implied prohibitions or restrictions with the purpose of avoiding something that may prove harmful. Although avoiding the negative effects of noxious influences was viewed as beneficial, Steiglitz proposed that protective avoidance measures "do not actually improve the vigor and vitality of the individual" (Steiglitz 1952, p. 30). Although removing hazards from the environment had certainly contributed to increasing the average life span, the problems of aging, he noted, "arise from within" and were associated with biological changes. Environmental controls would not serve to modify these biological modifications.

Constructive medicine, with its positive implications, had as its objective the attainment of optimal health for individuals. Because he regarded health as kinetic, "well" people could become even healthier. Steiglitz pointed out that it was common pediatric practice to provide guidance in nutrition, exercise, and living habits, and he questioned the merit of providing this information only for infants and children. Adults, as well, he noted, should be given the opportunity to improve their state of health. The benefits included improved vigor, greater work efficiency, enhanced endurance, increased resistance to infection, and more rapid recovery from illness.

Steiglitz believed the objectives of constructive medicine could be met with a number of methods. One of these methods was through gerontological research, which was necessary in order to answer perplexing questions about the biology of senescence and the causes of the disorders that often appear in the later years. Education, another method that Steiglitz proposed, was "intellectual nutrition." Education in health matters is essential if people are expected to follow suggestions in order to become healthier. On the preventive side, he noted that environmental controls to neutralize or remove health hazards were necessary. This type of preventive measure was a public health, en masse matter, but Steiglitz also advocated "individualized health construction." He recognized that in order to attain optimal health through constructive medicine, one had to focus upon the individual and his or her unique needs.

Another grandfather of the movement toward healthier lifestyles was Halbert Dunn, M.D., Ph.D. Dunn may have borrowed some of the ideas proposed by Edward Steiglitz and his "constructive medicine." During the 1950s, Dunn, a public health official, gave radio talks on various aspects of well-being. *High Level Wellness* (Dunn 1961) contained 29 short talks that Dunn had aired on radio. In this book, to characterize high level wellness he referred to the definition of health adopted by the World Health Organization: "Health is a state of complete physical, mental and social well-being, and not merely the absence of disease and infirmity" (Dunn 1961, p. 1).

Dunn agreed with this definition in that a complete state of well-being involves wellness of the mind, the body, and the environment, with the environment encompassing the family, community life, and a "compatible work interest." Like Steiglitz, Dunn agreed that being well did not simply refer to a state of "unsickness" and it existed in different degrees at various times. Simply stated, at times you may feel "more well" than at other times, without actually being "sick." An example might be when you experience a lack of energy or, conversely, when you "tingle with vitality." Dunn stated that most individuals, most of the time, find themselves at some point between the two extremes on this wellness continuum.

Dunn found the state of wellness to be far more interesting than that of sickness and questioned why doctors, nurses, and health workers were preoccupied with disease, death, and disability. He postulated that an "illness" focus represented the medical training orientation toward disease rather than toward wellness. He noted also, as did Steiglitz, that wellness is not a static, homogeneous state, but rather a state that is ever changing. Dunn defined wellness in the following manner:

> High level wellness for the individual is defined as an integrated method of functioning which is oriented toward maximizing the potential of which the individual is capable. It requires that the individual maintain a continuum of balance and purposeful direction within the environment where he is functioning (Dunn 1961, pp. 4–5).

Rather than striving for an optimum level of wellness, Dunn preferred to describe a "direction in progress toward an ever higher potential of functioning" (Dunn 1961, p. 6). Dunn described his conception of the nature of man to demonstrate how we are, indeed, capable of achieving wellness based on his definition. Rather than viewing mind, body, and spirit as separate entities, he viewed the person as a total personality where mind, body, and spirit meld and function in an environment that constantly undergoes change. An essential element in achieving wellness, Dunn wrote, is a "purpose for living." Although Dr. Dunn's unique ideas did not stir much controversy at the time, two decades later they influenced John Travis and Don Ardell, the two fathers of the wellness movement.

While John Travis was a medical student and intern, he began to view medicine in a manner that was quite different from his contemporaries. He thought focusing on disease made medicine into an occupation of "disease care." Travis later read Dunn's unique little book, *High Level Wellness,* which reflected some of his own thoughts (Grossman 1983). Borrowing from Dunn's ideas while adding many of his own, Travis developed an illness/wellness model to demonstrate how health should be thought of as a positive state of well-being rather than the absence of illness. This was accomplished by using a continuum, with premature death and high level wellness at opposite poles. At the midpoint of the two poles was a vertical line to demarcate a neutral point where no discernable illness or wellness existed. Moving from the neutral point in the center to the left pole toward premature death, one would encounter signs, symptoms, and disability. According to Travis (1986), this is where one would find traditional medicine, whose purpose is to cure disease. Seldom did modern medicine progress beyond the neutral midpoint, he suggested. Moving along the continuum from the midpoint to the right pole toward high level wellness, you would find education, growth, and self-actualization. Travis's brand of medicine commenced at any point along the continuum with the purpose of assisting the individual in moving as far to the right as possible.

In 1975 John Travis established his wellness center in California. Dr. D. C. Jarvis, in his book, *Folk Medicine* (1985), predicted that "the doctor of the future will be a teacher as well as a physician whose real job will be assisting people how to learn to be healthy" (Ardell 1977, p. 17). At Travis's Wellness Resource Center, the goal was exactly that. Those who were ill and in need of medical treatment were sent elsewhere to physicians; clients at the center were well and would go through a detailed program that would make them feel even better. Central to the program was education about stress control, physical fitness, nutrition, and self-responsibility. Travis believed that his clients should be aided in discovering how they were contributing to their difficulties. They were encouraged and taught how to take charge of their lives to achieve healthier lifestyles (Ardell 1977).

Donald B. Ardell, like Travis, has been called a father of the wellness movement. As a health planner, it was Ardell's desire to make the health care system more efficient. Within the medical system, his roles were educator, researcher, consultant, and administrator. He left his job because he believed that health planning bore no impact on the health care system, which indeed was a sad reality.

Although Halbert Dunn's 1961 text *High Level Wellness* may not have had a dramatic impact at its time of publication, it was quite an eye opener to Ardell who became acquainted with it in 1975. Ardell described Dunn's book as "something akin to being hit with a bolt of 'benevolent' lightening" (Ardell 1977, p. 5) as he then realized what had been lacking in health planning. In the initial phase of his interest in wellness, Ardell was also influenced by the work of Dr. John Travis. With his book *High Level Wellness: An Alternative to Doctors, Drugs, and Disease* (Ardell 1977) and public speaking engagements, Ardell made a major contribution in popularizing wellness. In his 1977 book, he presents many of the themes current in the wellness movement. Two of these ideas are central to today's health promotion programs in the workplace. First, attention to lifestyle and environment, he states, is crucial if one wishes to avoid illness. Second, he notes that medical costs can be reduced substantially if attention is paid to these two factors, which, if neglected, can contribute to unnecessary illness.

Ardell, in his wisdom, spoke about the need for wellness programs in the workplace. He pointed out the staggering amounts that corporations pay for employee medical benefits and suggested, in 1977, that these amounts could double by 1980. Ardell projected, with dismay, that the health of the work force was not likely to improve, nor did he expect it to improve in the future. Rather than spending money on treating disease, he proposed that "big and little businesses could probably increase productivity, lower absenteeism, improve morale and otherwise decrease the extent of illness by promoting wellness at the company's expense" (Ardell 1977, p. 186).Without fear of contradiction Donald B. Ardell can certainly be named as one of the foremost fathers of the wellness movement in the workplace.

HEALTH PROMOTION PROGRAMS: WELLNESS GOES TO WORK

Health programs in the workplace evolved primarily as a remedy for the growing health care costs that Donald Ardell wrote about in 1977. In the United States, over $300 billion were spent on health care in 1982. Of that amount corporations contributed $77 billion because of decreased productivity, increased health insurance costs, and absenteeism costs (Rosen 1984). To demonstrate how rapidly health care costs are climbing, expenditures in the United States in 1965 were $42 billion, $132 billion in 1975, and were projected to be $462 billion by 1985 (Kondrasuk 1984). While the overall inflation rate was 3.9 percent in 1982, health care costs rose by a staggering 11 percent (Hartman and Cozzetto 1984).

While Herbert Steiglitz was writing about and promoting constructive medicine in the 1940s, health promotion programs began to evolve in occupational settings. Those early efforts focused on safety regulations and recreational activities and were, for the most part, unrelated to health issues. They were implemented to boost employee morale and productivity. The few programs that did reflect health related concerns tended to be unidimensional, focusing on single problems and preventive methods, and they served only specific members of the workforce, namely executives. These early efforts did, however, serve as prototypes for the comprehensive programs that would follow (Davis 1984).

In time, the focus of occupational health promotion or wellness programs changed to health related issues. The explanation for this shift is as follows. Infectious diseases such as tuberculosis, polio, typhoid, and cholera were the leading causes of death in the early twentieth century. These diseases were later controlled — conquered through immunization, medication, clean water supplies, and sanitary measures. Today, most lives, some say as many as 50 to 80 percent, are claimed by lifestyle generated maladies, including heart disease, cancer, and stroke (Nelton 1984; Rosen 1984). People such as Steiglitz, Dunn, Travis, and Ardell have helped to point out that these so-called modern diseases are, to a great extent, a result of "what we do to ourselves" and have been deemed "diseases of choice." Lack of exercise, poor diet, smoking, and stress are frequently cited as major contributing factors to those illnesses. Workplace wellness programs could thus take on a new role in educating and encouraging employees to assume healthier lifestyles in order to avoid those diseases of choice. As well as having happier more productive employees, health care costs would decrease substantially.

Although Donald Ardell, in 1977, projected that the health of the work force would not likely improve in the 1980s, employee wellness programs, health enhancement programs, health promotion programs, and disease prevention programs have become the "latest business buzz words" (Brennan 1983).

REFERENCES

Ardell, D. B. *High Level Wellness: An Alternative to Doctors, Drugs, and Disease.* Emmaus, PA: Rodale Press, 1977.

Brennan, A. J. J. "How to Set up a Corporate Wellness Program." *Management Review* 72 (May 1983): 41–47.

Davis, M. F. "Worksite Health Promotion. An Overview of Programs and Practices." *Personnel Administrator 29* (December 1984): 45–50.

Dunn, H. B. *High Level Wellness.* Arlington, Virginia: R. W. Beatty, 1961.

Grossman, J. "Inside the Wellness Movement." *Health* 4 (1983) 10–15.

Hartman, S. W., and J. Cozzetto. "Wellness in the Workplace." *Personnel Administrator 29* (August 1984) 108–17.

Jarvis, D. C. *Fold Medicine.* Toronto: Random House, 1985.

Kondrasuk, J. N. "Corporate Physical Fitness Programs: The Role of the Personnel Department." *Personnel Administrator* 29 (December 1984): 75–80.

Nelton, S. "Teaching Employees to Be Healthier." *Nation's Business* 72 (July 1984): 71.

Rosen, R. H. "The Picture of Health in the Workplace." *Training and Development Journal* 38 (August 1984): 24–30.

Saxl, L. R. "Hot to Create a Healthy Health Promotion Program." *Pension World* 20 (December 1984): 44–45.

Steiglitz, E. J. *The Second Forty Years.* Philadelphia: J. B. Lippincott, 1952.

Travis, J. W. *Wellness Workbook.* Berkeley, California: Ten Speed Press, 1986.

2 Worker Education and Training in Health and Safety in the United States

Michael A. Vojtecky

INTRODUCTION

In December of 1970 the Congress of the United States enacted the Occupational Safety and Health Act to ensure in so far as possible healthful working conditions for the nation's greatest resource, its people. Among the many requirements of this legislation was a provision requiring the secretary of labor to establish education and training programs for workers in the recognition, avoidance, and prevention of unsafe or unhealthful working conditions (Public Law 91-596, 1970). In general, coverage of the act extends to all employers and their employees in the 50 states, the District of Columbia, Puerto Rico, and all other territories under federal government jurisdiction. The only persons not covered by the act are self-employed persons, members of immediate families who work on family farms, persons in workplaces already protected by other federal legislation, and employees of state and local governments.

Despite a lack of conclusive evidence concerning the effectiveness of worker education and training as methods for controlling workplace hazards, the authors and supporters of this legislation, and indeed the supporters of worker education and training in job safety and health worldwide, believed that because education was an accepted method for achieving behavior change in other contexts it would also be an effective behavior change agent in the workplace (Heath 1981). This desire to improve worker behavior with respect to health and safety practices rested on the assumption that the adoption of self-protective behaviors could reduce the risks associated with occupational hazards by reducing to some extent the frequency, intensity, or duration of exposures to such hazards.

Furthermore, there seemed to be an ethical concern for providing workers education and training regarding the hazards they encountered as part of their jobs. This concern reflected the general feeling in free societies that it is a basic right of individuals to be informed about the things that affect them. Thus, education about the effects of hazards and training in self-protective measures would become major tenets to be reflected in training requirements established under the law.

The education and training of all persons covered by the act, however, is an enormous undertaking even for a government with the resources of the United States. Thus, the secretary of labor has met this charge largely by delegating the responsibility for education and training in job safety and health to individual employers. Today there are more than 125 explicit training requirements in federally promulgated health standards. In addition, the Occupational Safety and Health Administration contends that there is an implied requirement in the law to provide training even when not specifically called for by a health standard (USDOL, OSHA 1983). The training requirements established under federal legislation typically, although not always, attempt to address five major points. These points are illustrated in Table 2.1 using the lead standard.

Although good in so far as they go, the requirements do not address the question of how education and training in job safety and health are to be conducted. There is typically no mention, for example, concerning the use of instructional techniques, length of training sessions, qualifications of trainers, identification of specific training needs, instructional objectives, development of learning activities, or program evaluation. Thus, the implication is that these things should be considered by the person directly responsible for the education and training program, that is to say, the employer or his representative.

This would seem to be entirely appropriate because workplaces, work processes, and workers may be vastly different even within the same industry and often within the same company. Therefore, the law contains a flexibility that allows employers to develop education and training programs specially suited to their particular needs while keeping in mind that certain fundamental aspects of education and training specifically noted in the health standard must be addressed.

TABLE 2.1
Examples of Training Requirements in Federal Standards

Requirement	Example (Lead)
Who is to be trained	"all employees who are subject to lead at or above the action level or for whom the possibility of skin or eye irritation exists."
When initial training is to be completed	"prior to the time of initial job assignment."
Minimum frequency with which training is to be conducted after initial training has been completed	"at least annually"
Content of the training program	"(a) the content of this standard and its appendixes; (b) the specific nature of the operations which could result in exposure to lead above the action level; (c) the purpose, proper selection, fitting, use, and limitations of respirators; (d) the purpose and a description of the medical surveillance program, and the medical removal protection program including information concerning the adverse health effects associated with excessive exposure to lead (with particular attention to the adverse reproductie effects on both males and females); (e) the engineering controls and work practices associated with the employee's job assignment; (f) the contents of any compliance plan in effect; and (g) instructions to employees that chelating agents should not routinely be used to remove lead from their bodies and should not be used at all except under the direction of a licensed physician."
Access to information and training materials	"The employer shall make readily available to all affected employees a copy of this standard and its appendixes. . . . In addition the employer shall include as part of the training program, and shall distribute to employees, any materials pertaining to the Occupational Safety and Health Act, the regulations issued pursuant to this Act, and this lead standard, which are made available to the employer." (by the U.S. government)

Source: Part 1910, Section 1025, paragraph L of Title 29, Code of Federal Regulations.

15

However, an important assumption underlies this provision for flexibility. The assumption is that the employer, or his representative, has a willingness and a level of expertise in educational matters sufficient to develop an education and training program that will meet both the needs of workers as well as the specific requirements of the law. The remainder of this chapter will be devoted to a review of private sector worker education and training programs from two different perspectives. First, we will examine what research has demonstrated to be successful methods for achieving changes in health related work practices. Second, we will examine the education and training practices of employers in the United States.

EDUCATION AND TRAINING IN JOB SAFETY AND HEALTH: WHAT WE KNOW

To early safety practitioners preventive efforts centered almost exclusively on accidents and traumatic injury. Although occupational disease was philosophically associated with safety, in practice it was rarely considered (Bird 1973). Similarly, although research relevant to safe work behavior was being conducted in learning psychology, social psychology, and behavior modification, this work was, for the most part, not integrated nor applied specifically to education and training for job safety and health (Margolis and Kroes 1975). Recent research in worker education and training, however, has incorporated much of what has been learned in these areas into comprehensive and coordinated plans for providing education and training in health and safety to workers. These comprehensive plans can be broadly described as consisting of instruction, psychological reinforcement, and the establishment of new norms for safe behavior. Let us now examine these elements more closely.

Instruction in health and safety is the planned communication of health knowledge to workers. Specifically, it is the presentation of information and the sequential arrangement of formal learning activities designed to influence health related decision making, values, attitudes, and practices (Fodor and Dalis 1981). Thus, its primary purposes are to develop the knowledge, awareness, and cognitive and motor skills necessary to perform a job safely.

The first step in the development of any instructional program should be to identify the program's learning objectives. Because instruction in job safety and health is meant to teach workers about the relationship between work and health, the identification of specific learning objectives must consider the job relatedness of a worker's health behaviors. The assessment of job relatedness can be greatly aided by analyzing the job situation to determine the job safety conditions and work behaviors that contribute to worker health (Rohmert and Landau 1983). Once identified these conditions and behaviors can be prioritized according to their potential contribution to health protection and risk reduction and translated into learning objectives ultimately aimed at the primary prevention of occupational health problems (Vojtecky 1985). For example, a learning objective may be that a worker should be able to specify the conditions under which respirator use is necessary. Another may be that a worker should be able to select the appropriate respirator for the job and to adjust the fit to his or her face.

Generally, the second step in the development of an instructional program is to construct the curriculum, that is to say, the detailed plan for instruction and learning activities that lead to the achievement of the learning objectives. Although a comprehensive discussion of curriculum design is beyond the scope of this chapter, general principles governing the development of learning activities have been applied to the workplace. Some of the most useful of these principles are presented in guideline form in Table 2.2.

Often the general instructional plan used by researchers included the presentation of information (including demonstration of recommended practices), opportunity for skill practice in the newly recommended work practices (both supervised and unsupervised), and feedback to the worker regarding knowledge and skill acquisition. These elements are typically repeated as often as necessary for the knowledge or skill to be learned. As with information giving, however, special consideration should be given to the ways in which skill practice and performance feedback are conducted.

The practice of new skills, for example, should be arranged so as to allow for the transfer of learning to actual job conditions. This means that skill practice sessions should be conducted at the job station, if possible, and, if not, in a setting as similar to the job station as feasible. In addition, ample time should be provided for practicing the new skill because the more often a skill is performed in a certain way, the more fixed the performance of that skill becomes. Finally, the feedback given to workers on performance of the skill should be immediate, complete, and, perhaps most important of all, understandable (Goldstein 1975).

TABLE 2.2

Useful Applications of Learning Principles

Principle	Example (E) and Rationale (R)	
Instructions should be specific to the work situation.	(E)	Workers should position themselves so that their faces are 18 inches or more from sources of evaporating styrene. These sources include nozzles of spray guns, containers of styrene and parts on which there are curing resins.
	(R)	Research suggests that transfer of task learning may be limited to teaching and performance situations that contain identical elements (Goldstein 1975).
Instructions should be detailed with respect to descriptions of safe behavior and safe conditions.	(E)	Overspray of styrene on ventilation booth filters should be kept to depths of less than one-half inch in chop spray booths and one-quarter inch in gelcoat booths.
	(R)	Understanding the definition of concepts to be learned facilitates learning. Clear descriptions should identify the knowledge a learner is supposed to acquire in a way that the structure of the knowledge (the relationship between behavior, conditions, and safety experience) is explicit (Posner and Rudnitsky 1982).
Instructions should be presented in a positive way.	(E)	Exhaust ventilation should be turned on any time a worker is in the work area.
	(R)	Demonstrating and describing desired behavior or the product of such behavior serves as a guide to learning. Thus, workers should be told what to do rather than what not to do (Posner and Rudnitsky 1982).
Instructions should present the rules or laws that govern the solution of problems.	(E)	For the example instruction used above, the underlying rules regarding the use of exhaust ventilation are 1. Dilute styrene concentrations 2. Remove evaporated and vaporized styrene. 3. Reduce styrene introduced into the ambient plant air.
	(R)	Learning is enhanced when a person understands the underlying concepts involved in a given task (Goldstein 1975; Bruner 1977).

Source: Behavioral Procedures for Reducing Worker Exposure to Carcinogens: Final Report (University of Kansas, 1981).

Giving information to workers about their performance seems to function as both a device for providing additional instruction as well as for reinforcing new learning. In the first instance this performance feedback appears to capitalize on the teachable moment created when a learner's initial attempts to mimic a demonstration are not successful. In the second instance performance feedback becomes a mechanism for reinforcing newly learned behaviors by providing knowledge regarding the results of those behaviors. Such results, when favorable, can serve to motivate the worker to continue in the new behaviors (Goldstein 1975).

Indeed the purpose to which all forms of psychological reinforcement are ultimately directed is to increase the probability that a newly learned behavior will recur in the future. And it should be noted that psychological reinforcement comes in many forms, of which performance feedback is only one. Other kinds of reinforcement often used in the workplace are pay raises and vacation time (positive reinforcement) and job suspension, loss of pay, and reprimands (negative reinforcement). However, it must be noted that the selection and correct use of a reinforcer is often difficult. Guidelines published by the National Institute for Occupational Safety and Health (McIntire and White 1975) suggest that the following steps be taken when selecting psychological reinforcers. First, identify reinforcers that already exist in the particular workplace. Second, identify reinforcers that can be used in the particular workplace to reinforce safe behavior. Third, evaluate the reinforcers identified according to their strengths and weaknesses in the context of the particular workplace. Finally, select the reinforcers that are most likely to be effective and least likely to conflict with one another.

An example of this process can be found in the work of Zohar, Cohen, and Azar (1980). In this project the goal of the education and training program was to increase the use of hearing protectors by metal workers. The researchers first identified a number of existing reinforcers. These included awards for safety performance, safety posters, and talks by managers with individual workers. Zohar and his colleagues next considered what could be potential reinforcers. For example, information about the attenuating effects of hearing protection, such as the amount of temporary hearing loss that occurred during work shifts when hearing protectors were worn, was not routinely given to workers, but it was determined that such information could be effectively presented to workers without undue difficulty. Disciplinary suspension was also considered as a possible reinforcer.

When considering the use of these reinforcers within an education and training program, the researchers did not choose some, posters for example, because past experience had indicated that they would be ineffective. Others were not chosen because, as in the case of disciplinary suspensions, conflict would have been created in the form of union and worker resistance and disruption in work schedules. Information feedback was the reinforcer finally selected because it had the potential to be effective without causing undue disturbance. Details of how this reinforcer was then applied can be found in the article by Zohar, Cohen, and Azar (1980). Some general psychological principles underlying the use of reinforcement are summarized in Table 2.3.

Interestingly, the research literature further suggests that the programed use of psychological reinforcers can be a short-term process becoming much less important when new group norms for safety behavior have been firmly established. Whether group norms for safety behavior can be established systematically through education and training is not known. It is known, however, that the establishment of uniform behavior patterns in individuals, so vital to the maintenance of preventive behaviors, depends to a large degree on whether other people close to you share the same feelings about the behavioral practices in question (Festinger, Schachter, and Back 1968). We also know that when physical reality is low the dependence on social reality or group opinion is correspondingly high (Festinger 1968). Because the apparent physical reality of a health and safety problem is typically low during the initial period of exposure, attention must be given to the existing social reality if workers are to adopt safe practices. One particularly important aspect of existing social reality for workers is the work group, the people who form the group one works with day in and day out.

Based on relevant research (Hare 1976; Noro 1984), some think that introducing formal methods for working in groups may significantly aid in dealing with the social reality of workers (Vojtecky 1985). These formal methods would probably consist of the following elements: identification of a group leader by group choice (that is, the group selects a leader); giving the group a purpose (by assigning the group the task of suggesting ways to deal with the occupational health problem); establishing procedures for the control of discussion (introducing aspects of well-established parliamentary procedures); specification of behavioral goals through group discussion and agreement (given a set of goals, norms define the kind of behavior that is necessary for or consistent with the realization of those goals); and formal summary and recording of

TABLE 2.3

Useful Applications of Psychological Reinforcement

Principle	Application (A) and Example (E)	
Positive reinforcement is used when an increase in a particular behavior is desired.	(A)	The reinforcement should have some qualities of reward.
	(E)	Knowledge of performance results, special privileges.
Reinforcement should be appropriate.	(A)	The reinforcement should be job related, commensurate with the behavior being changed, equitable, and should not produce undue conflict.
	(E)	Daily information about the attenuating effects of hearing protection.
Reinforcement should be applied immediately.	(A)	Reinforcement should be given immediately after the behavior has occurred. In this way there should be no confusion as to what behavior is being reinforced.
	(E)	Performance feedback should be given when performance is observed.
Reinforcement should be applied consistently.	(A)	A reinforcer should be consistently paired with a certain behavior and reliably applied across repeated occurrences of the behavior.
	(E)	Specific rewards (for example, tokens) should be given when the desired behavior is observed.

Source: Compiled by the author.

group consensus (by maintaining meeting minutes and by conducting and recording formal group votes).

These activities may articulate with the instruction and reinforcement components of the education and training program in the following ways: by providing a method for the social breakdown of an old behavior pattern before adopting a new one; by involving workers directly in the problem-solving process; by enhancing social methods of problem solving by providing a mechanism and social reference point for collectively judging new behaviors; and by providing a forum in which workers can make their opinions on health and safety known. Apparently, once new norms have been established it is likely that they will govern, to a large extent, worker safety behavior even in the absence of further instruction or reinforcement (Zohar 1980; Zohar, Cohen, and Azar 1980).

In summary, recent research projects have demonstrated the effective use of instruction and psychological reinforcement to achieve significant changes in health related work practices and ultimately work related health risk. In addition the results of some recent research suggests that group norms for behavior play a major role in determining patterns for safe work practice.

EDUCATION AND TRAINING PRACTICES IN THE UNITED STATES

The discussion that follows was developed largely from work done by Vojtecky, Kar, and Cox (1985) and Heath (1981; 1982). It describes salient characteristics of trainers and of education and training programs for job safety and health in the United States.

Trainers

Most health and safety training in the United States is conducted by individuals who are not specially prepared to perform the role of educator. Only 62 percent of occupational health professionals responsible for the education and training of workers in job safety and health have received training of any kind in health education (Vojtecky 1985). Furthermore, those who are not health professionals are unlikely to have received any training in health education (Heath 1982). In many cases the major qualification for the position of trainer appears to be a willingness to do the work. Thus, these individuals, although interested, are unlikely to be familiar with the types of learning principles and strategies that have been discussed earlier in this chapter.

If the person responsible for education and training is an occupational health professional, his or her professional training probably has been in industrial hygiene, medicine, nursing, safety engineering, or another health related discipline. If not occupational health professionals, the persons responsible for health and safety education and training are probably foremen or middle managers (Heath 1982). Presumably the use of noneducators to train workers can be partly explained by the opinion widely held, even outside the United States, that the health and safety trainer should know more about the job than about how to educate and train.

> The feeling seemed to be that in order to instruct workers in job safety and health subjects, the instructor must first have the confidence of the workers. A major factor in obtaining such confidence was believed to be having recent, extensive experience in the industry (preferably at the shop floor level) from which the workers come. . . . One thing that almost everyone agreed on was that an individual who knew how to teach, but who had little or no work experience in work practices or occupational safety and health, would not make an effective instructor in this area despite considerable additional training (Heath 1981, p. 393).

Ironically, such an attitude may exclude those best suited to develop education and training programs. Indeed, if such a criterion were applied to the researchers responsible for the projects referred to in the previous section of this chapter, those projects would probably never have been conducted. Yet the importance attached to appropriate health and safety training is reflected both in legal requirements and to some extent in the fairly substantial amounts of time given to education and training activities by those responsible for it. Within a specific profession, such as industrial hygiene, time spent in education and training activities can range from less than 10 percent to 100 percent of total work time. All occupational health professionals spend an average of 33 percent of total work time in worker health education. Given such time commitments it does not seem unreasonable to suggest that adequate preparation in education and training be required of those responsible for them.

Programs

Workplace health and safety education and training programs typically address aspects of health promotion, accident prevention, hazard protection, or some combination of these three broad content areas. The particular content of the program offered appears to be related to some extent to the professional background of the trainer. Industrial hygienists, for example, seem to be primarily involved in hazard protection education, yet this focus should not be unexpected because the responsibility of the industrial hygienist is the engineering control of workplace hazards. Similarly the interest and expertise of other health professionals can also be expected to influence their educational activities. Although professional background may predispose an individual to one type of program or another, legal requirements seem to be the greatest determinants of health and safety program content. As we have seen, federal law often specifies the content of education programs as well as the audience and the frequency of instruction.

These requirements notwithstanding, it is up to the employer, or his representative, to specify a program's learning objectives and the methods for achieving them. Unfortunately, many learning objectives proposed by health and safety trainers do not seem to reflect sufficient understanding of educational processes and may be inconsistent with a program's risk reduction objectives. For example, health related behavior change, all agree, is the basic objective of a health and safety training program, yet few trainers propose learning objectives designed to directly facilitate a behavior change. Rather the learning objectives formulated seem directed at increasing knowledge of hazards and changing attitudes toward safe conditions. Admittedly such factors may be strongly related to the behavior change desired, but in themselves they are not sufficient to achieve it.

Although the learning objectives of educational programs may change according to the circumstances of the situation in which a program is offered, it is unlikely that the explanation for the differences noted can be attributed primarily to differences in situation. At no time did an analysis of learning objectives conducted by Vojtecky, Kar, and Cox (1985) suggest that the learning objectives formulated depended on situational variables such as setting, size, content, or training needs. Rather the differences noted appeared to be associated with professional background. It appears that although nearly everyone agrees that education should lead workers to engage in risk-reducing behavior those with training in health education and those without such training differ as to how to accomplish this behavioral change. Thus, we may have a situation in which learning objectives for health and safety programs are selected independently of situational variables such as setting and substantive content but consistent with the noneducator's perception of what education should be.

If unfamiliarity with education, what it is to accomplish and how it is to accomplish it, is a major reason for the variance between program and learning objectives, this unfamiliarity should also be reflected in the educational methods chosen to reach the learning objectives. Indeed this appears to be the case. The general tendency in current training programs is to rely solely on methods of education designed to communicate information. Thus, lecture, media, and individual instruction are used often. Such methods are consistent with an educational program that has an increase in knowledge as its objective. If, however, an education program must also develop skills and facilitate the adoption of new behaviors, the nearly exclusive use of information-giving methods is likely to be inadequate to achieve all the learning objectives. The apparent lack of extensive opportunities for practicing and reinforcing new skills may be a major deficiency of many current training programs. Therefore, there may be some cause for concern that trainers may not know how to reach their ultimate program objectives. Finally, the effectiveness of the educational methods chosen are rarely, if ever, systematically and rigorously evaluated. Thus, most trainers do not know if they are realizing their learning objectives.

CONCLUSION

Interest in education and training in job safety and health in the United States can be explained partly as the result of the overall increase in interest and activity in occupational health and safety following the enactment of the federal Occupational Safety and Health Act. However, there also seems to be a developing interest separate from that stimulated by the law. It is becoming apparent, for example, that the escalating costs of health benefits and legal actions are also major incentives for industry to seek new ways to prevent occupational illness and injury. In addition, other benefits of illness and injury prevention may include reduced absenteeism, increased productivity, enhanced corporate image, and increased employee morale.

Moreover, it may be that engineering technology, usually the method of choice for controlling workplace hazards, has reached a plateau, for the present, in providing feasible control over workplace hazards. And it seems clear that appropriate workplace health education can significantly enhance the effectiveness of engineering control. An increasing body of research demonstrates the dramatic success of an integrated approach to hazard control consisting of both behavioral and engineering procedures (Komaki, Barwick, and Scott 1978; Zohar, Cohen, and Azar 1980; University of Kansas 1981; Cohen 1979; Laner and Sell 1960; Maples et al. 1982). Thus, an increased interest in worker education and training may also represent an attempt to extend the protection of workers through educational and behavioral technologies complementary or supplementary to engineering and personal protective equipment.

Finally, there is a growing interest in the relationship between occupational disease and lifestyle. It is now thought that the control of occupational disease cannot be approached as though exposures to specific hazards were restricted to time on the job (Blackwell, French, and Stein 1979; Hooper 1982). Many common consumer products, cigarettes for example, interact unfavorably with physical or chemical substances found in workplaces even when the exposure to these consumer products is outside the workplace (Blackwell, French, and Stein 1979).

As the emphasis on education and training continues to grow so will the need for adequately prepared trainers. The day is gone when anyone with an interest could be assigned the responsibility for health and safety training. The discipline of education is too sophisticated for such an approach; it demands professional preparation of its practitioners. For education and training to achieve their potentials as methods for combating occupational injury and illness, education and training programs must be based on well-established principles and conducted according to the highest standards of the education profession.

REFERENCES

Bird, F. E., Jr. "Safety." In *The Industrial Environment: Its Evaluation and Control.* Washington D.C.: U.S. Government Printing Office, 1973.

Blackwell, M. J., J. G. French, and H. P. Stein. "Adverse Health Effects of Smoking and the Occupational Environment." *American Industrial Hygiene Association Journal* 40 (1979): 38–47.

Bruner, J. *The Process of Education.* Cambridge, Massachusetts: Harvard University Press, 1977.

Cohen, A., M. J. Smith, and W. K. Anger. "Self-protective Measures against Workplace Hazards." *Journal of Safety Research* 11 (1979): 121–31.

Festinger, L. Informal Social Communication. In *Group Dynamics Research and Theory,* edited by D. Cartwright and A. Zander. 3rd ed. New York: Harper and Row, 1968.

Festinger, L., S. Schachter, and K. Back. "Operation of Group Standards." In *Group Dynamics Research and Theory,* edited by D. Cartwright and A. Zander. 3rd ed. New York: Harper and Row, 1968.

Fodor, J. T. and G. S. Dalis. *Health Instruction: Theory and Application.* 3rd ed. Philadelphia: Lea and Febiger, 1981.

Goldstein, I. L. "Training." In *The Human Side of Accident Prevention: Psychological Concepts and Principles which Bear on Industrial Safety,* edited by B. L. Margolis and W. H. Kroes. Springfield, Illinois: Charles C. Thomas, 1975.

Hare, A. P. *Handbook of Small Group Research.* 2nd ed. New York: The Free Press, 1976.

Heath, E. D. "Worker Training and Education in Occupational Safety and Health: A Report on Practice in Six Industrialized Western Nations." *Journal of Safety Research* 13 (1982): 121–31.

_____. "Worker Training and Education in Occupational Safety and Health: A Report on Practice in Six Industrialized Western Nations. *American Journal of Industrial Medicine* 2 (1981): 379–403.

Hooper, K. "The Hazard Evaluation System and Information Service: A Physician's Resource in Toxicology and Occupational Medicine." *Western Journal of Medicine* 137 (1982): 560–71.

University of Kansas. *Behavioral Procedures for Reducing Worker Exposure to Carcinogens: Final Report.* Lawrence, Kansas: University of Kansas, 1981.

Komaki, J., K. D. Barwick and L. R. Scott. "A Behavioral Approach to Occupational Safety: Pinpointing and Reinforcing Safety Performance in a Food Manufacturing Plant." *Journal of Applied Psychology* 63 (1978): 434–45.

Laner, S., and R. G. Sell. An experiment on the effect of specially designed safety posters. *Occupational Psychology* 34 (1960): 153–69.

McIntire, R. W., and J. White. "Behavior Modification." In *The Human Side of Accident Prevention: Psychological Concepts and Principles Which Bear on Industrial Safety,* edited by B. L. Margolis and W. H. Kroes. Springfield, Illinois: Charles C. Thomas, 1975.

Maples, T. W., J. A. Jacoby, D. E. Johnson, G. L. Ter Haar, and F. M. Buckingham. "Effectiveness of Employee Training and Motivation Programs in Reducing Exposure to Inorganic Lead and Lead Alkyls." *American Industrial Hygiene Association Journal* 43 (1982): 692–94.

Margolis, B. L., and W. H. Kroes, eds. *The Human Side of Accident Prevention: Psychological Concepts and Principles Which Bear on Industrial Safety.* Springfield, Illinois: Charles C. Thomas, 1975.

Noro, K. "1984: Small-group Activities and Quality Control Circles in Japanese Industry." In *Proceedings of the 1984 International Conference on Occupational Ergonomics,* edited by M. L. Matthews and R. D. G. Webb. Toronto: Human Factors Association of Canada, 1984.

Posner, G. J., and A. N. Rudnitsky. *Course Design: A Guide to Curriculum Development for Teachers.* 2nd ed. New York: Longman, 1982.

Public Law 91–596. Occupational Safety and Health Act of 1970. Statutes at Large, Vol. 84, p. 1590, Title 29, U.S. Code Sec. 1976.

Rohmert, W. and K. Landau. *A New Technique for Job Analysis.* Philadelphia: Taylor and Francis, 1983.

United States Department of Labor, Occupational Safety and Health Administration. "Training Guidelines: Request for Comments and Information." *Federal Register* 48 (1983): 39317–23.

Vojtecky, M. A. "Workplace Health Education: Principles in Practice." *Journal of Occupational Medicine* 27 (1985): 29–33.

Vojtecky, M. A., S. Kar, and S. G. Cox. "Workplace Health Education: Results from a National Survey." *International Quarterly of Community Health Education* 5 (1985): 171–85.

Zohar, D. "Promoting the Use of Personal Protective Equipment by Behavior Modification Technique." *Journal of Safety Research* 12 (1980): 78–85.

Zohar, D., A. Cohen, and N. Azar. "Promoting Increased Use of Ear Protectors in Noise through Information Feedback." *Human Factors* 22 (1980): 69–79.

II
Implementation of Health Education Programs

Providing for the establishment of health education programs in the workplace poses an exciting challenge. In order to effectively address the challenge we need to prepare certain plans and pursue specific steps. However, we must not be too hasty in launching our programs.

Santa-Barbara describes the relationship between a particular aspect of corporate culture and the requirements for a successful health education program in the workplace. He describes the sensitive nature of the target behaviors of such a program as well as the conditions required for altering these highly personal lifestyle behaviors. He argues that the companies who pioneered health education in the workplace possessed the uncommon characteristic of having a strong people orientation. This value greatly facilitated the program's success. In contrast companies now exploring health education as a cost-control mechanism may not sufficiently possess this people orientation to meet the delicate conditions necessary to sustain lifestyle changes in their employees. Health education programs implemented in corporate environments that are interested solely in cost reduction run the risk of not attaining their cost-effective potential, or they may fail altogether. Suggestions are made for determining whether the necessary corporate culture exists and for taking steps if it does not.

Klarreich describes the importance of establishing a health education committee as a vehicle to effectively launch a health education program. Key reasons for creating a health education committee, which is the "doorway to health education," are carefully described. The role of this group is explored and the ultimate products and results of a well-organized committee are reported. Additionally, the question of the relationship between health education and employee assistance is addressed. He argues that employee assistance programs have traditionally adopted an "interventionist approach," which has limited the scope of the programs and has restricted the services being offered to the client group. He further contends that a "preventive approach" via health education can only enhance the services delivered to employees and create a more comprehensive employee assistance program.

Planning is a significant process, no matter what the project, and is certainly vital when it comes to health education. Cantlon and Carter capture the primary planning considerations in developing health promotion programs. They detail the basic characteristics of successful programs and then describe the "how to's" to achieve them. Issues such as determining the shape of the program by identifying the corporate culture, organizational structure, nature of the worker and the workday, and participant "turn-offs" are each considered concretely. Emphasis is placed on creating an environment conducive to positive health, establishing realistic goals, ensuring management support, and having an adequate budget and staff. The chapter concludes with a set of action strategies to ensure a successful health promotion program.

A significant strategy often overlooked or downplayed is communications. That is, a system to convey to the employees what you wish to implement and accomplish. Rawson explores the steps and thought processes that are involved in effective communication planning. Successful health promotion campaigns, using case studies, are highlighted and practical tips are provided. She discusses essential guidelines, namely the "what," "where," "when," "how," and "why" of communications. She further describes the use of a "creative theme and creative media" to enhance the impact of the message being imparted. One begins to appreciate that designing a communications strategy almost requires as much planning as the health education program itself.

Marketing is another commonly misunderstood important ingredient. Fleming points out that the implications of the marketing concept for wellness programs extend beyond promoting, advertising, and selling. Its real utility is in the planning and development phases of the program. Marketing-based programs are based not on compliance-seeking strategies but on strategies that match management's capabilities and resources with employees' needs and wants. A case study of a marketing-based wellness program along with the documentation of its effectiveness is presented. The advantages of planning and development strategies that include marketing are illustrated by flexible, tailored programs, ongoing review and clarification of management objectives, modest start-up budgets, low-cost and low-risk experimentation with new program components, and a "win-win" situation for management and employees.

High technology has entered our working lives with a big bang. Computers have become necessities rather than luxuries because of their tremendous capacity to heighten efficiency and enhance productivity. Opper colorfully describes a new opportunity, computer communications and its application to health education. She considers the ways in which computer hardware, software, and systems can make the communication of health education possible. The basics of "on-line networking" are described, and the process of separating information from the networking system is explained. In her discussion, she details the importance of having the on-line networks meet institutional needs. The concluding section highlights her visions of the future, which leads one to believe that the applications of computer communications for health education are boundless.

3 Corporate Health and Corporate Culture

Jack Santa-Barbara

INTRODUCTION

This chapter is addressed to those considering the implementation of a health education program in the workplace. Its purpose is to sensitize them to the importance of corporate culture in determining the program's eventual success. It is recommended that before implementation, each company conduct a review of their corporate culture, to determine whether a health education program is indeed feasible, given the employee related values identified by such a review.

The particular aspect of corporate culture that is regarded as critical to the success of a health education program is a strong "people orientation." This corporate value is discussed in terms of what it contributes to altering employees' lifestyle behavior patterns, the targets of most health education programs. First, we discuss the issues of behavior change, resistance to behavior change, and the unique requirements for modification of these highly personal and sensitive lifestyle behaviors.

HEALTH CARE IS A PERSONAL RESPONSIBILITY

Most health care is self-care. By far, most health related activities are carried out by the individual and family members in the privacy of their home (Santa-Barbara 1979). How successful these practices are, to a large extent, determines the individual's need for using professional health care services. Therefore, these personal health practices, which are largely the responsibility of the individual, determine the costs of the health care system. The so-called "lifestyle diseases," which account for such a high proportion of the total health care budget (Lalonde 1974), are the result of personal activities over which the professional health care system has traditionally had little influence. These lifestyle diseases are the result of inadequate self-care.

Health education as a means of influencing health behaviors is a relatively recent phenomenon. Surveys indicate that health is highly valued by most of us. Yet in typically human fashion, we are generally ignorant about many basic facts of health care (for example, Pratt 1956; Haley, Aucoin, and Rae 1977), and even fewer of us act on what we know (for example, Wilson 1970).

Both health professionals and corporate leaders now view health education programs as a cost-effective means of influencing personal health behaviors of large numbers of people. The goals of health education are to increase the health status of large numbers of people and to concomitantly reduce health care costs. For example, the recent decline in smoking behavior by more than 40 million North Americans (McGinnis 1985) is a clear demonstration that change can occur. The financial savings to both the individuals involved and their employers is significant (Kristine, Arnold, and Wynder, 1977).

However, many lifestyle behaviors remain that continue to generate more health problems than the burgeoning health care system can handle. There are simply not enough health care professionals to treat these lifestyle diseases once they occur. More health care professionals and more expensive treatments in the traditional medical model are not the answer. Prevention of disease is the strategic choice for the future. Health education programs in the workplace represent a promising approach to disease prevention. There are benefits for both the individual employee and the employer, and, because of these benefits, the workplace provides an ideal opportunity for launching and sustaining the necessary lifestyle changes.

However, the current burden of responsibility for health care remains largely and solely with the individual and the family — the very source of the problem. The difficulties individuals and families have in maintaining a high degree of physical and mental health are many and varied and beyond the scope of the present chapter (for example, Pratt 1976).

HEALTH EDUCATION AFFECTS
SENSITIVE PERSONAL BEHAVIORS

The behaviors that are targets of health education programs are very personal and sensitive ones: exercise, eating, smoking, use of alcohol and drugs (both prescribed and nonprescribed), stress management, safety practices, interpersonal relations, and even certain sexual practices. At the best of times, attempts to alter behavior patterns meet with resistance, from both conscious and unconscious sources. Behavioral habits in these particular areas are, therefore, not easily changed. For example, many of these behaviors offer immediate gratification, but in the long run are extremely unhealthy. The Valium prescribed by one's doctor may provide quick reduction of anxiety. The extra sweets, or third martini, may provide a temporary sense of well-being. Bottling up one's feelings may avoid an unpleasant confrontation with a colleague or family member.

These are powerful rewards to counter. Most people consider their use to be a right they may exercise whenever they wish, and for which they need account to no one. Self-concept plays an enormous role as well. One's sense of self as competent and able to handle stress and one's sense of vulnerability and dependence on others are also at stake.

CONDITIONS FOR CHANGING LIFESTYLE BEHAVIORS

Altering such health-compromising behaviors requires even more effective reinforcers. These behavior patterns are likely to be altered only if individuals feel change is in their own best interest. Relevant and accurate information concerning the consequences of change, is therefore, important. Also critical is the individuals' sense of self-control, of making the decision to change of their own volition. We tend to be self-motivated when we feel we have the necessary competencies and that we are responsible for using these competencies (Deci and Ryan 1980).

Another important factor in altering ingrained behavior patterns is the creation of new social norms regarding health related behaviors. Many of our expectations and needs are influenced by our social environment. We compare ourselves to others and accept for ourselves what we see as approved or expected by others. Although health has been highly valued, there have not been strong norms and adequate information readily available to support healthy lifestyles. Given the pervasiveness of the lifestyle diseases in our society, the generally accepted norms have clearly been oppositional. For example, the use of alcohol, drugs, and food to manage our stresses is expected. Solving marital or family problems by abuse or separation and divorce is too readily viewed as acceptable. One of the goals of health education is to create new norms and the social and informational supports to bolster these norms on a continuing basis.

Health education programs that incorporate these principles are more likely to succeed than those that rely on coercive procedures or sanctions. These considerations about health education have important consequences for their application in the workplace.

INNOVATORS HAVE UNIQUE CORPORATE CULTURES

In recent years, corporate health management has become a growing concern for many businesses. The rapid escalation of the corporate share of health care costs has focused corporate attention on this issue. Pioneers in this field such as Johnson and Johnson, IBM, Mattel, and Control Data have implemented model health education programs and demonstrated considerable reductions in health care costs. Their success has led many other companies to implement, or at least consider, their own programs. However, such programs are not automatically successful. Companies that pioneered such innovative programs are generally different in important ways from other companies. In many instances these companies enjoyed almost ideal conditions in which to deal with the delicate requirements for behavior change described above. As well as borrowing what is appropriate, it is important to understand these differences. Most important is that particular component of an organization's corporate culture that determines how that organization relates to its employees' personal needs.

A PEOPLE ORIENTATION IS CENTRAL TO SUCCESS

A major characteristic that many of the pioneer corporations involved in health education have in common is a strong "people orientation." There is an intense and widespread belief throughout the culture of these organizations that employees' well-being is important to the success of the organization. This people orientation is not simply a motherhood issue but is expressed in multiple and tangible ways throughout the company. It is reflected in the physical environment provided for employees, the equipment and training they are supplied, management style, benefit plans, and even the way receptionists greet visitors. Respect for each employee, not only in terms of rights but also in terms of individual needs, is expected and reinforced by management.

Part of this respect is the belief that employees are adults who will reciprocate courtesy and consideration and who will demonstrate self-responsibility if provided the opportunity and the support they each need. This respect for the individual is often expressed by encouraging employee participation — on joint committees, in quality circles, or in deciding how best to accomplish a given task. Employee participation, mutual support, and respect for the individual's contribution to the company are all parts of a genuine people oriented corporate environment. Where the culture is strong, it permeates the entire organization.

A value system that respects the individual is perhaps the single most important element of a successful corporate health education program. In such an environment employees believe there is genuine concern for their well-being and that they will not be exploited by the company. The presence of this value system creates certain expectations among employees as well. Reciprocity is a basic form of social exchange (Gouldner 1960). Being treated well by a company leads most employees to treat the company well — to take their responsibilities seriously, to respect company policies, procedures, and properties, and, in short, to be productive. Employees who feel respected also tend to develop feelings of loyalty to the company and respect for management.

Another consequence of this type of corporate culture is the influence it has on employees' perceptions of themselves. Being treated well makes employees feel well and has a direct impact on their health. In fact, survey data (Palmore 1969) indicate that one of the most important factors influencing longevity was job satisfaction. One's occupational role is generally one of the most meaningful roles in one's life. If the meaning derived from work is positive and fulfilling, then the individual's health and well-being are enhanced. Employees feel good about themselves, are more energetic and enthusiastic, solve problems better, adapt to new demands more quickly, can manage the normal stresses of life more easily, and can provide more support to their colleagues when necessary.

The circle closes. A corporate culture that invests in people enhances their well-being. These healthier employees reciprocate by being more productive and by taking pride in their achievements. Productivity rises as employees' commitment and enthusiasm grow, and unnecessary health care costs are reduced.

The implementation of a health education program in this type of corporate culture is a natural extension of this value system. A people oriented value system creates excellent conditions for changes in life-style behavior. People do not feel coerced or exploited because they trust the company's motives. Programs in such companies respect the individual's right to choose participation, thereby enhancing the individual's sense of self-responsibility. The corporate program facilitates healthy lifestyles and establishes positive norms to which employees may aspire. There is a greater willingness by employees to at least try participation in these programs because such companies have the confidence and respect of their employees. Because people oriented companies naturally emphasize self-motivation and self-responsibility, the employees feel the choice is theirs to make and feel apprecia-tive toward the company for providing them with an opportunity for self-development.

A strong people orientation has been identified as one of the distinguishing marks of corporate excellence (Peters and Waterman 1982). It is not surprising that many of the examples of excellence cited by these authors are the same companies who have pioneered health education programs in the workplace. In this important way, these companies have been different from other companies. Those that overlook the importance of a strong people orientation as part of their corporate culture, when implementing a health education program, do so at some risk. However, given the growing interest in the cost-reduction potential of corporate health management, the likelihood of this risk occurring would seem to be increasing.

A GOOD REASON NOT TO IMPLEMENT A HEALTH EDUCATION PROGRAM IN THE WORKPLACE

One reason that health education programs have attracted increasing attention is the evidence demonstrating the potential cost reductions available to the employer (for example, Berry 1981; Cox, Shephard, and Corey 1981; Fielding 1985). This concern was undoubtedly a major consideration of the innovators in the field. It is surely a legitimate concern, and all companies would be well advised to carefully calculate their existing costs related to the effects of lifestyle diseases among their employees. Survey data indicate that senior management is very often unaware of these costs (Sapolsky et al. 1981). These costs are indeed considerable and deserve careful attention. Furthermore, and most important, they are largely avoidable.

Cost reduction as a consequence of employee health education is an interest, if not yet a priority, for many corporate leaders. In the United States, federal legislation has been proposed as an incentive to encourage employers to implement such programs (Cohen 1985). However, it must be remembered that most of the data to date are from programs implemented in companies with a genuine people oriented corporate culture. With the growing interest in health education being stimulated by economic considerations, there is the risk that attempts will be made to implement programs in companies where this value is absent or too weak to contribute to the program's success. A good reason not to implement a health education program, therefore, is where this corporate value is lacking and where the overwhelming motive is economic.

A health education program is unlike any other corporate benefit in that it focuses on extremely personal and sensitive behaviors. These programs are likely to have a positive impact on the bottom line only if employees alter their lifestyle behaviors. This will happen only if the program touches people in a very personal and supportive way. The conditions required to change the behaviors described above are less likely to be developed in the absence of a people oriented corporate culture. Serious backlashes could develop in terms of employees feeling they are being coerced, tampered with, manipulated, or preached to. Resentment and actual sabotage are possible, greatly reducing or eliminating the company's return on investment and failing to improve the health status of employees.

Health education programs do have enormous potential to contribute to both corporate productivity and employee (and family) well-being. A corporate backlash as a result of poor implementation would be most unfortunate for all parties involved.

ANALYZING CORPORATE CULTURE

A complete description of how to conduct a review of a corporate culture is beyond the scope of this chapter. Generally it entails a review of documents like mission statements, corporate management philosophies, and interviews and/or surveys of staff at various levels in the organization. Assistance from an external resource is often very helpful in order to provide an objective and impartial perspective. The review should use some procedure for going beyond the formal, explicit policy or philosophy and critically (and skeptically) examine how thoroughly and pervasively any explicit philosophy is actually operationalized. Such a review and its findings could have an effect on the organization that goes far beyond the implementation of a health education program.

USING A HEALTH EDUCATION PROGRAM
TO ALTER A CORPORATE CULTURE

If the review of the corporate culture indicates that a strong people orientation exists, then planning for the implementation of the health education program can proceed (as outlined by Fielding 1985, for example). If the review indicates that the corporate culture is lacking a strong and genuine people orientation, several options are open. Implementing a health education program may be deferred until the corporate culture is revised as required. The decision to review corporate culture is clearly likely to involve motivations other than implementing a health education program. Given the importance of a people orientation as a basic component of corporate excellence (Peters and Waterman 1982), there are sound business reasons for altering the corporate culture regardless of a company's interest in health promotion.

If a sincere commitment is made to develop a people orientation as part of one's corporate culture, another option may also be considered. As part of the revision of corporate culture, a health education program may be implemented as a means of introducing this new corporate direction and making it tangible. A well-designed health education program could be an excellent vehicle for conveying to all staff the concern the company has for their well-being. The use of social marketing techniques (Greenberg 1982; Kotler and Zaltman 1971; Lewitt 1981; Novelli 1980; Rothchild 1979) to promote the program will provide high visibility and involve staff in ways that will encourage their participation and support.

A well-designed and implemented health education program can benefit a company in more ways than reducing health care costs. By creating the conditions necessary for a comprehensive health education program to thrive and contribute to the reduction of health costs, a company will also be contributing to its own striving for excellence.

REFERENCES

Berry, C. A. *An Approach to Good Health for Employees and Reduced Health Care Costs for Industry.* Washington, D. C.: Health Insurance Association of America, 1981.

Cohen, W. S. "Health Promotion in the Workplace: A Prescription for Good Health." *American Psychologist* 40 (1985): 213–16.

Cox, M., R. J. Shephard, and P. Corey. "Influence of an Employee Fitness Programme, upon Fitness, Productivity, and Absenteeism." *Erogonomics* 24 (1981): 795–806.

Deci, E. L., and R. M. Ryan. "The Empirical Exploration of Intrinsic Motivational Processes." *Advances in Experimental Social Psychology* 13 (1980): 39–80.

Fielding, J. E. *Corporate Health Management.* Don Mills, Ontario: Addison-Wesley, 1985.

Gallaiford, N. "Another Reason to Go to Work: Keeping Fit and Healthy in the Workplace." *Human Resources Management in Canada.* Toronto: Prentice-Hall Canada, November 5, 1984, 315–20.

Gouldner, A. W. "The Norm of Reciprocity: A Preliminary Statement." *American Sociological Review* 25 (1960): 161–71.

Greenberg, R. "Developing Mass Education of Community Health Programs, a Social Marketing Approach." *Health Education,* Summer, 1982, pp. 6–9.

Haley, M., D. Aucoin, and J. Rae. "A Comparative Study of Food Habits: Influence of Age, Sex, and Selected Family Characteristics, II," *Canadian Journal of Public Health* 68 (1977): 301–6.

Kotler, P., and G. Zaltman. "Social Marketing: An Approach to Planned Social Changes." *Journal of Marketing* 35 (1971): 3–12.

Kristine, M., C. B. Arnold, and E. L. Wynder. "Health Economics and Preventative Care." *Science* 195 (1977): 457–62.

Lalonde, M. *A New Perspective on the Health of Canadians.* Ottawa: Government of Canada, Dept. of Health and Welfare, 1974.

Lewitt, T. "Marketing Intangible Products and Product Intangibles." *Harvard Business Review* 59 (1981): 94–102.

McGinnis, J. M. "Recent History of Federal Initiatives in Prevention Policy." *American Psychologist* 40 (1985): 205–12.

Novelli, W. D. "Tremendous Need is Seen Ahead for More Effective Social Marketing." *Advertising Age,* 1980, pp. 51–92.

Palmore, E. "Predicting Longevity: A Follow-up Controlling for Age." *Gerontologist* 9 (1969): 247–50.

Peters, T. J., and R. H. Waterman, Jr. *In Search of Excellence.* New York: Harper and Row, 1982.

Pratt, L. "How Do Patients Learn about Disease?" *Social Problems* 4 (1956): 29–40.

Pratt, L. *Family Structure and Effective Health Behaviour: The Energized Family. Boston:* Houghton Mifflin, 1976.

Rothchild, N. "Marketing Communications in New Business Situations or Why It's So Hard to Sell Brotherhood Like Soap." *Journal of Marketing* 43 (1979): 11–20.

Santa-Barbara, J. "Health, like Charity, Begins at Home." *Health Education* 18 (1979): 4–6.

Sapolsky, H. M., D. Altman, R. Greene, and J. D. Moore. "Corporate Attitudes towards Health Care Costs." *Millbank Memorial Fund Quarterly/Health and Society* 59 (1981): 561–85.

Wilson, R. L. *The Sociology of Health: An Introduction.* New York: Random House, 1970.

4 A Health Education Committee: The Doorway to Health Education for an Employee Assistance Program

Samuel H. Klarreich

AN INTERVENTIONIST PERSPECTIVE OF EMPLOYEE ASSISTANCE PROGRAMS

Employee Assistance Programs (EAPs) since their beginning have maintained a strong philosophy of intervention (Presnall 1981). In their early development around the 1940s, they were greatly influenced by two movements. First was the alcoholism program movement; second, was the personnel counseling movement (Presnall 1981). Both of these advancements addressed employee issues through intervention.

Personnel counseling was often handled by specially trained lay people who would counsel employees about particular job performance and attitude problems in order to correct matters so that satisfactory levels of performance could be restored. At the same time, alcoholism programs, which appeared in companies, typically involved company owners, organizational managers, and specialized lay persons who would attempt to intervene with those employees who had drinking difficulties and a variety of health related problems. Concurrently, the Alcoholics Anonymous movement was also beginning to grow and flourish and shape the development of EAPs (Trice and Sonnenstuhl, 1985). Their approach arrested employee problems through the use of constructive confrontation.

As personnel counseling programs and alcohol based programs continued to evolve in the business community, a new development occurred and influenced EAPs, namely the mental health movement

(McLean and Taylor 1958). For the first time, consultants such as psychiatrists, industrial psychologists, clinical psychologists, and clinical social workers began to find opportunities for providing service in various organizations. These professionals focused their activities largely on mental and emotional conditions that employees were experiencing. Their approach involved directly addressing concerns in an effort to bring about positive changes.

The turbulent 1960s saw emerging EAPs being influenced by two conflicting forces. On the one hand, there were mental health and its proponents who resisted the strategies of direct intervention and constructive confrontation in favor of other indirect methods involving empathy, understanding, and unconditional positive regard. Problems were viewed as failures to fulfill potential, as blocks to growth, and as deficits in new learning. On the other hand, there were alcoholism and its advocates who spurned mental health strategies in favor of direct confrontation and assailment of employee problems, namely "drinking." Alcoholism was regarded as a disease and required the same treatment as other diseases. Consequently, the emerging EAPs seemed to adopt either one philosophy or the other, and the way employees were approached clearly would reflect the particular bias.

During the 1970s, their seemed to be an amalgamation of movements, and EAPs reflected this development (Presnall 1985). The concept of a "broad-brush approach" became prevalent. EAPs employing a broad-brush approach dealt with mental health issues and alcoholism problems. Practitioners running EAPs employed such intervention strategies as constructive confrontation and constructive coersion in combination with counseling, psychotherapy, and referral to inpatient treatment units or day treatment units or outpatient units.

However, a new trend materialized in the late 1970s and is now flourishing in the 1980s. This is prevention through health education and fitness (Levine 1982). Health professionals realize that prevention involves early detection of problems, and early detection occurs through heightened awareness via health education. Additionally, prevention also encompasses self-responsibility for mental and physical health, that is, employees taking greater interest and care in their health and well-being. This trend has now affected the philosophical position of EAPs. EAP professionals are now paying greater attention to the issue of prevention (Parcell 1985). Practitioners have not abandoned the concept of intervention and treatment but are now beginning to recognize that teaching employees to avert problems can be as valuable an activity as traditional counseling or psychotherapy for problems.

There is every reason to believe ... that for every domestic, marital, or emotional problem bad enough to warrant assistance through an EAP, there are three others that depress productivity and affect overall functioning, but they do not lend themselves to therapeutic intervention in the usual sense. These are problems with which people are, in a way, "coping," but that sorely tax their resources in doing so. It is, nevertheless, from this larger population that future candidates for EAPs will come. Consequently, intervention at this earlier level has preventative functions. (Shain and Boyle 1985, pp. 294)

IS THERE ROOM FOR PREVENTION VIA HEALTH EDUCATION IN AN EMPLOYEE ASSISTANCE PROGRAM?

EAPs should include prevention as well as intervention, health education as well as counseling or psychotherapy. Are prevention and intervention that different? The Funk & Wagnall's dictionary (1977) defines prevention as "the act of intending or serving to ward off harm or disease" (p. 523). The dictionary defines intervention as "the act of modifying an action or expectation" (p. 341). Do not both processes intend change? Is it not possible that during intervention, prevention may occur? Is it not possible that during prevention, some intervention may occur?

Although both processes are on the same continuum of health care, prevention occurs temporally earlier than intervention. They often intend similar basic changes, but the means to produce these changes often differ. If both are designed to help and assist the employee, then are not both strategies important? How can we include intervention and counseling and not include prevention?

When examining the concepts of health education and psychotherapy the differences actually become obscured. Funk & Wagnall's dictionary (1977) defines education as "a systematic development or training of the mind, capabilities, or character through instruction or study" (p. 202). Furthermore, the dictionary (1977) defines psychotherapy as "the treatment of disorders by psychological methods such as ... re-education" (p. 534). It is safe to say then that both processes involve some training of the mind. Furthermore both activities involve some instruction. In fact, psychotherapy is often viewed as a process of education, in particular health education (Ellis 1973). Because both activities are designed to assist and educate, but may incorporate different methods to achieve their aims, are they not both important ingredients of an EAP. One would have difficulty explaining why psychotherapy and counseling can be included and health education cannot be included.

Will we not as EAP practitioners be providing a more comprehensive EAP service if prevention through health education becomes part of the program? Over the years, I think many professionals who have offered EAPs have come to the realization that once the chronic, long-standing employee problems have been resolved, there are very few remaining employees who require "traditional intervention and treatment" (Parcell 1985).

In the first 2 1/2 years of my program, there were a significant number of chronic and severe problems to manage. However, after these were successfully resolved, there remained very few severely troubled employees who still required assistance. Since that time, the majority of the employees whom I have seen, have come to the program to receive instruction in order to prevent minor problems from becoming more serious ones. They have come to the EAP not only because they may have heard of the success of the program but also, and more importantly, because health education lectures have occurred with regularity, and a significant number of employees have come to explore in greater depth information they gathered from these lectures.

It would seem, therefore, that it would be in the best interests of EAP practitioners to make certain that there exists a strong health education component to their programs. It would surely generate more cases, and there is not one EAP practitioner who is not concerned with the issue of case finding. It would also give rise to a greater variety of cases, which would enrich the work for the EAP practitioner. It would broaden the range of activities for the EAP practitioner, which again would enhance the job. It might also bring about a shift in the orientation of the EAP practitioner from an illness model to a wellness model. The EAP practitioner could begin to think in terms of degrees of wellness rather than degrees of illness when counseling employees. Finally and most importantly, it would provide a more comprehensive service to the employee. It is an exciting prospect and one that should be part of every EAP.

RATIONALE FOR A HEALTH EDUCATION COMMITTEE

It might be relatively easy for an EAP practitioner to say, "Well, it is time to start rolling out health education programs." The practitioner might then plan, implement, and deliver the programs. However, this is quite an onerous task especially when there exists a large body of employees. In fact, this could be a full-time job for certain professionals, and in many cases it is. In my program there exists a population of approximately 2,800 employees. If I were the sole health educator, virtually 100 percent of my time would be spent in health related activities. Because my other activities in the area of counseling, assessment, and referral are so vital to the EAP, it seems extremely reasonable and very feasible to have a Health Education Committee. Seven key reasons justified establishing a Health Education Committee in my organization.

Innovation

An important consideration is innovation. Isn't there an expression that "two heads are better than one"? When creating regular health education programs, it is important that novel, imaginative, and fresh ideas are forthcoming. There is a greater likelihood that such ideas might be generated if a number of individuals work together. Many of these ideas might then become topics for present and future health education programs. If one works in isolation, there is sometimes the tendency to "exhaust the idea bank" and then become somewhat demoralized and demotivated. When there is a committee, this tendency is minimized.

Support

Support is another key consideration. Often when one is called upon to deliver presentations to employee groups, encouragement, support, and recognition are important ingredients to inspire continued motivation. When working on a committee, one finds these elements a part of a regular and ongoing process. Support is also helpful from a group especially after a presentation is given. If the results of a presentation have not been as meaningful or as positive as one might expect, a person might become discouraged. Encouragement from a committee can often inject new energy and new vitality.

Division of Labor

Division of labor is a critical ingredient. Often when health education programs are regularly delivered, a considerable amount of work and preparation is required. If one individual performs all the duties, it becomes a very burdensome task. When a group is committed to health education, it becomes possible to create an orderly division of labor so that individuals can assume specific responsibilities for each presentation. Committee members can also rotate various tasks subsequent to each presentation to reduce the likelihood of boredom from repeating the same assignments.

Management Support

Management support is a very important element (Brennan 1985). Where there is a committee comprised of a variety of professionals at various levels of responsibility in the organization, management is more likely to approve a proposal to offer health education programs prepared by these individuals. The proposal will probably be more comprehensive and reflect what can and cannot be accomplished within a given organization. If presentations take place during working hours, it is probably essential that management support the project; otherwise, employees will probably not leave their work area to attend the program. Programs can be delivered after work hours; however, we have found that more employees attend when programs take place during the workday. In our case, with the wholehearted endorsement of management, the presentations were offered during the lunch hour. If employees know that management truly supports these efforts, they will take these presentations more seriously. Finally, if management gives its stamp of approval, this in principle indicates that it values the health and well-being of the employee.

Budget

Budget is another important consideration. If health education programs are to be properly established they will require funds for promotion, advertising, materials, printing, honoraria for invited speakers, and for occasional hidden costs. The committee can carefully plan and design a well-documented budget. In the process, members can debate with one another to ensure that items are precisely stipulated and properly justified. This effort will heighten the prospects that the budget proposal will receive approval, should the submission of a budget statement be required. An individual working alone might overlook many items, which might detract from the effectiveness of the proposal.

Speakers

Another important consideration is the issue of speakers. One benefit of having a Health Education Committee is that a number of the committee members might be potential speakers who can deliver various lectures. Committee members often have various degrees of expertise, various degrees of skill, and some of them might be very polished speakers. In fact, when you are forming a committee, it might be wise to seek out people who are not only committed to health education but also can deliver presentations. In our organization, a number of health education programs have been prepared and delivered by committee members. This has the added benefit of saving speaker costs.

On the occasion you reach out to the community to find a speaker, a committee makes the task easier. Usually any one committee member will know a number of people who merit consideration.With a pool of individuals to choose from the selection process to arrive at a speaker who is suitable for a given topic is greatly simplified.

Networking

The final item of importance is networking (Windsor et al. 1984). It is critical for an EAP professional to "network," not only outside his or her organization but especially within the organization. The EAP must become part of the organizational fabric. The EAP professional should know "the culture" and should be known as a key resource in the organization. When the EAP practitioner becomes part of a Health Education Committee, he or she automatically has the opportunity to establish important relationships with different professionals in different capacities. These relationships may foster other relationships, which ultimately will heighten the EAP's profile within the organization and enhance the networking process.

THE ROLE OF A HEALTH EDUCATION COMMITTEE

> An obstacle to conclusive program evaluation is that most organizations fail to set clear-cut goals for the program before implementation. . . . However, companies do appear to be catching on to the importance of establishing rational objectives before the fact. (Feuer 1985, p. 32)

Proper planning is critical to the establishment and the development of a health education program (Brennan 1985). If the health education program is to be regulated by a Health Education Committee, it becomes essential to understand clearly the role and responsibilities of this committee. The process that was pursued to properly design a Health Education Committee in our organization will illustrate the importance of planning.

The regional medical services director and I, the EAP director, were both very excited about the prospects of presenting health education activities. We were committed to the venture and were willing to expend the energy and the effort initially needed to establish a committee. We assigned ourselves the responsibility of cochairing the committee because during the formative stages it was important to have clear leadership. If there was a need for other individuals to take on the role of chairperson, at a later date, that change could be made. We invited two nurses, another regional medical director, an advisor from employee relations, a specialist from corporate communications (the department responsible for advertising and communications), and an organizational development (OD) specialist. Thus, eight people constituted the core of our Health Education Committee.

The OD specialist worked with the members for approximately two days. During this time, we went through a process called "Management by Objectives and Results." This was designed to clarify our thinking, specify our obligations, and elucidate our goals. If we were to present ourselves in a professional fashion and if we were to be held accountable, we needed to be certain, in our own minds and on paper, of our exact responsibilities and objectives. This was a very meaningful exercise for all. It forced members to come to grips with what we wanted to accomplish as a Health Education Committee. After we had completed the process, we had a document that indicated a clear direction for our committee.

The basic mission or responsibility of the Health Education Committee was reflected in the following words, "responsible for promoting health awareness to Toronto area employees through group educational programs." We deliberated over the notion of promoting health awareness, as opposed to promoting behavior change or attitudinal change. We decided that the simplest approach was to encourage health awareness because the issue of attitude change or behavior change was a more complicated endeavor that we might have difficulty justifying and being held accountable for. Although attitude and behavior change programs are important, these matters could more easily be addressed through the Employee Assistance Program or the Health Services or both.

Our general objective was as follows, "employees who are knowledgeable about personal health management." We hoped that our programs could influence employees in such a way that they would become more informed about their own health and well-being and as a by-product might manage their lives more effectively.

We decided upon a number of key result areas upon which we wished to focus our attention. The first was "dissemination of personal health knowledge." We agreed that it was important to ensure that the health programs were designed and delivered efficiently. It was further concluded that we would offer one health education program each quarter. Each program would have and would include communication literature in the form of bulletin board notices, posters, flyers, and mailings. There was concern about losing valuable information, so we decided to install a library of health educational material and to include a copy of the information from each program delivered.

The second key result area was "diffusion of health education programs." We had a desire to share our information with other regions of the organization. Other regions that had or had not yet established health education programs could benefit from the material that we had developed and presented, so we circulated our material and our results after each program was completed.

The third key result area was "management support." We thought that it was essential to receive full management support for our Health Education Committee's plans and efforts. As such, we documented our responsibility statement, objectives, and key result areas, and one of the cochairmen arranged meetings with various management groups. During the meetings he outlined the Health Education Committee's plans regarding health education programs for employees. After each presentation, he received unanimous support for this project. The management teams seemed very impressed with the careful and elaborate strategy completed by the committee and indicated that they could be counted upon for ongoing encouragement.

The next key result area was "program effectiveness." We were very concerned that the programs be delivered effectively and were careful to choose presenters who were skilled in public speaking and who were properly prepared to deliver their particular topic. In fact, we would on occasion encourage the presenters to rehearse their talk in front of the Health Education Committee to ensure that they were suitably prepared. Additionally, we included an evaluation questionnaire to be completed by attendees after each health education presentation. This questionnaire served two purposes. First, it provided data that would allow us to assess whether we had met our overall objective of health awareness. Second, it provided information that allowed us to assess the effectiveness of the presentation and the speaker.

The final key result area was "coordination with external organizations." We felt that it was important to maintain a liaison with other external organizations, groups, and associations that are involved in health education. They could provide us with information, materials, and helpful suggestions before we developed our programs.

With the objectives and key result areas detailed, the direction for the Health Education Committee became very clear. The process that we pursued was critical in the development and evolution of health education programming for our organization. Had we not gone through this process, the focus for our efforts and energies would have been very ill defined, and this would have hampered the programs and hurt the reputation of our committee.

PRODUCTS AND RESULTS OF A WELL-ESTABLISHED HEALTH EDUCATION COMMITTEE

Our Health Education Committee has already sponsored eight quarterly presentations. Some of the presentations were delivered by our own staff; other topics were delivered by invited speakers. The evaluations, upon analysis, indicated that each program met our objective although some presentations seemed to gain a more favorable response from employees than others.

The first presentation that the Health Education Committee sponsored was about stress. More than 800 employees had an opportunity to attend the presentation, which was delivered by one of the members of the committee. After the presentation was completed the reviews and evaluations were summarized. Comments such as, "certainly made me more aware of my day-to-day living," "it was very beneficial to all," "I am very glad I came," "it meant a lot to me, it was marvelous, thank you," were very common.

The next program was about fitness, again delivered by one of our committee members. The presentation received such comments as, "good awareness vehicle," "very informative," "great seminar; keep it coming." Comments suggesting improvements for future presentations were also noted and kept on record.

The third presentation was entitled "Everything Doesn't Cause Cancer." The communications package for this presentation was so prominent and eye catching that the Canadian Cancer Society indicated their interest in using our materials for their own advertising campaign. After each presentation, including this one, an information kit was distributed to the attendees. We felt that it was necessary to provide employees with facts that would further heighten their awareness about the given topic. The cancer presentation was attended by more than 200 employees. Comments such as "glad I attended," "very thorough and complete coverage," "more such seminars on health care," were again quite common.

The fourth presentation was entitled "Emotional Fitness." A film by Dr. Leo Buscaglia entitled "Speaking of Love" was presented. This rented film discussed in a very uplifting, positive, and humorous fashion the importance of living life to the fullest including loving, learning, and maintaining strong relationships. The communications package for this presentation was extraordinary. In addition, the handout material, after the completion of the film was extremely well received. More than 400 employees saw the film during six separate showings. Their comments included, "very dynamic presentation," "best seminar yet; I loved it," "a topic good for the soul," "highly innovative."

Before the start of the second season, the Health Education Committee developed a questionnaire that requested employees to indicate their preferences regarding future topics. A most encouraging and interesting phenomenon was the return rate of this questionnaire. One might expect only a 5 percent to 10 percent rate, but we received over 30 percent of the questionnaires distributed.The most prominent topic of interest was burnout. Additional topics of interest included nutrition/diet, aging, the coping process, weight control, and self-acceptance. Upon tabulating the results, the committee decided that it should respond immediately to the expressed needs of the employees. So the next presentation was about the topic of burnout.

The burnout presentation given by one of our committee members was entitled "Beat Burnout . . . Cool It." As usual, the communications package was well conceived. Additionally, the handout material was quite extensive and was received with enthusiasm. More than 500 employees saw this presentation and their comments were most encouraging with such statements as, "thank you," "continue these seminars; they are of real value," "very important topic well done."

The next presentation was about nutrition, delivered by two members of our education committee. Approximately 300 employees attended, and they were quite appreciative of the effort, with such comments as, "thanks for a great effort," "very informative," "thank you very much for caring about us."

The next topic was entitled "Body Shop." The committee decided to experiment with a novel approach. There was no formal presentation by a speaker. Instead a comprehensive package of information was developed about the heart. Also the logo of a body was designed for the package. Once prepared, copies of the material were distributed to all employees in the Toronto region. In the future, at the same time each year there will be a different vital organ described; the material will be placed in folders and distributed under the heading "Body Shop." We hope that employees will maintain an ongoing file of the information they obtain each year. The comments we received from the employees included "keep up the good work," "looking forward to the next mailing," "a proactive attitude was expressed."

The final presentation for the second year was designated "Emotional Fitness — Part II." This was another film by Dr. Leo Buscaglia entitled "The Art of Being Fully Human." Once again the communications package was exceptional, and the handout material that the attendees received was well accepted. The message again was very positive, enlightening, and emotionally inspiring to the more than 350 employees who attended.

We are now looking forward to our third year. The first presentation will be about "Marriage and Its Alternatives." The next quarter will include a novel approach to the topic of "Smoking"; the third quarter will involve another "Body Shop" handout, and the final quarter may cover "Alcoholism and/or Drug Misuse."

In summary, it is safe to state that the health education programs were well planned and delivered, and the results, on the whole, admirably met our objectives. There were other benefits. The profiles of the medical services, the EAP, and the human resources department increased tremendously. The programs also seemed to boost the morale of employees. After each presentation, employees usually left feeling as if they had gained something meaningful. On many occasions they indicated that "the company must really care if it supports health education efforts." The health education programs also were instrumental in generating new cases for the EAP. Typically, I would receive phone calls from employees who wished to set up appointments or to obtain more information and assistance because of the presentation they had just attended. This is what prevention and health promotion is all about.

SUMMARY: PUT THE CART BEFORE THE HORSE

It may become necessary to reconceptualize the current approach to dissemination of the EAP by shifting emphasis from managerial identification of problem employees to self-identification through education (Shain and Groeneveld 1980, p. 21).

Self-identification of problems and self-responsibility for health and well-being are important considerations for any employee of an organization (Cohen 1985). Early identification, early detection, and early prevention through self-motivated action are certainly essential to the health of that employee. It then becomes very obvious that health education has a significant role to play. Furthermore, if EAPs are concerned about and devoted to the health and well-being of employees, health education cannot be overlooked as a vehicle to achieve the desired health-related goals.

Once an EAP is committed to providing health education programs, it is necessary to institute an appropriate mechanism to assist in fulfilling this mission. What better way to start than by designing and setting up a Health Education Committee — "the cart before the horse"?

Rosabeth Moss Kanter (1983), in her book *The Change Masters,* an exceptional text in organizational behavior and organizational change, comments on successful and innovative organizations. She points out that successful organizations are usually based upon a spirit of collaboration. Successful organizations in order to flourish, to grow, and to innovate need to build coalitions. If the health education effort in an EAP program is to grow, to flourish, and be successful, collaboration and a coalition are important. What better way to achieve these than to put together a Health Education Committee devoted to the development and dissemination of health education programs?

REFERENCES

Brennan, A. J. J. "Wellness Comes to Work." *Management World,* February 1985, pp. 12–15.

Cohen, W. S. "Health Promotion in the Workplace: A Prescription for Good Health." *American Psychologist* 40 (1985): 213–16.

Ellis, A. *Humanistic Psychotherapy, the Rational Emotive Approach.* New York: Julian Press, 1973.

Feuer, D. "Wellness Programs: How Do They Shape Up." *Training,* April, 1985, pp. 25–34.

Funk and Wagnalls *Dictionary,* New York: Funk and Wagnalls, 1977.

Kanter, R. Moss. *The Change Masters.* New York: Simon and Shuster, 1983.

Levine, A. "American Business Is Bullish on Wellness." *Medical World News,* March 29, 1982, pp. 33–40.

McLean, A. A., and G. Taylor. *Mental Health in Industry.* New York: McGraw-Hill, 1958.

Parcell, C. L. "Which Road Are We Taking, Illness, Wellness?" *EAP Digest,* March/April 1985, pp. 18–25.

Presnall, L. F. *Occupational Counseling and Referral Systems.* Salt Lake City, Utah: Utah Alcoholism Foundation, 1981.

____. "Historical Perspective of EAPs." *The Human Resources Management Handbook: Principles and Practice of Employee Assistance Programs,* edited by S. H. Klarreich et al. New York: Praeger Press, 1985, pp. ix–xvi.

Shain, M., and B. Boyle. "Toward Coordination of Employee Health Promotion and Assistance Programs." In *The Human Resources Management Handbook: Principles and Practice of Employee Assistance Programs,* edited by S. H. Klarreich et al. New York: Praeger Press, 1985, pp. 291–303.

Shain, M., and J. Groeneveld. *Employee Assistance Programs.* Lexington, Massachusetts: D.C. Heath, 1980.

Trice, H. M., and J. Sonnenstuhl. "AA and EAP: The Historical Link." *The Almacan,* May 1985, pp. 10–13.

Windsor, R. A., T. Baranowski, N. Clark, and G. Cutter. *Evaluation of Health Promotion and Education Programs.* Palo Alto, California: Mayfield, 1984.

5 Developing an Action Plan for Health Promotion Programs

Angelica T. Canton and Betty J. Carter

INTRODUCTION

Identifying the seven major characteristics of a successful program is the foundation and starting point for devising a successful plan of action for health promotion. A program cannot be successful, regardless of how limited or expansive, without adequate financial resources. There must be sufficient funding for program development, implementation, and evaluation. Commitment to a phased-in approach often provides the time necessary to pilot-test various aspects of the program and win enthusiasm for a complete roll out to the entire population. Supportive management is necessary to gain the funding and personnel required to implement the program as well as to encourage and reinforce participation among employees. A capable director and staff who are well experienced in program design and operations, presentation skills, and group facilitation have a direct effect on initiating and maintaining a program as well as determining internal role models and leaders. These leaders set an example, provide support, and generate enthusiasm for the various health activities. In order to attain participation, programs need maximum visibility and publicity. Using existing communication vehicles is a direct way to reach the population. Last, a program needs to incorporate and maintain an element of fun. Providing information, offering skills and promoting healthy behavior is not enough. Programs should be enjoyable, help employees feel good about themselves and create comraderie among coworkers. Throughout the remainder of this chapter, we refer to these characteristics and offer suggestions on how to incorporate them as the program is shaped and implemented. The principal characteristics of a successful program are

- An element of fun
- Maximum visibility and publicity
- Available role models and leaders
- Capable director and staff
- Supportive top and middle management
- Commitment to a phased-in approach
- Adequate financial resources

DESIGNING THE PROGRAM

Four basic factors must be considered in designing a plan: identifying company/participant needs and wants, defining the organization, determining participant turn-offs, and exploring organizational requirements.

Identifying Company/Participant Needs and Wants

The needs of the company/participants can be identified most readily through a review of health insurance claims, summary and trend data, absenteeism records, and, when available, clinical indicators of risk factors from medical examinations (preemployment and annual physicals). Health risk appraisals (HRA) and informational surveys can be administered to subsamples of employees to identify current health habits, risk factor profiles, and employee-perceived needs for health promotion programs.

The importance of clearly identifying what participants want in regard to health knowledge and skills, rather than what they might need, cannot be overemphasized. Often participants know they have a specific health need (that is, to lose weight), but their more immediate want may be to communicate better with their supervisor to reduce stress.

Keying into the wants of employees is accomplished in many ways such as focus groups, feedback sessions or a Health Promotion Planning Team approach. This team represents the organization (by level, department, union, and management) and has as its prime function identifying the needs and the wants of the majority of employees.

Encouraging participation from key employee groups in early planning stages directs the ultimate program shape to address the needs of the potential participants. In addition, it increases participation and enthusiasm for the proposed health promotion activities to follow.

Defining the Corporate Culture

Organizations often can be depicted as having personalities similar to individuals'. Organizations can be paternalistic, for example, or they can encourage a more entrepreneurial atmosphere among their employees. Many organizations have values that are promoted and encouraged throughout the company. Some organizations tend to encourage employees to be more autonomous and individualistic; others would have difficulty operating other than by clearly defined roles and relationships. Some organizations feel comfortable in creating rapid change, others prefer the slow introduction of one change at a time.

Deal and Kennedy (1982) describe the corporate culture as "the integrated pattern of human behavior that includes thought, special action and artifacts and depends on man's capacity for learning and transmitting knowledge to succeeding generations." Marion Bower (1966) offers a more informal definition: "The way we do things around here." For a health program to be naturally integrated and accepted, it must take on some of the characteristics of the existing organizational culture.

Corporate Policies and Procedures

Corporate policies and procedures need to be considered when investigating how the company operates. Typically, administrative bulletins or handbooks are available. If not, ask someone who has been with the company a while. Information about how things are done is useful in many ways — from getting posters displayed to obtaining a room reservation to knowing who's in charge.

Organizational Structure

Answers to three major questions help reveal the organizational structure.

Which department/division will the health program be part of?

What are other departments doing that may have an effect on the proposed program?

How can the staff members of existing health related programs and the proposed program work together to coordinate rather than duplicate efforts?

Of importance to the proposed program are maximum exposure, cooperation between related departments, and sound networking among the personnel. Piggy backing on existing programs enhances everyone's effort, makes it more effective for the potential participants, and helps gain visibility more quickly.

One other important component to consider, when applicable, is the involvement of the union and its representation. Union groups need to be assured of the cooperation and participation of their members. Clearly, union representation is mandatory on any committee or task force identifying the needs and wants of employees as described earlier.

The Nature of the Worker and the Workday

The type of work performed and the organization of the workday need to be identified to plan a program that will be easily accessible to the majority of employees.

Are everyone's hours the same, or are flex hours available? Is lunchtime 30 or 60 minutes? When are breaks during the day? Is the nature of work structured or flexible? Are the employees on site or on the road? What is the ratio of white-collar to blue-collar workers? What are the predominate age and sex of the work force? If there is a preponderance of white-collar married women with young children, the conceptual framework of the proposed program will take a slant different from that of a program designed for predominately middle-aged, blue-collar men. Such information might best be obtained through an itemized checklist (Table 5.1).

Is there a corporate hierarchy of decision making, or can decisions be made at lower levels? Must decisions be approved at several levels? If so, planning ahead is essential.

Internal Resources. Identifying the various groups within the organization that could be helpful is essential. Establishing good relationships with them can mean success in starting a program.

TABLE 5.1
Checklist for Identifying the Nature of the Worker
and the Workday

Nature of worker and workday	Yes	No	Comments
Hours			
Flex time			
Structured time			
Lunch — 1 hr.			
Lunch — 1/2 hr.			
Standardized breaks			
(15–20 min. a.m./p.m.)			
Flexible breaks			
Structure			
Hierarchical			
Matrix			
One location			
Multiple sites			
Centralized			
Decentralized			
			Percentage
Type of Worker			
Blue-collar			
White-collar			
Service oriented job			
Desk job			
Physical labor			
Age of Worker			
18–34 years			
35–54 years			
55 yrs–retirement			
Retirees			
Sex of Worker			
Male			
Female			

Source: Compiled by the author.

Identifying what these support groups do, how they could be of assistance, and their willingness to help are all areas to explore.

Internal and External Staffing Resources. Staffing for a health promotion program can be accomplished in many ways, depending on funding. Using existing health personnel, outside vendors, community resources, and outside consultants are among the more obvious choices. Personnel presently working in another capacity within the organization may have a health or education background. They can be invaluable resources. Frequently they are enthusiastic and willing to help.

Determining Participant Turn-Offs

Successful health promotion planners are aware that offering too much too soon can overwhelm potential participants. Focusing on issues that have been determined to have widespread appeal is going to be more interesting and meaningful to participants. Expecting a high level of readiness to make lifestyle changes among participants can often be a mistake. Creating awareness and interest, which eventually leads to more behavioral oriented programs, tends to work better. For example, an organization may launch a comprehensive behavior modification program and promote it aggressively before the employees are adequately motivated to accept such an approach. Instead, offering basic health information and skills, lectures or seminars that require little initial commitment, and yet enable the participant to measure progress, may be more workable. As the credibility of the program and its staff becomes more established, increased interest, participation and commitment often follow.

Easy access to the program is one of the keys to participation and compliance. Participants will pursue programs that are easily accessible, offered at a convenient time (that is, lunch hour, break time, before or after work), and fit into their daily schedules. Programs that require participation for long periods of time (usually more than eight weeks) often fail. The exceptions are fitness programs in which the employee expects a long-term, sustained approach.

Health promotion programs, like any other educational process, need to maintain an element of fun. Participation activities, lotteries, fun runs and incentives all encourage continued interest. They give the participants something to work for, a healthy competitive atmosphere with their coworkers, and something to anticipate. Individuals enjoy learning, and the word spreads quickly when everyone is having a good time.

Confidentiality is an issue of concern repeated by many employees. The question of who has access to HRA's questionnaires, and health screening data cannot be overlooked. Will the health habits or status of employees affect any aspect of their job function or evaluation? Developing, enforcing, and publicizing confidentiality policies are ways to minimize this turn-off.

Organizational Requirements

The philosophy of the top management should be conducive to positive health practices. An organization that has not clearly defined smoking guidelines for its employees may be considered hypocritical when a smoking cessation program is launched. An organization whose cafeteria has only fattening, high calorie foods cannot effectively offer weight control programs. When nonconducive atmospheres prevail, the surrounding environment should receive initial attention in planning.

Supportive upper and middle management personnel, identified earlier as essential to a successful program, is a characteristic worth repeating. Attitudes, values, support, and interest and reinforcement can be clearly communicated through management example. Developing a network to reach top and middle management and convincing them of the importance of the program will assure their encouragement of employee participation.

Broad based goals can be identified to help create the conceptual framework for the health promotion program. In designing the program, short-term, intermediate, and long-term objectives, based upon anticipated outcomes, need to be determined. The following are among some of the objectives that can be established.

Short-term objectives can most often be measured in a 6 to 12-month framework. It is realistic to expect to be able to:

- Determine the value of the program offered to employees based on interest and participation.
- Receive employee feedback regarding various aspects of the program.
- Observe changes in clinical data from mini to maxi screening baseline data.
- Review testimonials and case studies to identify changes in specific awareness, knowledge, and skill levels.
- Identify natural leaders or role models within the employees population.

Health promotion programs often become well integrated between year one and two, so the kinds of changes that can be expected are more significant. Intermediate objectives include the following:

- Values can now be measured in terms of employee morale as well as participation.

- Absenteeism trends can be identified.
- Surveys can be taken to measure such variables as enhanced self-image.
- Continued change in clinical data results are evident and measurable.
- Increased participation results from the ripple effect of employee success stories.

Long-term objectives are the outcomes that enable a program to be maintained over time. These results are not seen for at least 3 to 5 years. They include such things as:

- Value to the corporation in terms of cost/benefit analysis.
- Productivity/organization effectiveness.
- Cost containment from reduced and more efficient health care utilization.

The shape of a program is determined to a great extent by budget allocation and staff. If a comprehensive behavior modification program is sought, obviously, more finances and resources need to be made available than for a program that is to be less comprehensive in scope and implemented more gradually.

INITIATING THE PROGRAM: ACTION STRATEGIES

After gathering information about the employee population and organization, it's time to put the plan into action.

Components of the Program

Two major components are considered in establishing any type of health promotion program. The health status and the educational approach need to be determined.

Establishing health status can be accomplished in a noninvasive way by administering a health risk appraisal. A more comprehensive method is to conduct any one of a number of screening approaches (from a simple blood pressure reading to a cardiovascular risk factor identification). How best to determine health status will depend primarily on the perceived needs and wants of the organization, its population, budget available, and the support from management. The most important feature of health screening is that personalized information is specifically related to the individual. This frequently enhances the motivation to begin to make change.

The educational approach depends on the objectives of the health program. Creating awareness can be the first and only objective of the program. The population can be made aware of their health status. This awareness can then be followed by a film or newsletter series in which issues that relate to the initial health needs and wants of the employee are highlighted. Specific awareness issues can be targeted and carried out.

If knowledge is the aim, the population can become more knowledgeable about their health status followed by a series of mini courses (three to four sessions) that emphasize a specific health topic. Information about foods high in sodium, cholesterol reduction, and the importance of exercise are examples. Increasing knowledge can also be the stepping stone to a more comprehensive approach.

Most health promotion programs aspire to create behavior change. Programs intended to change behavior provide the opportunity for employees to learn skill-building techniques enabling them to change health habits or behaviors based on their personalized health status. This approach also needs reinforcement, maintenance, and follow up. Many programs begin with an awareness approach and gradually proceed to the behavior change emphasis.

Budget Options

Health promotion programs can be financed in many ways ranging from the organization's to the employee's paying for the total cost. Sometimes the employee and employer divide the costs in half. Creative financing also is finding its way into the health promotion field. For example, the employer may sponsor a program through outside consultants and arrange to give employees a discounted rate for services. Organizations may also enter into an agreement with a local community resource and arrange for all participants to receive a corporate rate. Some companies reimburse employees for a percentage of the cost of joining a health related class or facility. Others find the cafeteria style benefits to their liking, having employees trade one benefit (sick days) for another (free participation in a health education class or program). Regardless of which method is used, a budget for a director or a small staff is needed to get the program started.

Presentation of Program and Budget to Management

As stated previously, allocation of funding needs to be supported vigorously by top and middle management. Often the support given is dependent upon the presentation made for the budgetary requests. The goal of the presentation is to give a clear, concise rationale for the program and its budget. The need for verbal and financial commitment as well as a demonstration of support by top and middle management should be stressed. An overview of the program components, the steps and timetable for implementation, the necessary resources to meet the program requirements, and the methods for monitoring and evaluating are all part of this presentation.

The objectives and expected outcome of the program should be stated clearly. Management needs to see the benefits for the organization as well as the benefits for the employees. Other points to make are how the program might affect employee productivity, employee morale, employee health status, escalating medical costs, company image, competitive edge in attracting new employees, and existing OSHA regulations.

Marketing of the Program

Think of what it would be like if a party were planned for months and no one came because the invitations were lost in the mail. Applying this situation to a health promotion program is not so far fetched. Determining the vehicles to be used in publicizing and promoting the program needs careful consideration and planning.

The materials that promote and advertise the program should always be written to inform, remind, and persuade the employee to buy the service or product that the program is offering. An attention-getting headline is always a good start. The benefits of the service must be clearly stated, and the participant must be asked to take some action.

The availability of a graphics department within the organization is ideal for preparing designing materials. Otherwise, an outside consultant or graphics firm is needed. The main point is to strive for continuity between the graphics and written message and make it appealing and fun to read. Successful programs choose a logo with a theme that is representative of the goals and objectives of the program. This logo is used on all communications to show continuity and coordination between all program efforts.

Determining who should receive promotional materials is the first step of distribution. Identify these employees by name, building, location and department. Next, decide on the frequency of distributing information and develop a time schedule. Examples of various scheduling options are listed below. Based on what you are promoting, you may want to use a combination of these techniques in your publicity planning.

Examples of Scheduling Methods

Flights or Waves
Schedule on a rotational basis a concentration of publicity followed by a break, followed by con- centrated publicity.

Build-up
Schedule publicity in a progressive manner. Start out slowly and increase frequency over time.

Regular Scheduling
Use publications or announcements schedules that have a specific and consistent frequency.

Blitz
Introduce in spurts publicity with impact.

Incentives, as a marketing technique, can help create motivation as well as to sustain it. Offering employees various kinds of rewards often keeps the momentum of the program going and gives it a boost when it may be losing its sense of newness. The type of inducements that are most successful include material incentives like financial rewards, health club memberships, product rewards (T-shirts, gym bags, hats) and time off or release time for program participants; educational incentives (that is, leadership training courses); social enjoyment rewards like marathon runs, picnics, or luncheons; and recognition incentives that publicize the success stories of participants in the company newsletters.

If a good planner considers all these factors, the program is sure to succeed. Like anything new, the program may take time to become popular. The more the participants are involved in planning, the more their pride of ownership and the larger the number of participants.

Creativity and fun should be the driving force in planning, implementing, and maintaining a health promotion program.

REFERENCES

Bower, Marion. *The Will to Manage*. New York: McGraw-Hill, 1966.

Deal, Terence E., and Allen A. Kennedy. *Corporate Cultures: Rites and Rituals of Corporate Life*. Menlo Park, California: Addison-Wesley, 1982.

6 Wellness: Make It Happen through Effective Communications

Anne Rawson

Today, many companies are realizing that it makes good business sense to promote wellness among their employees. These companies have found that managing the health of their employees is more profitable than simply managing their health insurance premiums. In boardrooms across the nation, wellness programs, from health seminars to fitness classes, from home study kits to employee assistance counseling are being applauded and approved. But, will they be successful? Will they enjoy the enthusiastic support of employees? With a little effective communications planning, the answer is yes.

Effective communications don't just happen; they result when a series of logical steps and thought processes are applied to the communication-planning activity. In this chapter, we explore these steps and thought processes. We highlight a number of successful health promotion campaigns as well as providing practical tips that can be used in any workplace to develop more creative, cost-efficient health communication programs.

DETERMINE THE ROLE OF COMMUNICATIONS

The first step in any health promotion program is to establish the specific role or roles that communications will play. Because communications provide a solution to a problem, the role of communications will vary depending upon the nature of the problem.

Let's take a look at three companies to see how the communication solution varies for each.

Company A

This company has theoretically agreed to embark upon a series of wellness seminars for its employees, but it is unaware of the topics that would be of the most interest and value to the employees.

In this case, the role of communications will be to obtain input by providing employees with a mechanism to contribute their ideas and suggestions. An employee panel, an employee questionnaire, or a series of two-way communication meetings may be considered.

Company B

This company has agreed to sponsor an ongoing health education program consisting of seminars on burnout, nutrition, emotional fitness, and physical fitness. The first lunch hour seminar is scheduled to take place in two months, and management will be evaluating the future of the program on the basis of employee attendance.

In this case, the role of communications will be to generate maximum awareness of the seminar among employees and persuasively encourage employees to attend.

Company C

Company C has been successful in designing an effective health communication campaign to promote its upcoming stress seminar but is concerned that a seminar alone will not effect desired behavioral changes.

In this case, the primary role of communications will be to keep the message top-of-mind among employees following the actual stress seminar.

In summary, the role of communications should always be identified at the start by clearly stating the nature of the problem to be solved. This is an essential step in communications planning.

DEVELOP COMMUNICATION GUIDELINES

Once the role of communications has been established, you are ready to start developing a health or fitness communication plan. You must now document all the key factors that will influence your communications, establish the communications objective, and identify the key communication strategies that will be employed to meet your objective.

There is often a tendency at this point to rush into the creative execution of your program. What should we say? How should we say it? When should we say it? Try to avoid this temptation. Experience has proven that when key communication issues are overlooked because of inadequate strategic planning, the effectiveness of the communications will ultimately be jeopardized.

Begin by researching the communication environment and develop your communication guidelines. Twelve key questions should always be addressed:

1. What is the objective of the planned wellness program? To increase awareness? To influence attitudes? To modify behavior? What response is desired from the audience?
2. What information will be communicated to employees during the program? Are scripts or speeches involved? Will material be obtained from existing literature? Obtain all details.
3. How will the information be communicated? When and where? Is it a seminar, a workshop, a lecture? Will it be held during office hours? On site or off site?
4. Who is the targeted audience? All employees or management? At which locations?
5. What do we know about this group? Is the target audience homogeneous? What are its demographic and psychographic traits?
6. What attitudes or concerns may this group have about the subject matter? Will it be receptive to the message? What are its preconceived ideas? Beliefs?
7. What are the values, norms, and sensitivities of the workplace in which the program will be promoted? Would you describe the organization's culture as one that recognizes people? Profits? Innovation? Technology? How would you describe the company if it were a person?
8. What lessons have been learned from previous wellness communication programs? Have employee surveys been taken?

Did certain communication vehicles work better than others?

9. What other employee communication programs currently exist within the company? What is the competitive environment in which communications will be received?

10. What vehicles are currently being used to communicate internally? Is there a company newsletter? Are there bulletin boards?

11. Are there executional considerations to be aware of? Brochures to be distributed? A health department logo to be used? Areas of the company where communications are prohibited?

12. How much money can we afford to promote the program? Is there an established budget or an acceptable promotional expenditure per employee?

Once you have answered these questions, you will have sufficient information to develop the communications objective and key strategies upon which the creative and media recommendations will be based. To demonstrate this information-gathering process further, let's explore a situation involving a large Canadian corporation that is planning to hold a wellness seminar for its employees.

Company D

The third in a series of health seminars is planned for employees at Company D. The topic is marriage and alternate lifestyles; a well-known writer and lecturer has been asked to address employees.

The medical department, which is sponsoring the seminar, hopes that as a result of attending, employees will feel more positive about their own relationships, will have a better understanding of what contributes to a successful relationship, and will appreciate that many different kinds of relationships can be viable and satisfying in the 1980s.

The lecturer will illustrate these points by exploring some of today's relationships including marriage, dual working couples, single-parent families, step-parenting, and common law marriage. The guest speaker is renowned in the field and is an enthusiastic, provocative, and entertaining speaker. (His speech outline is available.)

The seminar will be held during the lunch hour in a large on-site meeting room. It will take a lecture format with a question and answer period following the address.

The medical department hopes to attract a broad cross-section of employees. Employees at the company range in age from 21 to 65 with the largest segment falling within the 30 to 45-year-old age group. Sixty percent are men. Staff are equally distributed in management, clerical, and hourly paid functions. Approximately 60 percent are married, and 40 percent have children.

There is some concern that the audience may feel that the topic is irrelevant to their jobs and may question the appropriateness of a seminar dealing with such personal issues. There is also a question of the lecturer's credentials and his ability to address the subject matter meaningfully within one hour. These issues will have to be addressed carefully in body copy.

The tone of communications will be important as the culture of this organization is rather staid and conservative. The message must reflect the norms of the company yet be sufficiently provocative and entertaining so as to generate maximum interest.

Attendance has been excellent at previous seminars where communication activities were scheduled within two weeks of the planned seminar and extra communications were scheduled the day before. Cafeteria and lobby displays and innovative deskdrops have proven to be effective, low-cost communication vehicles.

Because this company is communication oriented, there is a constant flow of bulletins, newsletters, and mailouts arriving on employees' desks. Therefore, our message will be competing for their attention within a highly competitive environment. Employee videos, audiovisual presentations, and electronic messaging are other means of communication frequently used.

Finally, a budget of $3,000 has been approved to promote the seminar. This budget will influence the choice of media as well as creative devices that can be employed.

Communications Objective

With this information, the communications objective can now be established. This must be the one, clearly focused message that we want to communicate to our target audience. It will be most effective when it is stated in employee benefit terms. In the case of Company D, our communications objective will be as follows: The target audience will be aware that by attending a seminar on March 31 at 12:00 noon they will discover some interesting new information about relationships that will probably enhance their own.

Communications Strategies

The communications strategy is simply six or seven key statements that have been derived from the information gathered. The strategy will drive future creative planning. In the case of Company D, our strategies will be as follows:

1. Target audience: who is the most likely group to attend our seminar? Employees 25-49 years of age, male and female, who are interested in improving the quality of their relationships.
2. Objective: what do we expect the communication program to accomplish? To maximize employee awareness of the seminar and to persuade employees to attend.
3. Benefit: why should employees go to the seminar? To discover some interesting new information about relationships that may help make their own relationships more positive.
4. Support: how can we support this benefit or promise? Our guest speaker is renowned in his field, and his lectures have been highly acclaimed throughout North America. He is a dynamic speaker and a prolific author.
5. Tone: what is the best tone for our communications? Contemporary, personable, upbeat, yet sensitive to the norms of the corporation.
6. Executional considerations: what, if any, are the logistical or linguistical considerations? Must be adaptable in English and French and must incorporate the health department logo. Must include a recommended leave-behind.

With strategies in hand, the creative process can begin. A theme can be developed, media can be recommended, and copy can be written. What would your communications recommendation for this seminar include? The next section provides some creative and media tips to get you started.

DEVELOP A CREATIVE RECOMMENDATION

With a very clear understanding of the target audience, the message, and the communication environment, you can roll up your sleeves and think creatively. What would be the most interesting, innovative, eye-catching way to communicate the message that would meet the key strategies identified in your communication guidelines?

The Creative Theme

One means of contributing to the effectiveness of the communication campaign is to develop a theme that can be extended throughout all campaign elements. The theme may involve a specific graphic treatment, color treatment, mnemonic device, headline, or slogan. It should reinforce the key message of the communications or employee benefit. Often, ideas for themes will spring from the content of the seminar itself.

Take the case of the company that was planning an emotional fitness seminar featuring a video tape of well-known university professor and speaker Leo Buscaglia. In his video, Buscaglia speaks of living life to the fullest, of finding your real niche in life, and queries why the audience persists in striving to be second bananas when they could be number-one plums. This image inspired an interesting creative theme that proved to capture the imagination and curiosity of employees.

Two weeks before the luncheon seminar, a bulletin notice appeared on boards throughout the company featuring the bold headline: "Why be a second banana when you can be a number-one plum?" One week before the seminar, administrative personnel, located at key office entrances, donned buttons stating, "Be a #1 Plum." Two days before the seminar, employees were invited to "Pick a Plum" from boxes of fresh plums located in the cafeteria and lobby. Easel displays were placed on each floor of the building on the day of the seminar to reinforce the theme. Each communication element incorporated a mauve and white, two-color treatment, plum graphic or mnemonic device, and the "Number-One Plum" theme. The communication program was so effective that two additional screenings had to be arranged.

In summary, to be successful a theme should reinforce the key message that the seminar is trying to communicate. It should be interesting, eye catching, simple to understand, and should be reinforced by a color or graphic treatment.

Creative Use of Media

Having developed a theme, the next step is to decide upon the most effective means of delivering the message to employees. Look for new and imaginative ways of reaching your target audience. Several excellent examples come to mind. The first involved a communication campaign with the theme "Turn over a New Leaf on Life." One week before the seminar, a leaf was left on each employee's desk. Underneath each leaf was a small note that read, "A sign of things to come on May 21st."

In the second example, a nutrition seminar with the theme "Food: Facts, Fads, and Fallacies," a tent card was placed on each table in the cafeteria to advise employees of the seminar. Each card included a nutrition quiz. For example: "The British fed their sailors a teaspoon of lime juice everyday to avoid scurvy, and that's where the name "Limey" came from. Fact, Fad, or Fallacy?" The tent card was followed by a more unique medium: a popcorn vendor, whose machine posted a sign in the lobby: "Popcorn is a nutritious, low calorie snack. Fact, Fad, or Fallacy?" The vendor provided each employee with a bag of popcorn to promote the upcoming event.

As part of the media mix, an innovative medium will help generate that extra awareness for your program. But don't forget that a number of low-cost, effective communication vehicles can be considered as well. Here are just a few:

bulletin board notices	posters
easel signs	information kits
cafeteria placemats and trayliners	brochures and handouts
cafeteria tent cards	stickers
buttons and balloons	mementos
deskdrops	lobby displays
company newsletters	electronic messaging
coffee-wagon notices	paycheck stubs

Handouts

If the wellness program involves a seminar or presentation of any kind, an appropriate handout should be considered as a take-away for each employee. It can be designed to provide employees with additional information on the subject matter. A mememto can also be included that will keep the message top-of-mind. You may wish to consider including the following items in each employee's take-away.

The biography of the lecturer, guest speaker
A supplemental reading list
Available brochures on the subject
A quiz relating to the subject
A questionnaire for each employee to complete following the seminar to evaluate the effectiveness of the presentation
A memento incorporating the campaign theme
Question and answer cards

CONCLUSION

Designing effective communications campaigns to promote wellness within the workplace can be an exciting and rewarding experience. The secret is to gather and recognize relevant information, select the most appropriate rational or emotional appeal, and then communicate the message in a fresh and imaginative way.

Once you have developed a communications campaign you can test its effectiveness by using this quick reference checklist:

Will each of the elements in this campaign arouse
quick interest?   Yes_____ No_____

Has the mesasage been persuasively and
meaningfully communicated to the target
audience?   Yes_____ No_____

Is the execution of the campaign memorable?   Yes_____ No_____

Is the execution feasible given budget and
production specifications?   Yes_____ No_____

Will the recommended media vehicles most
effectively reach the audience in a timely
manner?   Yes_____ No_____

Does the campaign meet all the communication
strategies?   Yes_____ No_____

If you can answer yes to each of these questions, take a bow. You'll have a winning campaign on your hands, not to mention a motivated group of employees who will be competing for front-row seats at your upcoming wellness event.

7 Effectively Marketing a Wellness Program

Phyllis L. Fleming

"We've developed our wellness program. Now it is time to market it to the employees."

"It was a terrific lifestyle change program. We just couldn't market it right."

According to these statements, marketing is something that happens after the planning and development of the wellness program is done. It suggests that marketing is advertising, promotion, and selling. Marketing includes these components, but a problem arises in limiting definitions of marketing to them (Bonaguro and Miaoulis 1983).

Do employees need worksite wellness programs? "Of course, they do," we answer hastily and point to lifestyle data and morbidity and mortality statistics to support our retort. Do they know or think that they need wellness programs? If the response is anything less than strongly positive, we run the risk of putting ourselves in a position of marketing "what nobody wants and what nobody needs."

There is a difference between the health professional's definition of need and the perception of the employee who is the consumer of worksite wellness programs. This distinction must be made clearly in order for programs to be dynamic and viable. The basis for marketing worksite wellness programs is identifying and understanding the employees' definitions of need and using this understanding to plan, develop, and implement programs. This does not connote a dictatorship by the employee. Rather a matching process takes place between wellness program management with its resources and point of view.

When the matching process is successful, the management and the employee enter into an exchange. The employee may contribute participation, enthusiasm, dollars, and lifestyle change; all are of value to the management. Management may contribute fun, opportunity to socialize, hope, promise of health or longevity, self-esteem, and a new vigor; all are of value to the employee. Ideally, both the employee and management emerge from the exchange satisfied. This is the essence of the marketing concept (Flexner and Berkowitz 1979; Kotler 1982).

A more formal definition of marketing is "the analysis, planning, implementation and control of carefully formulated programs designed to bring about voluntary exchanges of values with target markets for the purpose of achieving organizational objectives" (Kotler 1982).

The marketing perspective is ultimately useful because it reminds the organization of the primary purpose for which it is set up and asks for *form* to follow *function* rather than the reverse" (Kotler 1982). Thus, following a marketing perspective, hospitals become more patient oriented than physician oriented. Universities become more oriented to students than to faculty. Wellness programs become oriented to the needs and hopes of potential participants than to the definitions of health professionals. Once again, the marketing perspective calls for a balance between organizational mission and resources on the one hand and consumer needs, values, and dreams on the other.

The implementation of the marketing perspective in wellness programs is not necessarily complex. It requires an openness to doing things differently based on consumer expressions of needs and values. This may mean putting aside the familiar health promotion program model that begins with a health risk or health hazard appraisal (Fleming and Flexner 1983).

The following case study provides an example of the utility and the effect of applying the marketing perspective to the planning, development, and implementation of a worksite wellness program.

DESCRIPTION OF THE WELLNESS PROGRAM

Site

A bank in downtown St. Paul, Minnesota, serves the agricultural banking needs of a four-state region. Its 585 employees are primarily white-collar workers in a multiple-level management organization. In

1982, the bank launched an organization-wide productivity initiative that had employee wellness as a central component. The Wellness Program began officially in October 1982.

Management Expectations for the Wellness Program

The long term goal of the Wellness Program was to enhance and improve the quality of life and productivity of bank employees at work and at home. To accomplish this, management specified six goals for the program. The goals are to help employees:

1. become more open to change, to perceive change as a challenge.
2. experience personal and organizational involvement and commitment.
3. establish sense of control and self-responsibility in shaping the future.
4. develop skills in exploring, planning, choosing, and understanding the positive effects of beliefs.
5. build self-acceptance and acceptance of others and develop skills to deal with different points of view.
6. incorporate positive daily lifestyle behavior in exercise, eating, and emotional well-being.

Initial programing addressed primarily the sixth goal of lifestyle change.

Channels for Employee Input into Program Planning

From its inception, the Wellness Program was committed to a marketing based planning strategy. The importance of systematically gathering employee input, rather than relying on impressions of employee perspectives, was recognized. Five channels for employee input into the Wellness Program planning process were developed. The first was an employee survey in May 1982 that asked, "Are you interested in a Wellness Program here?" "If you are, what are the areas of most interest to you?" Had the aggregate answer to the first question been negative, management was prepared to postpone the introduction of a Wellness Program. Response was positive, however, and, guided by response to the second question, five months later in October 1982, the Wellness Program began with two classes, weight control and aerobic exercise classes, and weekly Brown Bag lunch hour seminars covering a variety of wellness topics.

A baseline/evaluation wellness survey administered in October 1982 represented a second channel for employee input. In addition to describing current lifestyle behaviors and wellness attitudes and values, employees identified wellness related concerns and provided suggestions to open-ended questions. For example, concern for the nutritional quality of food in vending machines expressed in the questionnaire prompted the formation of a volunteer employee Nutrition Task Force. The Nutrition Task Force surveyed fellow employees to establish their needs and preferences, talked with vending machine suppliers, and investigated health department codes. At the recommendation of the Nutrition Task Force, health-promoting alternative foods were included in vending machines, and a trial of a catered soup-salad-sandwich bar was initiated in the bank's lunch room. The salad bar has since become a permanent offering.

Weekly Brown Bag lunch hour seminars provided a third channel for employee input. The seminars included traditional health promotion topics such as nutrition for cardiovascular health, how to begin an exercise program, and tips for breaking the smoking habit. The seminars also included less traditional topics including humor and health, physical risk taking and personal growth, and interpersonal relationships among men. Attendance at the various presentations and enthusiasm for topics and speakers were noted. Some that generated particular enthusiasm were developed into extended series. Courses in smoking cessation, Tai Chi Ch'uan, and stress reduction had their origins in the positive response at Brown Bag seminars.

A fourth important channel for employee input was informal communication with program personnel. The Wellness Program initially had no full-time staff. The director and secretary were well integrated into bank functions and activities. As a result, they interacted with many bank employees who made requests and provided suggestions. Out of this communication came installation of showers and provision of towels, soap, toiletries, hair dryers, and curling irons. Accessibility to a winter running track in an underground garage, signs to alert motorists in the garage to the runners, payment of entry fees for marathons, team T-shirts, support for softball and racquetball teams grew out of informal communication with program staff.

An eight-month follow-up evaluation/wellness survey administered in June 1983 provided a fifth channel. Concern for smoke-free environments expressed in the survey prompted the formation of an Environmental Task Force. Survey responses also contributed in part to the formation of a task force to address child care issues.

By June 1983, the merger of management objectives with employee perspectives evolved into a Wellness Program including:

The following courses: Aerobic Exercise, People Using Life Saving Exercise (PULSE), Tai Chi Ch'uan, Weight Control, Smoking Cessation, Stress Management, Cardiopulmonary Resuscitation, Taking Charge.

Weekly Brown Bag seminars covering physical, emotional, and spiritual aspects of wellness.

Lifestyle assessment.

Competitive sports program including basketball, running, softball, and bowling.

Volunteer employee task forces in nutrition, environment and child care.

Wellness Program facilities including an exercise room, with exercycle, shower facilities equipped with towels, soap, and personal hygiene supplies, curling irons, and hair dryers.

EFFECTIVENESS OF THE WELLNESS PROGRAM PLANNING STRATEGY

Evaluation Method

The central questions for evaluating the Wellness Program were whether a marketing based program would generate adequate participants and whether participation would lead to the objectives defined by management. Because initial programming primarily addressed the sixth goal of lifestyle change, these data are presented here.

The baseline and the eight-month follow-up evaluation surveys were administered in October 1982 and in June 1983, respectively. There was one mailing, with no follow-up, through intraoffice mail to all 585 employees. Responses were anonymous. No control group was available within the bank.

The wellness survey questionnaire was developed to operationalize the six major management goal areas. It also requested perceptions of past, current, and future health and demographic information. The October 1982 questionnaire was pretested with white-collar workers who were not bank employees for face validity, clarity, and flow.

The lifestyle practices section, which addressed the sixth management goal, was based on the seven lifestyle items researched by Belloc and Breslow (1972) along with additional nutrition behavior items based on dietary guidelines developed by the U.S. Department of Agriculture and of Health and Human Services (1980). The items are listed in Table 7.1. Response categories were ordered along a three-point frequency continuum.

Lifestyle change was analyzed by comparing responses to individual items in 1982 and 1983. The status of lifestyle practices in 1983 was operationalized by summing the frequency response scores for the ten items.

Participation in program components and utilization of program resources was reported in the June 1983 wellness survey. Table 7.1 contains a list of program components and resources. Participation was operationalized as the total number of Wellness Program components or resources, including Brown Bag seminar, courses, and wellness facilities used by a respondent.

Methods of Documenting Lifestyle Change

Lifestyle change was examined in two ways. The first way, labeled the aggregate comparison, compared responses of all respondents in October 1982 with responses of all respondents in June 1983. This comparison does not consider individual improvements and setbacks. Rather it examines whether employees as a group had made changes. As such, it provides an indication of whether the general environment and culture of the bank changed (Deal and Kennedy 1982). The aggregate comparisons address whether employees generally had adopted a different way of thinking and living related to their physical and emotional well-being. A one-tailed Student's T-test was used to assess the significance of the change.

The second way of examining change, called matched individual comparison, was used to compare the responses of individuals in October 1982 with the responses of these same individuals in June 1983. Because the questionnaires were administered anonymously at both time periods, matching individual responses from October 1982 with those from June 1983 was achieved by matching demographic variables.

Cases were considered to be matched if all the following criteria were met:

Sex matched

Age (the same age or plus one year) matched

Marital status was logically consistent; that is, if June 1983 respondents indicated that they were "single, never married," they could be matched only with a response of "single, never married," in October 1982. A response of "married" in October 1982, for example, would be logically inconsistent with the 1983 response.

Parental life/death status was logically consistent; for example, a respondent who reported his mother to be alive in 1983 would not be matched with a respondent whose mother was reported dead in 1982.

Matches were made on three of the following five variables: education level, position within the bank, marital status, place of residence, and number of children.

Again, a one-tailed Student's T-test was used to assess the significance of the change.

RESULTS

Three questions guided the evaluation analysis reported here. First, to what extent did employees participate in the Wellness Program? Participation provides an indicator that the program meets employees' needs and preferences. Second, did employees report that lifestyle change was occurring? The goal of lifestyle change represents a management perspective. Third, if lifestyle change did occur, can it be attributed to Wellness Program participation?

Respondents

Response rates for the single mailing of the October 1982 and June 1983 surveys were 47.1 percent (275 employees) and 45.8 percent (267 employees), respectively. Respondents to both surveys represent a cross-section of bank employees by sex, marital status, level of education, and position within the bank. In both survey groups, the percentage of females and of employees with higher education levels was slightly higher than for the bank as a whole.

Wellness Program Participation

In June 1983, 209 respondents (78.0 percent of the responding employees) participated in at least one Wellness Program component. One hundred respondents (37.3 percent) used at least one program facility besides wellness courses. The percentages of participation in and utilization of program components and resources are reported in Table 7.1.

The typical pattern of involvement was participation in one or two components (84.7 and 29.5 percent, respectively) and utilization of one or two resources (10.8 and 10.1 percent, respectively). Brown Bag seminars drew the greatest participation, followed by aerobics classes. The percentages of participation in Table 7.1 are slightly higher than the standards for participation proposed by Parkinson (1984). These standards include 75 to 80 percent attending an orientation

TABLE 7.1
Participation in Wellness Program Components
(n = 267)

Component	Number	Percent
Enrollment in program	212	79
At least one Brown Bag lunch seminar	178	66
Five or more Brown Bag lunch seminars	45	17
Aerobics class	67	25
People Using Life Saving Exercise (PULSE) class	42	16
Weight control class	27	10
Smoking cessation class	14	5
Taking charge class	10	4
Health risk appraisal	6	2
Use of:		
Toiletry supplies	68	25
Hair dryers or curling irons	60	22
Exercise room	50	19
Exercycle	35	13

Source: Compiled by the author.

session and a range of 1 to 50 percent participating in program components.

The possibility that Wellness Program participants are overrepresented in the responding sample exists. Whether this is the case and the distortion it causes if it is the case are impossible to estimate. Nevertheless, the data presented in Table 7.1 paint a picture of health participation.

Lifestyle Change

More important than participation is the question of whether lifestyle changes are reported. Changes in daily lifestyle practices are examined in Table 7.2.

Significant changes were reported in several areas of nutrition, exercise, and alcohol consumption practices in both aggregate and matched individual comparisons. Changes in the areas of smoking and sleep were not significant. Responses to the October 1982 survey indicated room for improvement in smoking behavior. Sixty-six (23.9 percent) respondents indicated that they smoked on a daily basis. Although a ten-week smoking cessation course was implemented in response to an employee request, enrollment in the course was small. Some participants informally communicated to Wellness Program staff that because the program was inexpensive they had enrolled out of curiosity and interest rather than commitment to quit smoking. Thus, smoking continues as an issue for the Wellness Program within the bank. There was less room for improvement in the area of sleep. In the October 1982 survey only 22 (8.0 percent) reported that they never slept seven to eight hours a day.

Relationship Between Lifestyle Change and Participation

Because improvements in lifestyle practices are occurring in the general population apart form participation in wellness programs, it is essential to link reported improvements within the bank to program participation.

The relationship between improvement in lifestyle practices and participation in the Wellness Program was examined both qualitatively

TABLE 7.2
Reported Improvements in Daily Lifestyle Practices from October 1982 to June 1983

Daily Lifestyle Practices	Aggregate Comparisons	Matched Individual Comparisons
	(1982 n = 275)	
	(1983 n = 267)	(n = 97)
	T values	T values
I eat breakfast.	1.62	2.97**
I eat three meals a day.	2.51*	2.26*
I drink more than three cups of coffee, tea and/or soft drinks with caffeine every day.	1.14	.93
I eat salty food, like pretzels, chips, pickles, or add salt to my food.	1.77*	1.52
I eat sweets.	3.13***	4.76***
I get regular exercise, like walking, swimming, biking, at least three times a week.	5.08***	3.77***
I maintain my ideal weight within five pounds.	2.35**	2.15*
I smoke cigarettes every day.	.82	.39
I get 7 to 8 hours of sleep every day.	.11	.42
I use alcohol in moderation (one or two drinks a day) or not at all.	15.26***	9.18***

*p ≤ .05, **p ≤ .01, ***p ≤ .001.

Source: Compiled by the author.

and statistically. The importance of this analysis is underscored by the absence of a control group to rule out alternative sources of explanation for the improvements in lifestyle practices. Employees provided perceptions of the relationship in the response to the open-ended question on the June 1983 survey: Do you have any additional comments related to the topic of wellness? Typical responses included, "I would not have started on my own." "I participated in aerobics and still do and feel 100% better both physically and mentally." "I think it's a great thing for employees and results in improved morale and productivity."

Hierarchical multiple regression (Nie et al. 1975) was used to examine statistically the influence of program participation in lifestyle change, using the matched individual data set. This analysis essentially asks whether the participation in the bank's Wellness Program contributes significantly to the prediction of total lifestyle practices in June 1983 independently of other variables. The analysis involves two steps. In the first step, the following variables measured in October 1982 are regressed against the lifestyle practices variables: sex, age, marital status, education level, position within the bank, lifestyle practices, and perception of health. In the second step, the independent contribution of the number of times the respondent participated is examined using an F test to assess statistical significance.

The results of this analysis indicated that the independent contribution of participation was significant at the $p = .05$ level, thus establishing a statistical link as well as a qualitative link between participation in the wellness program and reported lifestyle changes.

DISCUSSION AND CONCLUSIONS

In summary, a worksite wellness program that was planned, developed, and implemented from a marketing perspective succeeded in getting participation and reported lifestyle change and in linking the two together. This suggests that the marketing-planning strategy creates a unique opportunity for the managers of wellness programs. After clarifying management objectives, the manager goes next to the employee for guidance in shaping and building the program. Programs shift away from an interventions-seeking compliance to a facilitative process in which both management and employee objectives are maximized to the extent possible.

Commitment to a marketing-planning strategy should result in a program that is unique to an organization. Along with the apparent advantages of uniqueness comes the possibility that the program will not look like a typical wellness program with health risk appraisals and risk factor components.

Also, because management objectives and employee perspectives change, a marketing-based wellness program evolves, develops, and changes in response to emerging concerns, resolved problems, and the ebb and flow of interest. The program structure is never completely finished or static because it accommodates changing management needs, employee lifestyle concerns, and environmental pressures.

In the evaluation of the marketing-based Wellness Program described here, changes in self-reported lifestyle behavior are apparent as is the statistical link between these behaviors and overall program participation.

Use of the marketing-planning strategy offers several advantages in addition to facilitating program participation. Because the program evolves in response to management-employee communication rather than relying on complete preliminary program development, start-up budgets can be modest. Programs, because they are management and employee responsive, can be tailored specifically to the needs of the worksite and the interests of an employee population. Programs retain flexibility as they adapt to changing organizational cultures and external environments. Management goals and objectives are reviewed and clarified regularly as decisions are made regarding whether and how to respond to employee input. The marketing planning strategy encourages low-cost, low-risk experimentation with new program components. As employees respond to requests for input and see evidence of responsiveness to that input, their involvement in and support for the program is enhanced.

REFERENCES

Belloc, N. B., and L. Breslow. "Relationship of Physical Health Status to Health Practices." *Preventive Medicine* 1 (1972): 409.

Bonaguro, J. A., and G. Miaoulis. "Marketing: A Tool for Health Education Planning." *Health Education*, January-February 1983, 6–11.

Deal, T., and A. Kennedy. *Corporate Cultures.* Menlo Park, California: Addison-Wesley, 1982.

Dr. Seuss. *Dr. Seuss's Sleep Book.* New York: Random House, 1962.

Fleming, P. L., and W. A. Flexner. " . . . But Will It Sell? A Marketing Approach to Program Design." *Promoting Health* 4 (1983): 1–3.

Flexner, W. A., and E. N. Berkowitz. "Marketing Research in Health Services Planning: A Model." *Public Health Reports* 94 (1979): 503–13.

Kotler, P. *Marketing for Nonprofit Organizations.* Englewood Cliffs, New Jersey: Prentice-Hall, 1982.

Nie, N. H., C. H. Hull, J. G. Jenkins, K. Steinbrenner, and D. H. Bent. *Statistical Package for the Social Sciences.* New York: McGraw-Hill, 1975.

Parkinson, R. "Participation: Keystone in Health Promotion Evaluation." *Corporate Commentary* 1 (1984): 30–35.

U.S. Department of Agriculture, U.S. Department of Health and Human Services. *Nutrition and Your Health: Dietary Guidelines for Americans.* Washington, D.C.: U.S. Government Printing Office, 1980.

8 You Are Not Alone: Computer Networks Help People Learn from Others

Susanna Opper

At first the monsters were small. Charles just brushed them off. But they grew, instantly, and became huge. They loomed over him. Charles tried to run — but couldn't. He shouted, but no sound came out. Charles awoke, half-dressed, on his living room floor in Montpelier, Vermont. He reached for the bottle of whiskey, but it was empty. He threw it against the wall. The noise of the breaking glass brought him to his senses.

Charles weaved across the room to his computer. He flicked the switch and watched the familiar routine of lights while a dialogue went on in his head. "I'm not an alcoholic. Sure, I drink a lot sometimes. It's lonely here. But I'm not an alcoholic. Alcoholics are loud and abusive. I don't do that." He heard the electronic sound of his modem dialing and was welcomed to CompuServe, one of the largest nationwide electronic communication systems.

In seconds, he was typing out the dialogue he'd been hearing in his head to an on-line Alcoholics Anonymous meeting. But this wasn't your usual AA meeting. In fact, no one was really "there" at all. Each person was in his or her own home — one in California, another in Nebraska, a third in New York City. At 1 A.M. Charles had no physical place to go. But he did know where to find electronic help.

Within 20 minutes, Charles's on-line group had convinced him that he was, in fact, an alcoholic. They shared their own experiences with him, suggested his next steps, told him about other electronic meetings about alcoholism and recommended him to a local AA group. Charles went the next day, but he still checks in on-line at night when he wakes up and realizes there aren't any bottles around anymore — empty or full.

Charles is one of thousands of Americans who are learning about health and finding help and information on-line. Some of the most dramatic examples include people with diseases so rare that only 10 or 20 people in the whole country have experienced them and severely handicapped people, such as quadriplegics who may never have been able to "speak" to anyone else remotely before. Now through the miracle of telecommunications and a mouthstick, they can talk to anyone.

HOW ON-LINE NETWORKING WORKS

Before we consider in detail all the various ways in which computer communications are being used in health education today, we need to take a closer look at the technology: the hardware, software, and systems that make on-line networking possible.

Computer communications are transmitted over the telephone. The device that links the computer and the telephone is called a modem, a device that translates between the digital signals of the computer and the audio tones a telephone requires. Almost any computer can be connected to a modem. And some have modems built in like the 3 1/2 pound Radio Shack Model 100, which is now available for $400.

Regrettably, telecommunications is the most complicated area of computer applications. With the modem and the computer, one has two of the essential ingredients for electronic messaging. Charles needed two other critical elements to attend his nonspacial AA meeting. One was a program in his computer that would tell his machine how to telecommunicate.

Popular communications software is marketed under brand names such as Crosstalk and Smartcom. Several of the best programs are so-called "freeware" or "shareware." This means you can get the program free. If you find it useful, you send a fee to the developer. PC-Talk for the IBM PC and Red Ryder for the Macintosh are examples of this type of software.

Once you have the necessary equipment, communication can begin. The rest takes place outside the home or office. In order to communicate with other people, your computer needs to connect with another computer. And, when your computer reaches that other computer, you need somewhere to go. You may tap into a data base, share health education tips with other professionals, collaborate with others on the treatment of a problematic case, or simply seek information on a current interest. So how does your computer get to the other computer that has the information you want?

You may dial the other computer directly. For example, Michael Pejsach, Ph.D., runs a health education network in North Carolina. (He was formerly in Ames, Iowa.) To connect with his system, you would make a direct, long-distance phone call to his number. His computer would answer the call, and you would be asked to type in some identifying information. Thereafter, you would be recognized when you telephoned.

When you reached Pejsach's computer, you may find him on-line. That means he is receiving your message in real time. But more likely, he won't be there when you call in. Instead, your message to him will be stored until the next time he signs on. This is often referred to as "store and forward" and is one of the most important and most difficult concepts to grasp about electronic communications. Atemporal communication is so foreign to us that it takes time to adjust to the concept. In fact, the only truly effective way to experience this aspacial, atemporal technology is to try it. At the end of this chapter, we'll make some suggestions about how you can do that.

If Dr. Pejsach is not "at home" when you call, no matter. Stored on his computer are resource files, articles, lists of 800-numbers to get free health education, computer programs you can copy and use on your machine, and private mail to other users. And, of course, you can message Dr. Pejsach and the other health education professions who assist him in responding to electronic queries.

One more set of concepts is needed here. In Pejsach's computer there is information that you could use on your computer. You can literally copy it from his machine to yours and then use it any time you wish, without tapping back into his machine. This is called "downloading," down from his machine to yours. Similarly, you can "upload." That is, you can create something on your machine (without being connected to another computer) and then "upload" or transmit your file to the other computer, where it will be accessible to others.

Dr. Pejsach's system is called a bulletin board. He runs it as a nonprofit venture, seeking funding from contributions. CompuServe (where Charles joined AA) and The Source are for-profit ventures designed to enable the public to get information and communicate. These networks are accessed through packet-switching telephone hookups. This means someone can make a local call to reach a long-distance computer. Charles called a number in Montpelier. The others in his AA meeting had each called numbers local to them. And they were all hooked up to a computer that happened to be in Ohio.

Just to give you an idea of the magnitude of this phenomenon, at this writing, CompuServe has approximately 220,000 subscribers, up 70 percent in the last year. If this is the first you've heard of computer communications, you're not alone. At the end of 1984 only 6 percent of all homes had personal computers. Of those a mere 15 percent had modems. By mid-1985 modem sales were outstripping computer sales, indicating that many computer owners were moving into on-line applications. Still, what exists today is just the tip of the iceberg.

SEPARATING INFORMATION FROM NETWORKING

Ed Madara heads the New Jersey Self-Help Clearinghouse at Saint Clare's Hospital in Denville, New Jersey. Since its inception in January 1981, the clearinghouse has referred more than 5,000 people to Mutual Aid Self-Help groups (MASH). What sets Madara's agency apart from similar groups is the New Jersey organization's policy of creating what doesn't exist. If someone calls for help with Prader Willi syndrome or neurofibromatosis but no such group exists, someone from the clearinghouse will encourage the caller to start a group. Through their consultation and education services, more than 260 new groups have been formed.

A computer makes this possible. Madara's data base of over 3,000 groups meeting in New Jersey and more than 350 national self-help resources available to New Jersey residents is accessed each time the phone rings. In seconds staff or volunteers can tell the caller whether a group exists, where it meets, and whom to contact. Usually, groups meet in person, often by phone or conference call. But sometimes they get together by computer. The listing of agencies and the contact information are a data base. The meetings on-line are electronic networking. In one case, a computer stores files for records that aid human beings to provide information. In the other, people are actually meeting via computer.

The amount of information available from electronic data bases is enormous. Should you wish to know more, consult one of the books listed for reference at the end of this chapter. This discussion focuses on the many forms of interactive, on-line communications.

There are essentially three types of computer communications. The first is called "electronic mail." A misnomer like many of the new terms, this form of communication is one-to-one messaging. You and I know each other, and we share a common system. From time to time we send each other a message. This is the electronic analog of personal letters, something people used to write.

The second category is bulletin board systems (BBS). When it was written *The Computer Phone Book* (Cane 1983) listed over 2,500 of these one-to-many systems. An interesting example is Dr. Alan Clark's Health-Link. "This BBS is provided as a free service to all medical consumers," states the on-line message when you dial up the Atlanta-based system. "Dr. Clark is a family practitioner and is a native of Atlanta." At this writing Clark's system is "booted up" (computerese for turned on) by Dr. Clark at 5 P.M. daily and unplugged at 8:30 A.M. It's available 24 hours on weekends and holidays. A 24-hour system will be up soon. Clark promises to respond to inquiries within 24 hours. He even makes house calls within a 15-mile radius of his office.

According to Dr. Clark, "Most of the areas which Health-Link (HL) has really been a success is allowing access by laypeople from all over the country. Questions are left on HL which otherwise would go unanswered. Things [are] communicated on HL that people would not discuss or ask because of difficulty or timidness in reaching a physician."

Clark feels his electronic system has eliminated barriers to communication between physician and nonphysician. "[HL] is not for the elite or professional, it is for anyone with a computer and a medical question for a doctor (or group of doctors, since I have several other consultants here)," he adds.

The final communication scenario is what Participate Systems, Inc., founder H. Chandler Stevens calls "many-to-many." These computer exchanges, sometimes called computer conferencing, are electronic meetings, like Charles's AA session or an on-line conference for the disabled facilitated by Georgia Griffin, who is blind and deaf. She uses a braille printer to read what's transmitted. The special quality of this third communication model is that it approaches networking. You don't always know who will read your message, who will answer your need. But almost always, someone does.

An example of this comes from The Meta Network, a system set up by retired Colonel Frank Burns, who initiated an early electronic network for the U.S. Army. On Meta Net, a special session is set aside to "explore the leading edge of health and healing." It was on this network that one participant wrote:

> Hello, folks, I'd like to invite your suggestions for resources for a special — to me — case. My father has just received a diagnosis of early prostate cancer, not metastasized. . . . I'd like to get him some audio tapes devoted to healing imagery before he goes into surgery. . . . I'd appreciate hearing from anyone with experience in this area.

Several suggestions followed. The networker's next note:

> Thanks for all your suggestions. I'd like to report back that my dad has been using several presurgery audio tapes containing suggestion for stimulating the body's healing powers, and he's very pleased with them.

In summary, there are private messages, almost always available in an electronic messaging environment. There are bulletin boards, often small privately owned systems with only one phone line. And, there are public networks where people who don't know each other can meet. But businesses and organizations can also use this technology.

ON-LINE NETWORKS TO MEET INSTITUTIONAL NEEDS

Some health institutions and large businesses are using electronic communication to accomplish their work. Depending on when they started and what their mission is, these organizations are using different technologies. Each is molding available systems to meet their needs. In some cases, they are working around still awkward links and complicated or confounding structures.

According to Dr. Carl Cameron of the American Association of University Affiliated Programs for Persons with Developmental Disabilities, "We had a federal grant that worked." Their purpose was to discover a way to bring together existing electronic communication services that deal with disability-related issues. The goal was to bring them together through a single access point so as not to "keep eating federal dollars."

In August 1985, the entire system went on-line providing an interdisciplinary electronic environment for the care and treatment of the disabled. According to William Veatch, director of telecommunications at the Kennedy Institute for Handicapped Children in Baltimore, Maryland,

"The electronic network ties together The Kennedy Institute, a treatment, training and research unit affiliated with Johns Hopkins University in Baltimore, Development Disability Councils located in 50 states and four territories, an AMA-sponsored information referral system for developmental disabilities, and independent organizations for the care of the disabled such as the United Cerebral Palsy Association, to name a few." Users of the system are medical students and Board-Certified pediatricians studying for advanced degrees, nutritionists and physical therapists, nurses and social workers, and administrators of a myriad of programs designed to provide care to individuals with special needs.

The essence of electronic communication is speed and being able to accomplish something that wouldn't be possible any other way. There are many examples. Veatch provided one that could happen to anyone. "I was responsible for working with the keynote speaker at a national meeting several years ago. The speaker suggested that he address a case study and asked my committee to create one. But, he neglected to mention he would be away in Europe all summer and would return only days before the event. I learned of this five days before his departure. Because my committee was all on-line, we got the study written even though I was attending another meeting away from home. Without electronic connections this would have been totally impossible."

As I was writing this section, I got a phone call from Australia in response to an on-line message I'd sent about a trip I was planning to the Far East. Although in this instance I could have phoned or written, in fact, I wouldn't. And an extremely appealing business opportunity would have been missed.

VISIONS OF THE FUTURE

To know how computer communications will affect health education and other areas, we need to look to the experiences of today's pioneers.

The first university to offer complete, full-scale college degree programs on-line was New York Institute of Technology in Greenvale, New York. The programs are identical to typical, on-campus, four-year programs, but students do their classroom work on-line. Courses start every four weeks and students are required to finish within a set time period. During the course, they are expected to sign on at least twice a week and take an active part in discussions with the instructor and other classmates. Obviously, this method of instruction could be ideal for homebound students and others who live in remote areas with no higher education facility nearby.

The Western Behavioral Institute has pioneered a course for executives that combines on-line work with in-person meetings. And the American Association of Certified Public Accountants (AICPA) is evaluating the possibility of offering some on-line courses for accountants seeking to earn continuing professional education credits from the association.

At Exxon the experiment with computer conferencing began in late 1983. The system was inaugurated to network the activities of the company's organization development and training people. It hooks up specialists in remote parts of the Exxon system such as Wales, Brussels, Hong Kong, and Melbourne, with U.S. centers like New York City and Houston. Since it's inception, the network has evolved in purpose and membership, and it now includes line managers and others interested in organizations and management.

In two years, the system has allowed collaboration between outside consultants and Exxon staff for the design and delivery of a variety of programs and events. Often system users actually design programs on-line, getting together in person just before the event to fine tune the design. When one network member, a pioneer in organizational development and close friend and guru to many on the system, became ill with throat cancer, the community shared its concern on-line. When he died, the on-line mourning went on for days and included a real time, on-line meeting at the exact moment of his memorial service.

One of the most dramatic on-line meetings has been on the subject of the first-line supervisor. Recently promoted workers often fall between two camps, no longer one of the "boys," but still not accepted as "management." The discussion of this quandary, which brought several first-line supervisors on-line, has spawned a major effort in the company to resolve some difficulties in the workplace that had never before been directly addressed.

According to Bill Paul, founder of the system:

My motivation when starting this experiment was based on a vision I still hold about the potential of this medium as a critical mechanism for the creation of networks which are highly purposeful and very synergistic, networks which are able to act as a unified whole and cause significant amplification of individual effort. I am now more convinced than ever that this is possible, though less sure I know how to help it happen.

He continues, pointing to one of the challenges of electronic networking, "Expectation and needs may differ widely on such a network. This has often led to misunderstandings when talking about activities and priorities. People choose different levels at which to participate."

One of the key challenges in organizational use of electronic media is who's using it and how often? At the Kennedy Institute for Handicapped Children, signing on at least once a day is the norm.

At the leading edge is Digital Equipment Corporation. This quotation comes from an on-line participant there:

> I typically get 30 to 50 messages a day, most of which I answer in some way. My guess is that in the past five years, which is the period in which the system grew the most, communications increased by a factor of 100 in the company. People across the country work with each other as well as with people in the next building.

But there are questions, too. People started dialing up at night from home. Soon there was no line between work and nonwork.

> I like to think what we are doing is giving people more options about work, that it's a mutual benefit. I know of no sociological studies; the time frame has been very short. The phenomena began in 1978 or 1979. By 1982 to 1983 almost everyone was working at home. Today, the person who does not do some work at home on the computer is rare. My secretary was still sending messages to people at midnight the other night.

We started our inquiry into electronic networking with Charles, who found, late one snowy Vermont night, that he was not alone. We've seen professionals get help they couldn't have found any other way. And we end with people who are not alone when, perhaps, they should be, people whose compulsion to work is now exacerbated by expanded communications technology.

But in one way or another, electronic communication, in Ed Madara's words, "will revolutionize society, increasing the linkage of people, ideas and concerns, and providing innovative ways in which people will find and develop the mutual aid and support they need."

ADDRESSES FOR ELECTRONIC COMMUNICATION

CompuServe Information Service
5000 Arlington Centre Boulevard
Columbus, OH 43220
(800) 848-8199
$39.00 registration fee

Electronic Information Exchange System (EIES)
New Jersey Institute of Technology
323 High Street
Newark, NJ 07102
(201) 645-5211
$75.00 a month plus network connect-time charges

Health Education Electronic Forum
Michael Pejsach, Ph.D.
Appalacian State University
Department of Health Education
Boon, NC 28607
No charge

Health-Link
Dr. Alan D. Clark
565 Colonial Park Drive
Roswell, GA 30075
(404) 587-2464
(404) 587-2465 - direct to bulletin board
No charge

Source Telecomputing Corporation
1616 Anderson Road
McLean, VA 22102
(800) 336-3366
$49.95 registration fee

GLOSSARY

Computer bulletin board — a dial-up service, usually privately owned, through which callers can post and read messages, download programs, and get information, usually about a specific area of interest.

Computer conferencing — electronic, topic-oriented meetings conducted over space and time through a data communications network, often on an information utility.

Data base — any electronic depository of data and information, usually organized and maintained by a data base management system.

Download — the transfer of a program or data file from a central computer to a remote computer.

Electronic mail — electronic transmission of letters, messages, and memos through a communications network.

Hardware — any microelectronics device such as CPU, peripherals, disk drives, tape storage.

Information utility — generalized information service that maintains up-to-date information banks and other electronic services for public use.

Modem — (modulator-demodulator) a device that adapts a terminal or computer to a voice (or analog) communications network.

On-line — connected to another computer and available; on-line systems are also called interactive systems, which implies a conversation between the user and the computer.

Packet switching — a technique for handling variable traffic in a communications network. Packet switching breaks all messages to be transmitted into fixed length units called packets, which are routed to their destination by the most expedient route.

Program — a group of instructions that tells the computer how to perform a specific function.

Software — computer instructions such as operating system, data base management, word processing.

Store and forward — the temporary storage of message in a computer system for transmission to its destination at a later time.

REFERENCES

Cane, Mike. *The Computer Phone Book.* New York: The New American Library, 1983.

Gengle, Dean. *The Netweaver's Sourcebook.* Reading, Massachusetts: Addison-Wesley, 1984.

Glossbrenner, Alfred. *The Complete Handbook of Personal Computer Communications.* New York: St. Martin's Press, 1983.

Hiltz, Starr Roxanne, and Murray Turoff. *The Network Nation: Human Communication via Computers.* Reading, Massachusetts: Addison-Wesley, 1978.

Jenkins, Avery. "Teleconferencing." *PC Week* 1 (1984): 61 ff.

Kerr, Elaine B., and Starr Roxanne Hiltz. *Computer-Mediated Communication Systems.* New York: Academic Press, 1982.

Lipnack, Jessica, and Jeffrey Stamps. *Networking: The First Report and Directory.* Garden City, New York: Doubleday, 1982.

Livingston, Dennis. "Computer Conferencing." *Datamation,* July 15, 1984, p. 111.

Opper, Susanna. "Meetings of the Minds." *Data Training* 3 (1983): 20–25.

____. "Keep Corporate Teams on Target." *Computer Decisions* 16 (1984): 101–6 ff.

Strassmann, Paul A. *Information Payoff: The Transformation of Work in the Electronic Age.* New York: The Free Press, 1985.

III
Health Education Programs in the Workplace

Health education programs no doubt have caught the attention of the business community. As such, certain programs, endorsed by the company, have been developed and implemented by paid professional employees of that company, who offer these programs on an in-house basis. Other programs, possibly of a more specific nature, have been offered to corporations by external professional consultants who are prepared to deliver these programs to a given employee population, usually on a fee-for-service basis. Whatever the arrangement, this chapter describes prominent programs offered on an in-house basis as well as programs provided by professional consultants.

Jones describes Staywell, which is Control Data's employee wellness program and which is also sold as a product. He delineates the foundations of the Staywell program and its emphasis on integrating awareness, knowledge, and behavior change in order to reduce lifestyle risks and the attendant costs in medical care, productivity, and absenteeism. Comparisons are made with alternative methods of delivering health-related information to employees, and results of evaluation studies are given.

Lewis describes Health Plus which is Union Carbide's comprehensive health promotion and fitness program. She indicates that this program is designed to provide participants with the tools to manage their own health more effectively, emphasizing the dynamics of personal change and the organizational factors that support these changes. She offers an overview of the developmental process, the goals and the scope of Health Plus. Additionally, she outlines the Health Plus Fitness program and the Health Plus Learning Center. She discusses the productive relationships between the Health Plus program and the medical department as well as the benefits department.

MacKeigan and McCormack describe an extremely novel and fascinating approach to health promotion. They point out that providing health information not only to people in an organization, but more generally to people in the community who are in need, has been difficult, especially in Cape Breton. The major problem is to find an information delivery system that encourages use and is not prohibitively expensive. The Tel-Med program, a telephone tape library of health information, seems to have solved these difficulties. MacKeigan and McCormack indicate that in Cape Breton with a population of approximately 180,000, more than 154,000 health messages have been played in three years. They state that if an effective health information delivery system is put in place, it will have the strong support of the community.

Jacobson discusses an important health problem for the field of health education, back injury. She states that employee back injury is a painful, costly, and increasing concern, influenced by a multitude of physical, psychological, economic, and cultural factors. Control of the problem, she points out, demands a concerted effort by management, staff, supervisors, and employees in order to reduce the number and severity of incidents and to contain the costs of those that do occur. Research data demonstrates that it is possible to reduce up to 75 percent of the cost of employee back injuries. She proceeds to describe her systems approach to back injury control, which includes the formation of an advisory committee and task groups, the determination of back injury costs and the analysis of baseline data, the investigation and application of prevention strategies, and the exploration and utilization of cost containment procedures.

Neale describes a comprehensive people maintenance health program that combines an employee assistance program and a rehabilitation program. She states that the preventive aspect of utilizing business and industrial settings to address personal and other human problems is being recognized as having enticing potential gains for the company and the employee. She indicates that employee assistance programs are services designed to help troubled employees recognize, identify, and solve personal problems before they grow to serious proportions and interfere with job performance. When an employee is disabled and off the job, she points out that rehabilitation is the process that restores the ill or injured employee to self-sufficiency and gainful employment in the shortest time possible. Together these two components provide an extensive health program for those employees in need.

Stress has always been a topic of concern for business and industry. Health educators, in response to this concern, have offered a variety of stress management or stress reduction programs. However, McGehee points out that her discussion is not about what stress is or how stress can be managed or the latest research in stress management. The literature on these topics is profuse and easy to locate. Rather, she is concerned with the nature of stress management programs inside companies that have decided to make stress management a part of their employee development. Her discussion includes the reason behind a management program, the format of stress management programs, the selection of a stress management program, work issues and stress management, and the management of the stress response.

Although stress has been a constant concern, a serious and growing problem in industry today is burnout. Klarreich relates his health education program on burnout, which was extremely well received in his organization. He describes the nature of burnout, the myths associated with this phenomenon, and the societal and familial influences that contribute to this problem. He delineates a number of steps to "put out the fire." These include self-appraisal, alteration of expectations, communication to establish social support, and determination of a behavioral option. He indicates that the healthy employee of the future will be a "hardy employee."

Achieving excellence in the workplace has become the passion of most North American corporations. Pulvermacher presents a unique health education program, which he delivers as a workshop, to many corporate employees. He states that pursuing excellence requires the application of several fundamental skills. He reviews effective goal-setting strategies, methods for avoiding the trap of perfectionism, techniques for managing self-defeating attitudes and beliefs, harnessing stress advantageously, increasing one's self-discipline, managing conflict constructively, and communicating effectively.

9 StayWell: A Pragmatic Approach to Wellness in the Workplace

C. R. Jones

INTRODUCTION

Corporate wellness programs have been generating increased attention over the past decade. Business and health oriented periodicals regularly carry articles describing existing programs and discussing cost-benefit analysis and evaluation studies. Worksite wellness programs include a wide range of activities from well-funded programs with specialized staff and facilities to those consisting of occasional special-emphasis courses, on subjects such as smoking cessation, conducted by outside organizations. A study of Fortune 500 companies (Forouzesh and Ratzker 1984) revealed that 70 percent of the 239 responding companies had specific health promotion and wellness programs, with an average age of five to six years.

Health care expenditures in the United States totaled $384 billion in 1984, with private employers paying a substantial portion of that bill. In recent years, employers have become increasingly alarmed about the escalating costs of traditional employee health care, fearing that these trends would make quality health care affordable only to those with considerable personal wealth or to those being assisted by government transfer payments. At the same time, the federal government, also concerned about the growing impact of rising health care costs on the budget, has been looking for ways to reduce its expenses. One way of doing this is to shift the cost burden to the private sector, further increasing the cost squeeze on employers. Wellness programs are now being viewed by many employers as a partial solution to the health care cost problem (Marcotte and Price 1983).

CONTROL DATA'S STAYWELL PROGRAM

Control Data is a worldwide computer and financial services company. In the 1970s, Control Data recognized the trend in health care costs and began actively exploring and implementing cost containment measures long before the concept became popular. One of the strategies that emerged in this process was the need to shift from a focus on curative health care to preventive health care.

A tactic in this strategy was to develop a health education and promotion program that would encourage individuals to take responsibility for their own health and behavior. The foundation for this tactic was the work of Belloc and Breslow (1972). They reported that health status was significantly related to seven simple health practices. An individual could maintain good health by always eating breakfast, eating three meals a day and avoiding snacking, exercising moderately two or three times each week, maintaining normal weight, sleeping seven to eight hours each night, not smoking, and using alcohol only in moderation. Forty-five-year-old men who followed six or seven of these practices could expect to live 11 years longer than similarly aged men practicing three or fewer of them.

Development of StayWell

In 1978, Control Data obtained a computerized Health Risk Profile (HRP) as part of an acquired company. The HRP is a form of the health hazard appraisal, which was first developed by L. C. Robbins in the 1950s when he was chief of the Cancer Control Program in the U.S. Public Health Service.

By completing the HRP questionnaire, which includes questions on lifestyle and family history, along with some clinical measurements, persons can obtain a computerized assessment of their lifestyle-related health risks, as well as a risk age, an achievable health age (compared to chronological age), and suggestions on reducing health risks and reaching one's achievable age. This can be done by modifying personal behavior by stopping smoking, losing weight, or starting to exercise regularly.

Executive management believed that a health promotion and wellness program could be designed that would be effective in the workplace. Control Data had successfully implemented an employee assistance program in 1974. Known as EAR, an acronym for Employee Advisory Resource, the 24-hour telephone based counseling and referral program was helping an average of 15 percent of the company's employees and their families each year. Estimated annual savings in turnover, absenteeism, and medical costs contrasted very favorably with program operating costs. It was believed that similar positive results could be attained with a wellness program. Specific cost benefits hoped for were reduced health care costs, reduced turnover due to disability and premature death, reduced training costs associated with reduced turnover, decreased absenteeism, and increased productivity.

Improvements in these areas would help lower operating costs and help make the company more competitive. The program was named StayWell, and a team of professionals was hired to design and deliver the educational and training programs to employees and their spouses. The StayWell program includes these major components:

An Employee Health Survey (EHS) that provides a corporate-wide description of health risk status
An orientation to the program for all employees, on company time
The Health Risk Profile and screening, with interpretations of results in group sessions
Availability of lifestyle change courses in the areas of fitness, weight control, smoking cessation, nutrition, back care, and stress management
Action teams, employee-led groups that concentrate on specific activities and goals, such as worksite changes or lifestyle changes
Special events such as health fairs or hypertension screening.

Self-Study and the PLATO System

Control Data was also faced with the problem of effectively and efficiently delivering StayWell to employees all across the United States, from groups of several thousand to single individuals. Traditional classroom delivery methods with a facilitator or instructor could work well where there were sufficient numbers of employees but could not be cost-effective for small groups. In addition, there were employees who could not regularly or conveniently attend classes because of job factors such as travel.

In order to have risk-appropriate education materials available to all employees, Control Data developed computer-based and self-study versions of the lifestyle change courses. The PLATO system, Control Data's computer-based educational program, provides high quality, consistent education and allows each student to proceed at his or her own pace in privacy and at a convenient time. Self-study courses are another alternative that permits employees to study at their own pace, wherever and whenever convenient, and does not require access to a computer terminal.

"Bricks and Mortar"

As a practical matter, Control Data recognized that it would be prohibitively expensive to attempt to provide physical fitness facilities to all, or even a majority of, employees. Further, this approach would address only one lifestyle risk area — exercise. To affect all major lifestyle risk areas, a decision was made to concentrate on effecting behavior change through health education, which would be delivered in instructor-led classes, self-study, and PLATO computer-based materials.

No major investments have been made in physical fitness facilities. Where local management has been able to allocate available space, some facilities have rooms used for aerobic classes and setting up exercise bicycles and weight-training equipment. When new buildings are constructed and whenever possible in major remodeling, showers and lockers are installed for employee use. The major emphasis of StayWell, however, is giving people the awareness and knowledge they need to make responsible decisions for their own health.

Evaluation Is Essential

StayWell was designed with an evaluation component from the very beginning. The purpose of evaluation was to provide information on employees' health habits and risks, prioritize health problems and needs, identify opportunities for cost containment and resource savings, tailor StayWell products (such as course offerings) to identified needs, and evaluate effectiveness of health promotion programs.

These were the real questions being asked: what are the major health risks employees face? Will employees and their spouses participate in StayWell? Will the courses work? Will people change their behavior? And, finally, will StayWell lower illness-related costs?

PROGRAM RESULTS

StayWell was introduced to Control Data employees in a phased approach beginning in 1979. Care was taken to introduce the program at selected experimental sites. Other sites with comparable employee populations and compositions served as controls.

Risk Factor Change

Significantly different results between the StayWell and comparison sites were noted in a 1982 study of reported risk factor change, as shown in Table 9.1.

TABLE 9.1
Reported Risk Factor Change by
Lifestyle Change Course Participants
(in percents)

Course/Risk Area	StayWell Participants	Control Group
Smoking	37	21
Exercise/fitness	32	13
Weight control	19	11
Nutrition	15	8

Source: Control Data 1982 Employee Health Survey.

Absence Rates

It was also possible to determine differences in absenteeism rates between employees in certain risk groups. A group of 2,479 employees was sampled and asked to report the number of workdays missed in the past 12 months because of sickness. It was recognized that company records of sick leave utilization also include time reported as sick, but taken for personal reasons. This methodology was selected to try to isolate actual sick time usage. The high-risk employees consistently reported higher sick leave usage (Table 9.2).

Health Care Claims

When the evaluation team matched health care claims data with HRP data, it was found that high-risk employees cost significantly more for medical care than persons who were at low risk. From an analysis of HRP data, researchers confirmed that it was possible to measure the prevalence of lifestyle risks in the employee population and that enough of the population was at risk to warrant efforts to change some of these behaviors. Comparisons of high and low-risk persons on health claims data confirmed that high-risk lifestyles were costing millions of extra dollars each year in health care costs. Additional millions could be accounted for in disability claims, absenteeism, and lost productivity.

TABLE 9.2
Employees Reporting Absence from Work
Because of Sickness
(in percents)

Risk factor	Low Risk	High Risk
Smoking	14	19
Exercise	14	20
Weight	14	19
Blood pressure	15	18

Source: Control Data 1982 Employee Health Survey.

Do Employees Participate?

A key question to consider in such a program is whether employees will participate once it is available. In the case of Control Data and StayWell, the answer has been "Yes." At the time of this writing, StayWell was available to 80 percent of Control Data employees, and more than 58 percent of employees and 15 percent of spouses had enrolled in the program. O'Donnell and Ainsworth (1984) suggest that in the general population 10-15 percent are joiners and will get involved in anything available; 5-15 percent are the opposites of the joiners and will not get involved in anything, leaving 70-85 percent who need to be attracted or motivated to join.

Wellness programs such as StayWell generally have no problems attracting people who already practice relatively healthy lifestyles. The challenge to program administrators is to attract persons who are at serious risk on one or more of the targeted risk factors. The critical issue is what they do with the information from their HRP's — act on it or ignore it.

Although much anecdotal data exists to suggest at least reasonable rates of involvement in StayWell of persons with high risk lifestyles, it has been difficult to establish clearly the extent of such involvement. Participants are promised confidentiality when they enroll in StayWell and any research or evaluation effort requiring identifying and contacting high-risk individuals presents a threat to the program credibility. Currently, an effort is underway to resolve this problem by matching successive HRP's for individuals and reporting the findings as grouped data.

Course Effectiveness

Getting high-risk employees into relevant classes is helpful only if the courses effect positive lifestyle changes. One-year postcourse evaluation studies show the classes produce desired changes.

Smoking

Follow-up of participants in smoking cessation classes showed 30 percent of participants were not smoking at all. Of those still smoking, 44 percent were smoking less than one pack a day, and 24 percent were smoking more than a pack a day. The average precourse smoking level for these individuals had been 1.6 packs a day.

Weight Loss

A similar follow-up of participants in a weight loss course showed average weights at 171.3 pounds one year after the class, compared to 178.3 pounds at the start of the course and 170.2 pounds at the end. This suggests that participants were able not only to lose weight, but also to keep it off.

Nutrition

Studies of "How to Eat Right" courses also showed substantial changes in eating habits. See Tables 9.3 and 9.4.

Self-Study

Recent studies of the StayWell self-study courses show they have attracted participants of all age, sex, and job groups. Participants were asked to complete a questionnaire upon finishing their self-study courses. They reported

Eighty-seven percent thought the course was "good" or "excellent."
Participants in the weight loss course lost an average of 11.4 pounds.
Eighty percent of those taking the nutrition course use less salt, 76 percent eat fewer fatty foods, and 66 percent eat foods lower in cholesterol.

TABLE 9.3
Changes in Key Eating Behaviors
(in percents)

Behavior	Before	After
Use butter at table	63.8	5.1
Add salt at table	69.0	29.7
Sugar 3+ times a week	63.8	36.2

Source: Control Data 1982 Employee Health Survey.

TABLE 9.4
Changes in Daily Eating Habits
(in percents)

Item (five–seven days a week)	First Class	Last Class
Eat four or more servings of fruits or vegetables	41.4	70.7
Eat one or more servings of fruit or vegetables high in vitamin C	50.0	74.7
Eat at least one fruit or vegetable high in vitamin A	15.5	74.7
Eat four or more servings of grain products daily	53.4	75.9
Eat two or more servings of dairy products per day	48.3	72.4

Source: Compiled by the author.

Eighty-five percent of those in the fitness course exercise three or more times each week, compared to only 34 percent before taking the course.

Seventy-eight percent of those who took the stress management course now regularly use stress reduction techniques.

Thirty-five percent of the smoking cessation course respondents quit smoking.

Although these results do not show long-term sustained change (for example, one year later), they do suggest that these low-cost self-study courses are an effective means of facilitating healthy behavior change. A long-term follow-up is being planned to see if changes from self-study are sustained.

CONCLUSIONS

Many current wellness programs were implemented in the hopes of achieving benefits in such areas as health care cost containment, increased productivity, reduced turnover, and improved employee relations. Control Data believes that such benefits are possible. It developed its StayWell program with a comprehensive evaluation effort so as to improve the chances of realizing those benefits and obtaining a pragmatic assessment of the program's effectiveness.

Evidence demonstrates that we are being killed by unhealthy lifestyles. Efforts to create a more comfortable and safe environment ironically have produced conditions that contribute to eight of ten early deaths in the United States. These leading causes of death, including cancer, strokes, accidents, and heart disease, are strongly influenced by personal behaviors.

The premise of StayWell is that if people know how to reduce preventable risks and then choose to do something about these risks, health care costs can be reduced and people can live longer, healthier, and more productive lives. Experience with StayWell has shown that the prevalence of lifestyle risk can be measured in an employee population and that people with high risks cost more than people with low risks because of higher health care claims and absenteeism. Additional costs may be attributed to increased disability costs and lowered productivity due to absenteeism and poorer health.

Employees of both sexes and all ages, representing all job families at Control Data, do participate in StayWell and make positive lifestyle changes as a result of StayWell courses. Control Data has chosen to concentrate on increasing employee awareness of individual health risks and to offer educational/behavioral change courses relevant to these risks so that employees and their spouses can make informed choices about their own behavior. The results confirm that the StayWell program concept is valid.

Future refinements of the program will be directed toward finding effective ways to deliver the StayWell program to employees in small site locations and to increase participation levels. The self-study courses appear to be a workable solution to part of the small site delivery problem, and incentive programs are being developed to increase participation rates beyond existing levels.

REFERENCES

Belloc, N. B., and L. Breslow. "Relationship of Physical Health Status to Health Practices." *Preventive Medicine* 1 (1972): 409.

Forouzesh, M. R., and L. E. Ratzker. "Health Promotion and Wellness Programs: An Insight into the Fortune 500." *Health Education*, December 1984/January 1985, pp. 18–22.

Marcotte, B., and J. H. Price. "The Status of Health Promotion Programs at the Worksite — A Review." *Health Education,* July/August 1983, pp. 4–9.

O'Donnell, M. P., and T. Ainsworth. *Health Promotion in the Workplace.* New York: John Wiley and Sons, 1984.

10 HEALTH PLUS: Union Carbide's Health Promotion Program, a Comprehensive Approach to Employee Health

Deborah J. Lewis

INTRODUCTION

HEALTH PLUS is Union Carbide Corporation's comprehensive health promotion and fitness program. The HEALTH PLUS program seeks to enhance employee health and productivity through health promotion programs designed to have a positive influence on individuals, the organization, and the work environment. The program provides its participants with the tools to manage their own health with an emphasis on understanding the dynamics of personal change and the environmental/organizational changes that support these changes. This article describes the overall HEALTH PLUS approach to employee health and includes an in-depth description of the HEALTH PLUS FITNESS program, the comprehensive on-site lifestyle and exercise program, and the HEALTH PLUS LEARNING CENTER, program laboratory for health habits change and the focal point of the umbrella HEALTH PLUS program.

Subsequent sections of this article give an overview of the development, objectives, and scope of the HEALTH PLUS program; describe the HEALTH PLUS approach to health promotion with its emphasis on practical self-management skills as means to taking personal responsibility for health; provide an overview of the HEALTH PLUS FITNESS program and the HEALTH PLUS LEARNING CENTER; and outline developments in total health management programs, describing cooperative activities between the HEALTH PLUS program and the other two parts of the Union Carbide medical department (the Employee

Assistance Program and medical services) and Union Carbide's benefits plans administrators.

DEVELOPMENT AND SCOPE OF HEALTH PLUS

Development

HEALTH PLUS was started in 1979 at Union Carbide's New York City headquarters as a pilot program under medical department sponsorship involving 200 employees in a smoking cessation class, a weight management class, an aerobic exercise class, and a series of one-time lifestyle management seminars. The programs were implemented in response to concern over preventable employee health problems and were a natural extension of the Union Carbide medical department's tradition of quality employee health programs. Long-range plans included a health fitness center for the planned new headquarters in Danbury, Connecticut. The health promotion program was seen as a means to initiate preventive medicine programs for employees and establish a broader umbrella framework for the future health fitness program.

After Carbide's relocation to its new headquarters, the HEALTH PLUS program was gradually expanded to cover many aspects of preventive medicine and lifestyle management. To date, 2,500 of 2,900 headquarters employees have participated in a formal health promotion program with programs ranging in scope from individual counseling to small group seminars or courses to headquarters-wide special events. Topics have covered approximately 50 different subject areas with smoking cessation, stress management, exercise, and nutrition and weight management as the ongoing core programs. Additionally, HEALTH PLUS FITNESS, the comprehensive lifestyle and fitness program, was phased in, and the HEALTH PLUS LEARNING CENTER, a combination exercise and lifestyle education facility, was opened. The HEALTH PLUS FITNESS program currently has 900 participants and will have approximately 1,100 participants, or almost 40 percent of headquarters employees, when the last phases of initial implementation have been completed. The next stage of growth for HEALTH PLUS is a coordinated effort to roll-out programs to interested plant and office locations throughout the United States, may of whom are already seeking assistance from headquarters staff who serve as internal consultants.

Objectives

The objectives of HEALTH PLUS stem from the program philosophy that endorses the prevention of health problems in a comprehensive fashion, addressing the entire person's health needs and habits in programs that contribute to Union Carbide's business objectives and enhance personal quality of life and productivity. Specifically, the objectives fall into two complementary categories: individual and organizational.

The objectives relating to individuals are:

Prevention of cardiovascular disease (specifically heart attacks and strokes) through prevention and reduction of cardiovascular risk factors (tobacco smoking, elevated cholesterol, high blood pressure, physical inactivity, excessive stress, diabetes, obesity); prevention and early detection of cancer; prevention and rehabilitation of lower back pain; and the prevention of other health problems through programs that impart personal lifestyle management skills, actively involve participants in changing their lifestyles, and provide health self-management information

Enhancement of personal effectiveness and quality of life through the development of health as defined by dynamic health rather than lack of symptoms.

The objectives that support organizational business objectives are:

Economic: management and reduction of health care costs and costs resulting from disability, workman's compensation, and absenteeism as they relate to preventable, lifestyle-related causes.

Subjective employee relations parameters: recruiting and retaining high quality personnel and enhancing employee morale

Promotion of a healthy work environment

Promotion of organizational and personal changes to promote greater productivity

Management of occupational health issues as they relate to lifestyle.

Scope and Staffing

The comprehensive approach to health promotion is reflected in staffing for HEALTH PLUS programs. Staff includes a variety of health professionals from within and without Union Carbide. Program staff includes the program manager, a health fitness coordinator, three fitness specialists, and a part-time nutritionist. All work together with medical and employee assistance personnel to provide programs. In addition, employee leaders and community resources are used.

HEALTH PLUS is the comprehensive umbrella program that includes a variety of separate programs. In turn, each separate program is a microcosm of the total program addressing all aspects of lifestyle management and thereby enabling participants through physiological and behavioral synergy to manage their health more effectively. For example, the weight management program integrates stress management, time management, and exercise into its curriculum. A sampling of programs available to employees in 1985, not including the HEALTH PLUS FITNESS program to be described later, appears in Table 10.1.

THE HEALTH PLUS APPROACH TO HEALTH PROMOTION

Helping employees move beyond awareness of health issues to actually making changes in their lifestyles is the core objective and forms the foundation of the HEALTH PLUS program. The following is an overview of how this is accomplished through program implementation and communications and includes a description of general themes consistent throughout all the programs, the "Lifestyle Action Planning" approach to lifestyle change, how the Lifestyle Action Planning approach is applied in group programs, and how lifestyle change, in general, and HEALTH PLUS, in particular, are marketed and sold to employees.

Themes

HEALTH PLUS programs are planned and implemented according to themes that ensure a comprehensive approach to health and facilitate lifestyle change. Some of these themes are:

TABLE 10.1
Programs Available to Employees at Union Carbide

PERSONAL LIFESTYLE MANAGEMENT OBJECTIVES

Courses
Pacewalkers
Conditioning
Shape-up
Aerobics: all levels
Self-defense
Weight management
Smoking cessation
Good nutrition
Stress management
Lower back pain prevention and
   rehabilitation
Cross-country skiing
Triglycerides and cholesterol
Nutrition and cancer
Lifestyle education certificate
Health for the pregnant woman

Lifestyle Break Seminars
Diet and behavior
Women's fitness
Exercise myths and misconceptions
Osteoporosis
Aging and fitness
Family nutrition
Fitness and children
Athletic injuries
Breast self-examination
Testicular self-examination
Contac lenses
Skin care
Exercise and diabetes
Medical self-care

Special Events
Health fair
Nutrition book fair
Pacewalkers prediction race
Great American Smoke-Out

Ongoing Services
Weigh-in
Blood pressure checks
Fitness trail/parcourse
Individual counseling for nutrition,
   smoking cessation, stress manage-
   ment, and cancer screening
   Seminars follow-up

ORGANIZATIONAL BUSINESS OBJECTIVES

Programs to Enhance Productivity
Stress management and productivity
Time and stress management
Health self-management for managers
Stress management for work groups
Divisional safety meetings
Lower back pain prevention

Healthy Work Environment Programs
Smoking policy
Healthy snacks vending machine
Healthy alternatives in the cafeteria:
   educating employees
Cooperative program with employee
   store (for example, pedometers)

Source: Compiled by the author.

128

1. *On-Site Programs:* programs are offered on-site, demonstrating a commitment to employees and offering an internal referral system among medical and health promotion staff members.
2. *The Educated Consumer:* Carbide's health promotion programs are a partnership between staff and participants. Staff members provide guidelines on the how-to's of lifestyle change and specific health information, and the participant takes an active role in designing and implementing his or her own program.
3. *Personal Agendas:* programs are designed to be rewarding to the participants and to contribute to personal goals. Individual agendas are met through personal goal setting and through staff teaching styles that provide a supportive and motivational environment.
4. *Systems Approach to Change:* the total health system, consisting of participants, staff members, the work system, family, and friends, is taken into account.
5. *Fitting into Business Culture:* tying into the systems concept of change, HEALTH PLUS has been designed to fit into and contribute to the business setting. This includes staff members who are well rounded and trained in other areas in addition to their credentials in health promotion (that is, backgrounds including training in business and psychology), programs geared toward the accomplishment of long- (that is, health care cost-containment) and short-term (that is, daily productivity) business objectives, promotion of a healthy physical and social environment, and prevention and rehabilitation of occupational health problems.
6. *Lifestyle Laboratory:* HEALTH PLUS programs are "laboratories for lifestyle change," and the criterion for success is the extent to which changes are carried over to activities away from formal program activities.
7. *Programs Before Facilities:* an emphasis is placed on quality programs and staff over elaborate facilities and on the medical aspects of the program. The priority market consists of employees who need the programs most, rather than athletes.

The Lifestyle Action Planning
Approach to Lifestyle Change

HEALTH PLUS combines business planning skills with what's known about the dynamics of health habit change in a Lifestyle Action

Planning approach to motivating, planning, implementing, and maintaining individual lifestyle change. This approach includes personalized, but structured, programs that focus on practical skills for daily living.The following process forms the basis of all individual and group HEALTH PLUS programs:

Establishing a general personal goal (employee perspective) and matching the program to the need and motivating employees to participate (program management perspective)

Orientation

Baseline assessment: biometric parameters, health habits and attitudes, lifestyle management skills, past attempts at change, supports and obstacles to change

Planning: goal setting (long-and short-range) and prioritizing of goals, establishing specific action steps, identifying supports; contingency planning, provisions for record keeping and follow-up assessment. The emphasis is on gradual plans that can be integrated into busy lifestyles, plans that are based on realistic evaluation of what those lifestyles are.

Implementation of plan and ongoing assessment

Follow-up assessment; reinforcement (feedback and rewards for accomplishing personal goals); modification of plan to keep it realistic, interesting, and challenging.

How the Lifestyle Action Planning
Approach Is Applied in Group Programs

The Lifestyle Action Planning model and the themes that summarize the HEALTH PLUS approach are incorporated into group lifestyle change courses such as the smoking cessation and weight management classes in the following ways.

Each HEALTH PLUS lifestyle change course is a comprehensive program covering a number of other aspects of lifestyle in order to promote optimum health and create a synergistic effect by promoting realistic, gradual change in a number of lifestyle areas simultaneously. Examples of this are the stress management program in which guest speakers, course material, and homework assignments address exercise, nutrition, and general lifestyle management skills and the group exercise classes that address a total healthy lifestyle with supplemental mini-lectures and handouts.

Each course is designed to shift the responsibility for change from the staff member to the participants in a "doing," highly interactive way including:

Training methodology: interactive class sessions are built around a flexible plan to allow for integrating the participants' personal learning objectives into the course material and providing for extensive discussion and participant leadership. This occasionally entails substituting participatory exercises for elaborate but distancing audiovisual materials.

Course materials with self-assessment tools, multiple small action steps, and hands-on homework assignments, such as wearing pedometers as part of the weight management class

Homework assignments and class sessions that promote intelligent consumerism and develop specific self-management skills that participants can integrate into their lifestyles, such as ordering pretend meals from actual menus or learning to take their blood pressures

The Lifestyle Action Planning model followed that creates structured opportunities for behavioral and biometric assessments, realistic goal-setting, record keeping, gradual action steps, and follow-up assessment

The systems approach to facilitating long-term change is built into the group programs, with a guest speaker program that includes other health professionals from within and without Union Carbide, former participants, and the buddy pair and group system within the class and in home and office groups.

Incentive programs are used. They include charging a modest fee and then offering a credit toward future participation in other programs and offering certificates of achievement and other awards.

Selling the Product of HEALTH PLUS

An important aspect of the strategy to promote both individual lifestyle changes and an environment conducive to these changes is the way programs are marketed and sold to employees before and during ongoing participation. Programs are planned based on an analysis of headquarters markets that are segmented into several categories: health needs or limitations (for example, health risk factors), demographics and life situation (for example, single parents, older employees), seasonal programs and considerations, special interests, fitness levels, family participation, and job-related needs (for example, the business traveler). These categories influence the choice in content, format, scheduling, and marketing of all HEALTH PLUS programs.

The communications program is designed to sell a maximum number of employees on getting and staying involved. This is done with an extensive variety of programs and formats and with a broad selection of communications media. The programs are marketed to employees through the quarterly newsletters for fitness and overall health promotion programs, videotapes, special mailings, the Lifestyle Break health seminar and the health mini-lecture series, special events and displays, and literature racks. Although some of these activities do not involve ongoing lifestyle change, they serve several important related functions: extensive and effective communications efforts contribute to the perception that health promotion programs are part of the business world; they can serve as the first step to lifestyle change; and they increase awareness levels and enhance the positive reputation of HEALTH PLUS.

The communications approach is one that stresses the professional, positive, business-related, and voluntary aspects of the program. This is accomplished through both substance, that is the content of communications pieces, and, just as important, through a professional, upbeat style that strives through use of recurring graphic and content themes, program name, and program logo to create a clear identity for HEALTH PLUS. The importance of a high-quality and varied communications program is further underscored because the headquarters market is closed and stable. That is, if employees are not sold on the programs and kept interested, the program manager cannot go outside to explore other markets.

HEALTH PLUS FITNESS PROGRAM: LABORATORY FOR LIFESTYLE CHANGE

The HEALTH PLUS FITNESS program is Carbide's comprehensive lifestyle and fitness management program that provides participants with individually tailored, total health programs. The focal point of these lifestyle change activities is the HEALTH PLUS LEARNING CENTER, which combines a variety of lifestyle learning materials and activities with use of exercise equipment and group exercise areas. The center's activities are comprehensive, with programs covering many areas of health and lifestyle. This section describes the HEALTH PLUS LEARNING CENTER facility, how the Lifestyle Action planning model is used to provide participants with the tools to manage their own health in the HEALTH PLUS FITNESS program, some of the aspects of ongoing participation, and how changes are reinforced and progress tracked.

The HEALTH PLUS FITNESS Program and the Lifestyle Action Planning Model

Every participant in the HEALTH PLUS FITNESS program goes through a personalized and comprehensive Lifestyle Action Planning process. The process combines education about lifestyle management, in-depth self-assessment (biometric, psychological, and health habits and general lifestyle), and acquisition of health self-management tools. Each participant is viewed as a potential program hero regardless of health or fitness status.

Lifestyle Action Planning as applied in the HEALTH PLUS FITNESS Program involves these steps: establishment of need and preliminary commitment, orientation, health and lifestyle assessment, group information session, and individual consultation.

Establishment of Need and Preliminary Commitment

Employees enrolling in the HEALTH PLUS FITNESS program fall into two categories: those who have never participated in any HEALTH PLUS program, or, as is more frequently the case, those who have taken other programs and are self-referred or referred by staff members to the more comprehensive program. Priority for participation is given to those with the greatest health need.

Orientation

All potential participants attend group orientations where they have an opportunity to learn how the program works, what the steps involved in lifestyle action planning are, and what the responsibilities and privileges of ongoing participation are.

Health and Lifestyle Evaluation

Participants then go through a comprehensive health and lifestyle evaluation to obtain baseline data for the design of safe and effective total health programs and to start the process of involving employees actively in the management of their own health. The health and lifestyle evaluation consists of:

A comprehensive health and lifestyle questionnaire that takes 30-60 minutes to complete and covers personal and family medical history and the major areas of lifestyle management: exercise, weight management and nutrition, safety and medical self-care, stress management, and smoking.

Biometric parameters including a treadmill test (stress tests are given to those who are 40 or older or when indicated; those under 40 without significant family or personal cardiovascular risk factors receive a submaximal treadmill test), a blood fat profile (cholesterol, high density lipoproteins, and triglycerides), and a fitness test that is held on a group basis to involve participants in conducting their own tests. The fitness test measures body composition, trunk flexibility, weight, girths, blood pressure, and the number of sit-ups performed in one minute. Girth measurements are made for psychological, rather than health reasons; many people use these as one of their goals because girth measurements often have an effect on how people feel about themselves.

The health and lifestyle report forms the foundation of personal Lifestyle Action Plans and is a compilation of the results of the biometric tests and the information gained from the health and lifestyle questionnaire. It compares participants to standardized norms, provides an exercise prescription, and makes lifestyle change recommendations. A summary at the end of the report assigns participants to program type: the cardiac rehabilitation, the lifestyle management program for employees with significant health risk factors, or the general program for those with no or little risk factors. The report also includes referrals to other HEALTH PLUS programs such as smoking cessation or nutrition counseling.

Group Information Session

Employees receive the health and lifestyle report at the group information session along with preliminary information on the upcoming action planning session (individual consultation) and an overview on what can be expected from a typical visit to the HEALTH PLUS LEARNING CENTER. A staff member reviews the report on a group basis, pointing out the significance of the lifestyle and biometric parameters evaluated, which lifestyle changes reduce health risks and enhance quality of life and productivity, and how these changes can be made on one's own, in the HEALTH PLUS FITNESS and in other HEALTH PLUS programs. The staff member then gives a preview of the individual consultation, explaining how participants will have an active role in planning their own programs for lifestyle change and which specific, easy action steps can be made on one's own and carried over to family and outside life. Participants also have a dry run through a typical exercise session and learn how to complete their "Lifestyle Records," the form used to record their exercise activities and other HEALTH PLUS program participation, and how to take their pulse to monitor the intensity of their workouts.

Individual Consultation

The final step in Lifestyle Action Planning, the individual consultation, is the most important one. This is where the individualized, written plan is drafted that will form the blueprint for lifestyle change. The individual consultation is the culmination of the other previous learning experiences and is an important step in involving the participant in the design of his or her own program and in moving closer to self-responsibility and health self-management. It lasts an hour and includes, in addition to the creation of an action plan, the opportunity to address additional, often confidential questions that were not asked at the group information session. The Lifestyle Action Plan is a concise, one-page document that lists prioritized annual and three-month goals in all areas of health, specific action steps toward the achievement of these goals within and outside the context of the HEALTH PLUS FITNESS program, support sources, contingency plans, record-keeping provisions, and personal program awards criteria.

The emphasis is on tailoring programs to fit the individual, and particular consideration is given to designing programs to address special health or lifestyle needs, such as programs for the business traveler, single parents, older employees about to retire, pregnant women, or employees with psychological problems such as eating disorders or depression. Tie-ins are made to plans of therapy for those who are also participants in the Union Carbide Employee Assistance Program, the medical department program that addresses the needs of the troubled employee. Because the program is seen as a laboratory for changes to be carried over into all aspects of participants' lives, the Lifestyle Action Plan also incorporates plans for activities away from Union Carbide including family and friends, as well as plans for gradually integrating bits and pieces of lifestyle changes in all areas of one's life. After the Lifestyle Action Plan is written, personalized starting points on each piece of equipment are determined.

Writing the Lifestyle Action Plan is just the start of lifestyle change. The plan, once written, is not etched in stone. Rather, it's a living document that is changed according to progress in the program, changing needs, desire for variety, and changing lifestyle circumstances. The plan is revised on an ongoing basis as part of participation and at periodic intervals during follow-up assessments.

HEALTH PLUS LEARNING CENTER and Ongoing Lifestyle Change Activities

Ongoing activities in the HEALTH PLUS LEARNING CENTER, both those that are in the context of the HEALTH PLUS FITNESS program and those that are under the umbrella program, are geared to helping program participants become intelligent consumers of the health care industry and managers of their own health and to providing a balance and variety covering all aspects of lifestyle and health self-management.

Ongoing participation in the HEALTH PLUS FITNESS program involves participation in two types of activities in the HEALTH PLUS LEARNING CENTER: exercise and lifestyle education/change activities.

The exercise segment involves use of exercise equipment (treadmills, Nordic ski trainers, rowing machines, stationary bicycles, and weight training equipment) in executing the exercise segment of the Lifestyle Action Plan. A general framework for safe and effective exercise forms the foundation of the exercise segment (warm-up, aerobic exercise, muscular conditioning, and cool-down), but specific activities are chosen based on personal needs and likes. Participants monitor the intensity of their work-outs using heart rate checks and perceived exertion ratings and record their exercise activities, heart rates, and other health promotion activities on their Lifestyle Records. Activities and goals are changed on an individual, ongoing basis by staff exercise physiologists, and psychological and physiological parameters are taken into consideration. The Lifestyle Record also provides space for recording other health data such as blood pressures and weight.

Other lifestyle change activities and services in the HEALTH PLUS LEARNING CENTER that are available to HEALTH PLUS FITNESS program participants include consultation hours in nutrition, smoking cessation, and stress management, "help-yourself" lifestyle management files (for example, kits for the business traveler or special work-outs for those with certain medical problems), program newsletters, literature racks, bulletin boards with changing health displays and information on HEALTH PLUS, and informal counseling. In addition, each participant receives a manual that outlines the concepts and steps of Lifestyle Action Planning, gives information on key lifestyle change areas, and serves as a tool for personal lifestyle management. The manual is in binder form so that personal records, Action Plans, and articles of interest can be inserted.

Other HEALTH PLUS programs also take place on a daily basis in the LEARNING CENTER. Examples include smoking cessation and stress management courses, health fairs and other special events, one-time health seminars, and the "Lifestyle Education Series." The Lifestyle Education Series consists of 15-minute health and lifestyle mini-seminars for busy people covering the spectrum of lifestyle management topics, including medical self-care, weight management, blood pressure management, and nutrition for the business traveler. Employees who attend 10 core and 4 elective seminars are awarded Lifestyle Education Certificates. There isa flow between these other health promotion activities and the HEALTH PLUS FITNESS program, and those in this program receive 25 percent rate reductions when they enroll in other HEALTH PLUS courses.

Personalized Rewards

The HEALTH PLUS FITNESS program rewards progress toward personal goals and good attendance. Awards are granted on an ongoing basis and at periodic formal intervals. Program heroes are recognized in many ways using a variety of motivational techniques such as monetary awards, certificates, public recognition, credit certificates for participation in future programs, and symbolic prizes with the program name and logo such as program T-shirts, mugs, or gym bags. The awards categories are:

Personal Goal Achievers: those who reach their short-term priority goals
Star of the Month: elected from the pool of Personal Goal Achievers
Hours clubs: recognizing those who attend 50, 100, 200, 300, 400, and
    500 exercise sessions in the HEALTH PLUS LEARNING CENTER
Lifestyle Education Certificate winners
Lifestyle Management Program Graduates: those moving to the general
    program after earning their Lifestyle Education Certificates, having
    good attendance, and significantly improving their fitness levels
Certificate and rebate award winners in other classes

Formal recognition of the award winners is provided by their induction into the "Wall of Fame" bulletin board in the HEALTH PLUS LEARNING CENTER with lists of all award winners and photographs of the Stars of the Month. Their names and pictures also appear in the two program newsletters.

How Am I Doing?: Follow-Up Assessment

Follow-up assessment supplements ongoing record keeping and assessment. Three- and 12-month follow-ups occur during the first year of participation. In subsequent years, follow-ups take place at 12-month intervals. Exceptions to this are more frequent testing for employees with special medical problems. Formal follow-up entails completion of a questionnaire that serves as a feedback/marketing tool on the program, an opportunity to list perceived benefits of participation and lifestyle changes made, and provision for requesting Lifestyle Action Plan revisions, and a retest of the biometric parameters measured initially. The annual follow-up also includes an individual consultation and establishing new annual goals. Letters to participants with low attendance levels are an additional form of follow-up.

THE CARBIDE HEALTH MANAGEMENT PROGRAM:
THE TEAM APPROACH FURTHER EXPANDED

HEALTH PLUS is a fully integrated, comprehensive program addressing all the health needs of its participants as they relate to how lives are lived. It involves extensive cooperative efforts with other health professionals in the medical department including medical staff and Employee Assistance Program counselors, as well as cooperative efforts with other human resources and business groups throughout the headquarters and corporation. Current directions and future plans include greater integration into the organizational development of the corporation. The move in this direction is being achieved in many small steps, through:

Greater integration of the three parts of the medical department, HEALTH PLUS, medical services, and the Employee Assistance Program. In addition to extensive cross-referrals, which are now part of comprehensive, individually tailored personal employee health management programs, future directions will probably include joint computerized health questionnaires and integration of screening for HEALTH PLUS FITNESS in a formal way into the periodic physical examination program.

A health care cost-containment program that consists of fully coordinated cooperative efforts between the medical department health management team and benefits plans administrators. The move in this direction is being initiated through a task force that meets at frequent intervals and works on projects and communications issues.

Increased integration of personal health management and global health management business issues into business training programs. This is already occurring but will probably continue to grow.

Continued emphasis on a healthy work environment through such programs as stress management and through worksite health policies, such as policies on smoking.

Ultimately, these pieces join together to form an emerging picture of a health promotion program that is comprehensive in its own right and also fully integrated into the business setting, part of overall plans for the development of the organization, and contributes in an increasingly significant way to both human resources and business objectives.

11 Tel-Med: Delivering Health Information

A. L. MacKeigan and Kevin McCormack

INTRODUCTION

Sexuality, birth control, and venereal disease are emotionally charged topics of high interest to the public. In response to this interest, a variety of pamphlets, articles, and books have been written, but the question remains, "Does this information actually reach the people in need?" Too often the answer is, no. The problem with this traditional approach to health information is that persons seeking the information fear they will be identified. This fear causes inaction, which at best causes stress; at worst, it wastes time that could be used in treatment.

The difficulties lie not in the information, but in how to deliver it. The ideal delivery system would have a wide selection of information that the user could select and would be anonymous, universally accessible (within target area), immediately accessible, easy to operate, and not prohibitively expensive. After much study the Cape Breton Hospital decided to implement a Tel-Med program for the residents of Cape Breton Island.

TEL-MED

The Cape Breton Hospital, like many psychiatric hospitals, has been plagued for many years with a negative image in the community. Efforts to improve this image have generally created more suspicion than good feelings. It was felt that by developing a new, innovative program the

140

hospital could demonstrate that it had made significant strides in the last several years. The hospital could provide a valuable community service at the same time. To be effective the program would have to serve the actual needs of the community, rather than simply promote the hospital. In 1981 the decision was made to implement the Tel-Med Telephone Health Information Line at the hospital. This program, while unproven in Canada, had demonstrated wide public acceptance in the United States. Funding was secured from the Cape Breton Hospital's Charitable Foundation, and the program was implemented in April 1982.

Tel-Med is a library of prerecorded health messages available directly over the telephone. No additional equipment is needed other than a telephone to access this library. The program was originally developed in San Bernardino, California, by the local medical association. In the 14 years since its beginning, it has grown into a network of nearly 400 centers across North America.

The attraction of the program is its simplicity. A library of over 300 tapes can be played to any caller directly over the telephone. Each message is locally edited and gives credit to the hospital as well as an appropriate referral source within the area. The caller remains anonymous. To request a tape the caller asks for it either by name or by its designated number. This anonymity clearly encourages reluctant callers to receive needed health information. A tally is kept of calls received each day, and tapes selected.

A complete listing of tapes is available in the Yellow Pages. It is estimated that more than 97 percent of the homes on Cape Breton Island (population 180,000) receive the directory. This listing is supported by t.v., radio, and newspaper advertisements.

BACKGROUND

It is commonly believed that if individuals are aware of the warning signs of physical and mental problems, they will seek assistance more quickly. Further, the sooner the problem reaches professional attention, the better the prognosis. These concepts are generally defined as being prevention. The specific concern of Tel-Med is primary prevention. Goldston (1976) states:

Primary prevention encompasses those activities directed to specifically identified vulnerable high-risk groups within the community who have not been labeled as psychiatrically ill and for whom measures can be undertaken to avoid the onset of the emotional disturbance and/or to enhance their level of positive mental health. Programs for the promotion of mental health are primarily educational rather than clinical in conception and operation with their ultimate goal being to increase people's capacities for dealing with crises and for taking steps to improve their own lives (Goldston 1976, p. 2).

Although Goldston speaks directly of mental health issues, primary prevention also has implications for physical health. The telephone has been used extensively as a medium of health information in the United States over the past ten years. There are two major programs: Can-Dial, providing cancer information, and Tel-Med, a library containing a wide variety of topics. Evaluation on the Can-Dial program (Wilkison 1977) has revealed a number of interesting findings. Of those users surveyed, some 60 percent reported some positive results from their use of the program. Those positive results ranged from decisions either to quit smoking or to visit a doctor to get relief from anxiety concerning cancer. The Tel-Med system operates on a much larger scale than Can-Dial, with nearly 400 centers across the United States and four centers in Canada. A major study by Diseher (1979, p. 4) revealed a number of interesting findings.

Tel-Med met its objective to help persons recognize early signs of illnesses with approximately one-fourth of the adult respondents being encouraged to seek medical or dental care initially or sooner than they would have had they not used Tel-Med. Therefore, information on the Tel-Med tape(s) had a possible motivating influence on 25 percent of the adult users. In general, our data suggest that Tel-Med had an impact on the behaviour of approximately 40 percent of the adult Tel-Med users who reported they followed a suggestion made on a Tel-Med tape.

PROGRAM GOALS

The goals of the Tel-Med Health Information Line are:

1. To increase both the amount and the accessibility of information concerning mental and physical health issues on Cape Breton Island
2. To inform the community of the services that are already available within the community to deal with these problems
3. To encourage reluctant individuals to seek needed information by making the process totally anonymous

4. To demonstrate to the community Cape Breton Hospital's commitment to offer services that reflect the needs of the public
5. To evaluate those tape topics that by their use indicate the interests of the community and develop programs to better meet these needs.

Considering the first 36 months of this program, we can say that we have achieved a degree of success on all five goals.

Goal 1

In 36 months of operation, Tel-Med has played 154,650 health messages. This number represents 214.79 percent of the estimated call volume (2000 calls a month). There are approximately 44,000 residential telephones on Cape Breton Island.

Goal 2

Each Tel-Med message closes with the telephone number of the most appropriate community resources. Local agencies have reported an increase in self-referrals and changes in types of problems being seen.

Goal 3

It appears that Tel-Med has been very successful at encouraging reluctant callers to receive health information. It has not been uncommon for callers to disguise their voice or have a child place the call for them. Considering the volume of information disseminated, it is not presumptuous to feel information is reaching many people in need.

Goal 4

Over the last 36 months, the Tel-Med program has been closely followed by local, provincial, and national mass media. This exposure and various speaking engagements with service clubs have propelled the program into the homes of many of the residents of Cape Breton Island.

Tel-Med has had a dynamic effect on the public's perception of the hospital.

Goal 5

Statistics have just been compiled on the program. Some of the major areas of interest include human sexuality, birth control, rape, quitting smoking, parenting, and emotional problems.

TOPIC SELECTION

The statistics on topic selection offer an interesting view of the health concerns of the community. The majority of callers are women (47.3 percent), followed by children (29.1 percent), and then men (23.1 percent). It should be noted that the children category is based on the operator's perception of age based on voice and is rather unreliable.

The following list gives the major topic headings and their percentage of calls. These statistics are based on the period from April 1, 1984, through May 31, 1985.

Topic	Percentage
Alcoholism	1.82
Allergies	.46
Arthritis	.92
Assertiveness and self-confidence	1.64
Autism	.14
Birth control	5.46
Cancer	2.04
Common emotional problems	4.43
Dental care	.90
Death and dying	.66
Depression	2.65
Diabetes	1.31
Divorce and separation	1.55
Drugs	3.50
Feet, back, legs	.90
Gastrointestinal	1.46
Heart disease	1.54

Topic	Percentage
Interpersonal communication	1.21
Kidneys	.46
Liver	.11
Lungs	.93
Marriage and relationships	3.37
Men	4.72
Mental health	7.12
Miscellaneous	1.20
Nutrition	.72
Parenting	8.13
Pregnancy	4.79
Sexuality	15.70
Sight and hearing	.28
Smoking	1.61
Stroke	.16
Suicide	.65
Tension	1.39
Venereal disease	3.73
Virus	.03
Woman	8.79
Information for senior citizens	.52

Statistics over three years show the ten most popular tapes:

Tape	Times Played
Female Sexual Response	7641
Masturbation	5524
Male Sexual Response	5449
Homosexuality	3286
Herpes	2556
Marijuana	2080
Gimmics to Help You Quit Smoking	1960
Am I Pregnant?	1945
Rape	1939
What Is Depression?	1772

CONCLUSIONS

The telephone has proven to be a viable means of delivering health information. The Tel-Med program with its wide range of topics offers a health delivery system that has great public support. It is clear that the anonymity associated with the telephone and having the tape selected by number have encouraged many reluctant callers.

The current method of evaluating this program has significant disadvantages. While a record is kept on those tapes selected, there is no way to determine the users' motivation, whether they will use the information, or contact a referral agency.

IMPLICATIONS

The Tel-Med service at the Cape Breton Hospital is a community based service. It has proven to deliver a large volume of health information quickly, anonymously, and at reasonable cost.

A similar installation in the workplace would offer many advantages:

A viable way of making health information available

A medium to measure health concerns and to act accordingly

A system to inform employees of the programs that are available both in the workplace and the community

A program that can immediately respond to any health information or other informational needs

The system requires only part-time attention, freeing specialized staff so that more service can be provided.

The popularity of the program will increase good will between management and employees.

REFERENCES

Diseher, R., R. Michielutte, and V. Morrison. "An Evaluation of Tel-Med." Unpublished research paper, Bonan Gray School of Medicine, Winston-Salem, North Carolina, 1979.

Goldston, S. E. "An Overview of Primary Prevention Programming." *Primary Prevention: An Idea Whose Time Has Come.* Document No. (ADM) 77-447 for

Superintendent of Documents. Washington, D.C.: Government Printing Office, 1976.

Wilkinson, G. S., et al. "Can-Dial: A Dial Access Cancer Education Service." *International Journal of Health Education* 20 (1977): 158–63.

____. "Utilization of a Cancer Telephone Information Facility: A Comparison of Caller and Non-Caller Controls." *American Journal of Public Health* 68 (1978): 1211–13.

12 A Systems Approach to Back Injury Control and Other Wellness Interventions

Jeannette M. Jacobson

On a personal level, the problem of back pain strikes four of five people and often defies diagnosis. On a management level, employee back injuries undermine productivity and profits and often seem uncontrollable. On a societal level, the economic costs of the problem are far reaching because, in a growing number of cases, two workers are being paid for the productivity of one. The first worker is on the job; the second is on disability compensation for an industrial back injury. In the case of federal employees, our taxes pay for this employee benefit; in private industry, it's added to the cost of goods and services. With Japan's employee loss time rate reportedly 3 percent of the United States', this situation makes competition on the world market increasingly difficult.

Why have the incidence and costs of back strain increased to make this the commonest disabling disease of man? What do the experts say? Treatment practitioners find the source of the problem in the body; orthopedics find mechanical defects, neurosurgeons blame the disc, and physiatrists point to muscular deficiency. Counselors find the root of the problem in the mind; psychiatrists suggest emotional deficiencies, and psychologists find social or situational roots to back pain. Human factors engineers blame hazardous work environments, and safety professionals attribute most industrial back injuries to lifting and handling heavy materials. Lawyers apply logic — they simply blame the opponent.

In a few cases, back pain is caused by an identifiable disease, but most often a variety of underlying factors, trigger factors, and complicating factors combine to confuse the diagnosis. The idea that lifting training will solve the problem of employee back injuries, or the belief that "they're all a bunch of malingerers," so nothing can be done, is neither realistic nor good management. This is a complex issue and a human condition that will never be totally eliminated. It can be controlled, however, to a far greater degree than presently exists. Those with a vested interest in managing this problem must recognize that there are several levels of responsibility for both prevention and cost containment and that a team approach is needed to carry them out: no one can do it alone.

Professionals in the community have devoted relatively little effort toward primary prevention of back pain. With the exception of attempts to improve job designs, most research activity has been devoted to treatment of back pain, after the fact. Aside from lifting training, which is often outdated in concepts (Jones 1985), education is rarely studied for effect. An examination of three research papers on the subject of back pain and injury (Andersson 1981; Quinet 1979; U.S. Department of Health and Human Services 1981), offering a combined total of 564 references, revealed only one that mentioned education, teaching, or training in its title, a U.S. Labor Department bulletin.

Responsibility for preventing the pain and costs of employee back injuries appears to fall on the shoulders of business itself. The ability to do so is available within organizations and the community, but it must be organized in a manageable way. A systematic approach would combine the knowledge and skills of a variety of health, safety, technical, and human resources personnel who often work separately, and therefore perhaps ineffectively, on problems of this nature. The benefits of joint effort can bring fewer and less painful back problems for employees and impressive financial savings, as well as synergy with other employee wellness programs.

STEP ONE: FORM AN ADVISORY COMMITTEE

Because the causes of back pain and injury are revealed to be multiple, it is appropriate to argue that the solution, too, must be multilevel. An organization contains three major levels of responsibility:

Top management's responsibility to provide leadership and support for back injury control, once a plan, budget, and justification have been developed;

Supervisory and staff responsibility to organize and carry out selected
strategies for both prevention and cost containment;

The individual employees' responsibility for personal back care, once
education and follow-up support have helped them learn how to do
so.

The Advisory Committee

An advisory group or steering committee should blend the expertise
of company personnel and relevant community resource people in jointly
planning, developing, and evaluating a back injury control program.
Involve everyone with interest in or responsibility for back injury
incidents, claims, and cost control to help make the plan a more creative
and workable one. This might mean key supervisors and union
representatives, as well as safety and health staff members will serve on
the committee. Include personnel concerned with employee health
promotion and human resources development, along with employee
benefits managers.

A major goal of the advisory committee would be to draft a back
injury control policy and procedures document for top management
approval. Another would be to establish the program's data management
responsibilities, measurable objectives, and an evaluation plan. The
steering committee can develop the project's overall goals then elect task
groups to carry out specific objectives such as data or program research,
employee surveys, or action plans. A guidebook has been developed to
help such committees simplify planning and organization (Jacobson
1985).

Task Groups

In small companies, one or two individuals might focus upon specific
areas of intervention; in large organizations, teams could be given
responsibility for researching methods of prevention and cost
containment. Prevention strategies include job design, preplacement
screening, and employee education in back care and, potentially, in
physical fitness, stress management, nutrition, and weight control. Cost-
containment and disability prevention strategies include medical case
management, vocational rehabilitation, and modified-duty programs. The

more that task groups involve line employees and supervisors who are close to the problem and who understand both the environment and the operations, the more likely that recommended strategies will be appropriate and accepted by everyone in the organization.

STEP TWO: STUDY TRENDS AND COSTS IN BACK INJURIES

Backache: Modern-day Dilemma

Exact figures on the numbers of back injuries that occur annually in the United States and Canada are hard to come by because there is no central reporting agency and current data are often lacking. The number must be estimated from Department of Labor statistics, unemployment compensation figures, and clinical data on those who seek care. It's estimated that of Americans alive today, 70 million have had severe back problems, and the trends are increasing. Back pain is second only to headache as modern man's most common physical complaint. It is the single most common disability in the United States in those under the age of 45 and is exceeded in prevalence among the 45-65 age group only by heart disease and arthritis (Nordby 1981).

Industry Bears the Brunt

Snook (1980) reports that low back pain affects more than half of the working population at some time in their career. Approximately one of every five injuries and illnesses at the workplace are for back injury, almost 75 percent of these reportedly due to lifting. The most frequent and severe incidents occur to industrial workers in their late thirties and early forties, which seems to be a time when the combination of aging body tissues, overweight, and poor physical condition loses out to strenuous work tasks. Statistics show (Klein 1984) that the highest number of back injury claims are from truck drivers, miscellaneous laborers, and nurses; human bodies can be as difficult to lift and handle as cartons or containers, if not more so. The Bureau of Labor Statistics (1982) estimates that the average lost-time back injury case results in 14 days off work, also putting a burden on coworkers who must fill the gap.

Litigation and the Pareto Law

Best estimates are that $20-$30 billion a year are expended in the United States for back disorders, costing the nation more than all other industrial injuries combined. As predicted by the Pareto Law, most of the expenses are absorbed by relatively few cases. A California study by Liberty Mutual Insurance Company reported that 25 percent of their cases accounted for 90 percent of the costs; more than 50 percent of the expenses in these cases were for attorneys and legal fees (Martin 1975). Florida studies further estimated that payments to attorneys for back injury litigation were nearly as large as benefits settlements awarded permanently disabled workers; legal costs in these cases amounted to considerably more than medical care expenses. Although such data indicate a system out of balance, few companies keep track of legal fees.

STEP THREE: A THOROUGH DATA ANALYSIS

Improved Data Systems Are Needed

An organization's own industrial insurance statistics are the first key to back injury control, at least potentially. Traditionally, accident data have been recorded by insurance companies to assess risk and determine premium rates, not to diagnose cause or discover factors associated with risk. So, despite the extraordinary capacity of modern computers, safety or loss control personnel must often leaf through stacks of figures, hand-computing data for accident analysis, in order to detect patterns of injury, categories of cost, or justify a return on investment for loss control programs. Considering the price that industry pays for employee illness and injuries, this is like playing high-stakes poker with an Old Maid deck; you have the picture, but not the numbers to bet on.

Potential Gains Must Be Shown
Greater Than Program Expenses

Most managers will not likely allocate funds for prevention or cost-containment projects without impressive data to support a proposal. Historically, top management tends to think of what prevention programs cost, instead of what they can save. The first task is to show the potential savings in back injury control by documenting both the direct and the indirect costs of the problem and by estimating how much these can be reduced. Direct costs for insurance premiums— or for medical treatment and loss-time compensation, in the case of self-insured companies — are usually easy to acquire. It's important, however, to include the indirect costs of employee accidents and illness as well. The personnel department can often help determine or estimate these figures. Indirect costs are calculated in many ways, but the most commonly accepted method estimates indirect costs at 4.5 times the sum of direct costs.

The second task is to put a price on the solution by determining what materials or equipment should be purchased and if technical consultants or trainers will be needed. Many outside firms and consultants will provide itemized budgets and proposals upon request. It may be cost-effective to bring in temporary expertise during the start-up period to assure that selected strategies will be current and of high quality and to provide the extra effort that is needed at the start of projects.

The third task is to estimate the potential return-on-investment. The California State Compensation Insurance Fund and California Back School provided training to approximately 20,000 employees, in 35 firms, reducing injuries as much as 53 percent and costs as much as 62 percent, with minimum improvement on either factor of 32 percent. The school also provided training to over 30,000 Southern Pacific Transportation Company employees. They estimate the training prevented 271 back injury cases and 16,236 lost workdays. An inhouse program in Massachusetts (Fitzler 1982) reduced total cost per back injury claim by 74.8 percent. It shouldn't be hard to get senior management's support for prevention programs when percentage savings of this kind can be applied to a company's own back injury costs.

Valuable indirect and intangible benefits of a successful program should be pointed out as well. Improvements in productivity, employee morale, and health and safety attitudes are among potential benefits, as well as reduced suffering. These are difficult to quantify, but should at least be identified, because they incorporate highly relevant new management values of the 1980s into the balance of program costs and gains.

STEP FOUR: INVESTIGATE PREVENTION STRATEGIES

Job Design Task Groups

The word "ergonomics" derives from the Greek "ergon" meaning work and "nomos" meaning natural laws. Thus the definition of ergonomics could be "the natural laws of work." Specialists in ergonomics design job tasks that fit human characteristics, taking into consideration not only body dimensions and mobility but also the body's stress behavior and the information processing characteristics of people. Snook (1980) reports the proper design of manual material-handling tasks can reduce up to one-third of compensable back injuries. Such design, however, does not necessarily involve extensive modifications of the workplace. Often simply raising a work surface, adding a mechanical aid, or changing a container size may be sufficient. Ayoub (1982) describes several methods for redesigning jobs, such as limiting the weight of objects to be handled and changing movements required by workers. Vibration has a particularly high association with back pain, particularly when combined with sitting. Truck drivers have a four times greater than average likelihood for disc herniation than most people (Kelsey 1975).

Ergonomics is not the exclusive territory of scientists and professors. A job design task group of supervisors, interested line workers, safety managers, and even community people who know the work, can tour facilities, problem-solve, suggest work modifications, or specify employee training needs. Offices and medical care settings, as well as industry, need close examination.

Employee Screening and Placement Task Group

Because it is not cost-effective to screen all employees for all jobs, a reasonable practice is to determine which jobs are high risk and apply screening procedures in those cases. The philosophy in industrial back programs has begun to change from giving preemployment physical examinations, with the goal of screening less physically and mentally fit employees from the job market, to preplacement screening, which attempts to place workers in jobs suited to their physical limitations. Hirsh (1977) reports a test for abdominal strength is the single best tool for predicting future back pain; it is widely accepted that preemployment x-rays have not proven successful in predicting future back injuries. Ayoub (1982) reports the most valid screening method uses apparatus to measure the worker's physiological efficiency in terms of oxygen consumption, heart rate, and ventilation rate. Strength and endurance are equally important for back safety.

Because of Equal Employment Opportunity legislation and trade union interests, among other things, employee screening can be a sensitive issue. Detailed job descriptions that clarify to new workers exactly what is expected of them and provide medical practitioners with objective information for physical assessments are particularly important in the case of physically demanding jobs. The task group assessing this process should determine if adequate job descriptions exist and if they are furnished to physicians during employee physical examinations.

Employee Training Task Group

Employee education should motivate workers to take responsibility for their own back pain prevention. True success requires high-quality materials and instruction because time away from work is a valuable commodity that should be well spent. A good audiovisual, explaining why the human back is vulnerable to pain and injury, is very important in today's video-oriented society. A trainer who makes the problem personally significant and active demonstrations are also vital. When teaching postures and body mechanics, people must be given an opportunity to "understand with their bodies" what they understand with their minds. A first exposure to quality back care education often inspires employees to change personal habits, but true motivation may await the "teachable moment" when individuals have back pain or discomfort. It is important to see that employees have easy access to informative materials at this teachable moment, either in their own possession or in company supplies.

Follow-up support for basic education sessions is critical to long-term success and should preferably be furnished by supervisors at job sites, particularly in the case of high-risk jobs where heavy lifting, excess sitting, or vibration occur. Supervisors, however, may not always have natural skills or interest in such training activities. They may be highly capable in terms of operational training but lack experience in behavioral training, so quality materials and support should be furnished. A great many demands are placed upon supervisors, who are often expected to accomplish difficult goals without adequate training.

Back Facts Are Needed by Everyone

If four of five people will probably have back problems in their lifetime, everyone should know more about the sources of this problem. It is often necessary for individuals to become better informed than their doctors — who are able to find the exact cause of back symptoms in only 12 percent to 15 percent of the cases. There is rarely a single cause for back pain or injury. The back is a very vulnerable part of the human body, and people should understand factors that underlie or complicate perplexing and painful back problems so that they can take appropriate steps. The question is, "Where can they learn this?" No one but the owner can prevent back problems. We must never overestimate people's information or underestimate their intelligence. We must provide education.

Sorting out the Causes of Back Pain

Underlying Factors in Back Pain. The human back is highly vulnerable to the normal aging process, which begins in the early twenties. This can be seen in hair, teeth, and skin, for example, and is also known to occur in the spine. Not too many decades ago, the human lifespan was 30 or 40 years. Today, if people expect to live for 80 years, and be pain free, they need preventive maintenance for their spines. Back tissues begin losing their elasticity and showing evidence of normal wear and tear at a fairly early age. The process is increased by poor standing and sitting postures, by countless bends at the waist, overweight, poor nutrition, exposure to vibration, prolonged stress, and lack of physical fitness. So, long before discomfort may be experienced, underlying factors can hasten the spine's normal aging process, making individuals susceptible to future problems. The more the spine is abused and one's physical condition is neglected, the sooner difficulties may be experienced.

Trigger Factors in Back Pain. Commonly, victims of back pain attribute its onset to a specific physical event, such as lifting, twisting, maintaining an awkward position, or a sudden move. Discomfort may not occur immediately, but the problem is usually attributable to a point in time. In some cases, a single overexertion has placed unbearable demands on back tissues. In other cases, the individuals' basic lack of endurance has reduced their ability to meet physical demands and allowed them to fatigue more easily. Fatigued muscles and ligaments are more easily injured. Stress can also trigger pain because emotional tension is often accompanied by physical tension, resulting in accident-prone situations for "tight muscles in a weak back."

Complicating Factors in Back Pain. The majority of back disorders are self-limiting and disable the sufferer for only a few painful days, or weeks at the most. But in a significant number of cases, a back incident can lead to long periods away from work. Unfortunately too often, a prolonged recovery period is the result of delays or omissions in treatment or of unnecessary surgery. Late loss-time payments or disagreements about claims can lead to considerable anxiety or to financial and domestic difficulties for the injured worker. Neglectful or adversarial management/labor relations also create anger and resentment. Such factors lead to a sense of having no control, lowered self-esteem, depression and sick-role behavior — hardly an environment for recovery and well-being. If such events accompany chronic pain, the potential for litigation should come as no surprise.

Back Care Education and Other Wellness Interventions

Homo Sedentarius: A Sitting Duck for Back Pain. The most important underlying factor in back pain seems to be poor physical condition. Navy Lifeline studies in 1982 reported that 85 percent of back injuries were linked primarily to muscle weakness and that 75 percent of those with chronic back pain are obese. Weak abdominal muscles are considered to be the best single tool for predicting back pain. Strong abdominal muscles work as a team with back muscles to maintain the spine's optimal s-shaped curve. If weak abdominals fail to do their share of the job, lower back muscles become easily fatigued and vulnerable to strain. Both adults and children in modern culture walk too little and sit too much, driving to or from school and work and sitting much of the day on the job, at meals, and watching television. People should realize why prolonged sitting is so damaging to back tissues and learn how to alleviate this danger through the use of proper chairs. Not only lumbar support but also correct pelvic position is important and can be provided by cushions designed to maintain both.

Flexibility, Strength, and Endurance — A Back Saver Trio. Once people understand the role of fitness in prevention of back pain, they are more easily motivated to improve their physical condition. The belief that only aerobics will achieve fitness discourages many individuals from committing to an exercise habit. Yet back health can be improved by flexibility exercises that maintain lubrication, mobility, and range of motion in joints of the body while strengthening the muscles and tendons surrounding them as well. In addition to firm abdominals, strong leg muscles are important for good lifting practices.

Aerobic exercise increases stamina, reducing the likelihood of muscle fatigue and subsequent back strain during strenuous work or leisure activities. Brisk walking is not only preventive but often prescribed for patients recovering from back pain. Once employees learn about the extreme importance of physical exercise for both preventing and recovering from back strain, they are often eager to join or develop fitness activities at the worksite. Basic motivation isn't always enough; people need social support. We can often accomplish things in groups that we can't do alone.

Back Pain: A Tension Headache That Slipped. Nordby (1981) reports that from 25 percent to 50 percent of all back pain includes a psychological factor as either a major cause or the exclusive cause of the disability but suggests that organic factors may also be present. Anyone who has suffered from back pain is likely to have discovered that stress increases discomfort and reduces one's tolerance to pain. People have a tendency to consider their minds and bodies separately, but they are, of course, one intradependent system. Tension and emotional problems can actually trigger back muscle spasm, and they tend to do so in a weak or previously injured back. People in stressful situations may also be so preoccupied with problems that they fail to protect their spine through proper body mechanics, thus bringing on injury. Stress management is an important part of preventing back injury and controlling back pain, so worksite programs on both of these topics — as well as on fitness — can work together for employee health and well-being.

STEP FIVE: INVESTIGATE COST-CONTAINMENT STRATEGIES

Medical Care Management Team

The medical care management team should monitor injury cases, both to assure state-of-the-art treatment and to contain costs. The concepts of reducing the pain and reducing the costs of employee back injuries are two sides of the same coin. The employee's personal well-being and the company's financial well-being are not mutually exclusive. The higher the quality of treatment received by employees, the sooner they will return to productive activity and the better will be the financial picture for everyone — except perhaps the treatment practitioners. Management should keep this vested interest in mind when delegating — or disregarding — the responsibility of seeing that employees are returned to work as soon as is practicable. A study by McGill (1975) indicates that employees off work for more than six months have only a 50 percent possibility of ever returning to productive employment again; more than one year, only a 25 percent possibility; more than two years, almost nil. Permanent disability payments are expensive for the company and for the economy. Except for many federal employees, who may receive nearly as much income while remaining off the job as while working, disability payments are not a very lucrative income for most injured employees.

Many physical, psychological, and social factors interact to impede the recovery of back injury cases. Victims often suffer isolation, fear, blame, and many stressful lifestyle changes. Martin (1975) decries the failure of the worker's compensation delivery system in preventing long-term disability in workers, claiming the emotional stress factors related to occupational injury and illness are the single greatest cause of workmen's disability. Yet a team approach to solving this problem can be highly successful. Leavitt (1972) reports a medical case management system that reduced case duration 42 percent, loss time 87 percent, and total costs of back injuries 68 percent. Injured employees often need help to keep them from "falling through the cracks" in the insurance, medical, and rehabilitations systems. Management has much to gain by providing that help.

PRINCIPLES OF CHANGE TO REMEMBER

A systems approach to controlling back injuries in any organization must bear in mind that a system is already in operation and usually resists change. Anticipating this fact, as well as the difficulty of modifying personal habits, we can be fairly certain of a few important principles that must be incorporated into planned change in every way possible.

We Must Understand What Something Is All About Before We Try to Change It. Correct diagnosis is the key to planning and bringing about change effectively, so data collection and feedback are essential first steps. It's important not only to have "facts" but also to understand dynamics and "feelings" surrounding the existing situation. Having both will permit the most appropriate innovations and increase chances for success.

People Must Expect Benefit from New Methods in Order to Be Motivated. Change usually creates a discomfort, may even feel like punishment. Doing things differently can make one feel incompetent whereas the old ways were comfortable, so we prefer to hold onto them. Especially during the early uncomfortable stages of change, it's helpful if people have support, early rewards, and trust that the potential gains promise to be considerably greater than any possible loss or discomfort. When proposing a project, it's important to examine the motivations for change that may be present, or absent, in various levels of the organization. Without a payoff, why should anyone bother to support the idea?

People Involved in the System Must Take Part in Directing the Change. We can increase people's acceptance of innovation by getting them involved in setting goals, devising strategies for achieving those goals, and determining what they will personally accept as measures of success. Changes that people feel they cannot control are the most stressful, but with the perception that they can influence the process, and with the support of others during the process, stress can be more easily managed and resistance to change reduced.

We Mustn't Try to Change Everything at Once, but Approach It in Steps. Participation and communication require time and, often, willingness to share degrees of power — a reluctant process. Few individuals or organizations make abrupt changes in attitude, or sweeping changes, in a hurry. This might even be undesirable. So we are wise to plan for implementation in stages, while allowing adequate time for adjustments. What one organization considers "moving fast," another might consider crawling, so this principle must be applied to suit conditions. The important thing is that steps be defined, and achieved, so that participants can feel a sense of progress.

Development of a steering committee, task groups, and a systems approach may seem more trouble than it's worth. Yet more than back injury control is at stake. To survive and prosper in today's economy, companies must monitor and control all losses as well as they have always monitored profits, and worker's compensation insurance costs are an expensive part of doing business. The Worker's Compensation legislation was passed in the early 1900s to assure workers a modest income while recovering from work-related injuries. In the case of back injury, there is usually an attempt to confine the injury determinant to a trigger factor, described earlier. But the Worker's Compensation Law does not take into account the need to control underlying and complicating factors in back pain, and under the present system no one but the employer holds a financial incentive or a central position for doing so. The law will not change until a more effective system has been demonstrated — perhaps not even then. The mandate is for better management control of the problem.

Should obstacles be met in acquiring needed data, funding, or support, remember what Pogo once said: "Life is full of insurmountable opportunities!" Back injury control is surely one of them.

REFERENCES

Andersson, G. B. J. "Epidemiologic Aspects on Low-Back Pain in Industry." *Spine* 6 (1981): 53–60.

Ayoub, M. A. "Control of Manual Lifting Hazards: III. Preemployment Screening." *JOM* 24 (1982): 751–61.

Bureau of Labor Statistics, U.S. Department of Labor. "Back Injuries Associated with Lifting." Bulletin 2144 August 1982.

Fitzler, S. L. "Attitudinal Change: The Chelsea Back Program." *Occupational Health and Safety*, February 1982, 24–26.

Hirsh, T. "The Billion Dollar Backache." *National Safety News* 5 (1977): 51–58.

Jacobson, J. M. *Hands-On Backs: A Guidebook for Worksite Back Injury Control.* Seattle, Washington: J & J Resources, 1985.

Jones, D. F. "Back Injury Prevention — Are Our Programs Adequate?" *Professional Safety* 30 (1985): 18–24.

Kelsey, J. L. "An Epidemiological Study of the Relationship Between Occupations and Acute Herniated Lumbar Intervertebral Discs." *Int. J. Epi.* 4 (1975): 197–205.

Klein, B. P., J. D. Jensen, and L. M. Sanderson. "Assessment of Workers' Compensation Claims for Back Strains/Sprains." *JOM* 26 (1984): 443–48.

Leavitt, S. S., R. D. Beyer, and T. L. Johnston. "Monitoring the Recovery Process." *Industrial Medicine* 41 (1972): 25–30.

Martin, R. A. *Occupational Disability.* Springfield, Illinois: Charles C. Thomas, 1975.

McGill, C. M. "Industrial Back Problems: A Control Program." *JOM* 17 (1975): 258–59.

Navy Lifeline. "Back Injuries: A Spine-Tingling Tale," Part I: May/June, Part II: July/August, Part III: September/October. Washington, D.C.: U.S. Government Printing Office, 1982.

Nordby, E. J. "Epidemiology and Diagnosis in Low Back Injury." *Occupational Health and Safety,* January 1981, 38–42.

Quinet, R. J. and N. M. Hadler. "Diagnosis and Treatment of Backache," *Seminars in Arthritis and Rheumatism* 8 (1979): 261–87.

Snook, S. H. "Low Back Pain in Industry." Workshop on Ideopathic Low Back Pain, Miami Beach, Florida, December 1980.

U.S. DHHS (NIOSH). "Work Practices Guide for Manual Lifting," U.S. Government Printing Office, Washington, D.C., March 1981.

13 A Comprehensive People Maintenance Program: Employee Assistance Programs and Rehabilitation

Bette Neale

INTRODUCTION

Problems in Today's Society

The increasing complexity of modern society with the accompanying breakdown in traditional values and structures creates a wide range of pressures and stressors that challenges each of us.

The high mobility of the nuclear family has put great distances between family members. Almost one half of today's marriages end in divorce. The search for personal privacy causes neighbors to be strangers. The "cashless" society creates a false sense of financial worth. The decreasing value of the Canadian dollar, rising real estate values, and increased taxes make first-time home ownership a financial burden or an unrealistic goal for many young couples.

At the workplace, economic restraints and technological changes have caused many companies to downsize their operations, restrain growth, or close up shop altogether. Bankruptcies of small businesses are at an all-time high. Job security is a thing of the past. Early or forced retirement is a new reality for the maturing worker.

The Human Factor

We live in stressful times. Stress from any of the problems mentioned above put a strain on a person's mental and physical well-being.

Moreover, these problems do not remain in the private realm of a person's life. People are employees, too, and they bring their stresses to work every day.

All too often, the human factor in an organization is forgotten or ignored. Yet, without people, an organization cannot function. Human resources, the most important investment a business makes, are a company's most important asset. And, because people at work experience problems to varying degrees, business pays for the cost through decreased productivity, increased absenteeism, turnover, on-the-job accidents, mistakes in judgment, increased insurance premiums, grievance, and disability.

Consider the following statistics published by the Ontario government:

In 1979, the cost of absenteeism in Canada was $49 billion, 25 times more than the economic loss attributed to labor disputes.

Research at Canada Life Assurance Company shows that the cost of hiring and training a new supervisory level of employee is about $20,000.

A U.S. study indicates that to replace a top executive can cost as much as $600,000 (Fitness Ontario 1983, p. 5).

Wellness

Healthy employees and those programs that promote their health can help reduce the trend toward ever increasing health benefit costs, absenteeism, and decreased productivity. What employer wouldn't want to reverse these trends? Companies invest in ongoing maintenance for machinery or equipment. As a company's most valuable asset, employees deserve a health maintenance effort greater than that for equipment.

Laurence Green, the well-regarded Johns Hopkins University scholar, has written the most widely accepted version of wellness: "Health promotion is any combination of health education and related organizational, economical or political interventions, designed to facilitate behavioural and environmental changes conducive to health" (Goldbeck and Kiefhaber 1981, p. 20).

This chapter focuses on two forms of health promotion or wellness programs, employee assistance programs (EAP) and rehabilitation. At different ends of the wellness spectrum (EAPs are proactive and designed for the well person; rehabilitation is reactive and designed for the unwell person), they complement each other and are inter-active. Together, they constitute a total, comprehensive maintenance program.

EMPLOYEE ASSISTANCE PROGRAMS (EAP)

Employee assistance programs are establishing themselves as legitimate and cost-effective ways to benefit employees and increase company productivity. By promoting "well-being", an EAP reflects a preventive approach to managing pressures and stressors of everyday living. Traditionally, management has viewed an individual's work life and private life as separate and unrelated. However, as other traditions are breaking down, so, too, is this one. The correlation between job performance and personal problems is now widely recognized.

Personal problems are not always kept outside the office. A study on absenteeism conducted by researchers at the University of Western Ontario (Fitness Ontario 1983) reveals that 20 percent of employees are responsible for 80 percent of absenteeism as a result of personal or health problems. The more severe these problems, the more likely it is that work performance will be impaired, a fact that employers cannot afford to ignore.

What Is an EAP?

Simply put, an EAP is an offer of a helping hand. It is a program designed to help troubled employees recognize, identify, and solve personal problems before they grow to serious and costly proportions. It is not an attempt to pry into one's personal life or to punish people with serious personal problems. It is a starting point, a sounding board where people can examine their problems or differences with a trained professional who can assess the situation objectively and help the employee resolve it. EAPs do not provide long-term therapy or treatment, rather they are short-term, active counseling services specializing in the concerns of employed persons, their families, and their place of work.

As Richard J. Ferris, chairman and chief executive officer of United Airlines reports in an editorial opinion in their inflight magazine:

> Employee assistance programs save lives. They help people cope. They set workers back on track. In addition, they save dollars. G.M. says it has cut

lost work time 40 percent among workers entering its alcoholism program. Kemper believes it recoups the annual cost of its program by helping 3 middle-management employees each year. United's program has more than paid for itself in improved attendance alone. Companies with EAPs report fewer on-the-job accidents, reduced turnover, and training costs, more favourable insurance claims experience, increased productivity and improved relations among employees and between employees and their supervisors (1984, p. 4).

Key Elements

The EAP concept is simple, but for it to be successful it must be implemented thoroughly and professionally. The following are the key elements crucial to the success of any employee assistance program:

Management support: this must come from the highest level; without it the overall impact is seriously limited.

Labor support: if a union is involved at the workplace, an EAP is not meaningful unless supported by the employees' labor unit.

Confidentiality: privacy of the employee's concern must be guaranteed. Anonymity and trust are crucial to employee use of the program.

Accessibility: counselors and the counseling location must be easily available for maximum use and benefit.

Voluntary participation: solicitation of help is voluntary. Utilization can be strongly encouraged via a management referral, but an employee cannot be forced to participate.

Professional clinicians: licensed professionals — psychologists and social workers — who have the expertise to deal with a broad range of problems

Broadbrush approach: availability of assistance for a wide variety of personal problems, for example, family and relationship conflicts, mental and physical health issues, including stress, substance abuse, care of children or the aged, financial matters and legal questions

Insurance involvement: occasionally assistance alternatives are costly and insurance coverage can be of great assistance.

Employee and management training: crucial to both levels so that there is an understanding and support of the EAP process in the workplace

Publicity: ensures program visibility and reminds potential users of its scope. Publicity can be in a variety of forms including orientation/training sessions, posters, wallet cards, newsletters, videos, and education sessions. An attractive program name that does not stigmatize the program is particularly useful.

Follow-up and evaluation: to measure program effectiveness and overall corporate improvements. Results can be measured in both humanitarian terms, that is, opinion surveys, and monetary terms, that is, statistical studies, to assure a high level of performance and track the return on investment.

Whether a company has an inhouse program, where they hire their own EAP professional and have a counseling location on premises, or an out-of-house program, where they contract with outside professional service providers and counseling is provided off premises, the above components must be part of the structure for the program to be successful and maximize the return on the employer's investment.

Return on Investment

Translated in dollars and time, the return on investment in an employee assistance program can be significant.

General Motors' alcoholism program reports a 49 percent reduction in lost work hours and a 29 percent reduction in disability costs.

Kennecott Copper Company's insight counseling program reports a 53 percent reduction in absenteeism.

Kimberley-Clark's employee assistance program showed a 70 percent reduction in accidents for the year after participation as compared with the year before (Goldbeck and Kiefhaber 1981, p. 26).

Despite these and other statistics some still question the success of indications of significant behavior changes such programs create. These critics miss three essential points.

By offering an employee assistance program as a health benefit, the employer is making a very definite statement about concern for employees and their health.

There is no commonly accepted definition of success for these programs.

If a purported 50 percent positive outcome was shown to be only 10 percent, most employers would be satisfied: some progress is preferable to none at all.

It is very succinctly stated by President Stephen E. Clear, Savings and Loan Data Corporation of Cincinnati, who realized, after his company changed hands, that he would have a "sinking ship" to contend with if he did not find some kind of safety valve or release through which employees could deal with the stresses created by this change. "If my competitors never use an EAP, it'll be fine with me. I'll be in business longer than they will" (Wojah, 1984, p. 8).

REHABILITATION: WHAT IS IT AND WHY IS IT IMPORTANT?

Rehabilitation is the process that restores an ill or injured employee to self-sufficiency and gainful employment at the highest attainable level of skill in the shortest time possible.

For the disabled worker, the dilemma is twofold: first, the worker must face the shrinking and changing job market, and, second, new physical limitations often must be adjusted to before reemployment can take place. For the employer, the disabled worker is an added burden, one for whom benefits must be paid out with zero return in production.

Most disabled persons want to be self-supporting. This is not surprising when you consider that one-third of our adult waking hours are spent at work. It is the single most consistent aspect of daily life; it is where we find meaning, even social identity. When we define our social status by our occupation, it is easy to realize the importance of work in our lives.

Comprehensive Rehabilitation

No single path leads to successful rehabilitation. The nature of the injury or illness, the quality and timing of medical care, the emotional state of the individual, the level of motivation, one's employment record, the family situation — these and more, affect the results.

Learning to cope with a handicap is a painful process, physically, emotionally, and financially. The disabled employee must depend on others — the doctor, therapist, counselor, family, friends, and employer — to help in the adjustment to a new life.

For every physical disability there is an accompanying emotional reaction. The counselor can play an important, if not crucial, role in helping the employee and family cope with this emotional reaction, which, if not dealt with in a timely and appropriate fashion, can become disabling in itself. Physicians are taught to deal with the physical aspects of an illness or injury; all too often the emotional or psychological aspects are forgotten or ignored.

A comprehensive rehabilitation program model that reaches all parties and whose focus is to uncover and remove all obstacles to recovery will be the most successful. Rehabilitation is a team effort. It is not a passive act. It must have the employee's active participation plus the cooperation of the employee's family and rehabilitation team.

Comprehensive rehabilitation deals with the total experience of a disability — both medical and vocational, through a complete process involving medical, behavioral, financial, and vocational aspects. Such programs are most successfully managed by rehabilitation specialists who come from backgrounds in nursing, vocational counseling and placement, behavioral therapy, or other closely related disciplines and who are trained to guide the transition from medical care to vocational management.

Medical Care Coordination

Before a disabled individual can consider a return to work, he or she must be medically stable. The goal of this phase of rehabilitation is to ensure that the employee progresses toward optimal medical stability as rapidly and steadily as possible. The specialist can clarify treatments, tests or procedures, secure proper medical care and equipment, expedite facility or home placement and care, coordinate follow-up care, and assist the individual and family with attitudinal adjustments. Skilled medical management speeds medical recovery.

Vocational Management

When the individual has reached the state of maximum medical improvement, the physician can release him or her for work, with or without limitations and restrictions. The philosophy of rehabilitation is that the disabled, within their physical limitations, ought to work and, with professional help and guidance, can work.

The rehabilitation specialist analyzes the employment history and job environment and inventories past training and transferable skills and the individual's motivation. The first choice is always a return to the same employer, same job. If necessary, the specialist can help the employer recognize job modifications that may be necessary to accomplish this choice. If a return to the same job is not possible, an alternate position with the same employer is sought.

In the event that an employer is unwilling or unable to reintegrate a disabled employee into the workplace, outplacement activities such as labor market surveys, vocational testing, and job placement need to be implemented. The goal is always to return the individual to full-time, gainful employment.

The Key to Success and Savings

One thing is certain. The sooner a case is referred, the better the chances for successful rehabilitation. Careful and systematic screening for potential barriers to a return to work eliminates such barriers and helps individuals from settling into the "disability rut." Returning a disabled worker to gainful employment renews a sense of self-worth and financial self-sufficiency and saves employers thousands of dollars through reduced long-term disability or workers' compensations claims and replacement costs. Insurance companies that manage disability claims through rehabilitation have consistently generated a return of approximately $10 for every dollar invested in rehabilitation.

A Final Word

In the last few years evidence of positive benefit to cost ratios for worksite EAPs and rehabilitation programs has been emerging. The evidence shows that results are achievable.

There is profit for all, for business in better productivity and reduced labor costs and for individuals in a longer and more productive life.

REFERENCES

Berry, C. A. *Good Health for Employees and Reduced Health Care Costs for Industry,* Health Insurance Association of America, Washington, D.C., 1981.

Corneil, W. D. "Employee Assistance Programs Make Good Business Sense." *Canadian Pharmaceutical Journal,* October 1981, pp. 370–71.

Dickman, F. and W. G. Emener. "Employee Assistance Programs: Basic Concepts, Attributes, and an Evaluation." *Personnel Administrator,* August 1982, pp. 55–62.

Ferris, R. J. "Editorial Opinion." *United Airlines Inflight Magazine,* September 1984, pp. 4–5.

Fitness Ontario, Ministry of Tourism and Recreation: *A Decision Maker's Guide to Fitness in the Workplace.* February 1983.

Goldbeck, W. B., and A. K. Kiefhaber. "Wellness: The New Employee Benefit." *Group Practice Journal,* March 1981, pp. 20–27.

"Health Education and Promotion, Agenda for the Eighties — A Summary Report." Proceedings of a conference sponsored by the Health Insurance Association of America and the American Council of Life Insurance, Atlanta, Georgia, March 16–18, 1980.

Rehabilitation Forum 11, (1984): 1–32.

Rehabilitation Forum 11, (1984): 1–28.

Wojah, E. "How to Cut Five Thousand Dollars off the Cost of Each Employee." *Managing People, 1984, p. 8.*

14 Stress Management in the Workplace

Lockie Jayne McGehee

This chapter is not a chapter on what stress is, on how you can manage stress, or on the latest research in stress management. The literature on these topics has proliferated and is easy to find. This chapter is concerned with the implementation of stress management programs inside companies that have decided to make stress management a part of their employee development. An informal poll taken in the New York, New Jersey, Connecticut area shows that of all companies with an existing employee assistance program, close to 90 percent have already implemented some form of a stress management program. Other companies have attempted to include stress management programs either in their medical departments or in their training and development programs.

WHY HAVE A STRESS MANAGEMENT PROGRAM?

A variety of reasons for implementing stress management programs are ascribed to by the companies currently doing so. The major reasons include reducing health costs, improving productivity, and boosting employee morale. In many cases, stress management is part of a wellness program.

Stress-related disorders, including certain headaches, stomach disorders, chronic muscular pain, cardiac and respiratory conditions, and psychosomatic complaints have been linked to a large percentage of doctor's office visits and hospital tests and admissions. One goal of stress management programs is to provide alternate ways to respond to stress, to prevent potential disorders, and ultimately to reduce health costs. A more elaborated treatment of this link between illness and stress can be found in *Stress and Chronic Illness* by D. L. Dodge and T. W. Martin (1970), *The Stress of Life* by H. Selye (1976), and *Stress and Disease* by H. G. Wolff (1968).

Stress level has been found to be linked to worker productivity. Work by J. M. Ivancevick and M. T. Matteson (1980) and J. E. McGrath (1976) makes this link clear. Their work shows that at moderate amounts of stress, performance is at its highest. Stress in moderate amounts, such as from reasonable deadlines, a focus on quality, rational performance rating systems, a system of accountability, often motivates performance. When stress rises to higher levels and a number of stressors are affecting the individual, performance deteriorates. At times of high stress, an individual is not as effective in solving problems, and on-the-job performance is negatively affected. The goal of stress management programs in this case is to provide ways in which employees can cope better with increasing stress and continue to perform well on the job.

Stress management programs are usually popular with employees. Attendance at talks and workshops shows that the topic is a popular one. Many companies decide to implement these programs as morale boosters because they "can't hurt anything."

Stress management has become an integral part of most preventive medicine programs. These programs attempt to include education and training in a variety of ways so that the employees can safeguard their health.

THE FORMAT OF STRESS MANAGEMENT PROGRAMS

Programs are offered in a variety of formats, depending on the amount of time made available for the program and the number of employees able to participate in the programs. The 3 standard formats include lunch-time talks, half-day programs, and full-day programs.

The lunch-time talks usually occur in no more than an hour's time. They are presented to any size group and are designed to fit into an easily accessible hour of the employees' time. The goal of these programs is to educate employees on a single topic. There is typically not enough time for interaction between the presenter and audience, so the programs take the form of lectures and demonstrations. Topics often include: "what is the stress response?"; "how do we contribute to our own stress?"; "coping with deadlines"; "coping with too much work"; and other similar topics.

The workshops in half-day programs usually occur in three to four hours' time. They are designed to present basic ideas in stress management and allow time for the group to practice and interact around these ideas. Topics usually include relaxation exercises, time management techniques, identifying stressors, identifying the body's stress response, identifying thinking patterns that contribute to stress reaction, and better problem-solving and crisis-handling techniques.

These programs are most effective when they are provided over several months' time with the same group of employees participating in each of the workshops. The intervening time between the workshops provides employees time to practice some of the techniques that were learned. They can receive additional feedback on them when they reconvene. The half-day format appears to be one of the most effective ways in which to deliver stress management programs inside the company.

In the full-day format, the program is put into a single full day or several consecutive days for an intensified experience. The advantage of this program is that the employees who meet together are better able to interact freely and overcome their inhibitions about discussing their stress-related issues in the group. Another advantage to this format is that the ideas can be presented and practiced immediately, with each level of stress training building on previous levels. The disadvantage is that so many ideas are presented over the course of the day(s) that the employee may not be able to retain much of the information given. There is also no opportunity for follow-up after the program unless the employee seeks it out individually.

The "media" program is typically not included in descriptions of stress management workshops, but it has many of the benefits of the lunch-time talk series. A media program includes articles in the company's local newsletter, posters describing certain facts or information, announcements of stress management programs that may be appearing on TV or radio in the viewing and listening area of the employees and their families, and literature on local agencies that provide stress management programs in the area. One of the most useful tools in the media program is the local newsletter. Articles that focus on a single topic and provide some sort of self-checklist or "do you believe . . ." type of assessment that is currently being used in stress management programs provide the employees with information about themselves that might motivate further interest and exploration. Some questionnaires and checklists that are particularly useful can be found in work by Davis, McKay, and Eshelman (1982); Derogatis et al. (1974); Farquhar (1978); Friedman and Rosenman (1974); Gmelch (1982); Kranzler (1974); and Lakein (1973). When these materials are supplied in conjunction with a resource list for seeking help with stress, the articles can help serve the function of workshops.

Employee assistance programs (EAPs) are designed to handle various psychological and physical problems experienced by employees. Many employee assistance program staff members are trained in dealing directly with stress-related issues. Employees can refer themselves directly to the employee assistance program or referrals can come from supervisors and managers.

SELECTING A STRESS MANAGEMENT PROGRAM

Stress management has become a very timely and popular workshop, and numerous groups and professionals now offer stress management programs. Certain components in a stress management program distinguish a poor to mediocre program from a professional, state-of-the-art program. Any program that provides more than a few hours of material should have more than a single focus. For example, programs that focus solely on time management or on relaxation training are providing only one technique for stress management. Also, programs that focus only on identifying the stressors (those things in our work and personal lives that are sources of stress) and then spend the remaining time suggesting ways to change those outside sources of stress are neglecting one of the more powerful techniques in stress management, that of changing certain thoughts, perceptions, and beliefs about those stressors.

The following components are part of any comprehensive stress management program and should be found in the description of proposals to conduct these programs. Each of these components is necessary for a successful program, but, alone, none are sufficient.

First, the program must provide information on the physical consequences of stress and allow participants to assess their own physical response to stress. The content should help participants understand the physical stress reaction and decide if they need to seek medical advice and treatment.

Second, the distinction between stressors, outside negative events that precipitate the stress response, and the individual's stress response should be made. A program of assessing participant's beliefs and attitudes as they affect their reactions to stressors is a major part of an effective stress management program. An excellent resource for materials on changing beliefs and attitudes toward a more rational coping response is the work of Albert Ellis, and Robert Harper (1975). This component in the program helps participants deal with the difficult situations that they are not able to change. The participants thereby reduce the stress they experience.

Third, a component on relaxation training is a useful part of the program. Additional components on nutrition, breathing, exercise, and topics such as time management and assertiveness training are often included as part of stress management training if there is available time.

WORK ISSUES AND STRESS MANAGEMENT

Corporate Downsizing

Downsizing, or the reduction of personnel as large corporations divest, has become a frequent phenomenon in the corporate world. The resulting stressors include loss of job, change of job, change of job location, acquiring additional work, experiencing work underload, and change in management. Stress management programs are often effective during these times. One large corporation in the New York, New Jersey area implemented stress management programs after dramatic downsizing. The major issues raised by employees during the program included fear that they might be laid off, anxiety over what they perceived to be their new workload, anger with management for allowing the downsizing and for not providing more notice, and a feeling of loss concerning their colleagues and jobs. The physical symptoms being reported included muscular tension, headaches, stomach disorders, heart palpitations, lack of concentration, altered sleep and eating habits, and poor overall performance.

In this case, employees were taught that the cause of their physical problem was related to their stress response. They were helped to see that their poor performance was adverse to their goal of doing well in the company. The component of the program that was most effective for these employees was the "cognitive restructuring" or "changing irrational beliefs" component. These employees were demanding a superhuman effort from themselves, and, because they were certain that they could not meet these superhuman demands, they had become anxious about the potential outcome for themselves. The anxiety had resulted from the irrational demands they had placed on themselves. This anxiety was accompanied by all the physical manifestations of stress.

A second major cognitive element in the program included working with the stress symptoms related to anger and resentment. The anger and resentment were being evoked by employees' demands that management should have handled the situation better or differently. The demand that the reality of the downsizing and what had occurred should have been different was a major target area for the stress management program.

The case of corporate downsizing and the resulting stress illustrates that stress management programs need to have both a standard presentation on issues such as relaxation, health, and time management, as well as an individualized component for dealing with the participant's own concerns. The most effective technique for dealing directly with individual concerns in a time-limited presentation is that of dealing with the participants' irrational beliefs that are contributing to their stress reaction (Ellis 1962; Ellis and Harper 1975). Often, as in the downsizing case, most of the group, or even an entire corporate culture, will attempt to adhere to certain irrational, stress-evoking beliefs. If these beliefs are not revealed and dealt with in the workshop, participants may leave thinking that the techniques presented are good ones, but do not apply directly to their own situations.

The irrational beliefs that emerged in the corporate culture in which the downsizing occurred included:

Employees must never make mistakes or have any "glitches" in their performance; or the errors will be catastrophic for their career.

An individual who cannot always produce superhuman effort and perfect performance is not competent enough and, therefore, not adequate.

Companies must not treat employees unfairly or in a negative manner, and they must not have to go through something like downsizing.

Jobs should not have to change, and additional work or new work should not be required of employees.

Going through something like downsizing is too difficult and awful and cannot be tolerated.

A philosophy including such beliefs would create a great deal of stress for the person operating with it. Such a philosophy would also interfere with the individual's being able to use stress management techniques unless the situation itself had been altered in some manner. When changing the situation is unlikely, one must deal with the underlying irrational philosophies.

Rust-Out and Burn-Out

Work overload and frequent, often unmeetable, deadlines have become a way of U.S. worklife. This work pace is named most often as the cause of employee stress. A useful scale for assessing work overload is Dr. Gmelch's RO-BO Scale (Gmelch 1982). This scale is designed to illustrate whether there is some "rust-out" (RO) or some "burn-out" (BO) occurring in the user's worklife. Employees who have a workload that they experience as monotonous or unstimulating for long periods of time are candidates for "rusting out." Employees who have experienced heavy, difficult, and overstimulating workloads over extended periods are candidates for "burning out." Both rust-out and burn-out are forms of stress responses. In rust-out there is actually not enough stress or arousal for the employee, and boredom, frustration, fatigue, and dissatisfaction can occur. Physical symptoms often look similar to high-stress symptoms and include headaches, sleep disturbances, immobilization, and a number of typically depressed behaviors. Burn-out from overstress often results in frantic, irrational behavior, poor problem solving, and exhaustion as well as many other stress responses.

Because rust-out and burn-out often look similar to someone judging a stress response, it is useful to determine which is more of an issue for the employee. The techniques used in the stress management program will differ according to whether rust-out or burn-out is an issue. Both groups of employees may actually have a great deal of work to do, but one is actually dulled by the workload, and the other is overwhelmed by the workload.

Techniques for working with rust-out include developing risk-taking exercises, planning new activities, reviewing job descriptions, exercises focusing on success and enjoyment, and assertiveness training. In order to help employees use and integrate these techniques, it will also be necessary to deal with these common irrational beliefs surrounding rust-out:

Because I don't have much responsibility, I can't really handle improving my job. Once a failure, always a failure.

I am too inadequate to ask for more stimulating work.

Other people should give me more stimulating work without my having to ask for it or develop it.

I can't take a risk with more stimulating work because it would be too awful to fail.

It's too hard to create changes that will make my work more stimulating.

Techniques for working with burn-out will include time management, relaxation training, delegation exercises, overcoming perfectionism exercises, and learning to say, "no." In order to carry these exercises out and develop these skills, it will be necessary to recognize and dispute these irrational beliefs:

I must be perfectly competent in everything I take on, or I won't meet expectations.

I have to take on everything given to me even if I can't get it done, or I won't get the approval I need from others at work.

I can't delegate tasks because they might not get done as perfectly as I require that they get done, and that would be terrible.

I can't say, "no," to others because they would not approve of me or like me the way I must be approved of.

I have to feel frantic about my workload because something catastrophic will happen to my career if I cannot handle everything.

If participants can be shown they are actually operating according to these irrational beliefs, and if they can change these beliefs, they will be more able to utilize stress management techniques.

MANAGING THE STRESS RESPONSE

The integration of stress management programs into the workplace has brought about a new awareness on the part of managers that "managing the stress response" is a part of managing people. A major part of the "stress aware" manager's job has become the monitoring of the employees' responses in working situations. Because stress affects job performance and problem-solving skills, it is well within any traditional description of a manager's job to include an understanding of stress and to implement stress reduction techniques where appropriate. One resource available to managers is the EAP. Employee assistance programs attempt to train managers to make referrals to the employee assistance program. This referral is appropriate when mangers observe a marked performance decrease that might be due to psychological, emotional or health-related concerns. Because stress-related concerns have been cited by employees as one of the major causes of problems that have affected job performance, an understanding of stress is essential to the manager. A rapid referral to the employee assistance program can help remediate a potentially harmful stress response.

Training in stress reduction for managers is a useful technique in implementing larger-scale stress management. If managers are handling their own stress levels, they will be more likely to provide a more positive model for managing difficult situations and stressors. They will also have a better understanding of the value of such programs for employees. If managers have uncovered some of their own irrational beliefs about work, workload, and performance, they may be able to reflect a more rational, positive performance philosophy to employees. This attitude may aid in helping employees to develop more stress-free responses at work.

Stress management programs will have a multifaceted effect on the employees who are able to participate. The original goal of reduction of stress of the individual participant will be accomplished in an effective program. Additional and perhaps unexpected results from the program may also occur. Some of these results may include:

an increased awareness of ways employees can enhance their own productivity

the generation of valuable new techniques for managers in managing people in difficult times, during times of heavy workload, and during times of major change

an increased enjoyment by both managers and employees of work that might have been previously considered too difficult or too dull

a common language among employees for discussing stress-evoking events and a shared view on techniques for managing these events and problem solving

reduced absenteeism as a result of health or attitude improvement

improved morale due to an awareness of the company's interest in each employee's health and productivity.

In summary, there are no reasons not to implement such a valuable program. Costs for these programs are low. The time taken in the program is usually returned through enhanced on-the-job performance. Health costs and concerns are often reduced. Integration of such stress management programs should have positive and lasting benefits for any company pursuing quality in their operations.

REFERENCES

Davis, M., M. McKay, and E. Eshelman. *The Relaxation and Stress Reduction Workbook.* 2nd ed. Oakland, California: New Harbinger, 1982.

Derogatis, L. R., R. S. Lipman, K. Rickles, E. H. Uhlenhuth, and L. Covi. "The Hopkins Symptom Inventory." *Behavioral Science* 19 (1974): 1–15.

Dodge, D. L., and T. W. Martin. *Stress and Chronic Illness.* Notre Dame, Indiana: University of Notre Dame Press, 1970.

Ellis, A. *Reason and Emotion in Psychotherapy.* New York: Lyle Stuart, 1962.

Ellis, A., and R. A. Harper. *A New Guide to Rational Living.* Englewood Cliffs, New Jersey: Prentice-Hall, 1975.

Farquhar, J. W. *The American Way of Life Need Not Be Hazardous to Your Health.* New York: Norton Press, 1978.

Friedman, M., and R. Rosenman. *Type A Behavior and Your Heart.* New York: Alfred Knopf, 1974.

Gmelch, W. H. *Beyond Stress to Effective Management.* New York: Wiley, 1982.

Ivancevick, J. M., and M. T. Matteson. *Stress and Work.* New York: Scott Foresman, 1980.

Kranzler, J. *You Can Change How You Feel.* New York: RECT Press, 1974.

Lakein, A. *How to Get Control of Your Time and Your Life.* New York: Signet Books, 1973.

McGrath, J. E. "Stress and Behavior in Organizations." In *Handbook of Industrial and Organizational Psychology,* edited by M. D. Dunnett. Chicago: Rand McNally, 1976.

Selye, H. *The Stress of Life*. New York: McGraw-Hill, 1976.

Wolff, H. G. *Stress and Disease*. 2nd ed. Springfield, Illinois: Charles C. Thomas, 1968.

15 Burnout: A Real Fire or False Alarm?

Samuel H. Klarreich

INTRODUCTION AND RATIONALE

> "Perhaps no other area of interest . . . has demonstrated the proliferation of literature in such a brief period than has the topic described as burnout" (Eldridge, Blostein, and Richardson 1981, p. 315).

> "Burnout is one of the most . . . real and tragic afflictions of workers in the post industrial age" (Harrison 1983, p. 29).

There is no doubt that burnout is a real fire and not a false alarm. It is certainly prominent in the workplace, and employees at all levels in an organization, across all job categories, across all professions, across all levels of management, are prone to this phenomenon (Herzberg 1983; Kahn 1978; Meyer 1982).

Because it was a genuine concern to many employees in our organization, our Health Education Committee decided to present the topic of burnout to the employee population in the Toronto region. It was extremely well received and obtained high ratings from the evaluations completed by the attendees. Because it is such a prominent problem and because the program was so well received in our organization, I decided to present the topic as a chapter in this section.

There are two purposes intended: one, this chapter may prompt the reader to pursue the topic of burnout as a health education presentation, two, the reader may simply want to ponder the information for the purpose of self-enhancement. Health professionals, health educators, and employee assistance program practitioners are more likely to be prone to burnout than other groups (Zemke 1981; Pines and Maslach 1978; Larson, Gilbertson, and Powell 1978). In fact, the phenomenon of burnout evolved from an examination of the problems that beset health professionals (Hall et al. 1979).

A Vignette

Mr. "X" was raised in a "good" home environment. He went to University, was graduated successfully, and accomplished his educational objectives. He eventually settled into a meaningful career as a health educator. He married the woman whom he truly loved, and eventually he and his wife had two children to further enhance a seemingly strong marital bond. There were never any real financial problems. Mr. "X" had the home that he always dreamed about; he had two cars in the driveway; he had a number of "extra toys" including a video cassette recorder and a personal computer. For all intents and purposes, there was absolutely nothing to worry about.

However, recently Mr. "X" had become very irritable and edgy. He often thought to himself that there was "something missing." Nothing seemed to matter anymore. No matter what he accomplished, it did not seem to hold the same value. He appeared exhausted, tired, and was fed up with working so hard. Additionally his tolerance level had decreased considerably. He did not want to be in the company of anyone; he became annoyed easily with peers, colleagues, family, and friends. Basically, he had a strong desire to run away from it all, to hide on some deserted island, and just abdicate all his responsibilities.

Some of these signs and signals are regarded as being part of the syndrome known as burnout. Burnout can be explained as "the exhaustion of one's resources both physical and psychological caused by excessive striving due to unrealistic expectations which are typically but not always job related" (Freudenberger 1980; Maslach 1978). The emphasis is on excessive striving and unrealistic expectations.

ORIGINS OF BURNOUT

Societal Influences

Before burnout is more carefully described, it is very important to examine the origins of this syndrome. Many of mankind's psychological and emotional problems are associated with a distorted value system, an irrational belief system that ultimately influences feelings and guides behaviors (Ellis 1962; Guidano and Liotti 1983). Burnout is no exception. People who suffer from burnout seem to have an unrealistic set of values and beliefs with respect to what they think they can accomplish, what they think society owes them and what they think the job can do for them (Freudenberger 1980). Burnout victims seem to believe that their job will supply them with more than it is really able to offer to them. In essence these victims seem to be overly committed to idealism, unrealism, and thus experience many unfulfilled expectations, which over time take their toll.

In examining these internal constructs such as values and expectations, there are two key influences. First, there is the influence of society (Pines and Aronson 1981). What does society reinforce that conditions people to subscribe to certain values and not others, to uphold certain exaggerated and unrealistic expectations?

Society reinforces the notion that we must rise above our parents. If our parents achieved a certain level in their careers and in their financial status, we must make certain to go beyond that level of achievement. Furthermore society tells us that we must go out of our way to strive, drive, and achieve excellence and acquire respect from our community. We must have possessions; we must gain prestige, status, and security and accumulate all these wholesome ingredients that we richly deserve, today! If we are unfortunate enough not to have these ingredients of success, the subtle message is that we have somehow failed. We have failed ourselves, and we have failed those around us, and we must push, strive, and drive even harder in order to overcome our failings.

Television has taught its viewing audience to go after "the good life" and become part of the "Pepsi generation." Become a yuppie and have it all, the imported cars, the imported clothing, jump on the fast track and stay there.

Education and affluence has taught us basically to reject simpler lifestyles in favor of more complicated ones. If our lives are not filled with all the machinery, all the technology, all the gadgetry that is available, then life must be dull. If we are not wearing clothing with the "right" label, driving cars of the "right" make, owning homes in the "right" area, having the "right" neighbors, going to the "right" schools, meeting and having the "right" friends, then we must not be successful.

The sexual revolution in society has emphasized that today we must become sexual gymnasts and contortionists who experience and produce multiple orgasms. There are sex manuals that describe 101 different ways to achieve complete sexual satisfaction. There are instruments and tools galore that we are to bring into the bedroom in order to heighten and magnify the ecstasy of the sexual experience. In fact if these sensations and experiences are not taking place, then we are obviously sexual failures.

Relationships today, society informs us, must be filled with complete romance and complete happiness. In fact, many books, articles, and magazines discuss how to make relationships happier than they have ever been before. Techniques to improve and multiply happiness are constantly bombarding us. The implication seems to be that if this state of complete happiness is not achieved and maintained, then the legitimate option of divorce must be considered. This philosophy might partially account for the fact that almost one in every two marriages today ends in divorce.

We are informed on a regular basis that to get ahead in society today we must put forth "150 percent, 200 percent, even 500 percent." We must maximize our full potential because we use approximately only 10 percent of our potential, and the other 90 percent is wasted. Superathletes, supersalesmen, supermanagers, superexecutives — all tell us that stretching our limits is the answer.

However, is it not reasonably legitimate to believe that to get ahead we need to try to put forth 100 percent (in whatever way that is measured)? When we heed what society is telling us, we may develop a variety of unrealistic expectations and values that may lead to many frustrations and, in turn, ultimately result in the syndrome of burnout (Lasch 1979).

Familial Influences

Not only does society impact our value system; the family, the second key influence, has a tremendous power to shape our views (Freudenberger 1980). Families directly and indirectly shape our thinking and shape our approaches to everyday living (Packard 1972). Certain families have emphasized the fact that we should never accept defeat. If we accept defeat then we will truly fail and never succeed, as we must. Furthermore, we must never admit weakness because, if weakness is admitted, then surely someone will take advantage of it, and we will suffer in the process. Another guiding principle is that we must persevere at all costs. Subtly this implies that whether we are stressed or burned out, we need to keep on pushing, driving, and striving, and eventually we will realize our ambitions.

Another principle that is reinforced is that we must never let "our family down." If we fail, then we will feel not only guilty about our personal failure but also regretful about the fact that we failed our entire family. We must always pull ourselves up by the bootstraps and do the right thing — make good!

Once these views, expectations, and values are reinforced directly or indirectly by the environmental influences of society and the family, the individual is more or less primed (Fischer 1983; Lazarus and Folkman 1984). Once the individual comes into the workplace, his or her behavior will be guided and shaped by these values and expectations. It is not difficult to visualize how a person with these unrealistic expectations, accompanied by excessive striving, could begin to experience trouble.

THE PROCESS OF BURNING OUT

Burning out progresses through a series of sequential stages (Glicken 1984). Keep in mind that these stages do not necessarily need to follow one another in order for the syndrome to occur. What these stages basically indicate is a series of disappointments and nonfulfillments over a period of time. If not helped, the individual will eventually reach burnout.

Stage #1 is entitled "the eager beaver stage" (Lauderdale 1982). Here the individual has come to the job with extremely high expectations, a commonplace occurrence. The individual may think the following, "I can do anything"; "This job will do it all for me"; "I will make this world a better place to live"; "I will conquer all." When these cognitions are examined, one quickly realizes that this individual has rather omnipotent and grandiose thinking. This person is typically idealistic, purposive, and single-minded. Yet at the same time, this person, although filled with extremely high energy, is unrealistic with respect to what the job will provide, and with respect to what can be accomplished in the position (Veninga and Spradley 1981).

As time progresses, the individual slowly drifts into stage #2, entitled "disillusionment" (Freudenberger 1980). In this stage the person realizes that the job is not meeting expectations. So the individual tries harder as the value system dictates. However, in the process the person becomes somewhat confused, disoriented, impatient, and irritable but, nonetheless, pushes on and drives for success. Some confidence has been lost in the process but striving "to become a winner" will eliminate that loss.

Time continues and the individual slowly drifts into stage #3, entitled "frustration" (Lauderdale 1982). The individual understands that the job may never measure up, so desperation takes over. The person becomes angry, short-tempered, fatigued, exhausted, loses enthusiasm, and generally blames others for this predicament (Tubesing, Sippel, and Tubesing 1981). Cynicism, callousness, and detachment are strikingly prominent so that it is difficult for this individual to work successfully. More confidence is lost, yet the person attempts desperately to push ahead.

Finally, the individual moves into stage #4, entitled "despair" (Lauderdale 1982). The individual recognizes that "it's over." There is a tremendous sense of defeat, disgrace, dishonor, and the general feeling of failure. As such, alienation, isolation, and emptiness are prominent. There is a loss of energy and increased apathy. At this point the individual feels like running away from it all and abdicating all responsibilities. When this person wakes in the morning he or she feels like pulling the covers over his or her head and simply not getting out of bed.

If this syndrome persists, the individual will probably experience depression, considered to be the end-result of burnout (Herzberg 1983).

DISPELLING THE MYTHS ABOUT BURNOUT

Victims have interesting explanations to account for their burnout. They will commonly attribute their problems to external, organizational influences and typically blame the corporation for their woes.

In this section, I refer to these explanations as myths. They are myths simply because they are not the cause although they may be the triggering events. That is not to say that organizational influences, changes, and pressures are not real. They may, in fact, contribute to or reinforce the problem of burnout. However, the legitimate villains are the burnout victim's expectations with respect to the organization. Burnout victims have perpetuated a number of myths as the causes of their burnout. But underlying exaggerated expectations are the genuine menaces.

The first myth that burnout victims perpetuate is reflected in the statement that "My burnout is caused by work overload" (Glicken and Janka 1982). Because I have "too much on my plate and too little time to do it," that is the reason I am burned out. If my work overload were reduced, then my burnout would be eliminated. Now the condition of work overload may, in fact, be very real. However, the culprits are the underlying exaggerated expectations with respect to work overload.

If these underlying exaggerated expectations are not examined carefully, the burnout syndrome will still persist. Second, if, in fact, there is a work overload problem, this condition will not be resolved unless the exaggerated expectations are examined first. These expectations read as follows, "There is too much to do, but I have to do it all, and I have to do it perfectly well." Or "I should be able to handle everything, I need to be in control, and because I am not, I cannot do anything." One can quickly see that if these expectations were somewhat reduced, or even eliminated, then the issue of work overload, if it is an issue, could be reasonably resolved. The associated burnout symptoms also could be significantly reduced (Ellis 1972b).

The next myth sustained by burnout victims is summarized in the statement "My burnout is caused by work underload" (Glicken and Janka 1982). In other words, "There is not enough on my plate; therefore, I am experiencing burnout." Work underload may, in fact, be an issue. But unless the exaggerated expectations are examined first, the issue of work underload will not be resolved. And burnout will still persist as a very real problem. The exaggerated expectations read as follows, "I have to have more work, otherwise it means I am a failure." Or "I should be more productive, I should be more useful, and I should be more successful, and because I am not I will never be able to live it down." These internal statements need to be examined and ultimately changed before other changes are attempted (Ellis 1971).

Another myth put forth by burnout victims is summarized in the statement, "My burnout is caused by role ambiguity" (Glicken 1984). Again this condition may, in fact, be reality, but unless the exaggerated expectations are examined first, the issue will never be properly resolved, and the symptoms of burnout will never be significantly reduced. Some of the exaggerated expectations include the following, "I need my job, and I should be treated better, and because I am not, I cannot work at all." Or "I cannot stand this uncertainty and confusion because if I cannot be totally efficient, to hell with everything."

Another myth that has been perpetuated is summarized in the following statement, "My burnout is caused by inadequate resources to perform my job" (Glicken 1984). The exaggerated expectations underlying this myth include the following, "They have no right to do this to me; how will I ever get on the fast track?" Or, "I always have to do everything on my own and because I can't, I will truly fail." Here again these expectations need careful examination.

Burnout victims have maintained another myth summarized in the following statement, "My burnout is caused by uncooperative peers" (Glicken and Janka 1982). This issue, in fact, may be very legitimate, however, unless the exaggerated expectations are examined first, this concern will not be resolved, and the problem of burnout will not be properly addressed. These exaggerated expectations include the following, "They have no right to act that way toward me; I am a better person than that." Or, "I hate people like that because they will prevent me from achieving success." If these expectations persist, the burnout victim will be in a constant state of anger and hostility, and we know from the earlier description of burning out that anger, cynicism, and hostility only prolong and magnify existing difficulties.

Another myth that has continued is summarized in the following statement, "My burnout is caused by lack of feedback" (Glicken 1983). The exaggerated expectations underlying this myth include the following, "No one cares about what I do; therefore, I must only be average or below average and probably stupid." Or, "I need to be recognized, I need to be told I am worthwhile, and because I am not I will never succeed." It is these expectations that need restructuring before other changes are considered.

Another myth that has been preserved is summarized in the following statement, "My burnout is caused by too close supervision" (Glicken 1983). The exaggerated expectations supporting this myth include the following, "They don't trust me because they think I am incompetent." Or, "I should not be treated like a stupid child; how can I ever perform when I am treated that way?" As you can see these expectations are the key to unlocking the problem of burnout.

The next myth that has thrived is summarized in the following statement, "My burnout is caused by outdated policies and procedures"

(Glicken 1984). This organizational condition may, in fact, exist, but once again the exaggerated expectations need careful examination first. These expectations include the following, "This isn't the right or perfect way to run things; how can I ever be successful?" Or, "I am always the one who has to do everything perfectly well, perfectly right, and how can I in this crazy environment!"

Another myth that has grown vigorously is summarized in the following statement, "My burnout is caused by lack of stimulation and job enrichment" (Glicken 1983). The exaggerated expectations in this instance include the following, "What am I going to do? There is nothing interesting outside work success, and because I am not experiencing the right amount of work success, I am a failure." Or, "I need to be innovative, I need to be excited by my work, and because I am not right now, I feel miserable." It is these expectations that require careful reorganizing.

The final myth that has been perpetuated by burnout victims is summarized in the following statement, "My burnout is caused by lack of reward and recognition for my good work" (Glicken 1983). The exaggerated expectations supporting this myth include the following, "I need to feel that I am good, I need to feel that I am great, I even need to feel that I am outstanding." Or, "I have to know that I am just not capable or just not average, but I have to know that I am way above average." Or, "Someone has to tell me something good; otherwise, I know that I have truly failed."

I hope, from the above explanations, it has become quite clear that the exaggerated expectations are the true villains. These exaggerated expectations typically cause the individual to feel anxious, or depressed, or worried, or guilt-ridden. If these emotions persist, the resulting behavior can only be self-destructive. Once exaggerated expectations and disturbed emotions and self-destructive behavior become a regular pattern of functioning, the individual is burned out.

THREE STEPS TO PUTTING OUT THE FIRE

Self-Appraisal

There are a number of steps to take to put out the fire. The first step is entitled "self-appraisal." Self-appraisal is very important because it allows us to determine our level of disturbance, to assess the nature of our condition and to decide whether our life has so significantly changed that something needs to be done about the problem (Helliwell 1981, 1982; Pelletier 1984).

There are a number of questions to be asked, and if the answer is, "Yes," to many of these, it is reasonable to conclude that you are "burning out." Are you cynical about your work? Is work draining to you? Do you force yourself to do routine things at work? Does your job, which you worked so hard to obtain, seem meaningless to you right now? Do you identify so closely with your work that if it fell apart you would too? Is your department or section or work area a maze of red tape and foul-ups? Are your peers and colleagues "goofing off" all the time? Do you constantly want to be somewhere else rather than at work? Are your peers, colleagues, friends, and relatives no longer as exciting to you? Do your family members seem more distant and remote? Do you feel resigned rather than enthusiastic about your future? Do you look for more dangerous diversions in order to bring liveliness into your life?

The answers to the above questions will allow you to appraise the degree to which you are burned out, an essential first step before other steps are taken.

Changing Expectations

The most critical step is changing or shifting our expectations (Veninga and Spradley 1981). Altering expectations is not an easy task. However, there are a number of very important points to consider that will make the task a workable and feasible process.

First, it is critical to admit that you are "burned out." This may sound rather obvious, but it is a very important consideration (Ellis 1972a). For example, Alcoholics Anonymous stipulates that the first step to recovery from alcoholism is to admit that you are an alcoholic. With respect to weight loss programs, the first step in losing weight is to admit to yourself and to key people around you that you are overweight. If this strategy has already proven to be successful, then certainly it can be useful in this case. Admission, not repression, is obviously the first step to recovery.

What is equally important, if not more important, is to admit that you created the problem (Ellis 1978). You created the problem simply because you were the one who adopted those exaggerated expectations and unrealistic values. It was you, furthermore, that developed an unhealthy approach to problems. However, because you learned and developed a particular unhealthy style, you can also unlearn and develop a new approach. To admit that you created the problem empowers you to create a more healthy lifestyle.

You must not "damn" yourself for being burned out (Ellis and Harper 1975). Burnout victims are notorious for being extremely self-critical. Not only are they self-derogatory because they have failed, but also they become even more self-degrading because they have burned out. Self-criticism merely compounds the problem and prevents them from ultimately confronting the condition of burnout.

It is also important for burnout victims to challenge their low frustration tolerance (Ellis and Knaus 1977). Burnout victims are renowned for thinking that they can no longer tolerate anything, including the admission and pain of being burned out. They cannot tolerate lack of success, they cannot tolerate failure, they cannot tolerate working conditions, they cannot tolerate their peers. With these attitudes, they will certainly not be able to come to grips with their problems. Human beings are resilient. Many times daily, people overcome very severe crises and traumas. Once victims begin to realize that they are able to tolerate a significant amount, they are psychologically preparing themselves to face the unfortunate predicament of burnout.

Burnout victims need to acquire a philosophy of uncertainty (Ellis and Harper 1975). These victims typically demand guarantees and certainty in life. In fact, they want to know for sure that they will be truly successful and not fail. But human beings know very little for certain. Once burnout victims are prepared to accept this philosophy, it makes it easier for them to deal with the unpredictability of daily living. Furthermore, it will make it possible for them to deal with various failures, various setbacks, and various uncertainties, which occur regularly in the workplace.

It is important that burnout victims learn to minimize their musts, conditions for living, and prerequisites for life (Ellis 1971). These victims seem to think that living is equated with being successful. Success is defined in terms of a fantastic job, a great office, a hefty salary, a big house, imported cars and clothing, and other expensive items. If these were prerequisites for living, everyone would require them. But everyone does not and they continue to enjoy life comfortably. Burnout victims need to realize that they can certainly strive for these possessions but that they are not necessarily preconditions for living.

It is equally important to abandon the unrelenting demand and craving desire for success and achievement. To strive for success and achievement is important, but if one has a burning desire for it and it does not occur, then what remains? For the burnout victim, very little remains. Success and achievement are not related to a need in the same way that food or drink might be, but the burnout victim perceives that there is an exact similarity. This is grossly unrealistic.

To be antiperfectionistic is significant (Helliwell 1981). Burnout victims pride themselves on doing things perfectly well. However, if a project has not reached perfection, then the burnout victim becomes worried, even terrified, because failure is implied. Because failure is so unacceptable to the burnout victim, fear is generated that failure may occur again, which in turn may create a deterioration in performance. Some victims become so fraught with trepidation that they literally "stop doing" for fear that something may go wrong. They eventually achieve exactly what they fought so strenuously to avoid — failure. They have failed simply because they have stopped performing. Although it is laudable to strive for perfection, if it is not forthcoming it is necessary to continue.

It is important to be anti self-rating and not attach your ego to your achievements (Ellis 1972b). Burnout victims regularly rate themselves in accordance with what they do and achieve. If they perform well, it is proof positive that they are superstars and fantastic human beings. On the other hand, if they do not succeed it proves that they are stupid, ridiculous failures. Accomplishments are simply actions, but these alone do not determine who you are as a human being although burnout victims would vehemently dispute that. If you wish to rate, then assess your performance and learn from your mistakes, but, if you then rate yourself based on your performance, you may run into severe difficulties. Should you rate yourself negatively because you performed poorly, you will probably feel extremely miserable and eventually depressed. In that mood, it will be very difficult to accomplish anything. This is one of the most difficult principles for burnout victims to accept.

As a corollary, burnout victims should accept themselves unconditionally (Ellis 1985). These victims are experts at rejecting themselves because of their failures. However, a failing does not imply that you are a failure; it simply means that you have not performed well in a particular situation. Accept yourself with your defeats, with your accomplishments, with your idiosyncrasies. Then and only then, can you concentrate on the tasks at hand. Thereupon, you will be able to learn from your failures and gain pleasure from your successes.

Equally important is accepting others and their idiosyncrasies (Helliwell 1982). Burnout victims unfortunately do not do this well. They not only do not accept themselves, especially when they have failed, but they also find it difficult to accept others. Consequently, they feel angry and cynical and detach themselves from those around them. This disruptive behavior simply compounds the problem of burnout. Acceptance does not necessarily denote that you have to comply with what others say and do. You can certainly challenge the actions of others, but is is very important to accept them and their own weaknesses, frailties, and strengths. This will then considerably reduce anger and hostility toward others, and it will be possible to cooperate with peers and colleagues in order to resolve troublesome issues.

Another important item is to recognize that you do not necessarily need motivation and inspiration in order to do something. Also, you don't invariably need to "enjoy it and feel pleasure about it before you do it" (Ellis and Knaus 1977). Burnout victims are convinced that motivation, inspiration, pleasure, and joy are the essential ingredients to performance. But, on many occasions people have not felt like doing anything, yet they were still able to complete successfully any number of tasks. Once burnout victims recognize that the above ingredients are not preconditions to performance, it will make living easier.

The final point carefully to consider is to take risks in other areas of your life (Ellis and Harper 1975). Burnout victims principally specialize in one area, namely "work." First, these people believe that they are experts in their chosen fields of endeavor and feel most comfortable devoting all their time and energy to work. Second, these victims fear that if they extend their activities outside work, they may only achieve an average performance. This is so terrifying that these people rarely experiment and do not broaden their horizons. But do you have to excel at everything? Is that possible? Branch out and enjoy what the rest of life has to offer.

If you as a burnout victim, began to consider and test the above ideas, you would discover a significant shift in your expectations. No longer would your expectations be exaggerated; instead they would become more realistic, flexible, and adaptable. These elements are essential to a resolution of burnout.

Communication and Other Behavioral Options

After your expectations have changed, it is important to consider behavioral changes. Communication or dialogue is an extremely meaningful activity (Glicken 1983). Share your feelings and thoughts with close friends, relatives, and understanding colleagues, especially with those who will listen and may even offer feedback. Talk about how you have been feeling lately, what you have been thinking about, what you want from your job, what you hoped to achieve and what you have not achieved, what you invested in your job, what you expected that did not happen. This entire process is referred to as developing a social support system. Individuals who have strong support systems seem to develop greater resistances to burnout and other related disorders (Pines 1983; Veninga and Spradley 1981; Farber 1983).

There are other behaviors to consider; some entail considerable risk. A very common behavior is known as a diversion (Lauderdale 1982). Taking a weekend break, getting involved in athletics, and picking up a hobby are examples. However, you may be drawn to an activity to the extent that you deny that you are burned out. Your diversion may become too consuming. You may be so involved with the activity, that everything else is excluded. An excellent example of this is compulsive jogging. Some joggers are damaging their health because they are anxiously compelled to jog. In essence, any diversion, which includes no change in expectations, combined with a compelling urgency to engage in the activity may produce dangerous consequences.

Another option is referred to as major introspection (Lauderdale 1982). Here, you spend time discovering "what you are all about." In a sense it can be referred to as cerebral jogging. The individual thinks and rethinks without attempting to change the predicament or the situation. This is as dangerous as the previous diversion. The individual is mentally trapped and does not go beyond the thinking stage.

The third option is probably the most meaningful one. It can be considered a compromise between changing your expectations as well as changing some part of your routine (Lauderdale 1982). Changing your routine may entail altering your work environment to the degree that it can be changed, changing other parts of your lifestyle or changing both work and nonwork situations. On some occasions, the change in the work environment may be a major one. The individual may feel that it is necessary to leave a particular job or career in favor of another job or another career.

SUMMARY AND CONCLUSIONS

Without doubt burnout is a very real fire. However, the fire can be extinguished. I hope the reader has gained an appreciation of the steps necessary to stifle this fire.

Burnout victims, as well as individuals who are not yet burned out, must aim for a new condition entitled "hardiness." It indicates a commitment to thinking, feeling, and doing but not necessarily succeeding. If there is this commitment, you probably will succeed most of the time, although not all the time. Hardiness denotes a commitment to overall happiness, not specific glory and grandeur. If there is a commitment to glory and grandeur and it is not forthcoming, what then do you have?

Hardiness signifies a responsibility to go after challenges in all aspects of life, not necessarily to crave achievement in only one area. If you crave achievement in only one area and do not receive it, then what? Hardiness represents a responsibility to develop a strong support system. We are all "social animals" after all, and it is important to establish a social network and social relationships. Finally, it indicates a devotion to laughter and humor. What better way to celebrate life and living?

REFERENCES

Eldridge, W., S. Blostein, and V. Richardson. "A Multi-Dimensional Mode for Assessing Factors Associated with Burnout in Human Service Organizations." *Public Personnel Management Journal* July-August 1981: 314–21.

Ellis, A. *Reason and Emotion in Psychotherapy.* New York: Lyle Stuart, 1962.

____. *Growth Through Reason.* Hollywood, California: Wilshire Books, 1971.

____. *Executive Leadership: A Rational Approach.* New York: Institute for Rational Living, 1972a.

____. "Helping People Get Better Rather Than Merely Feel Better." *Rational Living* 7 (1972b): 2–9.

____. "Rational-Emotive Therapy and Self-Help Therapy." *Rational Living* 13 (1978): 3–6.

____. "A Rational-Emotive Approach to Acceptance and Its Relationship to EAPS." In *The Human Resources Management Handbook: Principles and Practice of*

Employee Assistance Programs, edited by S. H. Klarreich et al. New York: Praeger, 1985.

Ellis, A., and R. Harper. *A New Guide to Rational Living.* Englewood Cliffs, New Jersey: Prentice-Hall, 1975.

Ellis, A., and W. Knaus. *Overcoming Procrastination.* New York: Institute for Rational Living, 1977.

Farber, B. A. "A Critical Perspective on Burnout." In *Stress and Burnout in the Human Services Profession,* edited by B. A. Farber. New York: Pergamon Press, 1983.

Fischer, H. J. "A Psychoanalytic View of Burnout." In *Stress and Burnout in the Human Services Profession,* edited by B. A. Barber. New York: Pergamon Press, 1983.

Freudenberger, H. J. *Burnout: How to Beat the High Cost of Success.* New York: Doubleday, 1980.

Glicken, M. D. "A Counseling Approach to Employee Burnout." *Personnel Journal,* March 1983, pp. 222–28.

_____. "Response to Worker Burnout." *EAP Digest,* September-October 1984, pp. 48–53.

Glicken, M. D. and K. Janka. "Executives under Fire: The Burnout Syndrome." *California Management Review* 24 (1982): 67–73.

Guidano, V. F. and G. Liotti. *Cognitive Processes and Emotional Disorders.* New York: The Guilford Press, 1983.

Hall, R. C. W., E. R. Gardner, M. Perl, S. K. Stickney, and B. Pfefferbaum. "The Professional Burnout Syndrome." *Psychiatric Opinion* 16 (1979): 12–17.

Harrison, W. D. "A Social Competence Model of Burnout." In *Stress and Burnout in the Human Services Professions,* edited by B. A. Farber. New York: Pergamon Press, 1983.

Helliwell, T. "Are You a Potential Burnout?" *Training and Development Journal,* October 1981, pp. 25–29.

_____. "The Wages of Overwork-Burnout." *CA Magazine,* August 1982, pp. 83–87.

Herzberg, F. "Up the Staircase to Productivity Burnout." *Industry Week,* January 10, 1983, pp. 65–70.

____. "Remedies for Depression and Burnout." *Industry Week*, February 7, 1983, pp. 38–39.

Kahn, R. "Job Burnout: Prevention and Remedies." *Public Welfare*, Spring, 1978, pp. 61–63.

Larson, C. C., D. L. Gilbertson, and J. A. Powell. "Therapist Burnout: Perspectives on a Critical Issue." *Social Casework*, November 1978, pp. 563–65.

Lasch, C. *The Culture of Narcissism: American Life in an Age of Diminishing Returns*. New York: Norton, 1979.

Lauderdale, M. *Burnout*. New York: University Associates, 1982.

Lazarus, R. S., and S. Folkman. *Stress, Appraisal, and Coping*. New York: Springer, 1984.

Maslach, C. "Job Burnout: How People Cope." *Public Welfare*, Spring, 1978, pp. 56–58.

Meyer, J. H. "Burnout." *Executive*, July 1982, pp. 27–29.

Packard, V. A. *A Nation of Strangers*. New York: McKay, 1972.

Pelletier, K. R. *Healthy People in Unhealthy Places*. La Jolla, California: Merloyd, Lawrence, 1984.

Pines, A. M., and E. Aronson. *Burnout: From Tedium to Personal Growth*. New York: Free Press, 1981.

Pines, A. and C. Maslach. "Characteristics of Staff Burnout in Mental Health Settings." *Hospital and Community Psychiatry* 29 (1978): 233–37.

____. "On Burnout and the Buffering Effects of Social Support." In *Stress and Burnout in the Human Services Profession*, edited by B. A. Farber. New York: Pergamon Press, 1983.

Tubesing, D. A., M. D. Sippel, and N. L. Tubesing. *Rx for Burnout*. Duluth, Minnesota: Whole Person Associates, 1981.

Veniga, R. L. and J. P. Spradley. *The Work/Stress Connection: Hope to Cope with Job Burnout*. Boston: Little, Brown, 1981.

Zemke, R. "Trainer Burnout: What Is It and How to Avoid It." *Training HRD*, September 1981, pp. 97–98.

16 In Pursuit of
Personal Excellence

Gerald D. Pulvermacher

Like many others interested in the science of enhancing human performance, I, too, read *In Search of Excellence* (Peters and Waterman 1984). Quite frankly, I was not overwhelmed by its contents. I would not go so far as the famous management writer Peter F. Drucker (1984) who labeled the book "juvenile." The focus of the book was to enhance the corporate effectiveness of U.S. organizations and addressed the crisis that the U.S. economy was experiencing at the time. U.S. business was witnessing increased competition from the Japanese and reduced productivity from its work force and was in the midst of a recession. Organizations needed to be reminded of business basics, such as the importance of staying closer to their customers or the groups they were serving, listening to their employees (at all levels) so as to benefit from their observations, and creating an innovative, creative, and responsive work environment.

Although corporate excellence is a valuable goal, it occurred to me that one could not attain organizational excellence without first helping individuals within the organization achieve personal excellence and peak performance. In reviewing the literature regarding enhancing human performance, I found three major themes emerge as characteristic of individuals who are capable of achieving optimum levels of performance: a strong sense of self-esteem, maintaining a set of concrete, achievable goals, and an ability to harness and reduce self-imposed barriers to excellence.

Emerging from this philosophy are a number of principles that, when implemented, will bring one significantly closer to achieving personal excellence. These are setting realistic, achievable goals; developing and enhancing one's self-discipline; managing self-defeating attitudes and beliefs; reducing excessive worrying; utilizing stress advantageously; managing conflict constructively with individuals whom one relies upon to achieve goals; assertively expressing needs and wants; and actively listening and attending to the needs and goals of others.

COMBATING PERFECTIONISM

One of the major barriers to achieving excellence may well be our concept of excellence. If one adopts the "Madison Avenue" view of excellence, the conclusion might be reached that the only way to achieve is by attaining perfection. This view suggests that the only way to derive pleasure from an activity and enhance self-esteem is to set exceedingly high standards and aspire to achieve these goals. Failure to achieve perfection, if one adheres to this view, results in a lessened degree of satisfaction from goal attainment and a reduced sense of accomplishment. Thus, children who aspire to be gymnasts ought to shoot for scores of ten; men who want to find the ideal mate would be advised to find a perfect "10"; those who want to demonstrate financial success ought to drive Mercedes-Benzes; ideal parents rear perfect children; perfect marriage partners never fight; and the perfect employee never makes mistakes. Perhaps the epitome of this view was encapsulated by Vince Lombardi, the famous football coach of the Green Bay Packers, who said, "Practice does not make perfect, perfect practice makes perfect."

Ironically, the pursuit of perfection is more often than not self-defeating. As Bulka pointed out: "The human being is finite, therefore, imperfect. These imperfections make for individual uniqueness and irreplaceability, and also make perfection impossible. To attain perfection would make the person existentially dead, with nothing more to achieve, inviting the existential vacuum" (1984, p. 6).

Dr. David Burns, a psychiatrist at the University of Pennsylvania Mood Disorders Clinic, developed the Perfectionism Scale, which was subsequently used in several studies. In one such study (1980), 18 of 34 insurance agents in the Philadelphia Million Dollar Forum, who scored high on the Perfectionism Scale, earned $1,500 less each year than those who were measured as being nonperfectionists. The Perfectionism Scale was administered to students enrolled in the University of Pennsylvania

Law School who sought out counseling services; 80 percent of these students scored high on the scale.

Recent studies (Tiseall 1984) also suggest that although Type A behavior may well be a risk factor for heart disease, perfectionism is probably one of the personality variables that potentiates Type A as a risk factor. When one considers that the major characteristic of Type A individuals is their sense of time urgency, hurriedness, and impatience, it is logical to conclude that one who is striving for perfection under these circumstances will also experience elevated levels of stress.

Perfectionists are prone to disruptions in interpersonal relationships. Because perfectionists fear rejection if judged imperfect, they tend to respond defensively to criticism. The defensive behavior frustrates and alienates others, which usually invites further disapproval. Thus, rather than reduce their defensive responses, perfectionists conclude that they must continue to perform perfectly to be accepted.

Perfectionists are also reticent to become self-disclosing because they believe that people will judge them imperfect if various human foibles are discovered. In order to develop and enhance intimate relationships, however, it is necessary that one gradually expose inner feelings, thoughts, wishes, fears, strengths, and weaknesses. As a result of their unwillingness to do so, perfectionists often create their own barriers to intimacy.

Perfectionists are also likely to be found among individuals we label as being procrastinators. By virtue of trying to achieve the perfect product, they have difficulty determining the point of diminishing return and when a task should be considered complete. They also believe that their models for success are individuals who achieve personal goals with little effort, few errors, maximum self-confidence, and little, if any, emotional distress.

Perfectionists are also prone to apply their high standard to others and are inevitably disappointed. When these standards are not met, they often respond with anger and annoyance, causing resentment in others and leaving both parties exasperated and frustrated.

Clinically, it has been observed that perfectionists, when overwhelmed by their behavioral tendencies, often succumb to burnout, with corresponding feelings of depression. Perfectionists tend to avoid activities that they do not do perfectly and engage in activities that they do exceedingly well; ironically those activities that they perform well generally provide them with the least amount of pleasure. Thus they inevitably spend most of their time doing things they do not really enjoy.

Consequently, they become the architect of their own feelings of unhappiness, lethargy, apathy, and burnout.

Apart form the view that perfection will elicit affection and approval, perfectionists tend to maintain several other distortions in thinking. Perfectionists often exhibit all-or-nothing thinking wherein any performance short of perfection is judged undesirable. Therefore, a performance that is less than perfect is deemed a failure. Consequently, the perfectionist has few opportunities to experience satisfaction because perfection is rarely achieved.

Goals are made rigid and are not seen as tools for motivation; rather, goals are seen as standards for evaluation. Thus, perfectionists measure their self-esteem based on the attainment of these rigid, often unachievable goals.

Perfectionists also tend to convert basic desires into absolutistic demands. Thus, they frequently use phrases prefaced by words such as "should" or "must" rather than "prefer" or "want." Failure to achieve these "shoulds" results in viewing the consequences in exaggerated terms. For example, the perfectionist might say, "It is awful or terrible when I am not competent at everything I do," rather than, "I would prefer to be competent at all activities, but failure to do so only makes me human."

Perfectionists are also quite remiss at providing themselves with self-praise and believe that the way to attain perfection is through self-abasement and negative self-evaluation. Consequently, they tend to deflect compliments judging them as undeserved, or point out even minute shortcomings in their performance. They are also more prone to being vigilant for their faults than for their accomplishments or achievements.

Before writing *Tactics,* Edward de Bono (1984) interviewed more than 100 individuals, who in their chosen areas of endeavor, would be considered successful by most. De Bono attempted to identify the strategies these individuals deemed important for achieving excellence.

Maintaining a positive mental attitude was seen as essential. In so doing, one tends to experience defeat not as failures or setbacks, but as opportunities to make corrections, to add to one's learning, and to move forward. Defeats were not seen as occasions for remorse or self-recrimination. These successful individuals believed also in the value of being goal-directed. Goals provide a sense of purpose and meaning. Goals might be altered by experience or circumstance, but they were never far from consciousness. Finally, these individuals were characterized by their sense of being self-motivated rather than motivated by extrinsic factors, such as rewards or fear; in other words, they wanted to succeed.

GOAL SETTING

What are goals? Goals are plans, dreams, wishes, needs, and desires. Goals can be short-term or long-term. One needs both types of goals; without short-term goals one does not have a sense of being able to successively approximate the longer-term goals. Goals need to be S.M.A.R.T.; they need to be specific (S), measureable (M), achievable (A), realistic (R), and target-dated (T). Goals can be developed in most areas of human endeavor. Examples include career and professional goals, financial goals, material goals (house, car, boat, plane, cottage), educational goals (degrees, certificates, qualifications, skills, and languages), physical goals (weight, smoking, fitness, stress, sports), family goals, self-improvement goals (memory, public speaking, concentration, self-confidence, assertiveness, courage); social and community service goals (clubs, associations, politics), travel goals, creative goals (writing, painting, renovating, refinishing, building), and spiritual goals.

Once goals have been described and listed, they need to be graded in order of their priority and defined in S.M.A.R.T. terms. Next, one must clearly identify any potential obstacles that might stand between the individual and the goal. Additionally, it may well be necessary to identify additional knowledge that is required to achieve these goals and individuals whose cooperation is required.

Once goals are specified, activities leading to goal attainment need to be listed and prioritized. These activities become the building blocks for goal attainment.

GOAL ACHIEVEMENT AND IMAGERY

Research has demonstrated that one of the most effective ways to succeed in achieving goals is to rehearse mastering the activities leading to gaol attainment in imagination first. During training, for example, ski racers are taught to physically and mentally relax, then visualize the course and themselves moving down the course with great speed doing each turn as precisely as they would like to. They focus on their bodily sensations as they do the course, they feel the air against their face, they feel the bumps under their feet. They repeat this process two to three times a day, each training day. When they actually run the course, their performance improves.

Another example is business executives who would like to become less tense making oral presentations in conferences and meetings. After relaxing they visualize themselves in the conference room, delivering a presentation in a calm, confident, spontaneous, and articulate fashion. They see the smiles on the faces in the audience, the return of eye contact, themselves fielding questions, being applauded, and congratulated at the conclusion. After several practice sessions, they are far better able to perform in the actual situation.

In order to facilitate goal attainment an individual should learn to master the technique of relaxation and, in conjunction, practice imagery techniques relating to a particular goal. Too often people visualize and rehearse failure experiences; thus they increase the probability of future failures. By attaching feelings of relaxation, as well as mastery and control in past experiences to the imagination of current goals, the probability of goal attainment in the current instance is increased.

MANAGING SELF-DEFEATING ATTITUDES AND BELIEFS

Dr. Terry Orlich of the University of Ottawa (Smith 1984) stated that "the greatest barriers we confront in our pursuit of excellence are psychological barriers which we impose upon ourselves."

Undesirable, counterproductive behaviors and undesirable emotions are not the result of setbacks that we experience or expectations that are unfulfilled. Rather, the undesirable emotional and behavioral consequences that we experience are a function of our misinterpretation of life events. The misrepresentations are frequently exaggerations of their true impact. Thus, the same event can lead to quite different responses in different people. If you wanted to make someone angry at you and the person called you a name, you might be pleased. If you required a deduction for your income tax, a stock market loss might make you feel good. Feelings are not caused by events, otherwise everyone would have the same feelings toward any given event.

Drs. Albert Ellis and Robert Harper (1975) in *A New Guide to Rational Living* propose that we attack or dispute irrational beliefs so that we remain in control, goal-directed, and essentially safe from our own self-defeating nature. They propose that irrational beliefs be identified, disputed, and transformed into more realistic, rational thinking. They (1975) describe several irrational beliefs including:

I need everyone's approval and love for just about everything I do.

I should be able to do everything well.

If something bad might happen, I had better worry about it.

It is easier to avoid difficult things than to try and risk failure.

I will enjoy life more if I avoid responsibilities and take what I can get now.

Some people are bad and should be punished.

When things aren't going well, my life is terrible.

If things go wrong, I'm going to feel bad, and there's very little I can do about these feelings.

What has happened to me and what I have done in the past determine the way I feel and what will happen to me now and in the future.

People and things should be different, and perfect solutions should be found for everything.

One can readily recognize the relationship between accepting these beliefs and the increased probability that excellence will not be achieved. As a function of entertaining these attitudes, excellence would be equated with perfection, self-esteem would hinge upon attaining perfection, and negative self-evaluation would be the inevitable outcome of the nonachievement of goals. One would also be more prone to lamenting the past and worrying about the future; indeed, one would expect that if everything were going well, some inevitable gloom would be over the horizon. Risk taking would be minimized, consideration of catastrophic outcomes would be enhanced, and one would work only for the approval of others rather than for personal self-satisfaction.

COMMUNICATION SKILLS

Far too often people are unable to satisfy their goals and desires as a function of their reluctance to tell others what type of assistance they require to achieve their particular goals. The inability to assert one's needs and wants then becomes an obstacle in the path of achieving excellence.

Correspondingly, when one takes the risk of asserting one's needs and wants, there is an increased probability that the needs and wants of others, upon whom you may be relying, may conflict with your own. Thus the ability to resolve conflict constructively and to listen to the needs of others effectively become additional skills in the pursuit of excellence.

The goal in assertive behavior then is to express needs, wants, thoughts, and opinions without feeling guilty, anxious, or fearful. This differs from the goals of aggressive behavior, to dominate others, to assert one's own needs and rights without concern for other people's needs or rights, and to win at all cost.

The goal in nonassertive behavior is to be liked above all and to avoid conflict. Consequently, nonassertive individuals are prone to being frustrated in their quest for excellence and tend to lose the respect of others and their own sense of self-respect. Their inability to act in their own best interest becomes an ever-increasing obstacle on their road to excellence.

Aggressive individuals may from time to time achieve their goals, but they create a great deal of tension, anger, and a sense of vengefulness in others. The motive of the "boss" becomes to sabotage the efforts of the aggressive person.

To enhance the degree of cooperation in others, it is not only important to be able to articulate one's own needs and wants; it is also imperative to listen effectively to the needs and goals of others. Attending to others, as well as to oneself, demonstrates not only conviction in one's purpose but also demonstrates valuing and concern for others. A sense of mutuality develops wherein both parties set about devising strategies to satisfy the needs and goals of one another.

This does not imply that the ultimate goal or compromise is self-sacrifice; rather, both parties attempt to find a collaborative solution wherein both finish as winners. The advantage of the collaborative approach is that there is a mutual exploration of new approaches to satisfying wants; both parties are more likely to be committed to the strategies; the solutions tend to be more permanent; and there is greater satisfaction in a win/win situation. The competitive or aggressive approach tends to inhibit the exploration of new approaches, results in little or no commitment from the parties, and, at best, the solution is temporary, frequently leading to confrontation.

Admittedly, one can assume a collaborative approach to resolving differences while others will continue in an aggressive mode (winner/loser). The subsequent anger may lead to an undermining of the collaborative process. The assertive model suggests that when anger rises to threaten the collaborative process, the emphasis needs to remain on the problem, the issue, or the behavior, rather than on the person. Frequently attacking the person will only exacerbate and escalate the conflict. The outcome then is a loss of an ally in the quest for excellence. Furthermore, attacking the person leads to animosity and possible attempts at sabotaging one another's goals, directly or indirectly (passive-aggressive behavior). Utilizing relaxation techniques to reduce physiological arousal, walking away from the situation to rethink, responding in a nondefensive manner, knowing when to remain silent, and focusing on specifics rather than generalities are all essential characteristics in expressing negative feelings without damaging relationships or another person's integrity.

STRATEGIES TO ENHANCE PEAK PERFORMANCE

Several major steps need to be taken in order to achieve personal excellence. Set realistic (S.M.A.R.T.) goals; define the activities necessary to attain those goals; utilize relaxation and mental rehearsal techniques to facilitate goal attainment; collect data so as to provide opportunities for self-praise as well as for occasional necessary readjustments of goals; challenge self-defeating attitudes that interfere with goal attainment; and utilize active listening skills, assertiveness skills, and collaboration skills to enlist the cooperation of others who may be important allies in the pursuit of personal excellence.

REFERENCES

Bulka, R. P. *Logotherapy as an Answer to Burnout.* Toronto, Canada: International Forum for Logotherapy, 1984.

Burns, D. D. *Feeling Good: The New Mood Therapy.* Signet, New York: New American Library, 1980.

de Bono, E. *Tactics: The Art and Science of Success.* Toronto: Little, Brown, 1984.

Drucker, P. F. "Who's Excellent Now?" *Business Week,* November 3, 1984, pp. 76–86.

Ellis, A., and R. A. Harper. *A New Guide to Rational Living*. North Hollywood, California: Wilshire Books, 1975.

Peters, T. J., and R. H. Waterman, Jr. *In Search of Excellence*. New York: Warner Books, 1984.

Smith, C. "The Inner Race for Excellence." Toronto *Globe & Mail*, 1984.

Tiseall, P. "Fatal Habits." *Equinox* 21 (1984): 1–6.

IV
Research and Evaluation in Health Education Programs

Research and evaluation are critical ingredients to the growth and development of health programs, particularly health education and fitness. Research and evaluation permit the investigator to test the validity of certain health promotion efforts, to examine the effectiveness of specific health education programs, and generally make it possible to formulate decisions about the continuation of certain projects or the redesign of other projects.

Chapman presents a pragmatic view on the tools and techniques used to evaluate workplace health promotion programs. He argues that in contrast to rigorously designed and controlled evaluation research, practical program evaluation must balance the concern for validity and reliability of results with the very real constraints of limited staff time and limited financial resources for outside technical expertise. He points out that the challenge addressed in this chapter is one faced by the majority of workplace health promotion programs. The evaluation of a smoking cessation program is used as an example of how to use some practical evaluation tools to meet the challenge of program evaluation in worksite settings.

Yardley, in his comprehensive research chapter, discusses fitness and physical activity. In spite of reports indicating increased involvement in physical activity and fitness programs over the last two decades, he indicates that there is considerable need to develop strategies and methods that will increase the proportion of society involved in such pursuits. Moreover, people need to be motivated to be involved at high enough energy levels and to make physical activities part of their regular daily lifestyle in order to derive the benefits that may be gained. Through a thorough investigation of the research literature, Yardley carefully describes a number of person and situation factors that affect activity and exercise attendance and adherence. Such topics as the importance of studying human behavior, motivation, reasons for being active and inactive, goal setting and attainment, and choice and decision making are just a few of the areas considered. The workplace is identified as an excellent situation where these factors can be successfully manipulated to the benefit of employer, employee, and, ultimately, society at large.

Health and safety training are essential to the health protection of employees. The spiraling costs of health benefits and legal actions are the other critical reasons for industry and government to seek involvement in these prevention programs. Vojtecky and Berkanovic describe the ways in which program evaluation can be used to improve health and safety training. They argue that an insufficient amount of rigorous research has been conducted and that only a small percentage of those performing program evaluations have ever been trained to do so. Their chapter presents and discusses the elements of and the requirements for valid program evaluations. These are then applied to health and safety programs and are examined with respect to comprehensiveness, rigor, and usefulness.

With a reduction of health risks would there be a concomitant reduction in health care costs? This has been a controversial research question. Fielding first points out that epidemiological evidence linking health habits and serious disease has grown rapidly. Smoking, poor nutrition, obesity, stress, poor physical conditioning, and lack of exercise have been suspected as contributors to a wide variety of ailments and disorders. The above habits are regarded as risks. Can an employer-sponsored health promotion program reduce these risks? Furthermore, will the reduction of risk levels translate into health improvements? Fielding cites research that addresses these questions as they relate to the risks of smoking, hypertension, seat belt use, and stress management. If these health risks can be controlled through worksite programs and if health improvements occur, do they translate into health cost savings for the organization? Fielding cites additional research that addresses this question and formulates very interesting observations.

The previous chapters maintained a broad research focus upon particular topics within health education, namely, fitness, health and safety training, smoking, hypertension, and stress management. The next chapter adopts a more exclusive focus and discusses the StayWell health promotion program of Control Data Corporation. Anderson and Jose indicate that comprehensive evaluation has been a central component of the program from its beginning in 1979. They discuss individual elements of the program and also present the more global concerns, such as the evaluation objectives and strategies and underlying process model that guided both development and evaluation. Specific evaluation design issues are addressed, and the strategy of multiple quasi-experimental designs is formulated and recommended for long-term studies in dynamic real world environments. Questions appropriate to various levels of analysis — course, individual, and corporate — are also discussed. Numerous examples illustrate how evaluation has contributed to developing the StayWell program and enhancing its effectiveness.

17 Evaluation Tools for Use in Workplace Health Promotion Programs: Practical Applications

Larry S. Chapman

BASIC EVALUATION PRINCIPLES

Before embarking on the practical aspects of program evaluation, it is prudent that we establish a general framework for formal evaluation.

The basic purpose of formal evaluation is to derive valid and reliable conclusions about a series of activities, actions, or relationships. Program evaluation is generally focused on the structure, process, and outcome of organized activities designed to accomplish a particular goal or series of goals. Workplace health promotion programs usually strive to reduce the frequency and severity of illnesses and injuries in a specific target population in the workplace. Therefore, any evaluation effort for these types of programs should include an attempt to measure this outcome as well as the variety of other possible evaluation parameters.

Validity of evaluation results is usually defined as the extent to which the measurements taken actually measure what they were supposed to measure. Researchers or evaluators frequently argue about the validity of evaluation findings based on the occurrence of systematic error in some aspect of the study that is not eliminated or minimized by the research or evaluation design. Various generic threats to the validity of the evaluation results have been identified and classified in the research and evaluation literature. These include:

Threats to Internal Validity	*Threats to External Validity*
History	Interactions
Maturation	Reactive arrangements
Testing	Multiple variable
Instrumentation	interference
Regression	
Selection	
Attrition	
Interactions	
Address the question: are the conclusions of our evaluation valid for the group or population being evaluated?	Address the question: are the conclusions of our evaluation valid when applied to another group or population?

A detailed discussion of each type of threat to internal or external validity is available in the evaluation references identified at the end of the chapter.

The reliability of evaluation results is usually defined as the extent to which the same measurements give the same results on repeated applications. The concern here is the elimination or minimization of random error. Some of the same threats to internal and external validity often pose a problem for the reliability of evaluation measures and conclusions derived from the measurements.

In order to obtain maximum validity and reliability of evaluation results, it is necessary to structure carefully the design of the evaluation. A basic typology of different kinds of evaluation designs is as follows:

General Classification	*Evaluation Design*	*Increasing Validity and Reliability*
Nonexperimental	One-shot case study	
	One group pretest, posttest	
	Static group comparison	
	Nonequivalent control group	
Quasi-experimental	Separate-same pretest, posttest	
	Counterbalanced	
	Time series	
	Multiple time series	

General Classification	Evaluation Design	Increasing Validity and Reliability
	Equivalent time series	↑
Experimental	Pretest, posttest, control group	
	Solomon Four group	↓

A detailed discussion of the features of each of these basic types of evaluation and research designs can be found in the reference material at the end of the chapter. The key elements in designing an evaluation are issues to be evaluated, measurement(s) to be used, timing of measurement(s), data collection methods, use of control group(s), use of randomization of subjects, and length of the evaluation period.

REASONS FOR CONDUCTING PROGRAM EVALUATION

There are many possible formal and informal reasons for conducting a program evaluation. Some of the more appropriate reasons and less appropriate reasons for doing an evaluation are as follows:

More appropriate reasons
To make sure the program survives financially hard times

To improve the program's effectiveness or efficiency
To enhance employee ownership in the program
To answer internal or external critics
To determine which program strategies, tactics, and components contribute most to the program's success
To justify or restrict expansion or replication of the program
To compare the program to other programs

Less appropriate reasons
To justify weak programs by evaluating their stronger aspects
Because it's a "good thing" to do
Because it's expected
To "whitewash" the program
To inappropriately postpone decision making
To affix blame
Because everybody else is doing it

EVALUATION IN THE WORKSITE: REALISTIC CONSTRAINTS

It is important to recognize the realistic constraints that affect any effort to evaluate any type of program that is conducted in the workplace. By understanding these constraints, a person's expectations for the evaluation probably will be more realistic, and the evaluation probably will be conducted in a more appropriate manner. The same nine major constraints face virtually any effort to conduct research or evaluation in the worksite.

Program evaluation is usually a low priority item for managers and employees; therefore, compliance with data collection or survey requirements is usually problematic.

Financial resources for evaluation of worksite programs are usually extremely limited. Companies are often not willing to commit much money to improving the validity of evaluation results. Therefore the sophistication of the evaluation effort needs to be balanced against the resource commitment.

Program evaluation is often seen as a threat by program supporters and as a tool for program detractors to question the appropriateness of the program. Therefore, the evaluation process can become highly politicized, particularly where there is an undercurrent of mistrust.

Relevant, accurate, and timely human resource management (HRM) data that are critical to health promotion program evaluation are rarely available. Often the informational systems that are assumed to exist are not operational. Therefore, it is often necessary to set up or substantially revise existing HRM data systems in order to perform the evaluation.

The often changing priorities or the emphasis on crisis oriented management of senior managers frequently leads to poor implementation follow-through. Therefore, evaluation efforts need to be structured so that some controls exist on the follow-up stages of data collection.

There is a long time between behavior change and changes in the frequency and severity of illness or injury in the experimental population. Because of this, the business community does not automatically support the continuation of program activities and evaluation efforts over the long-term, because of their dynamic nature and emphasis on short-term results. The constantly changing environment of work organizations requires that the evaluation design be as nonintrusive and nondisruptive as possible so that evaluation does not pose so much of a nuisance that it is terminated prematurely by management.

Few individuals in business organizations understand the complexity of trade-offs involved in conducting research in the workplace. It is, therefore, prudent for those responsible for the evaluation to seek some level of outside technical expertise as early as possible in the evaluation process.

Decision makers rarely perceive the cyclic nature of marketplace economics and, therefore, frequently undervalue the evaluation of the organizational gains from a health promotion program. Therefore, it is often difficult to get an appropriate level of commitment from senior management to perform a balanced evaluation of both program operation and impact.

The variety of types of data that need to be collected in the evaluation of a workplace health promotion program often violates the organizational territory of several corporate staff groups. Therefore, the evaluation effort needs to have a clear statement of commitment from senior management.

POTENTIAL TECHNICAL PITFALLS

It's easy to conduct evaluation in the workplace, but it's extremely difficult to do good evaluation in the workplace. Good evaluation has few threats to internal and external validity and few weaknesses in the reliability of its measurements. A list of some of the major technical pitfalls in conducting evaluation of workplace health promotion programs follows: inadequate baseline data, pervasiveness of "halo" effect, large numbers of intervening variables, difficulty of getting good controls, difficulty of sorting out the effect of multiple interventions, lack of data processing capability, conflict of evaluation objectives with program objectives, instability of business environment, absence of well-designed program objectives, measurements often not standardized, little comparability between programs in different sites, strong effect of environmental factors on outcomes, small sample size, and lack of random assignment of subjects.

RECOMMENDED EVALUATION STRATEGY

In spite of all the limitations and constraints that plague those who want to evaluate a workplace health promotion program, an evaluation still needs to be done, and it is possible to arrive at a reasonable approach. There are several options for achieving a balanced approach. One particular option is to develop a modular evaluation approach that fits, in a complementary way, your own program objectives and your own specific program components. A model for this kind of modular evaluation strategy consists of several core evaluation modules diagrammatically portrayed as follows:

Evaluation Module	*Evaluation Concerns*
Program activities	Participation levels
	Participant satisfaction
	Participant feedback
Changes in attitudes and knowledge	Change in knowledge
	Change in attitudes
	Change in norms
Changes in participant behavior	Short-term behavior change
	Long-term behavior change
Changes in health status	Physiological changes
	Risk factor changes
	Health service use changes
Changes in organizational cost	Changes in organizational indicators
	Changes in organizational costs
	Cost-benefit determination

This evaluation strategy is designed to allow the evaluator to track changes through each of the major evaluation modules in order to strengthen the degree to which program effects can be attributed to program performance.

SAMPLE EVALUATION TOOLS

Each evaluation module may utilize one or more evaluation tools consisting of structured instruments for the collection of various kinds of information. Types of evaluation tools presented here include initial participant survey instruments, general workshop evaluation forms, follow-up participant survey instruments, and a direct data collection format. Figures 17.1-17.6 illustrate what these tools might look like and how they would be used. The examples address the evaluation of a smoking cessation program. Table 17.1 shows how the evaluation strategy is linked to each evaluation tool. These types of instruments can be adapted for use in the evaluation of other kinds of health promotion programs.

SUGGESTED TIMING FOR USE OF EVALUATION TOOLS

The evaluation tools identified in Figures 17.1–17.6 are examples that are designed for use in evaluating a smoking cessation program. The tools can be adapted to focus on fitness programs, weight management, nutrition, back care, and other health programs. The same format and timing can be utilized to conduct a modular approach to program

TABLE 17.1
Evaluation Tools for Smoking Cessation Program

Evaluation Module	Figure Number	Title of Evaluation Tool
Program activities	17.1	Questions for Inclusion in an Employee Health Survey
Changes in attitudes and knowledge	17.2	Beginning of Program Participant Questionnaire
Changes in participant behavior	17.3	General Workshop Evaluation Form
	17.4	End of Program Participant Questionnaire
Changes in healthstatus	17.5	Follow-up Evaluation Response Card or Mailer
Changes in organizational cost	17.6	Organizational Health Cost Profile

Source: Compiled by the author.

FIGURE 17.1
Questions for Inclusion in an Employee Health Survey

1. Do you smoke cigarettes? _____ Yes _____ No (If "No," skip to question #10.)

2. How many years have you smoked cigarettes?
    _____ Less than one year _____ 11–20 years
    _____ 1– 5 years _____ More than 20 years
    _____ 6–10 years

3. Do you smoke:
    _____ Unfiltered? _____ Filtered?
    _____ Low tar and nicotine?

4. On the average, how many cigarettes do you smoke each day?
    _____

5. How many times have you attempted to quit? _____

6. Do you now want to reduce your smoking? _____ Yes _____ No
    Or stop smoking entirely? _____ Yes _____ No

7. Would you be interested in attending a smoking cessation course?
    _____ Yes _____ No

8. In the morning, about how often do you experience smoker's cough?

    All the time   Often   Once in a while   Seldom   Never
         1   2   3   4   5

9. Did your family and friends support you in past efforts to quit smoking?

    All the time   Often   Once in a while   Seldom   Never
         1   2   3   4   5

10. Within the last month how many days were you absent from work for health reasons? _____

FIGURE 17.2
Beginning of Program Participant Questionnaire

Please answer the following questions in order for us to evaluate the program and to make sure the program is of help to you. Thanks for your help!

1. On the average, how many cigarettes do you now smoke each day?

    _____

2. Do you smoke:
    _____ Unfiltered?   _____ Filtered?
    _____ Low tar and nicotine?

3. In the morning, about how often do you experience smoker's cough? (circle one)

    All the time   Often   Once in a while   Seldom   Never
         1   2   3   4   5

4. About how often do you feel a shortness of breath? (circle one)

    All the time   Often   Once in a while   Seldom   Never
         1   2   3   4   5

5. Did your family and friends support you in past efforts to quit smoking? (circle one)

    All the time   Often   Once in a while   Seldom   Never
         1   2   3   4   5

6. Do you now want to reduce your smoking? _____ Yes _____ No.
    Or stop smoking entirely? _____ Yes _____ No

7. How badly do you want to reduce/quit smoking?

    _____

8. Why do you want to reduce (or quit) smoking?

    _____

    _____

Figure 17.2, Continued

9. Within the last month how many days were you absent from work for health reasons? _____

10. What are the health effects of long-term smoking?

   1. _____ 6. _____
   2. _____ 7. _____
   3. _____ 8. _____
   4. _____ 9. _____
   5. _____ 10. _____

Thanks again for your cooperation!

FIGURE 17.3
General Workshop Evaluation Form

Please answer the following questions in order to help us evaluate this session and improve future sessions. Your feedback is appreciated. Thank you for your help!

Please circle only *one* number for each question.

	No, not at all	A little	Moderate amount	A lot	Yes, definitely
Key:	1	2	3	4	5

1. Did you enjoy the workshop/s?

    1   2   3   4   5

    Comments? _____

2. Did the workshop help you?

    1   2   3   4   5

    Comments? _____

3. Was the instructor well prepared?

    1   2   3   4   5

    Comments? _____

4. Was the information presented at this program new to you?

    1   2   3   4   5

    Comments? _____

5. Did the workshop/s help motivate you to change?

    1   2   3   4   5

    Comments? _____

Figure 17.3, Continued

6. Would you recommend this workshop to others?

           1   2   3   4   5

    Comments? _____

7. How would you suggest improving the workshop/s?

    _____
    _____
    _____
    _____

FIGURE 17.4
End of Program Participant Questionnaire

1. Do you currently smoke cigarettes _____ Yes _____ No. (If "No," skip to question #4.)

2. If you currently smoke, about how many cigarettes do you smoke each day? _____

3. If you smoke, do you smoke:
    _____ Unfiltered?   _____ Filtered?
    _____ Low tar and nicotine?

4. In the morning, about how often do you experience smoker's cough? (circle one)

All the time	Often	Once in a while	Seldom	Never
1	2	3	4	5

5. About how often do you feel a shortness of breath? (circle one)

All the time	Often	Once in a while	Seldom	Never
1	2	3	4	5

6. Do your family and friends support you in your goal to reduce (or quit) smoking? (circle one)

All the time	Often	Once in a while	Seldom	Never
1	2	3	4	5

7. How many program sessions did you attend? _____

8. Within the last month how many days were you absent from work for health reasons? _____

9. What are the health effects of long-term smoking?

    1. _____   6. _____
    2. _____   7. _____
    3. _____   8. _____
    4. _____   9. _____
    5. _____   10. _____

Thank you again for your cooperation!

FIGURE 17.5
Follow-up Evaluation Response Card or Mailer

Hello! This card contains a couple of follow-up questions which will help us evaluate our smoking cessation program. Please take a moment to complete these questions and return (mail) it to us. We very much appreciate your feedback and cooperation!

1. Are you currently smoking cigarettes? _____ Yes _____ No. (If no, skip to question #4).

2. If yes, how many cigarettes do you usually smoke per day? _____

3. If you currently smoke, do you smoke:
   _____ Unfiltered?   _____ Filtered?
   _____ Low tar and nicotine brands?

4. Is there anything we can do to help you continue to be a non-smoker? (or to quit smoking again?)

   _____

   _____

5. Is there any way that we can improve our program in order for it to be of more help to you?

   _____

   _____

6. Would you like a refresher session? _____ Yes _____ No

7. Within the last month how many days were you absent from work for health reasons? _____

FIGURE 17.6
Organizational Health Cost Profile

The following information is intended to reflect the impact of the overall
health promotion programs on organizational health costs. One facet of
the health promotion program would be the smoking cessation program.
The information below is intended to be individually plotted on a line
graph over time and compared with expected trend lines. Where a
significant change is seen an assessment should be made of the estimated
contribution of the health promotion program. Where possible, control
groups should be utilized to improve on the estimation of the program's
contribution to the change in trends.

			Year		
Evaluation Indicators	1	2	3	4	5
Per capita health benefit claims cost	___	___	___	___	___
Worker compensation cost (per capita)	___	___	___	___	___
Sick leave absenteeism cost (per capita)	___	___	___	___	___
Disability claims cost (per capita)	___	___	___	___	___
Number of occupational injuries per 1,000 workers	___	___	___	___	___
Number of medical retirements	___	___	___	___	___
Number of terminations for health reasons	___	___	___	___	___
Number of inpatient hospital days per 1,000 covered lives	___	___	___	___	___
Number of employee health unit visits for acute illness per 100 workers	___	___	___	___	___
Number of International Classification of Disease (ICD) diagnoses linked to specific health promotion risk factors (Approximately)	___	___	___	___	___
Number of cases in diagnostic clusters related to smoking?	___	___	___	___	___

evaluation. The suggested timing for the use of the evaluation tools is as follows:

Figure	Title	Suggested Timing
17.1	Questions for Inclusion in an Employee Health Survey	Use the employee health survey annually at the same time of the year. Do the first survey as a baseline before the program is started.
17.2	Beginning of Program Participant Questionnaire	Distribute to participants at the start of the smoking cessation program.
17.3	General Workshop Evaluation Form	Distribute to participants at the conclusion of a workshop. Use periodically with multiple workshop sessions.
17.4	End of Program Participant Questionnaire	Distribute to participants at the conclusion of the formal workshop sessions.
17.5	Follow-up Evaluation Response Card or Mailer	Distribute to participants at 3 months, 6 months, and 12 months after the conclusion of the last program session.
17.6	Organizational Health Cost Profile	Ideally, collect a three-to-five-year baseline of data prior to initiation of the health promotion program and then collect annualized data thereafter.

CONCLUSION

Evaluating a workplace health promotion program is a difficult and complex undertaking. Balancing the concerns for evaluation validity and reliability with that of the cost of the evaluation in terms of financial and staff resources is an important challenge. In meeting that challenge it is possible to use an evaluation strategy that provides a practical analytic structure to our efforts and one that also helps to identify the measurements that have the best utility-to-cost relationships. The creative refinements that will come with experience will, we hope, help us all meet the challenge of practical evaluation.

REFERENCES

Attkisson, C., et al. *Evaluation of Human Service Programs.* New York: Academic Press, 1978.

Bernstein, I. *Validity Issues in Evaluative Research.* Beverly Hills: Sage, 1979.

Cash, W. B. "How to Calculate an Employee Relations Index." *Personnel Journal,* March 1979, pp. 172–74.

Chenoweth, D. "Fitness Program Evaluation: Results with Muscle." *Occupational Health and Safety,* June 1983.

Deeds, S. G. *Overview of Evaluation.* Centers for Disease Control, PHS, 1976.

Driver, R. W., and R. A. Ratliff. "Employers' Perceptions of Benefits Accrued from Physical Fitness Programs." *Personnel Administrator,* August 1982, pp. 21–26.

Fielding, J. "Preventive Medicine and the Bottom Line." *Journal of Occupational Medicine* 21 (1979): 79–88.

Fielding, J. E. "Effectiveness of Employee Health Improvement Programs." *Journal of Occupational Medicine* 24 (1982): 907–16.

Gori, G. B., et al. "Economics and Extended Longevity: A Case Study." *Preventive Medicine* 13 (1984): 396–410.

Green, L. W. "How to Evaluate Health Promotion." *Hospitals,* October 1, 1979, pp. 106–8.

Green, L. W. "Toward Cost-Benefit Evaluations of Health Education: Some Concepts, Methods, and Examples." *Health Education Monographs* (Supplement), 1974, pp. 34–64.

Grove, D., et al. "A Health Promotion Program in a Corporate Setting." *Journal of Family Practice* 9 (1979): 83–88.

Guttentag, M., and E. L. Struening. *Handbook of Evaluation Research,* Vols. 1 and 2. Beverly Hills: Sage, 1975.

Hartunian, N. S., et al. "The Incidence and Economic Costs of Cancer, Motor Vehicle Injuries, Coronary Heart Disease, and Stroke: A Comparative Analysis." *American Journal of Public Health* 70 (1980): 1249–60.

Health Services Research Center. *Baseline: A Newsletter of Information About the Evaluation of Health Promotion Programs.* Vol. 1, Nos. 2, 3, 5, 6, 7, 1982–present.

Issacs, S. "Chapter Five: Criteria and Guidelines for Planning, Preparing, Writing, and evaluating the Research Proposal, Report, Thesis, or Article." n.p., n.d.

Institute of Medicine. *Conference Summary: Evaluation Health Promotion in the Workplace,* National Academy of Science, New York, January 1981, p. 38.

Iverson, D. C. "Evaluation of Health Education/Risk Reduction Program." Unpublished paper, p. 11.

Jacobs, P., and A. Chovil. "Economic Evaluation of Corporate Medical Programs." *Journal of Occupational Medicine* 25 (1983): 273–78.

Morrison, R. B. "Cost-Effectiveness." *Journal of Physical Education, Recreation and Dance,* April 1982, pp. 51–53.

Ossler, C. C. "Cost-Benefit and Cost-Effectiveness Analysis in Occupational Health." *Occupational Health Nursing,* January 1984, pp. 33–38.

Phillips, R. M., and J. P. Hughes. "Cost-Benefit Analysis of the Occupational Health Program: A Generic Model." *Journal of Occupational Medicine* 16 (1974): 158–61.

Pyle, R. L. "Performance Measures for a Corporate Fitness Program." *Human Resource Management,* Fall, 1979, pp. 26–30.

Rosenstock, I. M. "General Criteria for Evaluating Health Education Programs." Paper presented at the 62nd Annual World Dental Congress, London, September 13, 1974.

Rutman, L. *Evaluation Research Methods: A Basic Guide.* Beverly Hills: Sage, 1977.

Shortell, S. M., and W. C. Richardson. *Health Program Evaluation.* St. Louis: C. V. Mosby, 1978.

Suchman, E. *Evaluative Research: Principles and Practice in Public Service and Social Action Programs.* New York: Russell Sage Foundation, 1967.

Sze, W. C., and J. G. Hopps, eds. *Evaluation and Accountability in Human Service Programs.* Concord, Massachusetts: Schenkman Books, 1978.

Thomas, P., et al. "Heart Disease Risk Factors in Los Angeles County Safety Personnel." *Journal of Occupational Medicine* 21 (1979): 683–87.

Van Peenen, P. F. D., et al. "Cardiovascular Risk Factors in Employees of a Petrochemical Company." *Journal of Occupational Medicine,* Vol. 27, March 1985.

Weiss, C. *Evaluation Research: Methods of Assessing Program Effectiveness.* Englewood Cliffs, New Jersey: Prentice-Hall, 1972.

18 Motivating People to Become Involved and to Stay Involved in Physical Activity

John K. Yardley

INTRODUCTION

Many reports and research surveys have documented an increased interest and involvement in physical activity, in the Western world, over the last two decades. A series of major physical activity studies undertaken by the Ontario Provincial Government have documented that all segments of the population are becoming more physically active. The Ontario Ministry of Tourism and Recreation (1983) reports that:

> 58% of Ontario adults are physically active at least once a week (p. iv);
> . . . A substantial number of people of all ages participate in some form of physical activity (p. v); . . . Older people have increased their activity even more than younger people! (p. 12).

In the United States the 1979 Perrier survey (Ontario Ministry of Culture and Recreation 1981) indicated that the increase in the percentage of people regularly involved in physical activity rose by 35 percent (from 24 percent in 1961 to 59 percent in 1979) since the early 1960s.

There has been a parallel growth of interest in the promotion of physical activity through government national fitness campaigns, for example, "Trim," Federal Republic of Germany; "Come Alive," New Zealand; "Life Be In It," Australia and the United States; and "Participation," Canada (Wankel 1985). This growth is also reflected in the development of national, provincial/state, and local government departments being involved in physical activity promotion and programing.

The commercial world has reacted to the boom with a tremendous increase in consumer goods and services aimed at those involved in physical activity. This is partially reflected by the staggering increase (184 percent in personal expenditure on consumer goods and services from 1961 to 1978, in constant 1971 dollars (Yardley 1984).

More and more companies are becoming interested in recreation and fitness in the workplace. This is linked very closely to the concept of corporate wellness and includes recreation, fitness, assistance, and service programs. Chubb and Chubb (1981) estimate that in the United States 50,000 companies are involved in helping provide recreation programs for their employees and spend in excess of $3 billion on those programs. The Ontario Ministry of Tourism and Recreation (1984) estimates that over 800 companies (10 percent to 12 percent of all companies) in Ontario have employee fitness programs and up to 30 percent have sports and recreation programs.

The physical activity and fitness phenomena that we observe in today's society have become pervasive. It is undoubtedly an important part of the health and welfare of the citizens of a country, community, and company. The benefits derived from such involvement in physical activity are so well documented that Morgan (1977) states that it is no longer fruitful to research beneficence of physical activity programs.

So why is it important to motivate people to become active and stay active? If approximately 50 percent of the population is involved in physical activity, then the other 50 percent are not involved. Most people who are involved in physical activity do so irregularly or at energy levels that are too low to gain any significant cardiovascular effect (Wankel 1985). Coupled with this low level of involvement is the adherence or drop-out problems. Wankel (1980) estimates that from 30 percent to 70 percent drop out of the physical activity program that they joined. If one in ten companies are involved in fitness programing then, nine in ten are not. Similarly, if three in ten provide sports and fitness programs, then seven in ten do not. A large number of injury, accident, absenteeism, and health cost figures document overwhelming economic evidence as to why society and employers need to be concerned with employees wellness. It has been estimated that absenteeism, in Canada alone, cost industry $5.5 billion in 1977 (Banister 1978). A host of lifestyle and health factors are complicated in costs to companies (Banister 1978).

Those burdens and costs can be alleviated because physical fitness programs have been experimentally shown to reduce those costs in industry (Collis 1974; Peepre 1980). Consequently the workplace is an ideal environment to promote and implement adequate physical activity programs, and therefore it is incumbent upon employers and employees alike to motivate people to become and remain involved in physical activity.

FITNESS DEFINED

Unfortunately many people associate "blood, sweat, and tears" with fitness. The recent upsurge in aerobic dance programs is dispelling these images to some extent. However, fitness is more than physical fitness, and physical fitness is more than cardiovascular conditioning. The concept of wellness that is creeping into use owes some of its origins to the idea that one can be positively healthy in mind, body, and spirit. According to Hockey (1985) the American Association for Health, Physical Education, Recreation, and Dance defines fitness as "that state which characterizes the degree to which a person is able to function efficiently. Fitness is an individual matter. It implies the ability of each person to live most effectively within his potentialities" (p. 8).

Functioning efficiently requires recognizing appropriate physical limitations, cardiovascular endurance, strength, muscular endurance, flexibility, and body composition (Hockey 1985, p. 11). Coupled with this has to be positive mental health, which some people would also link to a spiritual sense of well-being. The definition also indicates every individual is different, a factor that some group fitness programs and instructors forget. Finally, the work "potential" indicates that each person has positive health that can be approached through proper care. This indicates that fitness must be couched in an array of programs that include all aspects of lifestyle. Ignoring a major component could be likened to maintaining a car in all aspects except changing the oil; eventually this missed component will cause problems for the whole machine. It will become inefficient or, at worst, break down.

APPROACHES TO STUDYING HUMAN BEHAVIOR

If fitness is an individual matter, as the above definition indicates, then it goes without saying that individuals' behaviors can be determined differently and studied differently. The literature is in conflict concerning how best to study, analyze, and interpret what is observed in exercise behavior, as it does with all human behavior. There are three basic approaches known as trait, situationism, and interactionism (Bem and Funder 1978; Morgan 1980).

Trait Approach

The trait approach to studying behavior has been described by Endler and Magnusson (1976) as the "dominant force in personality research and theory." The underlying belief, in this approach, is that traits are the main determinants of behavior because they are "relatively stable behavioral dispositions that individuals exhibit over time" (Epstein 1977, p. 83). Morgan (1980) outlines that various studies utilizing the trait approach account for enough variance in exercise behavior, 20 percent to 45 percent, that it is useful for predicting exercise adherence behavior. The obvious practical application is that a trait measuring device could be used to help direct counseling toward those, entering exercise classes or beginning physical activity, who are measured as most likely to drop out. Unfortunately no one best instrument has been identified. Yardley (1982) identified no less than 14 different measuring instruments and models that had been used in a variety of exercise and sports research studies, with varying degrees of success. Also, because traits and attitudes are relatively stable and enduring, it is difficult to modify people's exercise behaviors — something to which all exercise instructors will testify! A variety of approaches, outlined in the rest of the chapter, describe potential methods. Again, however, no one person is the same as another, and no one method is clearly superior to another.

Situationist Approach

Situationism views the primary cause of human behavior as being determined by situation factors (stimuli in the person's environment). This approach is closely allied with behaviorism, which holds that people's behaviors (responses) are largely controlled by antecedent and resultant conditions in their environment, that is, eliciting stimuli and reinforcers. An extension of this is the so-called "neo-behaviorist" approach, for example, social learning theory, which maintains that an individual's behavior patterns are developed through social learning experiences based on modeling, reinforcement, and punishment (Bandura

1969). More recently this approach has been modified to allow the existence and importance of cognitive factors, as mediating factors, to enter explanations of behavior, for example, Bandura and Schunk (1981); and Grossberg (1981). The saying, "Success breeds success," is a reflection of this approach, and undoubtedly one major barrier to fitness is previous failure or lack of success.

In his review of exercise management, Martin (1981) indicates that a number of reinforcing techniques such as feedback, praise, token reinforcement, money, social reinforcers, contracting, and lottery interventions have been used in different settings with a variety of populations. However he states that, "application of behavioral technologies to the problem of exercise adherence is relatively new" (Martin 1981, p. 5). Exercise or physical activity class instructors and programers, therefore, can utilize a variety of inducements and reinforcers to attempt to attract and retain participants. The participant can mediate these factors as well because, as Brownell (1978) points out, a variety of self-control factors, such as self-reward, choice, and perceived control over one's own environment, can be utilized by participants to reinforce behaviors they wish to continue. With help and encouragement from others, for example, instructors, self-control techniques can be utilized to modify behavior and adhere to the behavior desired. Wankel (1985) points out, however, "that although reinforcement techniques can effectively modify short-term behavior, the maintenance of long-term behavior is frequently more difficult" (p. 125).

Interactionist Approach

The interactionist approach focuses on both the person and the situation and how the two interrelate (interact) in determining behavior. Magnusson and Endler (1977) state that, "persons and situations are regarded as indispensably linked to one another during the process of interaction. Neither the person factors nor the situation factors per se determine behaviour in isolation" (p. 4). Exercise programers who adopt this approach therefore, will emphasize equally cognitive and motivational components of the person factor, as well as situational components, to attract and retain participants.

Two approaches can be taken to the interactionist perspective. The first is to view behavior in a simplistic manner, using main factors, which are assumed to be additive and, therefore, more reinforcing (Magnusson and Endler 1977). The exercise programer would, therefore, intentionally use a few important person and situation factors to try to motivate people to attend and stay in programs. The simplicity of this approach makes it more amenable to application in actual situations, but it ignores the fact that humans are highly complex and individual in their needs and motives.

The other approach is considered to be more dynamic or interactive, where a host of person and situation factors form an interwoven structure that mediates human behavior (Magnusson and Endler 1977). This suggests a much more complicated and complex interactive view of behavior, and its complexity is its disadvantage. Cronbach (in Epstein 1980) concludes that, "once we attend to interactions, we enter a hall of mirrors that extends to infinity" (p. 119). This approach, conceptually, may be the more acceptable method, but it is not so practical as the first because the limits and relative importance of factors are difficult to determine.

MOTIVATION

Motivation is one specific concept whose importance has been frequently identified in the adherence literature, for example, medical compliance (Baekeland and Lundwall 1975) and physical activity adherence (Dishman, Ickes, and Morgan 1980). Again varying theoretical perspectives have been taken for the derivation and control of motivation. Birch and Veroff (1966) are clearly situationist (behaviorist) in their approach; they state, "other psychologists look for the determinants of action in behavioural terms alone . . . this is an approach in which we share" (p. ix). In contrast Deci (1975) clearly represents the cognitive point of view, which he defines as,

> This approach [the cognitive approach to motivation] asserts that humans process information and make choices about what behaviors to engage in. Implicit in this is the assumption that cognitions are causal determinants of behavior — an assumption that contradicts behavioral theories" (p. 95).

There does, however, appear to be a unification of these approaches that lends credence to the notion that an interactionist approach is the more fruitful way of studying and changing behavior. Central to this unification are the ideas of intrinsic interest, self-motivation, competency, and self-determination (Bandura 1977). Bandura and Schunk (1981) explain that "self directedness operates through a self system that comprises cognitive structures, and subfunctions for perceiving, evaluating, motivating, and regulating behavior" (p. 586). These subfunctions and cognitive structures provide the basis for the notion of intrinsic motivation that for participants is derived from their involvement in physical activity. Extrinsic motivation is derived from things other than involvement in physical activity, for example, the trophy, the praise, the reward, the tissue satiation.

This definition is not without its problems; Iso-Ahola (1980b) warns that many activities are engaged in for extrinsic and intrinsic reasons and that those reasons are subjectively defined. He says, "no matter how obvious extrinsic rewards may look to an observer, one cannot say for sure whether a person is engaged in an activity for extrinsic or intrinsic reasons" (p. 23). The primary importance of this approach to programers is that a

> cognitively based source of self-motivation relies on the intervening processes of goal setting and self-evaluative reactions to one's own behavior. This form of self-motivation, which operates largely through internal comparison processes, requires personal standards against which to evaluate ongoing performance" (Bandura and Schunk 1981, p. 586).

Obviously programers and instructors should be aware of the specificity and level of participants' goals and ensure that they are reasonable (within the participants' abilities) and provide feedback to help develop self-efficacy and feelings of competence. The self-perceptions of efficacy and competence "can affect people's choice of activities, how much effort they expend and how long they will persist in the face of difficulties" (Bandura and Schunk 1981, p. 587). The application of this to physical activity and fitness regimes is self-evident.

One area of research, in motivation, that has profound implications for how reinforcers and feedback are used in exercise settings is the effects of extrinsic factors on ongoing task motivation. Generally, it has been found that extrinsic factors such as rewards (for example, Deci 1971; Green and Lepper 1974; Lepper and Green 1975), surveillance (for example, Lepper and Green 1975), and competition (Weinberg 1979; Weinberg and Ragan 1979, and McCaughan and McKinlay 1981) decrease intrinsic motivation. However salience (Ross 1976) and contingency of rewards (McCaughan and McKinlay 1981; Ross 1976) have been shown to be important in ameliorating these effects. It is crucial, therefore, to ensure that rewards are given with regard to quality of performance and relevance of behavior. Rewards that signal competence may be particularly effective and strengthen behavior (Deci 1975). Rewards, competition, and surveillance (for example, being under the eye of an instructor) are fundamental to many fitness and physical activities and should be used with discrimination because they can adversely affect adherence.

SELF-REPORTED REASONS FOR BEING ACTIVE OR INACTIVE

Oldridge (1977) and Wankel (1980) report that people often begin exercising for different reasons than those they report for continuing. People often state that they begin exercising for health reasons, but Wankel (1980) reports that continued involvement is often more dependent on their reaction to the exercise program and/or the program's interference in their daily routine.

Iso-Ahola (1980a) points out that leisure behavior is dynamic; therefore, reasons given at one time, place or situation will not apply to all persons nor necessarily to that same person at another time and space. London, Crandall, and Fitzgibbons (1977) demonstrated that different people perceived the same activity as meeting different leisure needs, some even say the same activity in a diametrically opposing light. In practical terms, the person providing physical activity and exercise programs has to be aware of the reasons for people's attending and recognize that some people's reasons may be opposed to others, for example, some may enjoy socializing and interaction while others are just there to work out. It is important, therefore, that those responsible for programs emphasize those factors identified by participants as being important through ongoing evaluation. Particular attention to enjoyment and socialization during the program is important because they are powerful motivators and reasons for staying with physical activity. Moreover, group activity programers must be keenly aware of individual differences because providing for a wide variety of levels and interests is difficult to do effectively.

Romsa and Hoffman (1980) state that the main barriers to more involvement for active people are different from those reported by low-active and lower socioeconomic strata. They state that the more active group report, in order of importance, the following barriers, "supply factors . . . , then lack of time, and finally costs" (Romsa and Hoffman

1980, p. 321). The less involved and lower S.E.S. groups report lack of interest as their main barrier.

The workplace offers an excellent opportunity to remove all four barriers. Interest can be piqued by educational and promotional campaigns utilizing various media, for example, films, bulletin boards, newsletters, company newspapers, and special events. Programs offered at the worksite, or nearby, before work, during lunch, and after work at reasonable cost would appeal to those who perceive supply, time, or cost as barriers. An excellent document for information is the *Employee Fitness and Lifestyle Project, Toronto, 1977–78* published by the Canadian Minister of State, Fitness, and Amateur Sports. It outlines some extremely effective and interesting promotional and educational campaign methods and materials.

GOAL SETTING AND ATTAINMENT

Participants may set many different goals for themselves when becoming physically active. It has been found that the attainment of goals is an important factor in terms of performance and attendance in physical activity programs (Katell, Martin, Webster, and Zegman 1980; Orlick 1974; and Wanzel and Danielson 1977). Wanzel and Danielson (1977) report that goals that are too general or unlikely to be attained in the short run were unlikely to facilitate attendance. In Orlick's (1974) words the goals should be "realistic," "achievable," "short term" and "long term." He stresses that goals that are based on past performances or achievements and that are progressively increased provide a continuous sense of success, as they are achieved, and challenge, as they are reset.

Orlick (1974) also mentions the use of keeping charts because they graphically represent progress and keep the desired goals in the awareness of participants. Charts have been positively evaluated in experimental settings by Wankel and Yardley (1982) and Wankel (1985). The writer has seen a goal-setting chart produced by Xerox Corporation that is called "Fitness by Objectives," a play on the well-known management technique, Management by Objectives (M.B.O.). Participaction Network (no date) has produced a goal-setting booklet entitled *The Official Participaction Network Goal Setter*. It begins with the message, "This is not a book. . . . It's a piece of fitness equipment. You can't wear it, lift it, swing it, or ride it. BUT . . . you can use it to get more out of your fitness program." Goal setting and attainment is important. The Ontario Ministry of Culture and Recreation (1981) indicate that a sense of failure arises from dropping out of programs and makes low-active adults less able to take up activities again in the future. This is a type of learned helplessness and is a common psychological phenomenon (Iso-Ahola, 1980a).

It is therefore incumbent upon physical activity programers to provide opportunities for goal setting. Discrete monitoring should be used to ensure that the goals are realistic, attainable, and reset as they are reached.

CHOICE AND DECISION MAKING

Choice is fundamental to leisure. As Burton (1976) states, "the defining characteristic of leisure is choice. Choice or freedom from obligations, is a constant theme permeating the many varied interpretations of leisure throughout history" (p. 18). A theoretical model, a theory of reasoned action, has been formulated by Fishbein and Ajzen (1975) to help explain why choice is important in the decision to become involved in certain behaviors, for example, physical activity. This theory is based on the premise that people make rational decisions, utilizing the information they have available when they engage in volitional behaviors. Olson and Zanna (1981) explain this by stating that

> if people do not perceive any choice about performing or not performing some action, then their personal attitudes, beliefs, etc., cannot be expected to influence their behaviour — they will simply perform or not perform the act, as demanded by the external contingencies (p. 6).

Simply stated, the model predicts that a person's specific physical activity behavior is a function of that person's attitude and beliefs toward that physical activity. Empirical support for this model has come from studies, involving physical activity by Riddle (1980), who was concerned with jogging behavior, and Wankel and Beatty (1975), who considered exercise programs.

In terms of recruitment to a physical activity program, Heinzelmann and Bagley (1970) found that a small group discussion and decision-making method was more effective than a large group lecture method. The former method was supposed to allow for greater and closer involvement in the decision making and, therefore, greater commitment to the program. Olson and Zanna (1981) outline the implications of this model for educational and promotional campaigns aimed to encourage people to become involved in physical activity programs. They explain that the campaigns should be linked to specific, not general, activity behaviors; the focus should be on personal and evaluative consequences of the person's involvement in that activity; where possible, one should link the person's involvement to significant others, for example, co-workers; provide basic information about how to perform that activity; and convince the participant about the activity's compatibility with any lifestyle.

Wankel (1985) outlines a number of empirical studies that he carried out with associates utilizing a decision balance-sheet procedure first developed by Hoyt and Janis (1975) for use in physical activity programs. The procedure requires little specialized training, is simple, requires little time to implement, and has been found to significantly improve attendance in a wide variety of settings. Where possible, choice and individual decision making should be included in promotional campaigns and during the ongoing physical activity programs.

SATISFACTION

An important component of any physical activity program is the measure of satisfaction gained from it. Unless a person is satisfied with a physical activity program, he or she will be unlikely to persist in the program or join for a second time if it is a seasonal involvement. A number of writers have described this in terms of "fun" or "enjoyment" and have postulated that it is a central component in physical activity programs (for example, Jette 1979; Massie and Shephard 1971; Orlick 1974; Perrin 1979). However, as Wankel (1980) points out, there is a need to research the dimensions underlying fun or enjoyment because it is a general concept that provides little direction for practitioners. Some of the factors reviewed in this chapter are ingredients in the mixture that leads to a person's perception of satisfaction, for example, mastery of skills, perceived choice, feelings of competence, and achievement of goals.

An important contribution to the study of satisfaction is Csikszentmihalyi's (1975) model of the flow experience. This describes a holistic sensation that occurs when a participant perceives the challenges (action opportunities) presented in the physical activity as matching skills (action capabilities). When a situation is too demanding, for example, aerobic dance steps too complicated or energy demands too exhausting, for the participant's skill, a state of worry or anxiety ensues. Conversely if the activity is too easy, too simple, or not sufficiently demanding, the participant becomes bored. Group fitness programs, especially those led by an instructor at the front in time to music, are especially vulnerable to mismatching challenge to skill level. Similarly those individual activities, for example, jogging, where the novice tries to keep up with those who are experienced or trained also results in a mismatch. A good program is one that matches capabilities with opportunities that will result in experiences that then become intrinsically motivating or rewarding.

Crandall (1979) indicates that social interaction is important in the attainment of leisure satisfaction. In an exercise class, where people are congregating together, it is important for the class leader to consider the compatibility of people who are going to interact, and to create conditions whereby this interaction is facilitated. Peepre (1980) indicates that in the Canadian Employee Fitness and Lifestyle Project, "a number of special classes were offered. These included an 'Overweight' class, 'Over-45' class, walking and jogging clubs, 'Healthy Back' program, jazz and dance 'disco' class, and individualized programs for executives" (no page number). The wide variety of programs and people being able to choose a program suited to them contributed to their successful programs.

Studies by Tinsley, Barrett, and Kass (1979) and Tinsley and Kass (1978) provide evidence that needs, as expressed by participants, are often activity specific or, rather, more readily satisfied through one activity than another. These two studies, again, highlight that individuals vary in their needs and motivations, that activities vary in their capacity to satisfy those needs, and that the two must be matched for success to be assured.

PREVIOUS EXERCISE HISTORY AND HEALTH HISTORY

Considering that most people believe physical exercise to be a healthy activity, it is not surprising to find that previous exercise and health history affect attendance and adherence. Oldridge (1979) found that smoking was the single best predictor for quitting an exercise program (59 percent). Other researchers have found that biologic factors such as excess weight and high percent of body fat are discriminating factors for dropouts (for example, Andrew and Parker 1979; Dishman 1981; and Massie and Shephard 1971). This has to be tempered by Morgan (1977) who concluded that biologic factors accounted for very little predictive utility.

In a study reported by the Ontario Ministry of Tourism and Recreation (1982), Perceived Lifestyle Changes (a derived score based on open-ended responses to general lifestyle questions) was the best predictor as to whether participants in physical activity programs were active or inactive in the posttest period. The study, however, was unable to establish causal links because it states, "of these 21 participants, the majority (67 %) indicated that changes in physical activity *led to* other lifestyle changes. However, a sizeable proportion of the participants (33 %) indicated that other lifestyle changes (e.g. giving up smoking, etc.) led to, or preceded physical activity" (p. 36). No matter which direction the link is made it is important to consider programing for other lifestyle factors when promoting physical activity. In the workplace an ideal blend can be achieved through employee recreation programs (ERPs), employee fitness programs (EFPs) and employee assistance programs (EAPs).

The extent to which the participants remain free of injury is important in relation to adherence. Injury is a commonly reported reason for quitting physical activity programs (Boothby, Tungatt, and Townsend 1981; Morgan 1977; Pollock et al. 1977; Wanzel and Danielson 1977). Pollock et al. (1977) indicate that intensity of exercise is directly related to injury incidence and report that exercising at more than 90 percent of maximal heart rate, exercising more often than five days a week, and exercising more than 45 minutes a day significantly increases the incidence of injury. Instructors should be especially careful not to raise intensity levels too high especially for beginning classes. They should use quick and easy identification methods, previous history of exercise and health, to screen their participants. One such method is the Physical Activity Readiness Questionnaire (PAR-Q), developed by the British Columbia Ministry of Health (Stewart, Collis, Chisholm, and Kulak 1979).

OPPORTUNITY TO EXERCISE

Knowledge about physical activity programs being offered is one part of the opportunity spectrum. In the workplace the programer has a distinct advantage because the audience is captive and can easily be reached via bulletins, newsletters, flyers in paychecks or promotional activities in key areas, for example, the company cafeteria. The Employee Fitness and Lifestyle Project (Canada, Department of National Health and

Welfare n.d.) provides excellent advice on how these communication methods should be used and also provides overwhelming evidence of the efficacy of these methods.

Opportunity is more than awareness because a number of opportunity related factors can cause participants to not attend or quit. Cleanliness of exercise areas and appropriate changing, showering, and toileting arrangements are vital if an aerobic fitness or physical activity program is implemented. Teraslinna, Partenen, Koskela, and Oja (1969) and Wanzel and Danielson (1977) document that poor attendance can be elevated by increasing the distance to the physical activity facility. On-site physical activity centres are the best solution to this problem although this arrangement requires strong support from upper management to provide the necessary capital and opportunities. The Canada Life Assurance Company in the Employee Fitness and Lifestyle Project (Canada, Department of Health and Welfare n.d.) converted a disused basement to provide their employees with a convenient location. In spite of only having a 45-minute lunch break employees at Canada Life Assurance Company were able to show significant fitness improvement (Peepre 1980). Wanzel and Danielson (1977) indicate that flexible work hours and a variety of exercise program times are necessary to attract and retain participants in an employee fitness program.

LEADERSHIP

Central to any physical activity program are the programers or instructors. Simply by their authority or interaction with participants, especially in instruction situations, they can have a profound effect on the attendance and adherence of the exercise class participants (Franklin 1978; Orlick 1974; Wankel 1975; Wanzel and Danielson 1977). The leader can shape the environment, the atmosphere, the types of activities, dispense reinforcement or punishment, and act as a model. Faulkner and Stewart (1978) document how personal interest, shown by an instructor, can increase the attendance of irregular attendees. Wankel (1975) points out that a leader can unintentionally affect participants' attendance through expectations that are too high or too low. Wanzel and Danielson (1977) reveal a significant sex-of-participant interaction with instructors' personalities. In their study more women (11.1 percent) than men (1.6 percent) cited that they left the fitness program because of the instructor's personality; this was especially so for women under the age of 25.

Instructors can also be the reason for continuing a program. Andrew and Parker (1979) found that equal numbers of adherents and dropouts cited exercise staff as being the reason for their attendance or quitting.

Exercise and physical activity leaders must be aware of their influence (positive and negative) on exercise class participants. This is especially the case for classes where the instructor is male and the participants female, or vice versa, because males tend to have different goals and attitudes toward their physical activity that are different from those of females (Wanzel and Danielson 1977). In addition, instructors must be attentive to personality differences so that they (the instructors) do not become a reason for the participants leaving the program. Training and certification of instructors, for example, Y.M.C.A. or Fitness Ontario Leadership program, can help alleviate these problems.

Another form of leadership influence can be determined in the workplace. This is the influence of upper management who openly support company fitness and recreation programs. This was a key factor in the very successful program at the Employee Fitness and Lifestyle Project where it was noted that "the presence and support of senior personnel in the program was considered to be helpful in promoting the program to other employees" (Canada, Department of Health and Welfare n.d., p. 31). Lockheed employees, in March 1984, entered a 3-mile fun run, entitled "Beat the Boss," where they ran with the company president. The reaction from the president was noted in a N.E.S.R.A. *Keynotes*, "Calling the event 'very positive for Lockheed', president Dan Tellep was particularly impressed with the camaraderie that resulted from the run" (N.E.S.R.A. 1984, p. 3). Successful and attractive recreation and fitness programs are usually found in companies where senior management actively support the programs.

SOCIAL SUPPORT

There is considerable reference to the importance of social support in motivation for physical activity literature. The support can generally be classified into four types: family support, buddy support, group support, and leader support. Social support is given and received via a social network. Wellman (1981) states, "a support system is a social network: a set of nodes (e. g., persons) connected by a set of ties (e. g., relations of emotional support)" (p. 173). The network usually consists of people from the person's immediate family, friends, neighbors, and coworkers who provide guidance during periods of stress. This is applicable to physical activity, especially during the initial phases when considerable adjustment to one's life is made or when the body is dealing with the added stress of beginning regular, vigorous exercise.

Both Heinzelmann and Bagley (1970) and Andrew and Parker (1979) reported that spouses played an important role in the attendance of their partner in exercise programs. In the former study, the researchers found that 80 percent of husbands whose wives had positive attitudes toward the exercise program had excellent patterns of adherence; only 40 percent of those whose wives had neutral or negative attitudes had the same excellent attendance. Franklin (1978) suggests that spouses be periodically involved in an exercise program. Probably a better suggestion would be to try to attract couples or small groups of friends to exercise programs.

Another important consideration for family support is when one of the parents, but especially a mother, becomes involved in a physical activity program that results in the need for help with meals, cleaning up, someone to look after young children and, in one-car families, allowing her the exclusive use of the vehicle for those days or nights. Information form the Ontario Ministry of Tourism and Recreation (1982) study suggested "that very explicit and specific assistance with organizing one's family life to allow for physical activity is a key factor in becoming and staying active" (p. 38).

Another frame of reference to use, when considering social support, can be labeled buddy, friend, or peer support. Having friend or buddy support was found to be very important in the study carried out by Wanzel and Danielson (1977). They found a sex difference, females exercised more often with friends (61.9 percent) than did males (25.8 percent); an age difference, younger males and females (under 25) were inclined to exercise more with friends than were older participants (36 percent compared to 25 percent for over 45's); a job status difference, clerical workers exercised more with friends (40.9 percent) compared to management (15.4 percent); and a goal attainment difference for the under 25 group, 62.5 percent who exercised with a friend attained their goal(s) whereas 18.2 percent of those who exercised alone attained their goals(s). Therefore, it would seem, buddy support could be better utilized to affect adherence within a selected frame, that is, with younger people especially females who are not in managerial positions.

Buddy influence is pervasive in the leisure socialization literature, where it is indicated that peers, friends, and coworkers play an important role in affecting leisure behaviors. In particular, this influence appears to function as a result of positive social comparison and social feedback (Evans 1974; Evans and Lavoie 1978; and Heaps 1978). In physical activity programs there are many opportunities for social comparison and also for positive feedback from significant friends or, in the workplace, from coworkers. This positive atmosphere and camaraderie serve to enhance motivation to remain involved in physical activity.

Group involvement in physical activity has been found to be positively associated with interacting in a physical activity group (Brawley 1979; Faulkner and Stewart 1978; Heinzelmann 1973; and Massie and Shephard 1971). Brawley (1979) identifies a number of motivational factors that appear to be involved in affecting continued participation in fitness groups. They are the development of a group motive, which develops over time and is enhanced through group discussion and social interaction; the feeling of belonging that indicates group solidarity and, therefore, increases the attractiveness of the group; the presence of social obligation, which increases as solidarity and cohesion improves; social environmental factors that mediate interest and participation (for example, car pooling, buddy phoning, office co-workers); and the fitness group achievements or successes that allow for consequences such as social comparison and modeling to develop. These group factors are especially relevant in the workplace where benefits such as increased morale and decreased absenteeism and turnover could result from positive group physical activity experiences. The promotion of a positive, helping atmosphere in an exercise class would help moderate the stresses and strains associated with adherence to a fitness regimen.

The leader (class instructor) plays a central and crucial role in any group. Earlier in this chapter, the importance of the leader was emphasized. This is doubly so in the case of developing the framework and organization, within a class, that allows social support to flourish. Wanzel and Danielson (1977) point out that some participants respond well to the encouragement from the instructor; others, from their buddies and friends; and others, from peer group motivation. The social support given by these means can improve attendance and adherence. Social support has been empirically and experimentally verified in a series of physical activity research projects carried out by Wankel and his researchers and reported elsewhere (Wankel 1985; Wankel and Yardley 1982).

SUMMARY

Motivation for physical activity is a complex phenomenon and much is still to be learned in terms of how it can be manipulated to help people become involved and stay involved in physical activity. This chapter has outlined many strategies that can be used to help people become and remain active through good promotion and programing. The workplace offers an excellent opportunity for interventions and opportunities to be made available to a large segment of our society that is in need of improving its fitness. A wide variety of techniques and factors associated with attendance and adherence to physical activity were presented that can be used in the program by the instructor. Fitness instructors, recreation coordinators, and programers should attempt to utilize those techniques and factors in the promotion and implementation of their programs.

With a larger proportion of our society involved in programs that undoubtedly would benefit their health, everyone would win. The employer would have a healthier, more satisfied work force with a concomitant decrease in absenteeism and turnover. The employee would gain physiologically through improved physical fitness and psychologically through a greater sense of well-being. Finally, society would benefit from a nation of fitter, more efficient, and happier citizens.

REFERENCES

Andrew, G. M., and Parker, J. D. (1979). Factors relating to dropout of postmyocardial infarction patients from exercise programs. *Medicine and Science in Sports, 11,* 376–78.

Baekeland, F., and Lundwall, L. (1975). Dropping out of treatment: A critical review. *Psychological Bulletin, 82,* 738–83.

Bandura, A. (1969). *Principles of behavior modification.* New York: Holt, Rinehart and Winston

_____. (1977). Side efficacy: Toward a unifying theory of behavioral change. *Psychological Review, 84,* 191–215.

Bandura, A., and Schunk, D. A. (1981). Cultivating competence, self-efficacy, and intrinsic interest through proximal self-motivation. *Journal of Personality and Social Psychology, 41,* 586–98.

Banister, E. W. (1978). Health, fitness and productivity. *The Labour Gazette.* September, 400–7.

Bem, D. J., and Funder, D. C. (1978). Predicting more of the people more of the time: Assessing the personality of situations. *Psychological Review, 85,* 485–501.

Birch, D., and Veroff, J. (1959). *Motivation: A Study of Action,* New York: Brooks/Cole Publishing.

Boothby, J., Tungatt, M. F., and Townsend, A. (1981). Ceasing participation in sports activity: Reported reasons and their implications. *Journal of Leisure Research, 13,* 1–15.

Brawley, L. R. (1979). Motivating participation in the fitness group. *Recreation Research Review, 6,* 35–39.

Brownell, K. D. (1978). Theoretical and applied issues in self-control. *The Psychological Record, 28,* 291–98.

Burton, T. L. (1976). *Making man's environment: Leisure.* Toronto: Van Nostrand Reinhold.

Canada, Department of National Health and Welfare (n. d.). *Employee fitness and lifestyle project: Toronto 1977–1978.* Ottawa, Canada: Minister of State, Fitness, and Amateur Sports.

Chubb, M., and Chubb, H. R. (1981). *One third of our time: An introduction to recreation behavior and resources.* New York: John Wiley.

Collis, M. (1974). *Employee Fitness.* Ottawa, Canada: Minister of State, Fitness, and Amateur Sport.

Crandall, R. (1979). Social interaction, affect, and leisure. *Journal of Leisure Research, 11,* 165–81.

Csikszentmihalyi, M. (1975). Play and intrinsic rewards. *Journal of Humanistic Psychology, 15,* 41–63.

Deci, E. L. (1971). Effects of externally mediated rewards on intrinsic motivation. *Journal of Personality and Social Psychology, 18,* 105–15.

_____. (1971). *Intrinsic motivation.* New York: Plenum Press.

Dishman, R. K. (1981). Biologic influences on exercise adherence. *Research Quarterly for Exercise and Sport, 52,* 143–59.

Dishman, R. K., Ickes, W., and Morgan, W. P. (1980). Self-motivation and adherence to habitual physical activity. *Journal of Applied Social Psychology, 10*, 11–132.

Endler, N. S., and Magnusson, D. (1976). Toward an interactional psychology of personality. *Psychological Bulletin, 83*, 956–74.

Epstein, S. (1977). Traits are alive and well. In *Personality at the crossroads: Current issues in interactional psychology*, edited by D. Magnusson and N. S. Endler. Hillsdale, New Jersey: Lawrence Erlbaum.

Epstein, S. (1980). The stability of behavior: Implications for psychological research. *American Psychologist, 35*, 790–806.

Evans, J. F. (1974). Motivational effects of being promised an opportunity to engage in social comparison. *Psychological Reports, 34*, 175–81.

Evans, J. F., and Lavoie, N. F. (1978). Social motivation for physical fitness. In *Proceedings of the 6th Commonwealth Conference*, Vol. II. edited by P. Linsay and J. Vallance. Edmonton: University of Alberta.

Faulkner, R. A., and Stewart, G. W. (1978). Exercise programmes — recruitment/retention of participants. *Recreation Canada, 36*, 21–27.

Fishbein, M., and Ajzen, I. (1985). *Belief, attitude, intention, and behavior*. Reading, Massachusetts: Addison-Wesley.

Franklin, B. A. (1978). Motivating and educating adults to exercise. *Journal of Physical Education and Recreation*, 13–17.

Green, D., and Lepper, M. R. (1974). Intrinsic motivation: How to turn play into work. *Psychology Today, 8*, 49–54.

Grossberg, J. M. (1981). Comments about cognitive therapy and behavior therapy. *Journal of Behavioral Therapy and Experimental Psychiatry, 7*, 25–33.

Heaps, R. A. (1978). Relating physical and psychological fitness: A psychological view. *Journal of Sports Medicine, 18*, 399–408.

Heinzelmann, F. (1973). Social and psychological factors that influence the effectiveness of exercise programs. In *Exercise testing and exercise training in coronary heart disease*, edited by J. Naughton and H. K. Hellerstein. New York: Academic Press.

Heinzelmann, F. and Bagley, R. W. (1970). Response to physical activity program and their efforts on health behavior. *Public Health Reports, 85*, 905–11.

Hockey, R. V. (1985). *Physical fitness: The pathway to healthful living.* 5th ed. St. Louis: Times Mirror/ Mosby College.

Hoyt, M. F., and Janis, I. L. (1975). Increasing adherence to a stressful decision via a motivational balance-sheet procedure: A field experiment. *Journal of Personality and Social Psychology, 35,* 833–39.

Iso-Ahola, S. E. (1980a). *The social psychology of leisure and recreation.* Dubuque, Iowa: William L. Brown.

_____. (1980b). Toward a dialectical social psychology of leisure and recreation. In *Social psychological perspectives of leisure and recreation,* edited by S. E. Iso-Ahola. Springfield, Illinois: Charles C. Thomas.

Jette, M. (1979). An analysis of the lifestyle and fitness of male employees: Implications for physical activity programs. *Recreation Research Review, 6,* 53–61.

Katell, A. D., Martin, J. E., Webster, J. S., and Zegman, M. A. (1980). *Exercise adherence: Impact of feedback, praise and goal setting procedures.* Paper presented to a symposium at the meeting of the Association of Behavior Therapy, New York.

Lepper, M. R., and Green, D. (1975). Turning play into work: Effects of adult surveillance and extrinsic rewards on children's intrinsic motivations. *Journal of Personality and Social Psychology, 31,* 479–86.

London, M., Crandall, R., and Fitzgibbons, D. (1977). The psychological structure of leisure: Activities, needs, people. *Journal of Leisure Research, 9,* 252–63.

Magnusson, D., and Endler, N. S., eds. (1977). *Personality at the crossroads: Current issues in interactional psychology.* Hillsdale, New Jersey: Lawrence Erlbaum.

Martin, J. E. (1981). Exercise management: Shaping and maintaining physical fitness. *Behavioral Medicine Advances, 4.*

Massie, J. F., and Shephard, R. J. (1971). Physiological and psychological effects of training. *Medicine and Science in Sports, 3,* 110–17.

McCaughan, L. R., and McKinlay, S. (1981). Effects of success/failure and extrinsic rewards on intrinsic motivation using a competitive motor task. *Research Quarterly for Exercise and Sport, 52,* 208–15.

Morgan, W. P. (1977). Involvement in vigorous physical activity with special reference to adherence. *Proceedings, College Physical Education Conference, Orlando, Florida.*

____. (1980). The trait psychology controversy. *Research Quarterly for Exercise and Sport, 51,* 50–76.

N.E.S.R.A. (1984). Lockheed employees "Beat the Boss." *N.E.S.R.A. Keynotes, 14,* 1–4.

Oldridge, N. B. (1977). What to look for in an exercise class leader. *The Physician and Sports Medicine, 5,* 85–88.

____. (1979). Compliance in exercise rehabilitation. *The Physician and Sports Medicine, 7,* 94–104.

Olson, J. M., and Zanna, M. P. (1981). *Promoting physical activity: A social psychological perspective.* Toronto, Ontario: Ministry of Culture and Recreation.

Ontario Ministry of Culture and Recreation (1981). *Low active adults: Who they are and how to reach them.* Toronto, Ontario: Ministry of Culture and Recreation.

Ontario, Ministry of Tourism and Recreation (1982). *The relationship between physical activity and other health related lifestyle behaviours.* Toronto, Ontario: Ministry of Tourism and Recreation.

____. (1983). *Physical activity patterns in Ontario, II.* Toronto, Ontario: Ministry of Tourism and Recreation.

____. (1984). *A planners guide to fitness in the workplace.* Toronto, Ontario: Ministry of Tourism and Recreation.

Orlick, T. D. (1974). *Motivational factors related to adult participation in exercise programs.* Paper presented at the conference on Physical Activity and Cardiovascular Disease, University of Ottawa, June 1974.

Participaction Network, *The Official Participaction Network Goal Setter,* Toronto, Ontario (informal publication) 1985.

Peepre, M. (1980). The Canadian Employee Fitness and Lifestyle Project. An article reprinted from *Athletic Purchasing and Facilities.* December 1980.

Perrin, B. (1979). Survey of physical activity in the Regional Municipality of Waterloo. *Recreation Research Review, 6,* 48–52.

Pollock, M. L., Gettman, L. W., Milesis, C. A., Bah, M. D., Durstine, L., and Johnson, R. B. (1977). Effects of frequency and duration of training on attrition and incidence of injury. *Medicine and Science in Sports, 9,* 31–36.

Riddle, P. K. (1980). Attitudes, beliefs, behavioral intentions, and behaviors of women and men toward regular jogging. *Research Quarterly for Exercise and Sport, 51*, 66–674.

Romsa, G., and Hoffman, W. (1980). An application on non-participation data in recreation research. Testing the opportunity theory. *Journal of Leisure Research, 12*, 321–28.

Ross, M. (1976). The self-perception of intrinsic motivation. In *New directions in attribution research*, Vol. 1., edited by J. H. Harvey, W. J. Ickes, and R. F. Kidd. Hillsdale, New Jersey: Lawrence Erlbaum.

Stewart, G., Collis, M., Chisholm, D., and Kulak, L. (1979). Physical activity readiness: A pre-exercise screening plan for adults. *Recreation Research Review, 6*, 27–28.

Teraslinna, P. T., Partenen, T., Koskela, A., and Oja, P. (1969). Characteristics affecting the willingness of executives to participate in an activity program aimed at coronary heart disease prevention. *Journal of Sports Medicine and Physical Fitness, 9*, 224–29.

Tinsley, H. E., Barrett, T. C., and Kass, R. A. (1979). Leisure activities and need satisfaction. *Journal of Leisure Research, 9*, 110–20.

Tinsley, H. E., and Kass, R. A. (1980). Leisure activities and need satisfaction: A replication and extension. *Journal of Leisure Research, 10*, 191–202.

Wankel, L. M. (1975). *Leadership considerations for maximizing participation in sports and recreation programs*. An invited address to the Sport and Recreation as it Affects Women Conference, Lloydminster, Saskatchewan, October, 1975.

_____. (1980). Involvement in vigorous physical activity. Considerations for enhancing self-motivation. In *Fitness motivation: Proceedings of the Geneva Park Workshop 1980*, edited by R. R. Danielson and K. F. Danielson. Toronto: ORCOL Publications.

_____. (1985). Decision-making and social-support strategies for increasing exercise involvement. *Journal of Cardiac Rehabilitation, 4*, 124–35.

Wankel, L. M., and Beatty, B. D. (1975). Behavior intentions and attendance of an exercise program: A field test of Fishbein's model. In *Movement: Proceedings of the 7th Canadian Psycho-Motor Learning and Sport Psychology symposium, 1975*, edited by C. Bard, M. Fleury, and J. Samela.

Wankel, L. M., and Yardley, J. K. (1982). An investigation of the effectiveness of a structured social support program for increasing exercise adherence of high and low self-motivated adults. In *Proceedings of the Leisure Research Section. Canadian Parks/ Recreation Association Conference,* edited by D. Ng. Saskatoon, 1982.

Wanzel, R. S. (1977). Factors related to withdrawal from an employee fitness program. A paper presented to the American Association for Leisure and Recreation, AAHPER Conference, Seattle.

Wanzel, R. S., and Danielson, R. R. (1977). Improve adherence to your fitness program. A 3-part series, *Recreation Management,* July, 16–19; August, 38–41; September, 34–37.

Weinberg, R. S. (1979). Intrinsic motivation in a competitive setting. *Medicine and Science in Sports, 11,* 146–49.

Weinberg, R. S., and Ragan, J. (1979). Effects of competition, success/failure and sex on intrinsic motivation. *The Research Quarterly, 50,* 503–10.

Wellman, B. Applying network analysis to the study of support, in B. H. Gottlieb (ed.), *Social Networks and Social Support,* Volume #4 of the Sage Studies in Community Mental Health, Beverly Hills, Sage Publications, 1981.

Yardley, J. K. (1984). Leisure display: The great show-off in North America. *The Anthropological Association for the Study of Play Newsletter, 10.*

Yardley, J. K. (1982). *The effects of self-motivation and structured social support upon exercise program adherence.* Unpublished master's thesis, The University of Alberta.

19 A Strategy for Evaluating Occupational Health and Safety Training

Michael A. Vojtecky and Emil Berkanovic

Evaluation is a necessary activity for determining the worth of worker health and safety training programs. The worth of a health and safety training program can be judged in many ways. For example, it may be judged according to the program's usefulness to the participants, the sponsor, or society. The worth of a program may be judged according to the effectiveness of innovations and initiatives for program improvement or of program management and administration or in meeting various accountability requirements (Rossi and Freeman 1982). Thus, evaluation, or the estimations of worth, may be undertaken for different reasons and at different levels of comprehensiveness.

The basic assumption underlying the training of workers in job safety and health is that such training will increase safe behavior in the context of the work environment and thereby decrease health risks associated with the job. Thus, one reason for evaluating worker training programs is to test this assumption. In addition to the protection of worker health, however, effective training may also result in benefits to employers as well as to society in general. These potential benefits include the maintenance of a vital national resource, that is, a vigorous and healthy workforce; the reduction of health care costs and human resources development costs incurred by employers; an improvement in productivity; and an increase in the general well-being of society through the promotion of the health of its members and through the optimal allocation of scarce resources. Thus another reason for evaluating worker training programs is to determine the extent to which these benefits are being realized.

ELEMENTS OF EVALUATION

In brief, program evaluation is the systematic application of social and behavioral research procedures for the purpose of assessing the conceptualization, implementation, impact, efficiency, and adequacy of coverage of social intervention programs. When appropriate, as in the case of health and safety training programs, physiological and physical research procedures are sometimes included to provide additional information for assessment. Program evaluations can include any number of the following general elements.

Assessment of the Program Plan

An education or training program is an attempt to translate ideas about the determinants of behavior into learning activities that can produce changes in behavior. Therefore the program plan is a statement about the expected relationships between the program's activities and its goal. It represents the strategy for bringing existing behavior into conformance with the program's goal (Rossi and Freeman 1982). The evaluation of the program plan requires a critical examination of the hypothetical relationships proposed by the plan for logic, consistency, and empirical support.

Program Monitoring

Program monitoring is an assessment of the procedures and operations of education and training. Its purpose is to determine whether the implementation of the program is consistent with the design presented in the program plan. Thus the focus of program monitoring is the use of resources in terms of both what and how. In addition, program monitoring can provide information leading to the revision of a plan that is not succeeding.

Impact Assessment

Impact assessment seeks to determine the outcome of specific training methods by determining whether the training resulted in any changes in the safety related knowledge, attitudes, behaviors, or exposures of those trained. In addition the determination of the effects of these changes on morbidity or mortality or both is also often attempted.

Efficiency

"Efficiency assessments (cost-benefit and cost-effectiveness analyses) provide a frame of reference for relating costs and program results, the latter measured either in monetary terms or in terms of actual outcomes" (Rossi and Freeman 1982). Thus efficiency assessments are undertaken in order to determine the total cost per unit of impact. Because training programs often represent only one component of a system of varied activities designed to protect and promote worker health, it is essential that whatever resources can be allocated to occupational health programs are allocated in a way that is commensurate with the real benefits of each component.

Adequacy of Coverage

Adequacy of coverage refers to the extent to which a program is capable of reaching those for whom it is intended. Although there are frequently economies of scale in education and training programs, there are times when efficient, high-impact programs cannot be extended to everyone who might benefit from them. The reasons for this include lack of trained personnel, lack of material or monetary resources, and legal or bureaucratic restrictions.

The elements of a program evaluation are illustrated in Table 19.1. It is important to recognize that the table describes the dynamic processes through which social action programs move. Thus, it may be viewed as a map that can be used both to plan programs and to identify variables that need to be measured in order to monitor, assess impact, assess efficiency, and assess adequacy of coverage.

The examination of the appropriate variables alone, however, will not ensure a valid evaluation. The technical aspects of evaluation design and information collection must also be considered. A comprehensive discussion of appropriate evaluation research design is beyond the scope of this chapter. However, the main technical function of design is to control for factors other than program effects. Thus, a properly designed

TABLE 19.1
Elements of Program Evaluation

	Assess Program Plan	Monitor Program	Assess Impacts	Assess Efficiency	Assess Coverage
Resources	Activities				
Skills	Program processes	Activities conducted	Long-term learning	Cost per impact	Percentage of
Interests	Curriculum development	as planned	Changes in safety		target or at-risk
Money	Scheduling	Attendance	related behaviors		group covered
Location		Short-term learning			
Materials		Satisfaction			

Source: Adapted from Berkanovic and Gerber 1981.

evaluation will permit one to say how many of the changes observed are due to the program and how many of these changes are due to factors unrelated to the program.

Technically the first step in any evaluation is to establish a comparison criterion. Often this comparison criterion takes the form of a group of individuals who did not participate in the intervention program. Once a comparison group has been defined, the evaluator can plan the evaluation so as to compare changes in the participating group with changes in the comparison group. In other cases, standards such as industry experience can be used as a comparison for program performance.

In order to demonstrate the influence of program performance, the evaluation should make the conditions of the group experiencing the program as different as possible from the conditions of the comparison group. For example, if the training group receives a lecture on a health and safety topic the comparison group may receive none. In this way any subsequent differences in safety behavior observed between the two groups may be attributed to one or another of the effects of the lecture.

However, the content of the lecture is merely one component to which the target group may be responding. There may be cases in which other factors such as the attention the group receives or the manner in which the lecture is delivered may have more effect than the content.

There are several ways to isolate the effects of a program from other factors that might contribute to changes in the target group. For example, if experience at a job accounts to a large degree for safe performance a way must be found to separate the effects of experience from the effects of training. One way is to eliminate experience as a causal factor by assigning only inexperienced workers to the training. Another way would be to explicitly recognize the experience factor by keeping accurate records of the amount of experience each training program participant has and then comparing their performance to that of individuals of similar experience who have not been trained. A third way is to assign workers randomly to training and no training groups. This method allows the laws of probability to eliminate nonprogramatic effects. However, in many training situations, the random assignment of workers to different groups is unrealistic. Finally, the application of statistical methods for controlling the influence of nonprogramatic factors may be possible. If an evaluation is adequately designed, the analysis usually is straightforward, allowing the evaluator to get answers quickly.

In addition to proper design, however, attention must also be given to the accurate measurement of the factors of interest. In order to minimize errors in measurement, that is, mistakes in gathering and organizing information, the evaluator must be careful about the way in which the information is collected. The four primary ways to reduce measurement error are to use well established and reliable data collection tools such as standardized tests; to make the conditions under which tests are administered as standard as possible, for example, using only one protocol for administering tests; to ask only those questions the target group can and will answer; and to be as careful as possible in recording test results. By paying close attention to the problems of measurement error and evaluation design one can be assured of assessing the effects of the training program as accurately as possible. More complete discussions of evaluation design and methods for data collection can be found elsewhere; the reader is encouraged to refer to them (Green 1974; Campbell and Stanley 1963; Kerlinger 1973; Rossi and Freeman 1982).

CURRENT EVALUATION PRACTICES

It appears that the evaluation of ongoing health and safety training programs has for the most part been casual (Vojtecky and Berkanovic 1985; Vojtecky and Schmitz 1985; Heath 1981), if it is conducted at all. Thus the effects of ongoing training are largely unknown. We believe this situation arises, at least in part, from two events. First, a large number of training programs are informal rather than formal programs of instruction. Second, the evaluations conducted seldom conform to the principles we have outlined above.

In this section, we will present an overview of the current evaluation practices of those doing training required by the Occupational Safety and Health Act. The data were collected as part of a study directed by Vojtecky. They consist of questionnaire responses of 124 individuals who evaluate occupational health and safety programs. These 124 individuals were part of a random sample of health and safety trainers drawn from the registers of professional associations for occupational health specialists.

ASSESSMENT OF THE PROGRAM PLAN

In the United States about 74 percent of the health and safety training programs are described by those responsible for evaluating them as formal programs of instruction. If the existence of written lesson plans that describe the sequential arrangement of learning activities and teaching methods for reaching clearly specified learning objectives is used as a criterion of formality, only 49 percent of programs qualify as formal. Thus, there is seldom a detailed program plan in which the conceptualization of instruction and instructional methods can be assessed. Although 87 percent of the programs that describe themselves as formal report that they regularly review the content of their programs, that is to say the accuracy of the information presented, only 67 percent keep lesson plans on file.

PROGRAM MONITORING

Perhaps the most common method of program monitoring is keeping attendance records. About 90 percent of individuals responsible for formal programs of instruction keep training session attendance records. Thus, they are able to know who is receiving what training. In addition most individuals (91 percent) responsible for training keep copies of Material Safety Data Sheets and whatever films, slides, books, and pamphlets they use during training. It is likely that these materials are assessed for appropriateness of content with respect to the training program; however, it is not likely that individuals unfamiliar with educational theory and method can assess these materials for educational soundness. In addition, roughly 60 percent of evaluators also ask employees if they are satisfied with the training given, and virtually every business keeps a record of expenditures for their programs.

Unfortunately the information collected may be of little use. In only 34 percent of formal programs is the information collected during evaluations used for managerial activities, such as shifting resources. In 65 percent of these programs, it is used to change the program's content. In almost 20 percent of programs, the information collected is not used for anything at all. Understandably then about one-third of evaluators say they are dissatisfied with the evaluations they conduct.

IMPACT ASSESSMENT

In order to assess the effects of the program, about 30 percent of evaluators of formal programs ask employees to demonstrate correct work practices on the job subsequent to training. However, 70 percent of these individuals report that this information is collected casually through field observations conducted by supervisors and health and safety staff persons. A slightly higher percentage (42 percent) requires employees to demonstrate proper work practices correctly at the time of training. Only 19 percent require employees to take a written test regarding the content of the training, and 60 percent say that program effects are documented by changes in accident records, physiologic measures, or by supervisor reports.

With respect to the technical approach used in evaluation, about 40 percent of programs use a historical record-keeping design that documents process and, therefore, may be inappropriate for impact assessment. Twenty percent compare their program's results with common experience such as the industry's average experience. Another 20 percent use quasi-experimental designs including pre-post and time series studies; 10 percent use experimental designs featuring randomized controls. Interestingly, program type, size, and sponsorship are unrelated to how impact is assessed in these programs. It appears that little is being done that allows the rigorous evaluation of training program effectiveness.

MEASUREMENT OF EFFICIENCY

As we noted before, efficiency assessments relate program costs to program results. Because program outcomes are for the most part unknown, there is little basis for conducting a valid efficiency assessment. For this reason, neither our examination of evaluation practices nor the research literature has emphasized this type of evaluation. We believe, however, that assessing efficiency is important for determining which education and training program is optimal and for allocating resources among the different components of the total health and safety program.

PLANNING AN EVALUATION

Although the technical aspects of evaluation are of the utmost importance in the generation of valid information about programs, it is equally important that the evaluation be planned with respect to a number of nontechnical issues. The first step in planning an evaluation is to identify who the users of the evaluation will be and what they want to know. This can be a more difficult task than is apparent. Often several users can be identified who have conflicting interests. This is often true in occupational settings where both union and management have differing agendas for a program. Equally often, users have difficulty in identifying the specific kinds of information they want. Indeed, in this situation, the evaluator may expend considerable time discussing how different kinds of information might be used. Nonetheless, if the users cannot agree on what they want to know and on how it will be used, an evaluation is likely to be a waste of resources.

The second step in planning an evaluation is to determine both the form and the conditions under which evaluation information can be released. Again, the potential for conflict among several users can be great at this stage. It is important, therefore, for the evaluator to understand the restrictions various users might wish to place on the release of information and that there be clear agreement among the various users on those restrictions. Related to the problem of release, but usually easier to solve, is the form in which the information generated in the evaluation is most usefully presented. Often, different users would like different levels of detail, differing schedules for when information is delivered, and different emphasis in the analysis of the data. This problem can be solved by the generation of alternative formats, a task that is easily accomplished by those with access to a computer.

The third step in planning an evaluation is to conduct an evaluability assessment. The purpose of the evaluability assessment is to determine if the desired information can be gathered and if the restrictions on its dissemination can be maintained. In addition, the evaluator might also identify other information that could be gathered that might enhance one or more of the uses identified in step one. The evaluator should also determine at this stage what would have to be done technically to conduct the evaluation. Moreover, apart from the purely technical matters of measurement and design, the evaluator must consider who will actually gather the information and what impact gathering the information is likely to have on normal work routines. Finally, the evaluator should determine the cost of conducting the evaluation.

The fourth step in planning an evaluation is to present the various users with the results of the evaluability assessment. It is at this step that the users must decide if the evaluation is worth both its monetary costs and its disruptions of work routines. They must decide whether the information that can be gathered is sufficient to meet their needs as users and also the extent to which it can be restricted in the manner they desire. At this step, a go or no-go decision must be made.

The fifth step assumes an affirmative decision has been made to proceed with the evaluation. Here, the evaluator develops the detailed plan of the evaluation specifying all the technical procedures required by the measurements, specific measures, data collection, design, and analysis.

The final step is to assure that the evaluation plan can be implemented. This means that all data collection forms and instruments

TABLE 19.2
Steps in Planning an Evaluation

Step	Purpose
1	Identify users and what they want to know.
2	Determine the form and the conditions under which the evaluation information can be released.
3	Conduct an evaluability assessment: Can the information be obtained? Can the restrictions on its dissemination be maintained? What must be done technically to carry out the evaluation? Who will do the various tasks required by the evaluation? How will the evaluation affect normal work routines? What will the evaluation cost?
4	Present the results of the evaluability assessment to the users and decide whether to proceed.
5	Develop a detailed evaluation plan.
6	Develop a system to assure that the evaluation plan can be implemented.

Source: Adapted from Berkanovic, Gerber, and Landswerk 1983.

are available and ready for use, that the persons collecting the data are appropriately trained, that the individuals from whom data will be collected have been identified or that a means of identifying them has been developed, and that an analysis plan and schedule have been developed. These six steps are summarized in Table 19.2. Once these steps have been completed, the evaluation may be implemented with the hope that it can be completed to the satisfaction of both the users and the evaluator.

CONCLUSION

The basic question of great practical significance that evaluation may help answer is, "How can we improve current training programs?" Although our review of current evaluations seems to suggest that the majority of evaluations conducted cannot answer this question, this may be due primarily to the way in which those evaluations are conducted, not because education and training are ineffective or because current evaluation methodologies are unable to provide an answer. On the contrary, the few rigorous evaluations of demonstration training programs that have been done have shown the effectiveness of health and safety training as an additional control over workplace hazards. (Komacki, Barwick, and Scott 1978; University of Kansas 1981; Maples et al. 1982; Zohar, Cohen, and Azar 1980).

The evaluation of ongoing training programs must also be considered in the light of the qualifications of the evaluators to do evaluation. Only 23 percent of those responsible for conducting program evaluations have ever been trained, even at a superficial level, to do so. These individuals can hardly be expected to recognize the uses of evaluation, much less to know how to conduct it.

It is becoming more apparent, however, that the potential gain in employee health protection deriving from effective health and safety training is only one reason for conducting such training in the best possible way. The escalating costs of health benefits and legal actions are also major incentives for industry and government to become involved in prevention programs. In addition, other benefits of an effective health and safety training program may include reduced absenteeism, increased productivity, and increased employee morale. If industry is to realize these benefits fully, evaluation should play a major role in the management of health and safety training programs.

REFERENCES

Berkanovic, E., and B. Gerber. "Evaluating Cancer Control Programs in the Community." *Family and Community Health* 4 (1981): 75–85.

_____. *Contractors Final Report. Community Cancer Control/Los Angeles,* NCI Contract NO1-CN-75400. 1982.

Berkanovic, E., B. Gerber, and J. Landswerk. *Workshop Materials Prepared for the American Cancer Society.* 1983.

Campbell, D., and J. Stanley. *Experimental and Quasi-Experimental Designs for Research.* Skokie, Illinois: Rand McNally, 1963.

Green, L. W. "Toward Cost-Benefit Evaluations of Health Education: Some Concepts, Methods, and Examples." *Health Education Monographs* (Supplement No. 1) (1974): 34–60.

Heath, E. D. "Worker Training and Education in Occupational Safety and Health: A Report on Practice in Six Industrialized Western Nations." *American Journal of Industrial Medicine* 2 (1981): 379–403.

Kerlinger, F. *Foundations of Behavioral Research.* New York: Holt, Rinehart and Winston, 1973.

Komacki, J., K. D. Barwick, and L. R. Scott. "A Behavioral Approach to Occupational Safety: Pinpointing and Reinforcing Safe Performance in a Food Manufacturing Plant." *Journal of Applied Psychology* 68 (1978): 434–45.

Maples, T. W., J. A. Jacoby, D. E. Johnson, G. L. Ter Haar, and F. M. Buckingham. Effectiveness of Employee Training and Motivation Programs in Reducing Exposure to Inorganic Lead and Lead Alkyls." *American Industrial Hygiene Association Journal* 43 (1982): 692–94.

Rossi, P. H., and H. E. Freeman. *Evaluation: A Systematic Approach.* 2nd ed. Beverly Hills: Sage, 1982.

University of Kansas. *Behavioral Procedures for Reducing Worker Exposure to Carcinogens: Final Report.* Lawrence, Kansas: The University of Kansas, 1981.

Vojtecky, M. A., and E. Berkanovic. "The Evaluation of Health and Safety Training." *International Quarterly of Community Health Education.* 5 (1985): 277–86.

Vojtecky, M. A. and M. F. Schmitz. *Program Evaluation in Health and Safety Training.* Manuscript submitted for publication, 1985.

Zohar, D., A. Cohen, and N. Azar. "Promoting Increased Use of Ear Protection in Noise through Information Feedback." *Human Factors* 22 (1980): 69-79.

20 Economics and Worksite Health Promotion

Jonathan E. Fielding

REASONS FOR EMPLOYER INTEREST IN HEALTH PROMOTION

Employer-sponsored health promotion (wellness) programs are increasingly discussed as part of an overall strategy to better manage health benefit costs. In 1985 employers spent more than $100 billion for health benefits to employees, dependents, and retirees. More rapid growth in per capita health benefit costs compared with other benefit categories has made all employers actively seek approaches that can moderate future rates of increase and perhaps even lead to no growth in health benefit costs during a period of limited inflation.

But even if health benefit costs could be stabilized through a number of strategems, stabilization of the overall cost of ill health to an employer may not follow. Categories of health related costs include, in addition to health benefits, worker's compensation, absenteeism, short- and long-term disability, and the less quantifiable reductions in productivity associated with ill health (Fielding 1984). Totaling expenses for only the most quantifiable categories yields per employee health related costs as high as $7,000 to $10,000 a year (Fielding 1984).

Poor health habits are associated with higher costs in most of these categories. For example, Control Data Corporation has reported that in 1980 each smoking employee averaged 25 percent more in health benefit costs than each nonsmoker. Insurance claims for males age 40 or older averaged $1,498 for those within 20 percent of ideal weight versus $2,084 for those above 30 percent over ideal weight (Control Data

Corporation 1984). A smoker is estimated to cost an employer $300 to $800 more a year than a nonsmoker (Fielding 1982).

The epidemiological evidence linking health habits and serious diseases grows at an accelerating rate. For some habits, such as smoking, there are tens of thousands of studies. For example, smoking has been proven to greatly increase risk for heart and blood vessel diseases, many forms of cancer, a variety of acute and chronic respiratory ailments, and several serious problems for an unborn child (Fielding 1985). Evidence for the deleterious effects of poor nutrition, particularly elevated total serum cholesterol and obesity, is quite strong. Hypertension is known to be a major contributor to stroke and heart disease, and stress and poor ability to cope with it lead to a panoply of both physical and mental health problems (Tyroler 1986; Goldberger and Brezwitz 1982). Obesity and lack of adequate physical conditioning predisposes to back injuries, the highest category of costs under worker's compensation (Kelsey and Hochberg 1986).

Lack of exercise increases the chances of acquiring heart disease and muscle and joint problems and has been convincingly shown to be associated with decreased energy, alertness, and ability to work under stressful conditions (Fielding 1982).

For some serious diseases, including acquired heart diseases, some cancers, injuries, and stroke, contributing factors have been sufficiently delineated to be able to estimate their future rate of occurrence in a population based upon its risk characteristics. Table 20.1 estimates the expected and achievable (based upon risk reduction) number of deaths and serious incidents for each of these categories over the next ten years.

This type of risk profile can be readily developed by having a random sample of the employee population complete a questionnaire in which they provide risk-relevant information on their previous and current health status, health habits, and family history of certain health problems for which genetic composition can significantly affect overall risk. A limited number of easily ascertained risk-relevant biochemical and physiological parameters are added, usually height, weight, total serum cholesterol, blood glucose, and blood pressure. Body composition (percent body fat), high density lipoprotein cholesterol, and aerobic fitness are also sometimes assessed.

This information is fed into a computer program derived from a large number of epidemiological studies to yield an individual and group estimate of overall risk for the appearance of a number of serious health problems and related mortality over a defined future period, usually ten years. On a group basis prediction parameters are added, usually height, weight, total serum cholesterol, blood glucose and blood pressure.

REDUCIBILITY OF MAJOR HEALTH RISKS IN WORKSITE PROGRAMS

Even if one accepts the validity of predictions of future health based upon the risk profile, there remains the question of whether an employer-sponsored health promotion program can reduce those risks. Furthermore, will reductions of risk levels definitely translate into corresponding improvements in health? If so, how much time is required before improvements will be seen?

Demonstrations of reductions in known risk indicators associated with worksite health promotion programs are growing rapidly. A few examples are illustrative of the type of information available from such efforts.

Smoking

Twelve months after participating in a smoking cessation course sponsored by Control Data Corporation, 30.3 percent of employees reported not smoking, and a majority of those still smoking reported smoking less (Naditch 1984). A careful review of 22 formal, quantitative evaluations of worksite smoking cessation programs found that cessation results were similar to clinical smoking cessation programs, whose 6 to 12-month cessation rates usually range from 20 percent to 40 percent (Research Triangle Institute 1986). Johnson and Johnson's Live for Life program reports a 22 percent cessation rate over two years among all smokers at program sites, regardless of whether smokers formally participated in a smoking cessation program (Wilbur 1985). They attribute the results to a combination of formal smoking cessation programs, the institution of a smoking policy, and a large-scale communication campaign that stresses the benefits of quitting and urges peer support for those trying to quit.

The importance of smoking cessation for an employed population is underscored by the fact that smokers have an overall mortality rate during their middle years which is 1.7 to 2.1 times greater than nonsmokers (Fielding 1985).

Hypertension

The highest rates of control of high blood pressure reported in the medical literature are from worksite sponsored programs. For example, Massachusetts Mutual Life Insurance Company reported that a voluntary on-site blood pressure screening, referral, and follow-up program for their employees led to an increase in the percentage of hypertensive employees under control from 36 percent to 82 percent (National High Blood Pressure Education Program 1980).

A carefully controlled study in four automobile manufacturing plants screened 66 percent to 83 percent of the total working population at the four sites. After three years, of those originally found to have high blood pressure, and either referred to their doctor and careful follow-up or given on-site treatment, 86 percent to 90 percent had blood pressures below 160/95 mm Hg and 56 percent to 62 percent had readings below 140/90 (Foote and Erfurt 1983).

Seat Belt Use

A program to increase seat belt usage for employees of the Radford Ammunition Plant gave local restaurant tickets and tickets to the local university basketball games to employees chosen at random from among those observed using their safety belts as they entered the parking lot. Observed mean usage rates increased from 6.7 preprogram to 23.1 percent while the incentive program was in effect and were at 16.3 percent about one month after the special program ended (Geller 1982).

A similar program with a stronger educational component was launched by Teletype Corporation for approximately 1,500 employees. Based on direct observation, usage increased from 5 percent to 20 percent for blue-collar workers and from 19 percent to 38 percent for white-collar workers. One month after a second program, mean seat belt usage was 38 percent for blue-collar and 51 percent for white-collar workers (Geller 1982).

Stress Management

A controlled trial of a stress management program for workers found program participation was strongly associated with significant reductions in total blood cholesterol levels, cigarette smoking, and both systolic and diastolic blood pressures (Patel, Marmot, and Terry 1981). Many carefully developed studies, summarized in several recent papers, have shown stress management programs to lead to reductions of stress symptoms, visits to employer sponsored health facilities, absenteeism, (McLeroy et al. 1984; Murphy 1984) and problems with supervisors.

Not all reports of success in the literature are well documented. Some suffer from poor experimental design, lack of objective measurement of results, and limited information on the nature of the program. However, the consistency of results from different worksite settings is striking and strongly suggests that a well-designed, carefully planned program can be successful in ameliorating known risks for serious health problems.

Does reducing risk levels translate into reduced health problems? For example, does a hypertensive whose treated blood pressure is 120/80 have the same risk as his co-worker with the same blood pressure naturally. And how quickly does reduction of blood pressure lead to a reduction of risk for stroke and for heart and kidney problems?

For almost all risks that can be reduced in theory, the answer is that risk reduction leads to reduced illness, disability, and age-specific death rates. For example, blood pressure reduction in hypertensives yields a reduction in risk to a level roughly commensurate with the level attained. Excluded from this are those employees who may already have kidney or heart damage due to their elevated blood pressure. But the vast majority of hypertensives identified have at the time of identification no permanent changes based upon their condition. The fact that most life insurance companies provide coverage to hypertensives under adequate control without any surcharge is strong evidence for the reduction in risk (National Heart and Lung Institute 1975).

Ex-cigarette smokers eliminate their excess risk of heart attack within two years of quitting, and slowly reduce their excess risk of lung and other cancers over a 15-year period (Fielding 1985). Reduction in total serum cholesterol leads to a reduction in heart attacks and deaths from coronary heart disease over a period of several years.

Evidence is also increasing that some risk reduction programs may be more effective when sponsored through the worksite than when provided through the more usual clinical setting. For example, one multiyear study of hypertension screening and control reported a 48 percent drop out rate for those referred to clinics but only a 12 percent drop out rate for those in a worksite treatment program. In the same study 75 percent of hypertensives were able to achieve a reasonable level of control compared to 33 percent and 29 percent for clinics and physician offices (Alderman 1984).

The percentage of those with a particular health risk who are willing to enroll in a worksite sponsored risk reduction program can be quite high if the program is properly designed and promoted. Competitions for results appear particularly attractive. For example, at a worksite with approximately 2,000 employees, average enrollment in a weight management class was 20 to 30 while a weight loss competition pitting different divisions of the company against each other for only minimal financial incentives but a considerable amount of recognition drew close to 200 participants (Fielding 1985). A healthy smoking cessation competition among four competitive banks led to 88 percent of all smokers participating with 91 percent of these completing the program (Klesges and Glasgow 1986). The ability to achieve high participation and success rates in worksite sponsored health promotion programs suggests that for some health risks these programs may be both more efficient and effective than reliance on an individual's usual source of health care.

No randomized controlled experiment to determine whether those who begin exercising have a lower heart disease rate has yet been reported. However, the indirect evidence for such an effect is very strong. Middle-aged Harvard alumni who expend fewer than 2,000 calories in reportable physical activities a week have a 64 percent greater risk of having a first heart attack than their classmates who exercise more (Paffenbarger, Wing, and Hyde 1978). This effect is independent of whether they were athletes as students. Those unathletic in college do as well as the college athletic heroes if they exercise later in life. Conversely, having been a conditioned athlete in college provides no protection for those who do not continue a regular exercise program.

Reduction in obesity is associated with reduced blood pressure and total serum cholesterol; both are important risks for cardiovascular disease (Sorlie, Gordon, and Kannel 1980).

HEALTH PROMOTION AND EMPLOYER
HEALTH RELATED COSTS

Demonstrations that important health risks can be controlled through worksite sponsored programs leave financially oriented managers asking whether these changes in health outcomes can be equated with changes in health costs. Two types of evidence support such a conclusion. The first is application of simple logic. Given the convincing evidence that risks for serious diseases can be reduced and that the risks are causally related to problems costly to employers, such as heart disease, cancer, stroke, and injuries, one can predict a reduction in these events by knowing the pre- and post-program risk levels.

For example, Table 20.1 demonstrates the expected decline in adverse health effects if employee aggregate risks are reduced to specified attainable levels. Translating the reduced incidence of serious health problems into dollars is made more difficult by limited employer specific information on the cost of each event, such as a heart attack or a case of colon cancer. Few employers have accurately determined the cost of a heart attack in an employee of average salary and value to the organization. In the absence of exact numbers, reasonable estimates can be developed by reference to health care claims data, as well as records of absenteeism, disability, and workers' compensation claims. Using this approach, for example, an estimate of the average cost of a heart attack might be within a broad range of $25,000 to $100,000. Applying this to the number of heart attacks avoided through preventive efforts, an estimate of savings can be developed and a return on investment, in net present value terms, determined.

TABLE 20.1
Expected and Achievable Numbers of Deaths and Serious Health Problems over Next Ten Years for the XYZ Company

Category	Current Number	Percent of Average Risk	Achievable Number	Possible Reduction
Motor vehicle deaths	11	140	2	9
Heart attacks	110	130	67	43
Heart attack deaths	52	130	32	20
Strokes	33	110	27	6
Stroke deaths	11	110	9	2
Cancer deaths	24	120	16	8

Source: Compiled by the author.

The second type of evidence comes from a growing number of reports of the effects of worksite programs on elements of employer health costs. A few of these reports present the relationship between programs and health benefit costs. For example, a back injury prevention program by Capitol Wire showed a decline in worker's compensation costs from $108,000 for a total of 478,000 manhours in 1980 to $4,900 for 462,000 manhours in 1983, a 95 percent reduction (Morris 1984). Johnson and Johnson have presented data that the aggregate health care costs per employee in sites with their Live for Life program are significantly reduced compared to the control sites over a period of several years (Wilbur 1985).

The majority of reports, however, treat indirect health related costs, such as absenteeism. For example, a controlled study of teachers in Dallas found that those enrolling in an aerobic exercise program reported being absent 1.25 days fewer on average than the control group during the study period, despite comparable absenteeism among groups before the study (Blair, Jacobs, and Powell 1985). High adherers to an exercise program at a Toronto insurance company experienced a 42 percent decline in average monthly absenteeism compared to a 20 percent decline in both the test company overall and a control insurance company in the same city (Cox, Shephard, and Corey 1981). Seamonds found a significant reduction in absenteeism among employees who had a single stress management counseling session (Seamonds 1982).

Abundant reports exist from employee assistance programs (EAP) helping employees with alcohol and other chemical abuse problems. AT&T reviewed the work records of 150 employees referred to their EAP for two years before and two years after program referral. They reported dramatic improvements in absenteeism, tardiness, use of company medical facilities, and performance based upon supervisor judgment. On-the-job accidents declined from 36 in the two years before referral to five in the two succeeding years. At a conservative cost estimate of $4,000 a accident, savings from reduction in this accident rate saved the company over $100,000 (Occupational Hazards 1983).

General Motors reports that during the first year after entry into an employee assistance program, grievances and disciplinary actions against participants were reduced by about 50 percent, sickness and accident benefits by 60 percent, lost time by 40 percent, and on-the-job accidents by 50 percent. They estimated a three-year return of $2 to $3 for every dollar invested (Murphy 1979).

Despite the number of reports of impressive program results, the current evidence stops short of proof beyond a shadow of a doubt that investment in these programs will provide an acceptable return from a strictly financial point of view. The reports, both published and unpublished, have common limitations. First, only a limited number of studies, particularly in the use of control groups, have rigorous design.

Also some employers provided reports without the raw data from which researchers could reach independent conclusions or validate the company statements of results. Critics argue that those responsible for program operation within a company have a vested interest in stating encouraging results and may not have used the most rigorous analytic techniques in developing their conclusion.

Additionally, programs addressing the same health risk may be considerably different. A fitness program at one company may consist of the provision of showers and lockers without any supervision or organized activities. Another company's fitness program may sport a full gymnasium, with full staffing and extended hours of operation, as well as an on-site laundry service and a full slate of organized group activities for different sports and skill levels. Comparing results of these two programs is difficult.

The results of one program or group of programs have been extrapolated to the entire range of employers that might adopt similar programs. Such extrapolation, especially given the diversity of work forces and corporate cultures, truly presents problems. Can the results obtained in a manufacturing company with average age 48 and a 70 percent male work force be extrapolated to a retail operation with an average age of 29 and a 65 percent female work force?

And finally, few long-term studies have been done. Much of what has been reported covers a period of several months to several years, leaving questions about residual effects of programs over time.

REASONS FOR OBSERVED PROGRAM GROWTH

The absence of proof of savings does not appear to have deterred many employers from initiating health promotion programs for their employees. A 1982 survey of a random sample of California worksites with 100 or more employees found that, of respondents, 18.6 percent provided substance abuse programs, 18.4 percent mental health counseling, 13.0 percent stress management, 11.6 percent fitness, 10.1

hypertension screening, and 8.3 percent smoking cessation. Of particular interest was that the rate of initiation of new health promotion activities had grown at an exponential rate. One-half of all the cited activities had been established within the four years before the survey (Fielding and Breslow 1983). Preliminary results from a large nationwide random sample of worksites with 100 or more employees conducted in 1985 found that 51 percent of respondents had one or more health promotion activities. Provision of informational material only was not considered a health promotion activity for purposes of this study (Fielding 1986). Of worksites with 50–99 employees, approximately one-third were reported to provide one or more health promotion activities, using the same query method and program definition.

Employers are thus increasingly providing health promotion programs for their employees, and program growth rates appear quite high and even perhaps exponential. Reasons for such rapid growth are conjectural, but interviews with senior company officers as well as considerable anecdotal reports suggest four main contributing factors.

Improved employee morale is the first factor. There is a concensus that a well-run program has a major positive influence on employee morale. The financial effect of improved morale is difficult to quantify, but most senior executives feel it is worth a considerable investment to achieve. Employee evaluation of the Johnson and Johnson Live for Life program revealed a marked improvement in morale and job satisfaction in the intervention sites compared to the controls (Wilbur 1982). Employees of many companies sponsoring programs often cite the personal benefits they have achieved through participation and thank the company for showing through the program that it cares about each employee as an individual.

Second executives are willing to buy the value of organizational sponsorship of health promotion based on evidence of health effectiveness even if the question of return on investment remains open. In business, most decisions are made upon limited information. If the results of every decision could be virtually assured before it was made, there would be limited need for highly paid decision makers who are valued for their judgment under conditions of uncertainty. For example, IBM has implemented a wide ranging health promotion program entitled "A Plan for Life" and made it available to all employees, dependents, and retirees. After considerable discussion about the potential benefit of evaluating program impact on health habits and health related costs, it was decided that there was enough evidence to support a benefit to employer and program participants without the need for further study (Dickerson and Mandelblit 1983).

Third, competitive factors are causing many employers to ask themselves whether current and prospective employees will consider them progressive or a good place to work in the absence of worksite health improvement programs. For example, in the aerospace industry in southern California, many of the companies competing for engineers feel that the presence of health improvement programs is important for attracting and retaining engineers in a tight labor market. Some employers feel that having a program helps them to be considered an industry leader, at least with respect to personnel and benefit policies and programs.

Finally, a program often arises from a personal tragedy. A senior vice president who falls victim to a stroke that, in the opinion of his doctor, could have been prevented impels many a senior corporate officer to look at opportunities for the company to forestall further preventable mishaps. For example, a large engineering and construction company began a smoking cessation program within weeks after the chairman of the board, a long-time heavy smoker, was diagnosed as having lung cancer.

LINGERING QUESTIONS

While awaiting definitive evidence of a positive benefit to cost ratio, most worksites have established or appear to be on the verge of adopting some type of program to improve the health of their employees. Many questions remain about the most effective types of methodologies, how to maintain program momentum, appropriate communication techniques to encourage high levels of participation, and the permanence and effect of observed changes on known risks. Perhaps equally important, the degree to which programs should concentrate on the hard risks versus more subjective but also important health related characteristics, such as cheerfulness, feeling of fulfillment, humor, positive self-image, and others, needs to be carefully assessed. The fact that many employers are uncertain of program benefits and yet want to see whether the results of studies from other settings apply to their own employee group is necessary, if these employers are to fund research which may ultimately fill the holes in our current knowledge. The degree of employer willingness to use internal resources to perform rigorous internal studies or to cooperate with outside researchers will determine whether many basic questions are answered during the next decade.

REFERENCES

Alderman, M. H. "Worksite treatment of Hypertension." In *Behavioral Health: A Handbook of Health Enhancement and Disease Prevention,* edited by J. D. Matarazzo et al. New York: John Wiley and Sons, 1984.

Blair, S. D. Jacobs, Jr., and K. Powell. "Relationships between Exercise or Physical Activity and Other Health Behaviors. *Public Health Reports* 100 (1985): 172–80.

Control Data Corporation. *StayWell Evaluation Results.* 1984, unpublished.

Cox, M., R. J. Shephard, and P. Corey. "Influence of an Employee Fitness Programme upon Fitness Productivity and Absenteeism. *Ergonomics* 24 (1981): 795–806.

Dickerson, O. B., and C. Mandelblit. "A New Model for Employer Provided Health Education Programs." *Journal of Occupational Medicine.* 1983, pp. 471–74.

Fielding, J. "Effectiveness of Employee Health Improvement Programs. *Journal of Occupational Medicine* 24 (1982): 907–16.

———. *Corporate Health Management.* Reading, Massachusetts: Addison-Wesley, 1984.

———. "Smoking: Health Effects and Control, Part 1." *New England Journal of Medicine* 313 (1985): 491–98.

———. "Weight Loss Competition: Participation and Results at a Worksite." Unpublished paper, 1985.

Fielding, J. E. Preliminary report on national worksite health promotion program survey, under contract to Office of Disease Prevention and Health Promotion, DHHS, in progress, 1986.

Fielding, J. E., and L. Breslow. "Health Promotion Programs Sponsored by California Employers." *American Journal of Public Health* 73 (1983): 538–42.

Foote, A., and J. Erfurt. "Hypertension Control at the Worksite." *New England Journal of Medicine* 308 (1983): 809–13.

Geller, E. Scott. *Corporate Incentives for Promoting Safety Belt Use: Rationale, Guidelines and Examples.* Final report for NHTSA contract, Department of Transportation, 1982.

Goldberger, L., and S. Brezwitz (eds.) *Handbook of Stress.* New York: The Free Press, 1982.

"How Two Companies Curb Drug Abuse." *Occupational Hazards* 45 (1983): 93–96.

Kelsey, J., and M. Hochberg. "Epidemiology and Prevention of Musculoskeletal Disorders." In *Public Health and Preventive Medicine*, 12th ed., edited by John M. Last. Norwalk, Connecticut: Appleton-Century-Crofts, 1986, pp. 1277–95.

Klesges, R. C., and R. E. Glasgow. "Smoking Modification at the Worksite." In *Health Promotion in Industry: A Behavioral Medicine Perspective*, edited by M. F. Cataldo and T. J. Coates, New York: Wiley, 1986.

McLeroy, K., L. Green, K. Mullen, and V. Foshee. "Assessing the Effects of Health Promotion in Worksites: A Review of Stress Program Evaluations. *Health Education Quarterly* 11 (1984): 379–401.

Morris, Alan. "Program Compliance — Keys to Preventing Low Back Injuries." *Occupational Health and Safety*, 1984, pp. 44–47.

Murphy, L. "Occupational Stress Management: A Review and Appraisal." *Journal of Occupational Psychology* 57 (1984): 1–15.

Murphy, T. A. Remarks by Chairman, General Motors Corporation, October 5, 1979, at the Association of Labor-Management Administrators and Consultants on Alcoholism, Inc., San Diego, California.

Naditch, M. "The STAYWELL Program." In *Behavioral Health: A Handbook of Health Enhancement and Disease Prevention*, edited by J. D. Matarazzo et al. New York: John Wiley, 1984, pp. 1071–78.

National Heart and Lung Institute. *The Underwriting Significance of Hypertension for the Life Insurance Industry.* DHEW Publication No. (NIH) 75-426, 1975.

National High Blood Pressure Education Program. At Mass. Mutual Off-site Care and Good Monitoring Reduce Medical Costs, *Re: High Blood Pressure Control in the Worksetting.* National Heart, Lung, and Blood Institute, DHHS, 1980.

Paffenbarger, R. S., A. L. Wing, and R. T. Hyde. "Physical Activity as an Index of Heart Attack Risk in College Alumni. *American Journal of Epidemiology*, 108 (1978): 161–75.

Patel, C., M. Marmot, and D. Terry. "Controlled Trial of Biofeedback-Aided Behavioral Methods in Reducing Mild Hypertension." *British Medical Journal* 282 (1981): 2005–8.

Research Triangle Institute, University of Texas Center for Health Promotion Research and Development, and Project Hope. "Evaluations of Worksite Smoking Cessation Programs." Washington, D.C. Office of Disease Prevention and Health Promotion, DHHS. Unpublished preliminary contract report, 1986.

Seamonds, B. "Stress Factors and Their Effect on Absenteeism in a Corporate Employee Group." *Journal of Occupational Medicine* 24 (1982): 393–97.

Sorlie, M. T. Gordon, and W. Kannel. "Body Build and Mortality." *Journal of the American Medical Association* 243 (1980): 1828–31.

Tyroler, H. "Hypertension." In *Public Health and Preventive Medicine*, 12th ed., edited by John M. Last, Norwalk, Connecticut: Appleton-Century-Crofts, 1986.

Wilbur, C. S. *Live for Life: An Epidemiological Evaluation of a Comprehensive Health Promotion Program.* New Brunswick, Johnson & Johnson. Unpublished, 1982.

Wilbur, C. Personal communications, November 1985.

21 Comprehensive Evaluation of a Worksite Health Promotion Program: The StayWell Program at Control Data

David R. Anderson and William S. Jose II

The growth of worksite health promotion activities over the past decade has been truly dramatic. Much of this growth has been fueled by increasing awareness among employers that the cost of ill health is a major threat to the bottom line and that much of this ill health is directly attributable to controllable lifestyle risk factors. The widely documented magnitude of these costs (Cooper and Rice 1976; Fielding 1979) indicated to employers that the long-term return on investment in an effective health promotion program could be favorable. However, a large-scale worksite health promotion program is a major investment, and, as with any such financial commitment, management requires periodic reports on results. Continued funding decisions typically depend on positive indicators of program effectiveness at each major stage of implementation.

An important role of evaluation is to provide periodic indicators of program effectiveness. This role has been the focus of most published evaluation results of worksite health promotion programs. Many companies have reported substantial health behavior and risk change and cost savings from their health promotion programs (for example, Berry 1981; LeRoux 1981; Shephard, Cox, and Corey 1981). Unfortunately, most of these evaluation reports are based on preliminary, short-term, often correlational, results combined with numerous assumptions about related cost savings, rather than on systematic long-term evaluation (Fielding 1984a).

An equally important and often overlooked role of evaluation is to provide ongoing information that helps assure the ultimate success of each stage of program implementation. Such evaluation is critical to help program administrators assess organizational needs, design programs to best meet these needs, refine their initial design based on early feedback, and maintain a spirit of ownership and involvement in the program. The frequent tendency to neglect this role of evaluation, which ideally begins with the initial decision to consider a health promotion program, greatly reduces the likelihood of its ultimate success.

This paper describes the evaluation being done by Control Data of the StayWell health promotion program. From the program's beginning in 1979, this evaluation was planned as a comprehensive and systematic ten-year effort and was adequately funded to fulfill both important roles described above. This major commitment to evaluation by Control Data management was motivated partly by their determination to develop a successful program that would improve the health and productivity of Control Data employees and reduce the company's illness-related costs. A second important motivating factor was the extra burden of proof of program effectiveness required by the intent to market the StayWell program to external organizations.

STAYWELL PROCESS MODEL

Any effective program evaluation assumes the existence of a model of the process to be evaluated. Very early in the design of the StayWell program, evaluation efforts were guided by a behavior change model that was overly simplistic because it assumed that attitude and knowledge change were the necessary and sufficient conditions for behavior change. The assumption was that once knowledge was gained and attitudes correctly formed, the consonant behavior could automatically follow. This assumption led to a focus on imparting knowledge and changing attitudes rather than a more sophisticated behavior change approach guided by contemporary theory and research (Mischel 1973; Fishbein and Ajzen 1975; Bandura 1977a, 1977b; Walker and Thomas 1982). Early in the evolution of the program, it was realized that this model was inadequate. The revised process model that currently guides our design and evaluation is outlined in Figure 21.1.

The current model assumes that initial attitude change, knowledge change, and behavior change are correlated in an unspecified manner because of the effect of the program. Then, to the extent that these initial changes are evaluated positively by the individual and supported by the

FIGURE 21.1
StayWell Process Model

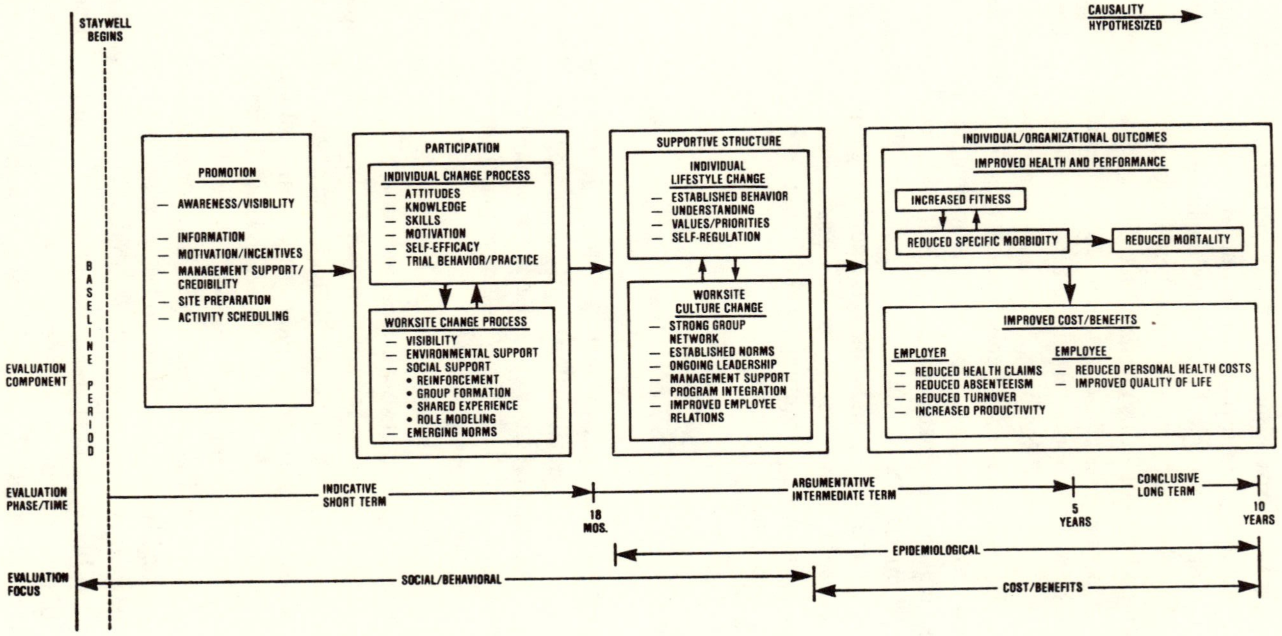

Source: Control Data Corporation.

286

environment, the changes will be maintained and incorporated into the individual's lifestyle on a more long-term basis. This model acknowledges the inherent long-term nature of the behavior change process and emphasizes the importance of environmental components including both social support and physical worksite alterations (Parsons, Bales, and Shils 1953; Homans 1961).

The authors believe the model is comprehensive in its treatment of the behavior change process, in that it encompasses individual knowledge, skills, and attitudes, incorporates a behavior change process, and emphasizes both internal and external reinforcers in establishing long-term behavioral changes. In addition, it models the linkage between behavior changes and reductions in risk factors that lower morbidity and mortality, thus reducing employer costs.

The current model has implications for design and evaluation that are substantially different from the original model. Three of the most significant changes in the program precipitated by this model are focusing courses on behavior change rather than knowledge and attitude change, incorporating social support formally into the program through the vehicle of action teams, and calling attention to the critical importance of the physical worksite environment.

STAYWELL PROGRAM

History of Implementation

Implementation of the StayWell program at Control Data began in pilot form in 1979. Systematic phasing in of the program to sites throughout the company began in 1980. Evaluation activities in the next few years led to the refinements of the original process model and to numerous alterations in the program. By mid-1983 the company had achieved a mature program ready for evaluation of long-term outcomes. Most significantly, by this time courses had been revised based on evaluation results, and the action team concept had been developed and implemented. By the end of 1984 the StayWell program had been introduced at sites encompassing from 75 percent to 80 percent of Control Data's U.S. employees, further preparing the evaluation to focus on issues of long-term outcome.

In addition to the internal implementation of the StayWell program, Control Data sells the program directly to a number of corporate customers. The StayWell program is also delivered to additional corporations through a nationwide network of authorized distributors that market and deliver the program in defined territories.

Current Program Description

The StayWell program currently consists of a number of discrete, but interrelated components:

Employee Health Survey to provide population level data
Preimplementation site planning and management orientation
Orientation sessions that explain the program to prospective participants
    and invite them to enroll
Health Risk Profile and screening
Health Risk Profile interpretation session
Instructor-led Lifestyle Change courses
Self-study Lifestyle Change courses
PLATO computer-based Lifestyle Change courses
Action teams, ongoing employee-led groups focused on specific wellness
    activities or worksite issues
Special events, periodic promotions highlighting specific wellness ideas
    or concerns.

Major lifestyle risk factors addressed by the program and monitored in the evaluation include exercise, weight, cholesterol, smoking, hypertension, and seat belt use. The Health Risk Profile identifies for participants their level of risk in each of these areas and tells how specific behavior change affects their overall risk.

Courses to address lifestyle risk factors are currently available in fitness, smoking cessation, managing stress, nutrition, weight reduction, and back care.

Each component has been designed so that it can stand alone and still have a demonstrable effect. However, when these components are used together in the context of a comprehensive program they seem to work synergistically (Fielding 1984b). While this observation has not been formally evaluated, existing data suggest that this interconnection produces a net program impact substantially greater than might be expected based on the performance of individual components. This is consistent with the process model because the implementation of a comprehensive program serves to alter the corporate culture of the worksite relative to health-related knowledge, beliefs, and practices. The altered corporate culture then supports norms directed toward healthy, risk-reducing activities, thereby increasing the probability of successful long-term behavior change.

STAYWELL PROGRAM EVALUATION

Most health promotion programs have an evaluation component. The evaluation component of the StayWell program is unique, however, both in terms of its comprehensive scope and the corporate investment in it. A full-time department was funded from the beginning to plan and execute the evaluation. The evaluation plan has addressed virtually every aspect of the StayWell program. Issues representative of the broad base of the evaluation include:

Employee participation patterns and rates
Spouse participation
Risk factor analysis
Program and behavioral adherence rates
Course evaluation
Instructor evaluation
Evaluation of media (instructor-led, self-study, PLATO computer-based
    education)
Evaluation of incentive plans
Evaluation of data collection techniques (for example, participation
    tracking, health diaries, surveys, biological measures, claims data)
Behavior change and maintenance
Illness-related costs (for example, health care claims, sick leave,
    disability, workers compensation, life insurance)
Program cost-impact modeling
Customer support
Marketing support.

Formative and Summative Evaluation

In comprehensive program evaluations where elements of the evaluation take place over a wide time span, it is often useful to formulate the evaluation plan in terms of the concepts of formative and summative evaluation (Morris and Fitz-Gibbon 1978; Wechsler 1984). For purposes of the StayWell evaluation, formative evaluation refers to the more short-term outcomes related to changes in an individual's attitudes, perceptions, and behaviors. It also includes evaluation of process elements of the program such as the efficacy of courses, effectiveness of personnel, program promotion, and other aspects of implementation. Summative evaluation refers to the long-term outcomes related to risk reduction and cost-benefit analysis.

Evaluation Objectives

As Green et al. (1980) have noted, one must move from the lower-level, immediate concepts and process concerns that can be evaluated in the short run (that is, formative evaluation) to the more long-term goals of risk reduction and cost impact analysis (that is, summative evaluation). Accordingly, a systematic evaluation was planned to address the many issues of interest in a logical, sequential order. While the range of StayWell evaluation activities has been enormous and varied, all of these activities can be organized under four broad objectives:

To assess need in the eligible population for specific program components and implementation strategies
To evaluate the overall process to develop and refine the program, including participant reactions, course effects, course completion rates, and changes in participant knowledge, attitudes, skills, and behaviors
To assess the effect of behavior change on risk factors
To assess the cost-benefit impact of the StayWell program.

The first two objectives address issues related to formative evaluation. The third and fourth objectives are long-term concerns of summative evaluation.

Evaluation Design

The theoretically ideal approach to evaluating the effect of any treatment or intervention is a true experimental design. Carefully planned research using true experimental designs allows strong causal interpretations to be made because these designs eliminate alternative explanations for group differences. However, it was not generally possible to use true experimental designs for evaluating the StayWell program; individual participation is voluntary, entry of individuals into the program is not controlled, and implementation sites were not determined randomly. In fact, experience gained through this evaluation suggests that true experimental designs in a long-term, real-world program like StayWell are almost inherently obtrusive and fraught with demand characteristics (Orne 1962). Such problems make their use questionable in most circumstances similar to those confronted in the StayWell evaluation.

Although a true experimental design was not possible, a number of alternative approaches for evaluating the impact of the StayWell program were utilized. These approaches or designs are called quasi-experimental because, although they have many characteristics in common with true experimental designs, they do not permit the certainty of causal inference of a true experimental design (Cook and Campbell 1979).

Each of these quasi-experimental designs has certain inherent weaknesses (for example, nonrandom sampling, self-selection into treatments, lack of adequate comparison groups), which leaves results of individual designs supporting StayWell impact open to alternative causal explanations (for example, history, selection, mortality, regression). Consequently, the strategy for evaluating the StayWell program has been to use a variety of quasi-experimental designs both within and across specific evaluation studies. Specific designs have included matched sites, pre-post, time-series and multiple time-series. The rationale underlying this strategy is that, although each design has certain inherent weaknesses, the specific weaknesses vary across designs. Thus, to the extent that results using a number of designs all support the same conclusions, a fairly strong causal inference can be made.

MULTIPLE LEVELS OF ANALYSIS

Evaluation of the StayWell program focused on several levels of analysis and addressed questions specific to each level. Three levels of analysis were identified: course, individual, and corporate.

Course-Level Analysis

At the course level of analysis, formative evaluation questions related to the acceptance and effectiveness of the course were addressed.

Courses were evaluated by participants on a pre-and post-course basis and, where feasible, after one year. Questions addressed included: did participants like the course? Did they think the content was appropriate to their needs? Did they learn helpful skills? Did they intend to make any changes in their lifestyle or behavior? How successful were they in actually making and maintaining desired changes (one-year follow-up)?

As a result of this type of course-level analysis, major modifications were made to the StayWell instructor-led Lifestyle Change courses. Early courses, it was discovered, relied too much on mere dissemination of information. Analysis revealed that participants wanted a more "how to" orientation. In the absence of such a skills-oriented approach, it was found that the desired behavior and lifestyle changes were not taking place. In addition, completion rates were quite low for the initial set of courses.

In 1983, redesigned courses were piloted. Striking results in the desired direction were noted. The overall completion rate went from 52 percent with the original courses to 81 percent with the newly designed courses. Behavior change and satisfaction with the courses also increased.

The course-level analysis was carried out systematically over the years, and the course modifications that resulted created a high level of confidence that the courses work. But courses that work, although of critical importance, are not the whole story in health promotion. Another critical ingredient is getting the eligible population, particularly those with one or more risk factors, to participate actively in the program. The individual-level analysis addresses this and related issues.

Individual-Level Analysis

At the individual level of analysis, answers were sought to questions related to participation levels and patterns of program involvement. Questions addressed at this level of analysis include: what are the relevant demographic characteristics of participants in each element of the program? Do individuals who participate actually lower their risk levels? Are individuals at risk actually joining the program? Are individuals participating in activities relevant to their needs and risk factors?

Several important findings resulted from investigations at this level of analysis. For example, comparing job types with degree of participation early in the program indicated that certain employee groups were not participating in courses. These job groups were sales, marketing, and customer service representatives, whose frequent travel makes it difficult for them to maintain regular participation in a course.

To meet the needs of these individuals, self-study courses were developed. The self-study courses, while missing the potentially motivating interaction of instructor-led courses, provide all the materials needed to assist a person in making positive lifestyle and behavior changes. As such, they are well suited for program delivery at small or remote sites where it is difficult or expensive to provide instructors. In addition, many individuals who do not like to attend courses or feel awkward in group discussions also found the self-study courses useful. Recent evaluation of the self-study courses indicate they are well liked by participants and effective in initiating behavior change. One-year follow-up evaluation of these courses is currently being planned.

To meet self-study needs in locations where computer access is available, computer-based interactive versions of the courses have been made available on the PLATO computer-based education system. The PLATO system provides individualized, self-paced instruction on demand. Evaluation to determine the viability and effectiveness of this alternative delivery mode is ongoing.

Action teams were added to the StayWell program to enhance and strengthen the social support and environmental components identified in the process model. The social support provided helps individuals maintain behavior changes initiated in the Lifestyle Change courses. This support is often essential in the early maintenance phase of behavior change. Analysis of individuals' reactions to action teams indicated that the most effective teams were not led by course instructors, but by co-workers. Leadership by employees created more of a sense of ownership and responsibility and, hence, more effective behavior change and maintenance of behavior change. As a result, all action teams are now employee-led and structured by employees to meet their specific needs. Because the support and reinforcement of positive behavior change is so important during the critical transition period between course completion and internally motivated, long-term lifestyle change, action teams are now considered an essential element in the success of the StayWell program. This support has helped reduce the widely reported recidivism of other programs with similar goals (Hung and Bespalec 1974; Morgan 1977; Volkmar et al. 1981).

Corporate-Level Analysis

At the corporate level of analysis, an effort is being made to answer questions related to outcome measures such as changes in employee attitudes and perceptions, risk factor change in the population, and program cost-benefit. Some issues appropriate at this level of analysis are the following: what are employee attitudes toward relevant corporate goals? What are employee perceptions of health-related changes in the worksite environment? How are illness-related costs related to risk factors? How are illness-related costs related to StayWell participation? How are illness-related costs affected by risk factor change? How cost-effective is the StayWell program, and what is its cost-benefit? As a comprehensive process? As individual program elements?

Some of the data required for corporate-level analysis were collected through annual corporate-wide employee surveys (Employee Attitude Survey, Employee Health Survey). However, much of the data necessary for the corporate-level analysis, particularly cost-benefit analysis, required the creation of a single data base to unify individually identifiable information captured and stored in several separate corporate data bases. The three primary sources of information for the StayWell evaluation data base are:

Employee personnel files
    Demographics
    Health care coverage
    StayWell eligibility information
    Sick leave usage and costs

Health care claims information
    Diagnosis
    Costs
    Hospitalization data

StayWell participation information
    Health Risk Profile results
    Detailed program participation records

Changes in employee attitudes and perceptions are short-range corporate-level questions for which answers are available. For example, it is known that the existence of the StayWell program at a worksite greatly increases employee perceptions that the company is supportive of good employee health practices. Among StayWell participants, 79 percent agreed that there was support at work for practicing a healthy lifestyle; only 42 percent of respondents at non-StayWell sites agreed with this statement. In addition, a "halo effect" was found at worksites where StayWell was implemented; 64 percent of those not participating in StayWell still agreed that there was lifestyle support at work. A similar pattern of responses emerged when respondents were asked if they agreed with the statement that co-workers were improving their health habits. Among StayWell participants, 42 percent agreed; 30 percent of the nonparticipants at StayWell sites agreed; but only 20 percent of the control site employees agreed. Both of these findings suggest that a change in cultural values and norms is occurring at StayWell sites, creating a worksite environment more conducive to positive behavior change.

Corporate-level questions related to risk factor change in the population and to program cost-benefit are inherently long-term questions, and many of the answers are not in yet. It is a fact, however, that high-risk individuals cost Control Data more in health care claims and absence due to illness than do low-risk individuals. Data relevant to risk factor change and cost-benefit questions are currently in the process of being analyzed. Some very preliminary cost impact results will be available in the coming months, and evaluation of the potential return on investment of the StayWell program will continue to increase rapidly as more data accumulates in the data base. However, knowledge of the full effects of the StayWell program on company illness-related costs and participant health and performance will still be emerging well into the 1990s.

CONCLUSION: EVALUATING THE STAYWELL EVALUATION

The unprecedented scope of the StayWell evaluation provided an ideal opportunity to learn a great deal not only about the StayWell program and how to maximize its effectiveness but also about how to evaluate worksite health promotion programs. Because the evaluation literature that existed when the StayWell evaluation began contained few practical guidelines to direct its course, most of the current evaluation expertise was gained through experience. Early in the history of the StayWell evaluation, significant time and resources were invested in several methodological approaches that, although very effective in appropriate circumstances, did not work well in the present context.

For example, one early approach was to use a matched site design to monitor program impact. However, it soon became apparent that in a dynamic organizational environment such as Control Data, with frequent employee transfers and organizational change, this evaluation design was not a viable long-term approach. Fortunately, data collection efforts had not been invested exclusively in a matched site that was subsequently divested. This experience made it clear that the frequent recommendation and use of matched site designs in the literature stem from the limited short-term scope of most other evaluations of worksite health promotion programs.

A second example of a valuable idea that did not succeed was an ambitious venture into the realm of health diaries (Verbrugge 1980). The intent of this ill-fated project was to gain an in-depth understanding of the interrelated health behaviors and morbidity experience of entire households and to determine the impact on household patterns of StayWell participation by individual members of the household and, conversely, the moderating influence of existing household patterns on StayWell participation and its effects. In fact, the health diary project did yield tremendously rich data on household health patterns. Unfortunately the multiple administrations of diaries required to evaluate the StayWell program became bothersome to participating households, and the increasing costs in incentives and staff follow-up required to maintain high participant cooperation soon overwhelmed the potential value of this project. Again, it was fortunate that not all the resources of the evaluation had been invested in this relatively unproductive methodology.

Despite some of these early setbacks, the substantial investment by Control Data in evaluating the StayWell program has been very rewarding. Valuable data has been collected by focusing on existing corporate data bases, keeping administrative procedures simple, and emphasizing easily quantifiable self-reports coupled with objective biological measures. An impressive body of findings has been accumulated (some of which C. R. Jones summarizes in Chapter 9 of this text supporting the efficacy of the StayWell program in addressing important health needs, attracting widespread employee involvement, and facilitating lasting lifestyle change. A unique data base that will support the successful long-term summative evaluation of the StayWell program has been developed and continues to expand. Perhaps most significant, the evaluation team has taken advantage of its accumulated experience by developing practical and effective tools (Anderson 1983; Peterson, Jose and Anderson 1985) that enable other organizations to assess their health promotion needs and evaluate program effectiveness.

REFERENCES

Anderson, D. R. "A Computer Simulation Approach to Projective Cost Analysis in Corporate Benefit Planning." Proceedings of the Nineteenth National Meeting of the Public Health Conference on Records and Statistics, August 1983. DHHS Publication No. (PHS) 81-1214.

Bandura, A. "Self-Efficacy: Toward a Unifying Theory of Behavioral Change." *Psychological Review* 84 (1977a): 191–215.

_____. *Social Learning Theory.* Englewood Cliffs, New Jersey: Prentice-Hall, 1977b.

Berry, C. A. *Good Health for Employees and Reduced Health Care Costs for Industry.* Washington, D.C.: Health Insurance Association of America, 1981.

Cook, T. D., and D. T. Campbell (eds.). *Quasi-Experimentation: Design and Analysis Issues for Field Settings.* Chicago: Rand McNally, 1979.

Cooper, B. S., and D. P. Rice. "The Economic Cost of Illness Revisited." *Social Security Bulletin,* February 1976, pp. 21–36.

Fielding, J. E. "Preventive Medicine and the Bottom Line." *Journal of Occupational Medicine* 21(1979): 79–88.

_____. *Corporate Health Management.* Reading, Massachusetts: Addison-Wesley, 1984a.

_____. "Evaluation of Worksite Health Promotion: Some Unresolved Issues and Opportunities." *Corporate Commentary* 1 (1984b): 9–15.

Fishbein, M. A., and I. Ajzen. *Relief, Attitude, Intention, and Behavior: An Introduction to Theory and Research.* Reading, Massachusetts: Addison-Wesley, 1975.

Green, L. W., M. W. Kreuter, S. G. Deeds, and K. B. Partridge. *Health Education Planning: A Diagnostic Approach.* Palo Alto, California: Mayfield, 1980.

Homans, G. C. *Social Behavior: Its Elementary Forms*. New York: Harcourt Brace, 1961.

Hunt, W. A., and D. R. Bespalec. "An Evaluation of Current Methods of Modifying Smoking Behavior." *Journal of Clinical Psychology* 30 (1974): 431–38.

LeRoux, M. "Cashing in on Wellness: Companies Discovering That Fitness Can Trim Soaring Health Care Costs." *Business Insurance*, September 21, 1981, pp. 1, 36–37.

Mischel, W. "Toward a Cognitive Social Learning Reconceptualization of Personality." *Psychological Review* 80 (1973): 252–83.

Morgan, W. P. "Involvement in Vigorous Activity with Special Reference to Adherence." In *National College of Physical Education Proceedings*, edited by L. I. Gedvilas and M. E. Kneer. Chicago: University of Illinois, Office of Public Service, 1977.

Morris, L. L, and C. T. Fitz-Gibbon. *Evaluator's Handbook*. Beverly Hills: Sage, 1978.

Orne, M. T. "On the Social Psychology of the Psychological Experiment: With Particular Reference to Demand Characteristics and Their Implications." *American Psychologist* 17 (1962): 776–83.

Parsons, T., R. F. Bales, and E. A. Shils. *Working Papers in the Theory of Action*. Glencoe, Illinois: Free Press, 1953.

Peterson, K. E., W. S. Jose II, and D. R. Anderson. "The Employee Health Survey: A Complement to Health Risk Appraisal." Paper presented at the meeting of the Society of Perspective Medicine, San Francisco, 1985.

Shephard, R. J., M. Cox, and P. Corey. "Fitness Program Participation: Its Effect on Worker Performance." *Journal of Occupational Medicine* 23 (1981): 359–63.

Verbrugge, L. M. "Health Diaries." *Medical Care* 18 (1980): 73–95.

Volkmar, F. R., A. J. Stunkard, J. Woolston, and R. A. Bailey. "High Attrition Rates in Commercial Weight Reduction Programs." *Archives of Internal Medicine* 141: 426–28.

Walker, L. R., and K. W. Thomas. "Beyond Expectancy Theory: An Integrative Motivational Model from Health Care." *Academy of Management Review* 7 (1982): 187–94.

Wechsler, W. D. "Program Evaluation." In *Health Promotion in the Workplace*, edited by M. P. O'Donnell and T. H. Ainsworth. New York: Wiley, 1984.

V
Critical Issues Relevant to Health Education Programs

Because programs of health education and fitness are ever growing and expanding in the many workplaces of our society, issues typically surface. Some issues may be resolved; others may be merely brought to our attention for reflection. However, if this discipline is to continue to evolve in a professional fashion, the critical issues must at least be addressed.

Derr tackles the challenge of attempting to differentiate three major program styles: health education, fitness, and wellness. He discusses the possible outcomes and potential problems of each particular program. He further points out that whatever program is established, it is important to create and communicate a corporate healthy lifestyle approach that meets the needs of both the employee and the employer.

A controversy that has surfaced repeatedly is whether health promotion programs reflect health care cost-containment strategies or human resource development projects. Edington calls our attention to this problem of motive and indicates that because health promotion programs are relatively new ventures for business and industry, their administrative locations are not consistent across organizations. This lack of consistency brings with it a clear difference in philosophical goals. He describes the major differences between the goals of health care cost containment and human resource development and further points out that these differences ultimately influence the long-term direction of health promotion programs. The conclusions seem to be that those programs that become integrated into the "cost of doing business" will achieve the most importance in the organization and will become ingrained into the "culture" of the organization.

When we think about health promotion, we usually conjure up approaches designed to affect our physical health and well-being. Backer broadens our perspective by suggesting that health promotion programs offer significant opportunities for enhancing individual and group creativity in the workplace. Relationships between worker health and creativity, however, have been little studied, and few existing health promotion programs are coordinated with whatever the organization may be doing in creativity development. He discusses how health promotion programs can be used to increase energy levels needed for creative work, to help workers cope with the special stresses of creativity, to prevent

301

burnout of creative personnel, and to offer alternate means of stimulating creative inspiration. As more scientific evidence emerges about the creative process and how to facilitate it, additional tie-ins between creativity and health promotion can be expected.

Employee fitness and lifestyle programs have been one of the most prominent topics of interest in occupational health settings. Cox critically examines employee fitness and lifestyle programs and indicates that, despite the lack of a sound scientific rationale, these programs have increased quickly over the last several years in North America. He provides summary information on the key issues facing corporations and individuals contemplating the establishment of these programs in the occupational environment. These issues include the present state of knowledge, the benefits of fitness and lifestyle programs, the cost effectiveness of employee fitness programs and the joining behavior and compliance of employees with these corporate sponsored programs.

Another program gaining increasing notability in the workplace is smoking control. Parkinson and Ericksen point out that the control of smoking in the workplace requires a knowledgeable and sensitive approach by today's business managers. The roots of the smoking problem are now clearly evident in the public health and epidemiologic research findings. They stress that given the adverse health effects associated with cigarette smoking and the fact that companies pay a major share of the medical and disability costs of employees and their dependents, it is of medical and economic interest for industries to search out viable means to control this problem. They precisely highlight the employee relations, legal, economic, and health promotion issues that companies are facing and review the potential strategies available for managing smoking in the workplace.

Because health promotion programs have grown so rapidly so, too, have the opportunities for employment. Many professionals from a variety of disciplines are competing for the opportunity to manage these programs. But, what about their training? Rotondo draws our attention to the issue of training. He indicates that a broad range of experience and skills is required and that only competent practitioners can direct these programs properly. He describes the necessary skills that a practitioner must have to provide a comprehensive health promotion program in the workplace. They include coordination and administration, promotion and marketing, clinical and program delivery, organizational development, evaluation and reporting, and supervisory and interpersonal skills.

After all is said and done, the final issue facing us is selecting a health promotion program. Powell points out that corporations have varied reasons for offering health promotion programs. Regardless of the reasons for deciding to conduct health promotion programs, many corporations are faced with a decision. It concerns the issue of the source of the programs. The company can either develop its own programs, or it can contract with an outside organization that already provides the particular service either with its own staff or trains others to do so. Powell indicates that many corporations choose to contract with an outside organization that offers wellness programs. For these companies it becomes extremely important that high-quality programs are selected. He delineates what criteria should be employed when evaluating health promotion programs. The topics he addresses include program content, program effectiveness, cost, program materials, marketing support, program training, quality control, and program updates.

22 The Difference between Health Education, Fitness, and Wellness Programs and the Importance of Communicating These Differences

W. Dennis Derr

INTRODUCTION

As various programs are developed by business and labor to address issues of employee healthy lifestyle, a crisis in the communication of program goals and objectives has developed.

This crisis is complicated by the numerous variations in program design, individual and public debate over what constitutes a healthy lifestyle, and the standards by which to measure it. For some people maintaining a desired weight within one of the many weight and height tables is considered healthy. Others claim standardized tables do not allow for big bones, body fat content, or muscle mass. The recent death of running guru Jim Fixx added fuel to the fire on the preventative benefits of running, and the tobacco industry continues its discounting of scientific findings connecting smoking to lung cancer and cardiovascular disease.

The average employee exposed to this plethora of conflicting health advice is justifiably confused by the sophisticated marketing and debate over health.

Healthy lifestyle is, to a great deal, dependent on individuals' perceptions, influenced by the sociological culture and subcultures in which they participate. For a business to create a health program promoting lifestyle changes among employees, it must first examine its options for communication and study the sociological culture bias and perceptions of its work force. Additionally it needs to create a program, goals, objectives, and identification that are acceptable within the corporate and sociological culture. Also it must effectively communicate the desired change to the population.

CULTURE AS A COMMUNICATIVE INFLUENCE

North America is a diverse area of blended cultures and norms. What is considered to be the norm in southern California may be unacceptable in the Midwest. Even with a shared common language regional dialects and cultural bias exist. These differences create different interpretations for identical words or phrases between individual health cultures.

A major conflict neglected in communicating an employee health program is requesting an individual to participate in a lifestyle change when the culture in which they work and live will not support their endeavor toward change. When individuals or small groups attempt change within a nonsupportive environment, they face high levels of frustration and feelings of failure.

To begin bringing about a revolution in health related lifestyles, attention must be given to the health culture of employees rather than focusing exclusively on the individual. Cultural norms of our sociological environments determine, to a large extent, what we do or do not do regarding health. These cultural norms influenced by individual perception of our cultural group (ethnic background, workplace, work status, community religious beliefs) offer shared expectations and standards for health lifestyle behaviors and information processing. In certain cultural or family groups, overeating is expected, a sign of love and respect for the food preparer. To diet is not understood culturally neither are the long-term effects of overeating.

Allen (1980), in a discussion of corporate health programs, suggests that health norms can be valued as either positive or negative, enhancing our state of health or detracting from it. To measure the value of health norms, Allen recommends use of a survey instrument entitled "The Lifegain Health Practices Indicator." The survey measures perceptions of individuals or a corporations normative influences that interfere with positive health practices. By responding yes or no to a statement, that is, "For people to be a few pounds overweight," of a positive or negative health norm that relates to one or more of their cultural groups, people can present a valuable view of cultural influences.

To a large extent, society and the subcultures created by corporations are influenced by an acceptance of negative health practices. Despite overwhelming evidence of the lifesaving aspects of auto seat belts, few regularly use them. The norm for many is negative; despite indisputable evidence, they ignore the safe choice, that is "to buckle up." Individuals attempting recovery from alcoholism face a difficult road as the society, through the media, encourages consumption of alcohol.

It is a cultural belief that individuals change solely on their own, the "up by the bootstrap" thought process. Economically deprived individuals are viewed as unable to gather the inner strength and fortitude to change their situation. Putting responsibility solely on the self is a cultural bias that fails to recognize the most important of human needs, "companionship."

In health lifestyle education a similar belief system often inhibits success. "Fit," "well," or "illness-free" individuals criticize the "unfit," viewing their condition as a personal failure of inner strength or weakness. This lack of support toward change goes beyond the individuals to be translated into whole cultures. Through various messages a corporation can be viewed as nonsupportive. To sponsor or encourage weight loss among employees while the company cafeteria pushes greasy, high-calorie food selections offers conflicting values for individual change. Sponsoring smoking cessation classes on the worksite without addressing nonsmokers' rights in the corporate smoking policy ensures a high recidivism among participants. Without organizational support beyond the traditional initial brochure, business health programs will fail. When health education and motivational activities toward behavioral change are presented in a nonsupportive culture (corporation), they are as successful as an obese person holding in his or her stomach to look thinner. Very quickly the little available support fails, and the individual returns, tired and discouraged, to the original shape. Support must be reflected in all aspects of the employee's culture.

DEFINING PROGRAM FOCUS

Corporate health programs promoting lifestyle changes come with numerous titles. These titles range from catchy names, "Health Love," "Love Life," "Health Wise," "Fit-Life," "Health & Wealth," to more direct names, "Wellness," "Fitness," or "Health Promotion." If a program has a subtitle, it often defines a program's focus as either a wellness, fitness, or health promotion program, reflecting the program objectives.

Because most programs fall into one of these categories, it is important to explore the common definitions, similarities, differences, and possible perceptions of what a program may provide.

Public or corporate health education and promotion programs have existed as long as public concern over individual or general health issues has existed. Based on the familiar public health model, the underlying belief of these programs is that by informing an employee of a specific health issue through educational materials, seminars, or direct advertising, a change in behavior will take place. These public service announcements, "PSAs," as classified by the media, are the familiar advertisements of late night T.V. encouraging us to lose weight, check our blood pressure, or buckle up for safety.

Corporate health education programs often take a similar approach. Although corporations may personalize programs by offering individual or small group discussion with a nurse educator or other professional, the underlying premise is that participants or recipients will gain new and motivational insight regarding their own health through one or more of the following areas:

educational brochures, films, or posters regarding individual risk factors such as smoking, obesity, dietary habits, and exercise

films and posters advocating self-identification and self-scoring of health risk factors, often including lifestyle recommendations to eliminate or reduce risk factors

ongoing educational materials through the various corporate communicative media or mailings

educational lectures or seminars led by health professionals during work or nonwork time periods.

This approach can be considered very productive. The change in percentages of Americans smoking cigarettes since the first 1964 Surgeon General's Report on Smoking and Health is the simplest example. The public response to realizing a connection between smoking and lung cancer resulted in a significant drop in the numbers of smokers during the past 20 years (1984 Surgeon General's Report). Obviously not all the credit can go to the 1964 report or warnings on cigarette packaging. Numerous public and private organizations began offering assistance, motivation, and support to quit smoking, and, most recently, the cultural acceptance of smoking has changed from tolerance to intolerance.

This classic example, however, also points out one of the distinctive deficiencies of a health education design. Educating or increasing awareness of a health problem provides only the initial step in behavior change. Without supportive assistance and motivation any attempt at long-term change will undoubtedly fail. Health education programs place the responsibility for change on the individual who may not have group or cultural support for change, let alone the inner fortitude to effect change.

Traditional health education programs focus on specific diseases or illnesses as a motivating factor, ignoring potential for a healthy lifestyle. Many corporate health education programs do discuss healthy lifestyles, but the main emphasis too often is on illness. In this style of program, recipients can be satisfied if they meet the minimal requirements for nonillness. This model of education is best exemplified by the response of physicians in performing routine physical examinations. Finding no current signs or symptoms of disease the patient is pronounced healthy when at best the patient is not exhibiting any current illness.

Health education must move beyond the not-sick model of thinking.

FITNESS PROGRAM DESIGN

The underlying concept motivating fitness programs is that as technology has replaced physiology as the source of human productivity, our survival as a culture no longer depends on our physical ability to do hard labor. The consequences of this cultural change is an assortment of degenerative diseases besetting a society whose muscles and cardiovascular systems have weakened seriously as a result of little or no physical activity. Corporate physical fitness programs allow sedentary employees to participate in vigorous exercise thereby achieving better physical health, arresting or reversing the degenerative affects of a sedentary lifestyle.

Numerous articles are available in the literature implying a direct relationship between physical fitness and increased productivity and mental abilities. A most recent study at Tenneco Co. (Bernacki and Braun 1984) investigated the relationship between exercise and overall measure of job performance. In this study of white-collar workers, a statistically significant association was demonstrated between above average job performance and exercise adherence. However, a comparison of current performance with previous performance for all groups in the exercise program showed no significant changes. From this the authors conclude their findings suggest a positive but probably noncausal, relationship between above average job performance and exercise adherence in a corporate fitness program.

The Tenneco study and others like it are encouraging many corporations to enter into a specific corporate fitness approach on a perceived belief that single focus efforts will bring about broad behavioral change. However, many pitfalls await this single style fitness program design.

Unrealistic Goals and Expectations

To assume that participation will demonstrate a measurable difference in job performance is quite unrealistic. Many aspects of job performance are difficult to measure empirically and are subject to the perceptions of the person responsible for reporting performance. Further clouding of measurable results is that many who will choose to participate in corporate sponsored physical activities are those already physically conditioned. Setting up a "preaching to preacher" situation.

Limited Availability on Restricted Focus

Many corporate programs on fitness limit the availability of equipment, exercise measurement, and related programs to a select group, quite often management. Studies by Edington (1984) indicate that a correlation exists between social class, education level, and concern about health issues and related lifestyle. The higher the education and social class, the more the likelihood to practice a healthy lifestyle or be accepting of health and lifestyle issues. By limiting the program to those in upper management a program may only be reaching those who are already fit.

Culturally Biased and Restrictive Design

The fitness revolution is a middle- and upper-class activity. The fitness movement in the media is directed at the upper, middle, and professional class of people with formal education beyond high school. The media approach to female aerobic exercise programs is similar.

Traditional fitness programs do not fit the cross section of cultures existing in corporations. When expanding the program into the rank and file, the cultural differences must be addressed to ensure that the program does not attract only the fit or socially accepting individuals.

Perks Versus Established Program

Fitness programs, the purchase of equipment, and hiring of staff may be viewed by upper management as an employee benefit or perk to retain or attract employees. Programs offered as a perk send a strong cultural message of exclusion to the lower ranks of employees further blocking their acceptance or support of the program should it be further expanded. The perk style program will also be quite dispensable when budgetary restraints are needed.

WELLNESS AND COMPREHENSIVE PROGRAM MODELS

As the concept of corporate health education promotion has expanded over the past ten years, "wellness" has become the watchword of the movement. Wellness projects more than an image of being well, more than the absence of pathological symptoms or disease. It has come to portray an overall state of robust good health and mental health. Wellness programs, being comprehensive in scope, provide knowledge, identification, and support opportunity for changing those behaviors associated with the major causes of death and disability, cardiovascular disease, cancer, accidents, musculoskeletal disorders, as well as mental illness, and substance misuse.

Wellness models approach behavioral health changes with many of the following major components.

General Health Education and Health Risk Appraisals

Appraising an individual's health risk ranges from simple paper-pencil self-appraisals to in-depth computer analyzed appraisal that may be tied into an extensive physiological examination. Most appraisals offer some form of recommendations and feedback on changing unhealthy lifestyles and maintaining desired change. The depth and sophistication of the appraisal depends on the amount a corporation or individual desires to spend. Some feel health risk appraisals offer the first step in individual awareness of detrimental lifestyle practices and point out the positive projected improvement in longevity through behavioral change. Many appraisals will include a corporate profile providing an accurate view of corporate health and lifestyle. Corporate profiles are useful in planning activities related directly to corporate needs.

Medical Identification Programs

Wellness programs allied with or in the corporate medical setting can offer numerous identification programs to reduce health risk and to influence behavioral change. Most popular are hypertensive identification programs and cholesterol testing. Utilizing medical staff and supportive agencies, an entire work force can undergo hypertension screening. A three site industrial hypertension screening program (Erfurt and Foote 1984) demonstrated the potential of worksite based programs to improve hypertension control among employees. Additionally with intensive follow-up and monitoring of identified hypertensives the annual cost per hypertensive employee was statistically lower than the cost per employee receiving treatment and follow-up with a personal physician. Similar results could be expected in a blood serum cholesterol monitoring program. Both hypertension treatment and recommendations for lowering blood serum cholesterol levels support numerous changes in lifestyle that can provide a direct motivated referral into other program activities.

Smoking Cessation

Thousands of epidemiological studies have demonstrated an unquestionably strong relationship between smoking and the incidence of heart disease, stroke, chronic obstructive lung diseases, and, most notably, cancer of the lungs, esophagus, oropharynx, and bladder (1984 Surgeon General Report). Studies from the Health Interview Survey (National Center for Health Statistics 1979) revealed that 33.7 percent of persons age 17 and over smoke.

When an individual is able to quit smoking, the smoking related increased risk for serious diseases declines after cessation. For the average smoker, cessation will reduce cardiac and heart disease mortality risk from 200 percent to 150 percent of that of nonsmokers within one year, and in five to ten years the mortality rate for ex-smokers is virtually equivalent to nonsmokers (U.S. Surgeon General's Report 1979).

Numerous programs, public and private, assist individuals in quitting smoking. Program cost ranges from free or a nominal donation to over $600. Controlled experimental data on the successfulness of worksite programs is virtually nonexistent. However, based on reports of other settings (Danaher 1980) from 15 percent to 80 percent of the participants are successfully able to quit. Many worksite programs consider success to be 20 percent to 30 percent smoke-free participants after one year.

The costs of smoking to corporations in lost time and medical benefits paid makes even a 20 percent to 30 percent success rate cost-effective. One estimate (Kristein 1980) of the annual cost to industry for each smoker is $400 when both health and safety related costs are figured in. Supportive cultural efforts by the corporation should include enforcement or creation of a realistic smoking policy that encourages a smoke-free environment, monetary rewards for continued abstinence, and public recognition of successful participants.

Weight Loss Dietary Programs

Losing weight in a chronically sedentary society is quite diffi-cult. Millions of dollars are spent each year by overweight individ-uals in an attempt to lose weight via diet books and medications and in weight loss clinics or special support groups. Claims for success are as outlandish as the methods despite overwhelming evi-dence that for a majority of individuals weight loss is dependent upon the number of calories consumed versus the number of calories burned.

Wellness programs wishing to incorporate weight loss programs have numerous professional and nationally accepted programs at their disposal; most rely upon the concept of mutual support and various company incentives. Recent studies (Seidman and Sevelius 1984) show most programs can be successful if attrition rates can be minimized. The difficulty as reported in the literature (Volkmar, Stunkard, and Baily 1981) comes in the maintenance of the weight loss over time. Employers may want to support maintenance of weight loss through incentives, follow-up, or continued support groups and through supporting moderate exercise programs for recent weight losers, dependent upon the number of resources available.

Fitness Programs

Program components on fitness, that is, regular exercise, are supported by epidemiologic studies in Europe and the United States (Kannel 1979) demonstrating a significant relationship between the physically active and lower age-specific rate of cardiovascular incidents and deaths. National surveys (Pacific Mutual Life 1979) found only 37 percent of adults getting regular exercise. A longitudinal study of Harvard alumni (Paffenbarger 1978) found that those alumni expending fewer than 2,000 calories a week at work or play had a 64 percent higher risk of heart attack than the more active.

Industrial fitness program components operate in hope of reducing participants' known risk factors, illness, reimbursable insurance claims, and absenteeism and of improving productivity morale and attitudes.

Problematic to this hypothesis is that most often those participating in a corporate exercise program enter the program with lower risk characteristics than the nonparticipants. This raises the question of what real benefits can be derived from exercise programs. As an adjunct to an overall wellness effort, a fitness program can offer many enhancements to employees and the employer, provided the costs of program and or facilities do not overshadow measurable savings.

Other Program Components

Related programs offered in a comprehensive wellness program can range as far as the interpretation and budget of the corporation will allow. Additional program components include:

Stress management — Seminars, materials, and assessments of managing both work and home related stress can be offered.

Sponsorship of events — Corporations can contribute to community athletic events, fun runs, marathons, bike races, and walkathons through both money and employees, demonstrating support for healthy activities.

Discount club memberships — Either as a perk or standard procedures, corporation can subsidize or negotiate a reduction in fees at community exercise facilities or private clubs for both employees and their dependents.

Flexible benefits — Some corporations now offer employees the choice of placing their benefit dollars in nontraditional areas of preventive health maintenance, that is, exercise facilities as a part of the overall employee benefit package.

Recognition rewards — Individuals achieving notable success in changing a health risk behavior can have their effort validated additionally by the recognition in company publications or gift rewards for their efforts.

SUMMARY AND CONCLUSIONS

With over 60 percent of adults over 16 employed, the worksite is an ideal area to address and support changes in health behavior. However, employer and employee perceptions of behaviors to be changed must be similar.

Health issues are governed by factors of media trends, cultural influences, age, and, most important, group and individual perceptions and interpretations. Employers desiring to change risk behaviors, thereby creating a healthy collective lifestyle, must be aware of the perceptions and cultural biases of the work force. They must recognize perceptions and biases can vary from one work force location to another. Similarly the expectations for success must be viewed as achievable by the work force, not solely by the program director.

Successful programs in changing health risk behaviors are those that:

Understand and communicate effectively realistic program concepts and goals to its work force

Provide allowances for cultural and sociological biases for and against changing health behaviors

Offer a comprehensive program allowing each person a beginning point for individual needs and desires

Support changes in health risk behaviors by recognizing individual and group accomplishments through incentives or media recognition

Support the goals and objectives of the program through changing the
corporate culture to modify its perceived message

Continually evaluate program effectiveness, employee preceptions, and
needs

Offer programs for changing health behaviors to all employees regardless
of status in the work force.

The creation, support, and growth of worksite programs to change
health related behaviors require continual in-depth analyses of the
corporation as a sociological entity and of the population within the
entity. The health practices that increase individual risks are not always
homogeneous, and individual success is based upon numerous
influences. Corporations recognizing the influences on health behavior,
willing to accept the recidivism of employees' attempts at change as a
beginning point rather than the end, will be able to communicate effective
support. Those with rigid standards and expectations based upon less
than analysis of both culture and perceptual influences will find failure
and frustration.

GLOSSARY

Cultural norms — beliefs, values, and behaviors considered acceptable
within a specific ethnic or sociological group.

Fitness — a state of physical well-being with concentration on muscular
strength and aerobic conditioning.

Health culture — beliefs, values, and behaviors related to health within a
specific ethnic or sociological group.

Healthy lifestyle — the incorporation into daily living of positive
health behaviors that are believed to enhance overall health and
longevity.

Health norms — beliefs, values, and behaviors on health that can be
positive or negative but are considered as acceptable practice.

Health promotion — the advocacy of healthy behaviors through various
educational techniques.

Negative health practice — health related behaviors that, despite overwhelming evidence of the detrimental effect on health, are continued by individuals as a normal daily routine.

Nonillness model — the approach to health that advocates no current symptoms of disease equal health.

Wellness — the overall state of robust health and healthy lifestyle both physically and psychologically.

REFERENCES

Allen, Robert F. The Corporate Health-Buying Spree: Boon or Boondoggle?" *Society for Advancement of Management Advanced Management Journal* 6 (1980): 9–14.

Bernacki, E. J., and W. B. Braun. "The Relationship of Job Performance to Exercise Adherence in a Corporate Fitness Program." *Journal of Occupational Medicine* 26 (1984): 529.

"Changes in Cigarette Smoking and Current Smoking Practices among Adults: United States, 1978." Advance Data, No. 53, September 19, 1979. National Center for Health Statistics, DHEW. Washington, D.C.: Government Printing Office, 1979.

Danaher, B. "Smoking Cessation in Occupational Settings." *Public Health Report* 95 (1980): 119–26.

Edington, D. W. *An Evaluation of the Henry Ford Hospital Employee Quality of Life and Optimal Health and Planning Program.* Unpublished technical report, 1984.

Erfurt, J. C., and A. Foote. "Cost Effectiveness of Work-site Blood Pressure Control Programs." *Journal of Occupational Medicine* 26 (1984): 892–900.

Health Maintenance. Newport Beach, California: Pacific Mutual Life Insurance Company, 1979.

Kannel, W. B. "Some Health Benefits of Physical Activity: The Framingham Study." *Archives of Internal Medicine* 139 (1979): 857–81.

Kristein, M. M. *How Much Can Business Expect to Earn from Smoking Cessation?* Council on Smoking and Health National Conference: Smoking and the Workplace, Chicago, January 9, 1980.

Paffenbarger, R. S., A. Wing, and R. T. Hyde. "Physical Activity as an Index of Heart

Attack Risk in College Alumni." *American Journal of Epidemiology* 108 (1978): 161–75.

Seidman, L. S., and G. G. Sevelius. "A Cost Effective Weight-Loss Program at the Worksite." *Journal of Occupational Medicine* 26 (1984): 725.

Smoking and Health. A Report of the Surgeon General's Office on Smoking and Health. U.S. Department of Health Education and Welfare, DHEW Publication No. (PHS) 79-50066. Washington, D.C.: Government Printing Office, 1979.

The Health Consequences of Smoking: Chronic Obstructive Lung Disease. A Report of the U.S. Surgeon General. U.S. Department of Health and Human Services. Washington, D.C.: Government Printing Office, 1984.

Volkmar, E. W., A. J. Stunkard, and R. A. Bailey. "High Attrition Rates in Commercial Weight Reduction Programs." *Archives of Internal Medicine* 141 (1981): 426–28.

23 Health Promotion: Health Care Cost Containment or Human Resource Development?

D. W. Edington

INTRODUCTION

It is not unusual for a new idea, a new technology, or a new service to have difficulty in finding a "home" within a complex organization. Examples of this can be found in universities, government bureaucracy, or private corporations. The confusion often is compounded by issues related to "turf" or political considerations as well as the more legitimate concerns such as quality control and efficiency of operation. The delivery of health promotion services is an example of a new concept searching for the proper niche in the organization.

The individual components of a comprehensive health promotion program are not new. Recreation programs, as an example, have existed in many corporations for over 50 years. What is new is the comprehensive approach to total fitness, employee well-being. The benefits individual and organizational of comprehensive health promotion programs are responsible, in part, for the confusion. Healthy employees benefit all aspects of the organization (see Figure 23.1). The concepts are not new, but the recent recognition that health promotion programs affect the bottom line is new, and thus, the struggle to find a home in the organization.

Since the early 1970s the surge in the popularity of health promotion programs grew, in part, out of the concern for cardiovascular disease and the boom in the physical fitness interest. In many organizations high-level executives became interested in their personal physical fitness and then transferred that interest to the organization. In most cases there was no

FIGURE 23.1
Impact of Healthier Employees on the Organization

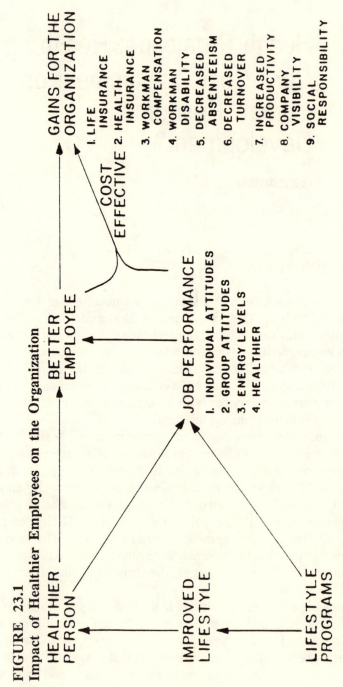

Source: Compiled by the author.

theoretically "natural fit," but the program was positioned wherever made the most sense at the time. As the exercise boom broadened to include other aspects of a healthy lifestyle, the fitness revolution matured into the health promotion and self-care concepts.

Employee service groups, which often expanded from original recreation programs, were cognizant of employee needs and sometimes expanded to include the health promotion concepts. This was relatively unusual before the early 1980s because employee services departments were expanding into other areas of employee needs including recreation, travel, and ticket sales. Health promotion and wellness programs were generated, most often, by employee requests, including those of the corporate officers.

Even more recent (since the late 1970s) is the concern for health care cost containment. Health care costs began to rise as much as 20 percent a year. This rise coupled with the economic downturn in the late 1970s and early 1980s magnified the economic impact of health care on organizations. Many organizations formed health care cost containment committees or task forces with memberships often representing all phases of the organization. Among the many health care cost containment strategies proposed by the committees was often a health promotion or wellness strategy. This strategy is generally accepted as an effective, long-term (5-7 years), and popular strategy to reduce utilization of the health care system. Health promotion is popular in the sense that it does not reduce employee benefits but, in fact, adds to the quality of worklife.

The strength of the cost containment movements plus the success of the popular business publications in the late 1970s and early 1980s, espousing the importance of a concern for people, increased the pressure for wellness programs. The pressures built so rapidly (in less than ten years) that programs were initiated with little knowledge of a proper structure.

By the mid-1980s a random selection of any ten wellness programs would show them in no less than four different places in the organizational structure. Examples of what would be expected include employee services, medical, human resource development, organization development, health care cost containment committee, employee assistance program, buildings and grounds, personnel, benefits, direct assistants to corporate officer, training, wellness and health promotion, and other.

Not all of the above are unique because many functions overlap and have different names in different organizations. Given the various geneses of wellness programs, the various legitimate goals, and the newness of the concept, it is not surprising to find the variety of homes for these programs. The question becomes, "Will health promotion and wellness programs ever achieve a singularity of purpose or find a common place in the organizational structure?" It will be the early 1990s before the question will be answered through empirical techniques.

GOALS OF HEALTH PROMOTION AND WELLNESS PROGRAMS

The Fitness Research Center at the University of Michigan is often asked to aid organizations in designing wellness programs. The recommended strategy is to write with the organization a strategic plan for wellness. The first step in that plan is to identify the goal of the proposed wellness program. When the subject is introduced, almost without exception, the two primary motivations for the wellness program are concern for people (helping people become all they can be) and health care cost containment (helping people stay healthy). Fortunately, these two motivations are not mutually exclusive and, in fact, can be synergistic over the long term (5 to 7 years). Sometimes one motivation clearly dominates, and the strategic plan must clearly reflect that concern.

Health Care Cost Containment

The goal of health care cost containment is to reduce or to stabilize health care expenditures. Reasonably, this has become an important short-term goal of many organizations. This is clearly attested to by the enormous growth of health care cost containment consulting companies with their computer programming and tracking systems. Health care cost containment committees are finding that techniques such as increasing deductibles, establishing preferred provider organizations, health maintenance organizations, second opinions, and extensive claim reviews are effective in reducing the immediate health care cost increases. How effective these become in the long term are not yet known.

Another technique that these committees have been willing to explore is that of wellness programs. It is quite believable that if you provide alternatives for employees to stay healthy and to maintain their wellness levels, they will eventually use the health care system to a lesser degree.

While the typical cost for health care is approximately $1,500 a person each year, cost for wellness programs range form 1 percent to 5 percent of that cost. The cost can escalate to 10 percent to 30 percent if extensive facilities, such as exercise gymnasiums, swimming pools or other equipment such as weightlifting equipment, are involved in the wellness program. Many organizations are seeing wellness programs as their long-term solution to health care cost containment.

Human Resource Development

The goal of human resource development programs is to develop people in a variety of areas. More and more evidence is accumulating that healthier people and the more productive people are one and the same. Although causality cannot yet be established, a clear relationship between these two factors is apparent. Management training companies such as Blanchard Training and Development have observed this relationship and have even begun marketing a program, "Get Fit" modeled after *The One Minute Manager Gets Fit*. The University of Michigan's Division of Executive Education began in 1983 to include a healthy lifestyles section in its month-long business executive education programs.

Bookstores in the early to mid-1980s revealed two major trends. On one side of the bookstore were the popular business books, including *The One Minute Manager, In Search of Excellence, Megatrends, Working Smarter,* and *Passion for Excellence*. On the other side of the bookstore were the self-help books about exercise, nutrition, weight control, and stress management. It was encouraging to see these trends come together at the worksite as wellness programs. The overall theme of the popular business books was the concern for people while the overall theme of the self-help books was how to take care of oneself. The directors of human resource development programs observed this trend, and in some organizations these directors began to establish a claim to this training area.

INTEGRATION INTO THE FUTURE

The future of health promotion programs is unclear at best. First of all it is not clear whether the programs will continue to weave their way into the main fabric of the organization or whether they will remain on the surface and disappear with the passage of time. The second uncertainty is their placement in the organizational structure. The issues are not trivial because ultimate survival in an organization depends upon the degree of importance attached to the activity, primarily in relation to the bottom line projections. If health promotion programs are to survive and become integral parts of organizations, they either must prove themselves through cost-benefit studies or become integrated into management's thinking so that they are accepted as important contributors to the goals of the organization.

The emphasis on health care cost containment was a major boost to health promotion programs in many organizations. The health care cost containment issue probably will not be a long-standing issue in organizations because methods are being found to counteract the escalation of health care costs. Programs tied to the health care cost containment committees need to be alert to this and become established in the more traditional organizational structure. If wellness programs prove cost beneficial, it is likely that these programs will be transferred to mainstream departments.

Human resource development is somewhat trendy and could swing away from the concern-for-people emphasis and become more training oriented. Health promotion programs tied to human resource development groups need to be aware of this possibility and continue to emphasize the important relationship of healthy people and productive employees. Health promotion programs need to broaden their perspectives to include the total development of the individual and development of the healthy person in the healthy workplace. If this is done, health promotion probably will continue to exist and flourish in productive organizations.

In summary, the positioning of the program in the organizational structure may not be as important as the concepts espoused by the program. Those programs that espouse developing healthy people in healthy workplaces will be the most enduring of all the programs and will survive in prosperous times as well as in economically depressed times.

24 How Health Promotion Programs Can Enhance Workplace Creativity

Thomas E. Backer

> Creativity is not a luxury. Ideas are as important as genes. . . . Wisdom is becoming the new criterion of fitness.
>
> Jonas Salk (Helvarg 1984, p. 195)

As we hurtle full-out into an information based economy, enhancing workplace creativity becomes ever more important to organizational success. Information is the one resource that is not depleted by use (Otto and Joseph 1984). In fact, using it can improve it, and the most dramatic improvements come from creative ideas. Such improvements increasingly are the means by which businesses remain competitive and profitable.

Creativity also is needed to invent new products and services and to devise strategies for living with technology's side effects. From the Model T to the Volkswagen Bug, from video games to personal computers, industry is replete with examples of how a good idea, well executed, can drive a company's fortunes.

Today more than half the Fortune 500 corporations provide in-house training in creativity development (Rice 1984). Many business schools offer graduate courses in creativity, and institutions such as the Center for Creative Leadership in North Carolina specialize in continuing education in this domain. Even government bureaucracies and the military are looking more seriously than ever before at how to enhance the creative productivity in their work forces (Backer 1985e).

But both individuals and organizations are discovering that just learning how to have more good ideas is not enough. Creative work takes enormous personal energy. The work itself, the work environment, and the personalities of creative people provoke many stresses that can inhibit creative productivity or even lead to burnout. Creative people need an appropriate context for their work, a total environment that can be custom-tailored to individual needs, helping to maximize creative output.

For the last 12 years, I have been exploring creativity development and its practical applications for individuals and organizations (Backer 1983a, 1983b, 1985c, 1985d, 1985e). Much of my work has been concentrated in the performing arts, the visual arts, and the film and television industries in Hollywood. After working with approximately 20,000 individuals, I have no doubt that physical and emotional health are intricately connected with creative productivity. But in reviewing the literature, I could find no explicit references to creativity development as an objective of health promotion programs. A 1985 series of interviews with leaders in health promotion produced similar conclusions. Many companies with outstanding health promotion programs also have creativity development efforts, but the two are rarely, if ever, coordinated.

Yet the framework for coordination already exists in many forward-thinking organizations. For example, health promotion programs often have "enhancing peak performance" as a stated goal. Part of peak performance is creativity, perhaps even more so now than in the past, as individual and group creativity is viewed as ever more critical to organizational success. Moreover, several observers (for example, Pelletier 1984) have concluded that the best current programs are the multiple-service, holistic ones. Adding a creativity-enhancement component seems entirely compatible with the state-of-the-art health promotion programming.

Such a strategy also is consonant with one of Pelletier's (1984) ten basic tenets of effective health promotion programs — that they respect workers' individual needs and unique circumstances. And health promotion programs generally are prevention oriented, which fits with the aim of preventing creative burnout and conserving creative resources.

The three issues of personal energy, stress and burnout, and alternate methods for enhancing creativity all relate quite directly to health promotion programs now operating in thousands of workplaces. Enhancing a health promotion effort by giving specialized attention to work force creativity can stimulate greater benefit without much increase in overall costs. Results may be especially dramatic with personnel overtly identified as creative, for example, scientists and designers. What follows focuses on these so-called "key creative personnel" although fostering creativity at all levels in a workplace also is important.

The strategies suggested here are just now being explored in medical and behavioral research, so of necessity much of the discussion to follow is rather general — ideas and speculations rather than operational techniques. But enough evidence already exists to encourage organizational leaders to coordinate actively their health promotion and creativity development activities.

PERSONAL ENERGY

In their biographies and other accounts of the creative process, people who do creative work refer constantly to the total, consuming energy the work requires (Ghiselin 1952; May 1975; Arieti 1972). Many report working days or even weeks virtually without stopping. Project-oriented work, such as making a feature film or designing a new consumer product, may be especially demanding. Poor physical health can interfere with, or even stop altogether, peak performance. Innovators working in organizational settings have the further challenge of getting their good ideas to the marketplace, a process also requiring intense energy and commitment (Rosenfeld and Servo 1984).

Absenteeism, lack of concentration, greater propensity for accidents and injury, and other side effects of poor health also can cripple a workplace's creative forces. Key creative people may be removed from the scene temporarily or permanently. Moreover, the energy used in coping with these by-products of ill health cannot then be used for creative endeavor. Especially for companies battling to keep a competitive edge, even a temporary energy drain can spell disaster.

Naturally, workers with little in the way of creative responsibilities are affected by energy limits too. It's common sense that we all have only so much energy, and whatever is drained away by ill health or its side effects can't be used for other activities, such as work. But increasingly business organizations find that their most creative people are, in Buckminster Fuller's terms, "trimtabs," small sails that help guide the entire ship. Where such enormous leverage effects are involved, attention to energy level is even more important.

STRESS AND BURNOUT

Poorly handled stress is one of the greatest impediments to creative productivity (Backer 1985c). Every year, thousands of creative people, from rock stars to design engineers in high-tech firms, suffer so much stress that they simply burnout; they lose the capacity, and the desire, to be creative. Many thousands more suffer in their creative productivity. Stress depletes energy, creates anxiety that impedes or blocks altogether the process of creative inspiration, and generates interpersonal tensions that make team creativity more difficult.

In a recent Los Angeles *Times* article (Isenberg 1983), a half-dozen leading artist/producers in theatre and music were profiled. All had suffered a burnout so serious that they felt it imperative to take a leave of absence. Fruedenberger (1980) and others have chronicled the incidence of burnout in highly competitive, creatively oriented executive positions. Avoiding burnout means learning to identify and cope with sources of stress in both work and personal life.

Everyone in modern life faces stress, but at least three sources of stress are special for creative people. First, the nature of the work itself is stressful. Creativity is about risk and about change, and so is stress. The two are bound together inextricably, like Siamese twins. Coming close to the edge to find something new is the bedrock of creativity. Although race car drivers, trauma surgeons, and coal miners all face risks, creative people are especially vulnerable to their risk-taking activities because deep emotions are likely to be exposed in the act of creating. Dredging up material from one's unconscious is a hallmark of creative inspiration (Arieti 1972) and also has its psychological stresses, especially because even today we still understand very little about how the creative process really works.

Second, certain psychological characteristics of creative people are likely to induce stress. Campbell (1977), in a summary of many years' research on the psychological correlates of creativity, identifies among the core attributes "psychological turbulence" and "preference for complexity over simplicity"; both traits obviously increase a person's likelihood of living under stress. Moreover, those working as part of a creative team may be affected by attributes in their creative colleagues as well; a group of turbulent people working together is bound to generate some stress!

Third, creative environments, whether the research and development department of a large chemical company or a motion picture studio, are places where uncertainty is a way of life, with many associated stresses.

Many creative workplaces involve unusual working hours, a lack of separation between work and personal life, and often a lack of understanding and support from top management regarding the creative process.

ALTERNATE METHODS FOR STIMULATING CREATIVITY

Evidence is accumulating (Arieti 1972; Harman and Rheingold 1984) that there are a number of ways to promote creative inspiration and that there are wide individual differences in what works best. Benson (1984), for example, cites his Relaxation Response as helpful in stimulating creativity. Yet this approach may not work for all people. Heide (1985) found that relaxation techniques are actually anxiety producing for some high-energy, achievement-oriented people, including many doing work that is largely creative in nature. In laboratory studies Martindale (1975) and others have found that there can be even a negative relationship between relaxation and creativity.

Thus, alternate methods for stimulating creativity need to be explored. One that is part of most health promotion programs is physical exercise. Ghiselin (1952) is one of many writers reporting that creative people often speak of exercise as immediately preceding creative inspiration. Mozart, for example, often had his best musical ideas while walking quietly in the country after a good meal. Both Albert Einstein and Thomas Edison in their autobiographies speak of creative ideas forming in their muscles as they exercised. In working with thousands of creative people in workshops and classrooms, I found the incidence of reported creative inspiration during exercise to be so high that I now recommend a regular exercise program as the single best way both to increase resistance to stress and to facilitate personal creativity. People find their own ways to make a connection between the two. For example, one television writer reported that once she began noticing how many of her best ideas came while jogging, she started carrying a small pad and pencil on her run to jot down the ideas as they occurred (Backer 1985c).

The basis for such a relationship between exercise and inspiration is not hard to intuit. Virtually every analysis of the creative process includes reference to an incubation period, a time of relaxed concentration during which there is an opportunity for creative ideas to form and bubble up from the unconscious (Neurnberger 1984). This is what novelist Saul

Bellow refers to as "dream space" (Backer 1985c, p. 87). Exercise is one way to facilitate this state, simply because the mind and body are focused on an activity that is diverting but not distracting (as is, for example, concentration on another intellectual subject). Both physical movement and creativity involve overlearned skills that are practiced largely at an unconscious level.

Moreover, exercise stimulates the flow of endorphins in the brain, the natural painkillers that produce "jogger's high" and also are known to reduce depression and elevate mood (Sime 1984). Elevated mood is clearly associated with creative activity, especially if the individual had been depressed before the creative burst (May 1975).

We are just beginning to understand the relationship between creativity and exercise, through both case studies and laboratory research. However, there is already enough anecdotal evidence (especially because exercise is well known to have other benefits) to warrant some experimenting with creative people and the exercise components of health promotion programs.

CREATIVITY ENHANCEMENT AS A HEALTH PROMOTION COMPONENT

Experimenting with exercise, stress reduction, burnout avoidance, energy maintenance, or other health-creativity connections, however, should not be haphazard. A number of systematic approaches to enhancement are possible.

Health Promotion Policy

Having a written organizational policy on how a program is to serve an organization's key creative people can help, both in stimulating program design and in focusing attention on the special needs of the creative work force. This also reflects a top management commitment to providing a conducive work environment for creativity. The workplace's key creative staff should be involved directly in formulating this policy, using their own creative ingenuity to help make it effective.

Creativity Development Activities

Creativity development activities can be offered through the health promotion program (active cooperation with the company's existing creativity development program should be sought, of course). This arrangement helps to develop a general understanding of the linkages between health and creativity. It also provides a chance to address specific issues such as the relationships between stress, exercise, and creative productivity. For example, most creative people have little awareness of how much influence their physical health can have on creative prowess (Backer 1985c).

Health Promotion Activities

Specially tailored health promotion activities can be offered for key creative people. Structurally these can be scheduled to favor unusual work hours, the intermittent needs for intensive services in project-related work, and interface between health promotion and creativity development. For example, at the Center for Creative Leadership, fitness consultant and psychologist Joan Kofodimis offers exercise classes as an ongoing part of the center's creativity development programs. The 30-minute classes typically are given at the end of each seminar day. They involve simple stretching and muscle relaxation exercises, combined with education on the role of fitness in effective work performance.

In Hollywood, fitness consultants now come to the film and TV studios, to give personalized workouts to performers and key executives. A company also could organize an exercise program to be followed by quiet times in a secluded environment, to further enrich the creativity-stimulation value of exercise.

The content of health promotion activities also can be targeted for creative people:

Substance abuse education and counseling can focus on the attempts creative people often make to cope with stress and to enhance their creative powers through using alcohol and drugs. The evidence is overwhelming that such tactics do not work for either purpose (Barron and Harrington 1981; Arieti 1972), but they persist among the myths of creativity for many people. For example, clients of the Entertainment Industry Referral and Assistance Center (an industry-wide substance abuse program serving the film and television industry in Hollywood) often say they started using drugs or alcohol for stress reduction or for promoting creativity (Backer 1985b).

Exercise and fitness training can include specific attention to the benefits of exercise for creative inspiration.

Stress management seminars and counseling can focus on the special stresses of the creative process and ways to handle them. Because stress management is currently the fastest-growing area in health promotion (Fielding and Breslow 1983; Pelletier 1984), there are still chances to design original stress management programs for this purpose.

Mental health counseling can include attention to the problems of creative work as they affect the family and on ways to handle the significant degree of "psychological turbulence" that seems a trait of most creative people.

Modeling Effective Behaviors

Managers of creative people can model effective behaviors. Especially on creative projects where the leaders set the tone for everyone else's behavior, a manager who takes time for fitness classes or for stress management activities can be highly influential. Over the last several years, I have been teaching stress management to film and television directors at the Directors Guild of America. A key topic in these classes is how directors can serve as role models for the actors, camera operators, and others in the high-pressure environment of the TV or movie set.

Intervention

Individual direct interventions may be necessary with key creative people in trouble. For example, I have been called in as a consultant by the managers of successful creative people to help with everything from dietary changes — particularly limiting junk food — to dealing with drug and alcohol problems, to handling interpersonal difficulties in the individual's private or work relationships, to increasing daily exercise and sleep requirements, to meditation and yoga training. A comprehensive program of activities may be necessary to salvage a key creative person who is teetering on the edge of burnout or severe health problems.

Organization Redesign

Increasingly, organizations where much creative work goes on are retooling entire environments to stimulate creative productivity. Specialized health promotion programs can, of course, be a part of this redesign. For example, Jonas Salk at the Salk Institute in La Jolla, California, says that the design of his institute's offices, from interior furnishings to choice of site, was governed by the goal of developing an environment where creativity would be maximized (Helvarg 1984). Rosenfeld and Servo (1984) report establishing an Office of Innovation for Kodak Research Laboratories, designed to help innovators deal with the stresses of getting their ideas to the marketplace. Ward (1985) describes a comprehensive environmental design for Hallmark Card's Technology Innovation Center, where the special care of 700 creative people takes place. And increasingly, industrial parks are being designed to lure high-technology firms by providing an environment with special appeal for these firms' creative staffs. One example is the Woodbridge Technology Center in Scottsdale, Arizona ("A Center for Corporate Creativity" 1985).

In a 1985 series of interviews I conducted with creative staff at Calty Design Research, Inc., in Newport Beach, California, several aspects of the physical environment were mentioned as significant for creative effectiveness. One is the beautiful seaside setting of this organization, which is the U.S. design subsidiary of Toyota Motors. Another is the relative isolation of the workplace for Toyota's U.S. and Japanese corporate headquarters. A third is the clean, uncluttered architectural and interior design (interestingly, several staff said their own creative processes were stimulated best by a more diverse, "messier," environment, again highlighting the need for custom-tailoring of the creative context to fit individual needs and preferences). Finally, this small company is unusual in that it has its own tennis court and resident tennis pro, affording exercise opportunities for staff in addition to such activities as walks on the nearby beach.

CREATIVITY AND ORGANIZATIONAL SUCCESS OVER THE LONG HAUL

As with other human resource development issues, organizations face choices between short-term profits or long-term success in dealing with issues of health promotion and creativity. Coordinating certain programs might admittedly be expensive in the short run, but long-run benefits can be great (other activities, as suggested here, may cost very little). Peters and Waterman (1982) say that the best-run companies tend to look at the long haul, including the overall maintenance of human resources. So it seems only a matter of time before companies begin to explore more systematically the relationship between health and the creativity of their best innovators.

Evidence is growing that certain qualities or norms within the work environment can promote either burnout or peak performance, such as creativity (Jaffe, Scott, and Orioli, 1984). We can do some exciting experimenting on both the values and the structures of workplaces with respect to health and creativity. The workplace is, in fact, a natural environment where behavior can be observed and where organizational and social structures can be used in the design of interventions (Krantz, Grunberg, and Baum 1985).

Dialogue and sharing of strategies for enhancing creativity through health promotion is certainly needed. Managers of health promotion programs can share with each other and with their counterparts in creativity development programs. Symposia at professional conferences and further writing on this subject also would seem to be of great value.

Recent reviews on creativity (for example, Barron and Harrington 1981) make it clear that there is still more that we do not know than we do about this complex, mysterious subject. Controversy rages even on seemingly simple matters such as definition of the word "creativity," itself. Yet progress is being made. Behavioral studies in the laboratory and in the real world are telling us more about the correlates of creativity; brain waves and other physical phenomena associated with the creative process are being studied intensively.

As we learn more about the nature of creative activity itself, we doubtless will learn more precisely how health promotion activities can stimulate creative productivity. This presentation is admittedly only a bare beginning. Following through is important for health promotion, however, if for no other reason than economics. If health promotion programs can be shown to protect and expand a company's vital creative resources, their overall worth is better demonstrated. There already is evidence that organizations are demanding that their health promotion activities show such types of concrete payoffs (DeMuth et al. in press). Gathering evidence on the availability of health promotion activities to stimulate creative productivity may, in the long run, help such programs in their quest for survival.

J. M. Keil, advertising executive with Dancer Fitzgerald Sample, reminds us that it is important simply to believe that "creativity and management can co-exist in a profitable environment" (1985, p.2). The glue of that coexistence is using the organization and power of management to help structure and support creativity through programs such as those in the health promotion arena.

REFERENCES

"A Center for Corporate Creativity." *Scottsdale Scene,* September 1985, pp. 72–75.

Arieti, S. *Creativity: The Magic Synthesis.* New York: Basic Books, 1972.

Backer, T. E. "Shielding the Flame: Stress Management for Creative People." In *Creativity Week V: Proceedings,* edited by S. Gryskiewicz and J. Shields. Greensboro, North Carolina: Center for Creative Leadership, 1983a.

____. "Beating the Stress Syndrome." *Adweek,* February 14, 1983b, p. 20.

____. "Career Development Consulting with Creative People." *Consulting Psychology Bulletin* 36 (1985a): 21–24.

____. "Drug Abuse Prevention and the Entertainment Industry." *Prevention Networks,* in press, 1985b.

____. *Creativity and Stress.* Submitted for publication, 1985c.

____. "Unleashing Creativity: Lessons Learned from the Entertainment Industry." Submitted for publication, 1985d.

____. Sanforizing Creativity. Submitted for publication, 1985e.

Barron, F., and D. M. Harrington. "Creativity, Intelligence, and Personality." *Annual Review of Psychology* 32 (1981): 439–76.

Benson, H. *Beyond the Relaxation Response.* New York: Times Books, 1984.

Campbell, D. *Take the High Road to Creativity and Get off Your Dead End.* Allen, Texas: Argus Communications, 1977.

DeMuth, N., J. Fielding, A. Stunkard, and R. Hollander. "Evaluation of Industrial Health Promotion Programs: Return-on-Investment and Survival of the Fittest." In *Health Promotion in Industry: A Behavioural Medicine Perspective,* edited by M. F. Cataldo and T. J. Coates. New York: Wiley, in press.

Fielding, J. E., and L. Breslow. "Health Promotion Programs Sponsored by California Employers." *American Journal of Public Health* 73 (1983): 538–42.

Freudenberger, H. *Burnout: The High Cost of Achievement.* New York: Anchor-Doubleday, 1980.

Ghiselin, B. *The Creative Process.* New York: New American Library, 1952.

Harman, W., and H. Rheingold. *Higher Creativity.* Los Angeles: Tarcher, 1984.

Heide, F. J. "Relaxation: The Storm before the Calm." *Psychology Today* 19 (1985): 18–19.

Helvarg, D. "A Conversation with the Old Master." *San Diego* 5 (1984): 194–200.

Isenberg, B. "Burnout: The Pressure Backstage." Los Angeles *Times,* February 20, 1983, pp. 42–44.

Jaffe, D., C. Scott, and E. Orioli. "Peak Performers Thrive in a Supportive Open Corporate Environment." *Business and Health* 2 (1985): 52–53.

Keil, J. M. *The Creative Mystique.* New York: Wiley, 1985.

Krantz, D. S., N. E. Grunberg, and A. Baum. "Health Psychology." *Annual Review of Psychology* 36 (1985): 349–83.

Martindale, C. "What Makes Creative People Different?" *Psychology Today* 9 (1975): 44–50.

May, R. *The Courage to Create.* Toronto: Bantam, 1975.

Neurnberger, P. "Mastering the Creative Process." *The Futurist* 20 (1984): 33–36.

Otto, N., and E. C. Joseph. *The Emerging Information Age.* Minneapolis: Anticipatory Sciences, 1984.

Pelletier, K. "Healthy People in Unhealthy Places." New York: Dell, 1984.

Peters, T., and R. Waterman. *In Search of Excellence.* New York: Harper and Row, 1982.

Rice, B. "Imagination to Go." *Psychology Today* 18 (1984): 48–56.

Rosenfeld, R., and J. Servo. "Business and Creativity." *The Futurist* 20 (1984): 21–26.

Sime, W. E. "Psychological Benefits of Exercise." *Advances* 1 (1984): 15–29.

Ward, B. "Centers of Imagination." *Sky* 14 (1985): 72–80.

25 Implementation of Fitness and Lifestyle Programs: Critical Issues

Michael H. Cox

INTRODUCTION

In the early 1950s, a small but persistent movement to promote physical activity began in North America. This movement gained momentum in the 1960s when an "Act to promote physical fitness" was adopted in Canada and the President's Council on Physical Fitness was established in the United States. Subsequently, federal, provincial, and state governments across Canada and the United States have promoted physical fitness in earnest. These fitness movements have resulted in an increased awareness and understanding of physical fitness and other aspects of a healthy lifestyle.

However, the impact of these programs on initiating exercise behavior is not clear. Certainly, the recent Canada Fitness Survey has illustrated that a majority of Canadians still are not physically active on a consistent basis. This lack of realization of community goals to improve lifestyle has helped lend credibility to the concept of corporate fitness programs.

Since the 1974 Canadian conference on employee physical fitness, (Health and Welfare, Canada 1975), corporate physical activity and lifestyle programs have flourished in North America. More than 50,000 firms in the United States (Pyle 1979a) and up to 1,000 companies in Canada (Salmon 1981) are involved in some aspect of employee fitness programming. The President's Council on Physical Fitness receives at least 20 inquiries a day from business firms interested in establishing employee fitness programs (Pyle 1979a, 1979b).

In Ontario, the government-funded Fitness Ontario Program has assisted more than 500 companies in developing physical activity and lifestyle programs for their employees. Support for employee fitness programs, although largely unsubstantiated, has been increasing for several reasons.

A new philosophy toward work values that emphasizes self-fulfillment is replacing the more traditional value systems of money, status, and possessions (Kerr and Rosow 1979). Several studies have consistently shown little relationship between life satisfaction and indexes of living standards (Campbell 1976). Because the extrinsic motivator of salary may no longer be the only criterion of job success (Frankenhaeuser 1977), employee fitness programs may be a natural addition to the intrinsic factors relating to quality of working life and employee motivation.

An increasing interest in "primary prevention" of disease has developed in both the private and governmental sectors (Milio 1966). The corporate concept of preventive medicine may be interpreted as keeping personnel in "proper operating condition" (Pyle 1979a). In this regard, health education programs alone have not been particularly successful (Cohen and Cohen 1978). Few studies have shown changes in behavior whereas most studies have demonstrated a wide discrepancy between health knowledge and attitudes and health actions (Green 1970); Shephard et al. 1980). Moreover, Haggerty (1977) has stated that "alterations in behavior rather than knowledge or attitudes should be the end result of intervention." Thus, a program of physical activity in the workplace may have not only physiologic benefits (Heinzelman and Bagley 1970; Rhodes and Dunwoody 1980; Dedmon et al. 1979); it may reinforce proper lifestyle behavior patterns as well (Keir 1976; Garry 1980; Council on Scientific Affairs 1981). Several authors (Heinzelman and Bagley 1970; Rhodes and Dunwoody 1980; Dedmon et al. 1979; Durbeck et al 1972) have shown that employee fitness programs improve functional capacity and "risk" profiles consistent with other scientific training studies.

Rising national health costs, workmen's compensation payments, high levels of worker absenteeism, and retarded growth in productivity have caused companies to be more concerned about human resources (Milio 1966; Garry 1980; Roys 1979; Everett 1979). In response to such concerns, research has shown that employee fitness programs may improve health (Garry 1980; Roys 1979; Shephard, Corey, and Cox 1983), reduce absenteeism and turnover (Lindén 1969; Cox, Shephard, and Corey 1981), change attitudes and feelings (Rhodes and Dunwoody

1980; Howard and Mikalachki 1979), improve energy levels, and reduce fatigue (Banister 1978; Shephard 1974).

The North American population will age considerably in the next two decades (Denton, Feaver, and Spencer 1980; Kettle 1980). Furthermore, demographic shifts indicate that there will be a drop in the number of young workers (Denton, Feaver, and Spencer 1980). Compared with the last two decades, the growth in the labor force will increase at a decelerating rate in the 1980s (Kettle 1980). The decline in the number of young workers entering the labor force will demand highly competitive recruiting strategies by many companies, particularly for highly skilled and professional personnel. The problem of aging in the workplace has many corporations seeking to change human resource policies and manpower planning strategies (Baytos 1979). Some authors (Skinner 1968; Sidney and Shephard 1976) have suggested that employee fitness programs may help workers adapt to retirement and thus reduce the need for hospital care for the elderly. In any regard, the modification of human resource policies will be dictated in the decades ahead by an older work force, and there will be a greater demand for innovative policies in employee benefits and the work environment.

EMPLOYEE FITNESS PROGRAMS: PRESENT STATE OF KNOWLEDGE

Despite the growing popularity of employee fitness programs, sound scientific data relative to their effects have been sparse (Heinzelman and Bagley 1970; Bjurstrom and Alexiou 1978; Howard and Mikalachki 1979; Fielding 1979; Jetté 1980; Koerner 1973; Laporte 1966; Ryan 1980; Yarvote et al. 1974). Furthermore, the nature of employee fitness programs has been such that the results of most studies have been based on uncontrolled research. In general most employee fitness research lacks sound control populations and is predominantly cross-sectional in nature, leaving the question of self-selection conspicuously unaddressed. Correspondingly, many reports that testify to the benefits of employee fitness programs have been limited to managerial journals and physical fitness magazines intended for the lay population (Pyle 1979a, 1979b; Garry 1980; Megalli 1978; Lauzon 1982; Cox 1984; Oldridge 1984; Berkanovic 1976). Howard and Mikalachki (1979) have suggested that the lack of objective data stems from data restriction policies of specific organizations, the lack of necessary program evaluation because of the company's inherent faith in the probable benefits of a physical activity program, and the lack of expertise in the design of program evaluations. Moreover, even though employee fitness programs have been effective in improving fitness levels (Shephard and Cox 1982), little scientific evidence suggests that these programs have had a direct or specific benefit on employee health or in the workplace.

Nevertheless, based on the limited success of other programs directed at altering lifestyle behavior (Cohen and Cohen 1978; Somers 1974; U.S. Senate 1975), it has been postulated that a combination of methods could be used to broach the question of injudicious lifestyles (Haggerty 1977). Of the methods suggested, changing the occupational environment is an attractive approach; the advantages include large population numbers in a relatively concentrated and accessible area, required attendance at the worksite, possible impact over a wide range of socioeconomic and education levels, an already established employee communication network, reinforcement of positive changes in behavior through company incentives, ability to cooperate with other programs, such as providing nutritional management in conjunction with the company cafeteria, the possibility of making company time available for lifestyle awareness programs, and in most cases, a convenient and cost effective environment to conduct employee fitness and lifestyle programs.

BENEFITS OF EMPLOYEE FITNESS AND LIFESTYLE PROGRAMS

Although the workplace has been considered an ideal setting for health promotion and disease prevention (Peters, Benson, and Porter 1977), little objective evidence exists pertaining to specific program successes (Howard and Mikalachki 1979). Pravosudov (1976) cites no less than 20 Soviet studies showing positive results of physical activity on health and economic efficiency; however, the exact experimental design of these studies has not been made clear. Benefits of employee fitness programs that the Soviets have reported include a 10 percent to 15 percent improvement in work output, a significant decrease in medical claims, a 30 percent decrease in industrial accidents, and a decrease in absenteeism of three to five days per worker each year. (In North America this could represent a reduction of up to 45 percent to 50 percent in absenteeism.)

Two Romanian studies state the need for employee fitness programs, but report no experimental findings (Barhad 1979; Pafnote, Voida, and Luchian 1979). Further, one other European study only reports improvements in physical work capacity (Ilmarinen et al. 1978).

In the United States, evaluation of employee fitness programs has centered on physiological gains. A number of North America's larger programs have reported improvements in physical work capacity and reduction in coronary heart disease risk factors (Koerner 1973; Martin 1978; Bjurstrom and Alexiou 1978; Dedmon et al. 1979; Ryan 1980; Rhodes and Dunwoody 1980) but offer no data pertaining to absenteeism, turnover, or productivity.

Establishing a link between programs of physical activity and worker performance has been difficult (Shephard 1974) although actual program results, such as physical changes, have been easier to substantiate. It follows that specific program results may lead to certain company benefits (Table 25.1). Howard and Mikalachki (1979) have cited three major pathways in which program results (improvement in fitness) may be related to positive company effects. The three pathways concern energy levels, attitudes, and health (Figure 25.1).

Increases in cardiorespiratory fitness could improve physical work capacity and influence physical fatigue. However, among white-collar workers this may not be a major factor (Cox, Shephard, and Corey 1981). Improvement in fitness levels for them could possibly influence the onset of mental fatigue (Howard and Mikalachki 1979), reduce injuries caused by impaired judgment due to mental stress (Pravosudov 1976), and improve employee motivation on the job (Cox, Shephard, and Corey 1981). Despite the measurability of such variables, the relationship between fitness and company productivity would not be readily evident (Shephard 1974; Howard and Mikalachki 1979).

Improvement in cardiorespiratory fitness could conceivably influence attitudes in two major directions: mood elevation (Cox, Shephard, and Corey 1981), as well as a more positive self-image may develop (Shephard 1977), and organizational loyalty may be improved (although improved loyalty may be due more to the institution of a new program than to an increase in cardiorespiratory fitness). In the former case, elevation of mood could influence reactions to minor infections and improved self-concept or self-esteem. An interaction between employee fitness programs and company productivity may eventually be shown in health as it relates to fitness. In the latter case, a more positive attitude toward the company may lead to improved job satisfaction and in turn

TABLE 25.1
Potential Company Benefits Related to an Employee Fitness Program

Program Results (Employee Benefits)		Program Effects (Company Benefits)
Improved physical fitness		Reduce long-term Protection/disability premiums
Increased cardiovascular efficiency		
Increased strength		Reduced Workmen's Compensation Board costs
Increased flexibility		
Reduced body fat		
Reduced cardiovascular risk factors	Improved employee health	Reduced short-term (weekly) indemnity insurance premiums
Reduced resting blood pressure		
Reduced body fat		
Reduced blood lipids		
Reduced stress		
Increased awareness of personal health maintenance		Decreased absenteeism due to illness and/or employee dissatisfaction
Improved nutritional habits		
Weight control		
Reduction of stress		
Improved individual self-concept	Greater employee satisfaction	Reduced employee turnover
Increased positive attitude		Decreased employee replacement costs
Improved worker relationships		
More active personal and family lifestyle		

Source: Adapted from Cowan and Cox (1979).

343

FIGURE 25.1
Program Result Pathways Whereby an Employee Fitness Program May Create Benefits to a Company

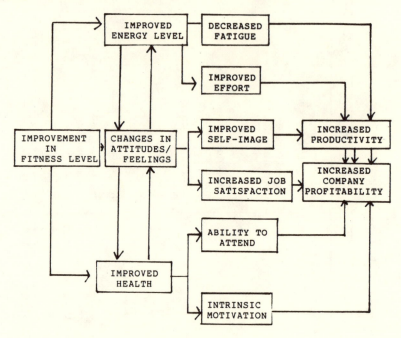

Source: Adapted from Howard and Mikalachki 1979.

affect worker performance. However, this change may be due more to the program itself than to an improvement in fitness.

Improved cardiorespiratory fitness may influence some areas of health. In particular, cardiovascular diseases (Fox 1972; Morris et al. 1953; Paffenbarger 1975) and certain problems associated with obesity (Shephard 1977) may be influenced by routines of physical activity although, as of yet, no optimum level of cardiorespiratory fitness has been ascertained that relates to an optimum level of health (Pollock 1978). (Pollock suggests a Vo_2 max of approximately 44 ml/kg.min $^{-1}$ independent of age.) A cross-sectional study administered in Ontario (Kelly, Nednick, and Goode 1976) showed health care costs to be lower among subjects with a high level of cardiorespiratory fitness. Further, the authors estimated that 5.5 percent of the Ontario Health Insurance Plan (OHIP) budget could be saved if residents aged 20-69 years had an average or better level of fitness. However, due to the nature of the experimental design, the question of cause and effect was left unanswered.

If attendance on the job were affected by health and if it can be postulated that fitness may in turn affect health, then possibly absenteeism due to illness and/or turnover offer the most concrete measures when assessing the relationship between fitness and company productivity. Many factors may influence work attendance; however, Steers and Rhodes (1978) cite job satisfaction and illness as the most significant factors. Further, the cost of absenteeism in Canada exceeds the cost of strikes by a factor of 11 (Timbrell 1979). Moreover, Ontario industry considers turnover and absenteeism to be its most serious problems (Robertson and Humphrey 1978).

Since absenteeism and turnover can be considered tangible evidence, longitudinal studies relating these variables to changes in fitness may elicit bottom-line data in respect to company productivity.

COST EFFECTIVENESS OF
EMPLOYEE FITNESS PROGRAMS

Fitness advocates have hypothesized that a firm implementing an employee fitness program would realize substantial economic gains. However, very little objective information exists as to the economic value of increasing the physical activity level of employees (Bond, Buckwalter, and Perkin 1968; Bryson 1970; Everett 1979). Two major problems have generally existed when attempting to evaluate the investment return of employee fitness programs: the appropriateness and measurability of factors that would be included in a return on investment model (Fitness Ontario 1984) and short-term appraisals of factors that need a longitudinal evaluation (Pyle 1979a; Howard and Mikalachki 1979).

The corporate demand to measure the value and effectiveness of an employee fitness program has been in line with the general business philosophy that any budgeted program meet specific criteria so that the corporate body can objectively support the endeavor. Measuring cost effectiveness or the development of performance measures thus far has had little success. Howard and Mikalachki (1979) maintain one problem has been the lack of understanding and proof in respect to "the links in the chain between exercise programs and positive outcomes." Further, attempting to assess results with global variables, such as productivity, often leads to spurious and inconclusive findings. Because corporate productivity has traditionally been difficult to measure (especially in the short term), it does not seem likely that a fitness-productivity relationship would be apparent. However, based on the assumption that an employee fitness program may improve employee attitudes and an increase in fitness levels may reduce short-term leave for illness and other causes, reduced absenteeism may be one factor in productivity that might relate to an improved state of worker physical fitness.

Several factors can be incorporated into a return-on-investment model. However, at present only a few may be measurable: recruitment, productivity, health care costs, and absenteeism and turnover.

Several firms have suggested a physical activity program to be a useful recruitment tool (Smalley 1978). However, quantifying of this factor would be difficult. Further, if an employee fitness program reduced company turnover, company recruiting practices might have a lesser priority.

The measurement of individual productivity has been extremely difficult, particularly in white-collar industries. Because so many factors affect productivity, results in this area may be less than accurate (Pyle 1979a). Moreover, evidence that improved fitness increases productivity has been relatively nonexistent (Fitness Ontario 1984). Cox, Shephard, and Corey (1981) showed no direct fitness-productivity link, and Finney (1979) demonstrated a consistent level among productivity measures.

In Ontario reduction of corporate health care costs would be difficult to study, because OHIP payments and premiums for Workmen's Compensation and life insurance policies do not reflect a corporation's experience. However, it might be possible that corporation taxes or short- and long-term disability premiums could be adjusted so that corporations with better health experience could have an advantage. One study (Kelly, Nednick, and Goode 1976) has recommended reduced health premiums, income tax incentives, and insurance policy premium reductions to motivate and encourage participation in physical activity programs.

Absenteeism and turnover represent two easily measured variables. A dollar value can be determined by taking the average daily cost of an absent employee and multiplying that figure by the number of days of reduced or increased absenteeism. In the case of turnover, cost of training a new employee might be examined. For example, Pyle

(1979b) estimates "one less heart attack a year within the executive group underwrites the cost of the fringe benefit (the employee fitness program) for the entire group."

An employee fitness program was studied in Toronto during the late 1970s. The purpose of the study was to determine by controlled trial the effects of a well-regulated employee fitness program on fitness levels, lifestyle characteristics, worker performance, and job satisfaction. Methods and results of this study have been previously described (Shephard and Cox 1982; Cox, Shephard, and Corey 1981; Lauzon 1982; Shephard and Cox 1980; Shephard et al. 1983; Shephard, Corey, and Cox 1983). After six months of program operation, subjects who adhered to the fitness program showed advantages relative to the control population in fitness and work attendance (Cox, Shephard, and Corey 1981), in modification of risk behavior (Shephard, Corey, and Cox 1983), and in reduction of health care use (Shephard, Corey, and Cox 1983). Based on the reduction in absenteeism and health care cost, as well as a decrease in yearly turnover, a calculated net gain per employee was $174.00 a year (Fitness Canada 1985).

Although the data is impressive, further research is needed to substantiate these gains. Perhaps, further trials of an extended period will provide convincing proof of a long-term effect relative to the corporate bottom line.

BEHAVIOR AND COMPLIANCE

One assumption relative to employee fitness program efficacy is that a majority of employees will join and eventually regularly attend the corporate sponsored program. Unfortunately, most studies have focused on the probable benefits of augmenting an employee's level of fitness, with little regard to evaluating what techniques and characteristics are associated with maximizing initial participation and establishing long-term adherence patterns. Any employee fitness program must carefully consider the program management function and the subsequent program methods so that maximum employee participation is ensured. Success in maintaining optimum program adherence by the greatest number of employees by definition will lead to the most positive results in terms of employee and company benefits. Nevertheless, studies of recruitment and subsequent exercise adherence in employee fitness programs are almost nonexistent (Cox 1984).

A recent study in our laboratory (Cox, Verde, and Godin 1986) has shown that employees adhering to the fitness program had specific positive beliefs relative to carrying out exercise a few times a week. That is, they perceived the program convenient, worthwhile, healthy. They thought it would help them be physically fit, improve their appearance, and relieve tension. Their high intention to exercise was also related to the perception that exercise was enjoyable and exciting and to the belief that important referents to them supported their behavior. Noncompliers, however, had difficulty establishing a link between exercise and a healthy lifestyle. Interestingly, noncompliers seemed to have a latent positive attitude toward physical activity, however, this attitude was inhibited by lack of support from family and close friends. Moreover, noncompliers were likely to consider physical activity time consuming and not a prudent way to fill free time. Furthermore, this group did not perceive society's attitude or beliefs about exercise as positively as did the high adherents.

Because the majority of employees surveyed in the study seemed to have a latent positive attitude toward physical activity, it would be prudent for management to share some responsibility for facilitating behavior (exercise adherence) in accordance with existing attitudes by the development of a supportive cultural environment.

Besides providing moral and information support, the corporate management could supply tangible support through flexible working hours, encourage participation by allowing exercise to be performed on company time, utilize existing employee communication networks, expand the existing employee fitness program and integrate it with community health endeavors, and provide babysitting and daycare services to enable spouses to be involved in the existing program. While the corporation is modifying the cultural norm, it would be the program director's responsibility to provide programing that is dynamic, constantly changing, meeting the clients needs with a sense of uniqueness.

SUMMARY

Present research and practical experience suggest that employee fitness programs may have a beneficial influence upon the employee and employer. Although all the mechanisms for positive results that have been related to such programs are unclear, it seems that enough evidence is present to proceed at least cautiously with further program implementation. Particularly, if the object of the employer is worker satisfaction, decreased absenteeism, and improved employee health and morale, it may not matter exactly how these gains are achieved as long as the methods are effective. Further, if the response to such programs has both a humanistic benefit and an economic effectiveness, wider use of this technique may be warranted.

REFERENCES

Banister, E. "Health, Fitness and Productivity." *Symposium Proceedings for Human Performance in Business and Industry,* 1978; 9–22.

Barhad, B. "Physical Activity in Modern History." *Physiologie,* 1979; 16:2, 117–22.

Baytos, L. "Nine Strategies for Productivity Improvement." *Personnel Journal,* 1979.

Berkanovic, E. "Behavioral Science and Prevention." *Preventative Medicine,* 1976; 5:92–105.

Bjurstrom, L. A., Alexiou, N. G. "A Program of Heart Disease Intervention for Public Employees." *Journal of Occupational Medicine,* 1978; 20:521–31.

Bond, M. B., Buckwalter, J. E., and Perkin, D. K. "An Occupational Health Program." *Archives of Environmental Health,* 1978; 17:405–15.

Bryson, D. D. "Health and Productivity." *Ergonomics,* 1970; 13...5, 561–68.

Campbell, A. "Subjective Measures of Well-Being." *American Psychology,* 1976; 31:117–24.

Cohen, C., Cohen, E. "Health Education: Panacea, Pernicious or Pointless." *New England Journal of Medicine,* 1978; 718–20.

Council on Scientific Affairs. "Physician Supervised Exercise Programs in Rehabilitation of Patients with Coronary Heart Disease." *JAMA,* 1981; 245:1463–66.

Cowan, D., Cox, M. H. "The Benefits of a Corporate Fitness Program." Paper presented at the Industrial Accident Prevention Association, National Conference, Toronto, Canada, 1979.

Cox, M. H. "Corporate Investment in Human Resources: A New Twist." *The Canadian Business Review*, 1982; 9:9–14.

____. "Fitness Life-Style Programs for Business and Industry: Problems in Recruitment and Retention." *Journal of Cardiac Rehabilitation*, 1984; 4:136–42.

____. Shephard, R. J., Corey, P. "The Influence of an Employee Fitness Program upon Fitness, Productivity, and Absenteeism." *Ergonomics*, 1981; 24:795–806.

Cox, M. H., Verde, T., Godin, G. "Exercise Compliance in Corporate Fitness Programs." *In preparation*, 1986.

Dedmon, R. E., Gander, J. W., O'Connor, M. P., Paschke, A. C. "An Industry Health Management Program." *Physician Sports Medicine*, 1979; 7:56–57.

Denton, F. T., Feaver, C. H., Spencer, B. G. "The Future Population and Labour Force of Canada: Projections to the Year 2051." *Economic Council of Canada*, 1980.

Durbeck, D. C., Heinzelman, F., Schacter, J., Haskell, W. L., Payne, G. H., Moxley, R. T., Nemiroff, M., Limoncelli, D., Arnoldi, L., Fox, S. "The National Aeronautics and Space Administration — US Public Health Service Health Education and Enhancement Program." *American Journal of Cardiology*, 1972; 784–90.

Everett, M. D. "Strategies for Increasing Employees' Level of Exercise and Physical Fitness." *Journal of Occupational Medicine*, 1979; 21:7, 463–67.

Fielding, J. E. "Preventive Medicine and the Bottom-Line." *Journal of Occupational Medicine*, 1979; 21:79–88.

Finney, C. "Recreation: Its Effect on Productivity. A Recent Study and Its Unexpected Results." *Recreation Management*, 1979; 21:10.

Fitness Canada. "Fitness and a Productive Exercise." *Fitness Works*. Fitness and Amateur Sport, Ottawa, 1985.

Fitness Ontario. "Cost Benefit Guide to Fitness in the Workplace." Sport and Fitness Ontario, 1984.

Fox, S. M., Naughton, J., Gorman, P. A. "Physical Activity and Cardiovascular Health." *Modern Concepts of Cardiovascular Disease*, 1972; 41:4, 17–20.

Frankenhaeuser, M. "Job Demands, Health, and Well-Being." *Journal of Psychosomatic Research*, 1977; 21:313–21.

Garry, W. "Integrating Wellness into Learning." *Training ad Development Journal*, 1980; 48–54.

Green, L. W. "Status Identity and Preventive Health Behavior." *Pacific Health Education Reports*, 1970; 1:1–13.

Health and Welfare, Canada. "Proceedings of the National Conference on Employee Physical Fitness." *Department of National Health and Welfare*, 1975.

Haggerty, R. J. "Changing Lifestyles to Improve Health." *Preventive Medicine*, 1977; 6:276–89.

Heinzelman, F., Bagley, R. W. "Response to Physical Activity Programs with Their Effects on Health Behavior." *Public Health Report*, 1970; 905–11.

Howard, J., Mikalachki, A. "Fitness and Employee Productivity." *Canadian Journal of Applied Science*, 1979; 4:191–98.

Ilmarinen, J., Rutenfrang, J., Knauth, P., Ahrens, M., Kylian, H., Siuda, A., Korallus, J. "The Effect of an On-The-Job Training Program — Stairclimbing — on the Physical Working Capacity of Employees." *European Journal of Applied Physiology*, 1978; 38:25–40.

Jetté, M. "The Participation of Canadian Employees in Physical Activity." *Canadian Journal of Public Health*, 1980; 71:109–11.

Keir, S. "Keynote Address 2." *Canadian Journal of Public Health*, 1976; 67 (Supplement No. 2): 27–30.

Kelly, N. A., Nednick, H., Goode, R. C. *The Relationship between Physical Fitness and Cost of Health Care*. Ottawa: Quasar Systems, 1976.

Kerr, C., Rosow, J. M. *Work in America: The Decade Ahead*. Toronto: Van Nostrand, 1979.

Kettle, J. *The Big Generation*. Toronto: McCelland and Stewart, 1980.

Koerner, D. "Cardiovascular Benefits from an Industrial Physical Fitness Program." *Journal of Occupational Medicine*, 1973; 15:700–7.

Lindén, V. "Absence from Work and Physical Fitness." *British Journal of Industrial Medicine*, 1969; 26:47-54.

Laporte, W. "The Influence of a Gymnastic Pause upon Recovery Following Post Office Work." *Ergonomics*, 1966; 9:501–6.

Lauzon, R. "The Bottom Line — Employee Fitness." *The Canadian Business Review*, 1982; 9:6–8.

Martin, J. "Corporate Health: A Result of Employee Fitness." *The Physician and Sports Medicine*, 1978; 135–37.

Megalli, B. "Employee Fitness Programs: Philanthropic Venture or Shrewd Investment." *The Labour Gazette*, 1978; 174–82.

Milio, N. "A Framework for Prevention: Changing Health-Damaging to Health-Generating Life Patterns." *American Journal of Public Health*, 1966; 66:453–39.

Morris, J. N., Heady, J. A., Raffle, P. A., Roberts, P., Park, J. W. "Coronary Heart Disease and Physical Activity of Work." *Lancet*, 1953; 3:111–20.

Oldridge, N. "Efficacy and Effectiveness: Critical Issues in Exercise and Compliance." *Journal of Cardiac Rehabilitation*, 1984; 4:11–20.

Paffenbarger, R. S., Jr., Hale, W. E. "Work Activity and Coronary Heart Mortality." *New England Journal of Medicine*, 1975; 292: 545–50.

Pafnote, M., Voida, I., Luchian, O. "Physical Fitness in Different Groups of Industrial Workers." *Physiologie*, 1979; 16:2, 129–31.

Peters, K. R., Benson, H., Porter, D. "Daily Relaxation Response Breaks in a Working Population: Effects on Self-Reported Measures of Health, Performance, and Well-Being." *American Journal of Public Health*, 1977; 67:10, 946–52.

Pollock, M. L. "How Much Exercise Is Enough." *The Physician and Sports Medicine*, 1978; 6:50–64.

Pravosudov, V. P. "Effects of Physical Exercise on Health and Economic Efficiency." Proceedings International Congress of Physical Activity Sciences, *Physical Activity and Human Well-Being*, 1976; 11–16.

Pyle, R. L. "Performance Measures of a Corporate Fitness Program." *Human Resources Management*, Fall, 1979a; 26–30.

———. "Corporate Fitness Program — How Do They Shape Up?" *Personnel*, 1979b; 58–67.

Rhodes, E. C., Dunwoody, D. "Physiological and Attitude Changes in Those Involved in an Employee Fitness Program." *Canadian Journal of Public Health*, 1980; 71:331–36.

Robertson, G., Humphrey, J. "Labour Turnover and Absenteeism in Selected Industries: Northwestern Ontario and Ontario." *Component Study No. 10,*

Ontario Ministry of Labour, and Employment and Immigration Canada, 1978.

Roys, K. "The Impact of Increasing Leisure Time on Society and Corporate Administration." *Proceedings from the NIRA*, Atlanta, 1979.

Ryan, A. "Employee Fitness Programs: A Round Table." *Physicians Sports Medicine,* 1980; 8:64–72.

Salmon, A. "Physical Activity in the Workplace." Ministry of Tourism and Recreation, Fitness Ontario, 1981.

Shephard, R. J. "A Brief Bibliography on Fatigue and Fitness." *Journal of Occupational Medicine,* 1974; 16:804–8.

____. *Endurance Fitness.* 2d ed. Toronto: University of Toronto Press, 1977.

Shephard, R. J., Corey, P., Cox, M. H. "Health Hazard Appraisal — The Influence of an Employee Fitness Program." *Canadian Journal of Public Health,* 1983; 73:183–87.

Shephard, R. J., Corey, P., Rengland, P., Cox, M. H. "The Impact of Changes in Fitness and Lifestyle upon Health Care Utilization." *Canadian Journal of Public Health,* 1983; 74:51–54.

Shephard, R. J., Cox, M. H., "Some Characteristics of Participants in an Industrial Fitness Program." *Canadian Journal of Applied Sports Sciences,* 1980, 5:2, 69–76.

Shephard, R. J., Cox, M. H. "Step-Test Predictions of Maximum Oxygen Uptake before and after an Employee Fitness Programme." *Canadian Journal of Applied Sports Science,* 1982; 7:197–201.

Shephard, R. J., Morgan, P., Finucane, R., Schimmelfing, L., Brown, P. "Factors Influencing Recruitment to an Occupational Fitness Program." *Journal of Occupational Medicine,* 1980; 22:389–98.

Sidney, K. H., Shephard, R. J. "Attitudes towards Health and Physical Activity in the Elderly: Effects of a Physical Training Program." *Medicine Science Sports, 1976*; 8:246–52.

Skinner, J. S. "Longevity, General Health, and Exercise." In *Exercise Physiology,* edited by H. B. Falls. New York: Academic Press, 1968.

Smalley, J. Personal Communication. Vice-President, Human Resource Department, Canada Life Assurance Company, 1978.

Steers, R. M., Rhodes, S. R. "Major Influences on Employee Attendance: A Process Model." *Journal of Applied Psychology,* 1978; 63:4, 391–407.

Somers, A. "Recharting National Health Priorities: A New Canadian Perspective." *New England Journal of Medicine,* 1974; 291:415–16.

Trimbrell, D. *Globe and Mail,* October 4, 1979, p. 1.

U.S. Senate Hearings on National Health Promotion and Education, 1975. Subcommittee on Health, May 7–8, 1975, Washington, D.C., Senate passed S. 1467.

Yarvote, P. M., McDonagh, T. J., Goldman, M. E., Zuskerman, J. "Organization and Evaluation of a Physical Fitness Program in Industry." *Journal of Occupational Medicine, 1974;* 16:589–98.

26 Workplace Smoking Control in the United States: Economic, Health, Legal, Programmatic, and Policy Issues

Rebecca S. Parkinson and Michael P. Eriksen

ASSESSMENT OF THE ISSUES

Health Effects

Cigarette smoking is the number one preventable cause of premature death and disability (USDHEW 1979b). Since the first major report on smoking, published by the United States Surgeon General in 1964, the evidence of the adverse health effects of smoking has continued to grow. Warner (1984) has recently observed that the number of lives annually claimed by smoking is equivalent to the airline industry experiencing three jumbo jet crashes a day for one year. Recent epidemiological research relates smoking to at least 30 percent of all cancers (Doll and Peto 1976) and cites it as the major cause of lung cancer in both men and women (*Cancer Facts* 1983). With an estimated 83 percent of all lung cancers in men resulting from smoking and another 43 percent of female cases of lung cancer attributable to smoking, lung cancer is now the leading cause of cancer death in women, surpassing breast cancer (*Cancer Facts* 1983). Ironically, lung cancer is one of the most preventable of all the cancers.

Cigarette smoking is responsible for a host of other health-related problems, cardiovascular disease being the most prevalent. Thirty percent of all deaths in the United States are due to coronary heart disease, and at least 30 percent of these deaths are attributable to smoking (USDHHS 1983). Smoking is related to 80 percent of the deaths from respiratory disease (USDHHS 1984). It is also linked to cerebrovascular disease, peptic ulcers, cancer of the larynx, kidney, pancreas and other major organs (USDHHS 1982). Smoking has been shown to have adverse effects on the fetus, increasing the risk of spontaneous abortion, low birth weight, and neonatal death (USDHEW 1979b).

Smoking prevalence varies by age, sex, educational level, occupational status, and presence of other lifestyle risk factors (Remington et al. 1985). The prevalence of smoking among workers is 36 percent: 38.9 percent for males and 32.9 percent for females. Blue-collar workers have higher smoking rates than these averages: 50 percent for males and 39 percent for females (OASH 1980; OSH 1981). More lost workdays are reported for smokers than for nonsmokers: 33 percent more in males, 45 percent more in females. Smokers experience higher bed disability than nonsmokers: 14 percent in males and 17 percent in females. These excess disability figures are dose-related (USDHEW, 1979a). Other studies report that smokers have a 50 percent higher health care utilization rate, add an additional two to three days a year of absenteeism, and experience increased work accidents and disability reimbursements (USDHEW 1979a; Luce and Schweitzer 1978). The significance of the health effects of smoking is thoroughly reviewed in recent articles by Fielding (1985a) and Jackson and Holle (1985).

The interaction of smoking and the occupational environment is of particular concern for those interested in the control of workplace smoking. In 1979, the National Institute of Occupational Safety and Health (1979a) identified six ways smoking can interact with the occupational environment:

Toxic agents in tobacco smoke may also occur in the work environment, thus increasing exposure to this agent.

Workplace chemicals may be transformed into more harmful agents by smoking.

Tobacco products may serve as vectors facilitating the entry of toxic agents into the worker's body.

The toxic effects of smoking may combine additively with workplace toxic agents.

The toxic effects of smoking may combine multiplicatively with workplace toxic agents.

Smoking may contribute to accidents in the workplace through loss of attention.

The importance of the interaction of smoking and the occupational environment should not be underestimated. Suta and Thompson (1983) recently studied blue-collar automotive workers and discovered that excess lung cancer mortality rates were almost entirely attributable to smoking. The importance of smoking as an occupational health hazard has been recently reviewed by Collishaw, Kirbridge, and Wigle (1984).

In addition to the direct effects of smoking on personal health, a growing body of research supports the impact of passive, or secondhand, smoke on nonsmokers. Although the specific effects of passive smoke are still being researched and debated, there is substantial agreement that side-stream smoke adversely affects the health of children (Vogt 1984; Weiss et al. 1983) and irritates the senses (Epstein 1975), especially among individuals with preexisting conditions such as asthma, bronchitis, rhinitis, and allergies. It also has been cited as a potential cause of cardiovascular disease (Garland et al. 1985; National Research Council 1981).

During the past five years, the studies on passive smoking have been conducted worldwide. U.S. researchers, White and Froeb (1980) and Kauffmann, Tessier, and Oriol (1983), found a decrease in small airway lung function among nonsmokers chronically exposed to secondhand smoke. This decrease resembled the lung function tests of light smokers. Japanese researchers cited evidence of lung cancer in nonsmoking wives of husbands who smoke (Hirayama 1981). Greek researchers Trichopoulos and associates (1981) found a statistically significant risk of lung cancer in the nonsmoking wives of husbands who smoked. Additional U.S. studies by Correa et al. (1983); Miller (1984); Hammond and Selikoff (1981); Friedman, Pettitti, and Bawol (1983); and Jarvis, Russell, and Feyerabend (1983) all confirm the evidence of lung cancer risk in nonsmoking wives of husbands who smoke. Recently, studies by Sandler, Wilcox, and Everson (1985) have demonstrated an increased cancer risk in adulthood among children who were exposed to parental smoking in their early years. An overview of the health effects of passive smoking on children and adults was recently published by Fielding (1985a).

The previous discussion has briefly outlined the severity of health problems facing smokers, with mounting evidence from international research pointing to a prudent avoidance of exposure to cigarette smoke even by nonsmokers. How these two health warnings affect industry and the strategies for controlling this health problem are the subject of the following discussion.

Economic Impact

It is agreed that increased health care utilization and disability by smokers translates into higher health care costs for employers. But there is significant debate over the extent of the economic impact of smoking on the health care costs of business and industry. The economic costs of smoking include more than increased health care expenditures; they include life, fire and accident insurance, maintenance expenses, and lost productivity. One economist, Marvin Kristein (1983), has estimated the annual cost of smoking to the employer to be in excess of $600 annually per smoker.

Describing the economics of smoking, Kristein breaks out five cost centers: insurance, absenteeism and sickness, productivity, involuntary smoking, and occupational health costs. Kristein calculates that an employer pays an additional $75–$150 a year in health insurance for each employee who smokes. He estimates that excess costs associated with fire, accident, and life insurance add $5, $17–$34, and $20–$33 respectively. Absenteeism and sickness benefits add an additional $50–$80 per smoker annually. (This estimate also includes any leftover effects of absenteeism among ex-smokers.) Productivity loss included by Kristein, such as work time lost because of the smoking ritual, clean-up costs, and damage to furniture and equipment, add $166 per smoker annually. Two other cost centers cited by Kristein, passive smoking and occupational hazards, add $27–$56 annually per involuntary smoker and $72 annually for occupational health liabilities. These figures bring the total economic cost for smoking to $336–$601 annually per smoker.

Another economist, William Weis (1981) cites productivity losses equal to or above $1,800 a year. Weis totals his calculations at $4,700 per smoker annually. The significant difference in estimates between these two economists serves to demonstrate the debate surrounding the economic impact of smoking. However, the importance of the problem is underscored even by Kristein's conservative estimates.

Legal and Policy Assessment

Recent years have shown a significant increase in state and local organizations lobbying for smoking ordinances and legislation. Industry has felt increased pressure to defend itself in litigation involving "nonsmokers rights" and to make efforts to respond proactively to anticipated legal demands. In general most industries believe that workplace smoking control is best handled by the industry itself, leaving the decision making to the people who are the most sensitive to the employees' needs. Only a minority of industries have taken a proactive stance on the question of smoking policies and legislative action. However, time, social pressure, and the litigious nature of society now have created an avalanche of actions forcing industry to respond.

Legal relief from the smoking problem has been sought by nonsmoking employees to remedy the situation they face in public and work places. Such legal action was taken in the following cases over six different issues.

Common Law Duty to Provide a Safe and Healthful Workplace
    Shrmp vs. *New Jersey Bell Telephone Co.*
    Smith vs. *Western Electric*
    Gordon vs. *Raven Systems and Research Co.*
Entitlement to Early Disability and Retirement Benefits
    Parodi vs. *Merit Systems Protection Board*
Entitlement to Worker's Compensation Benefits
    Fuentes vs. *Worker's Compensation Appeals Board*
    Brooks vs. *Trans World Airlines*
Entitlement to Unemployment Benefits
    Alexander vs. *CA Unemployment Insurance Appeals Board*
    Gibson vs. *Starkist*
    Apell vs. *Moorestown (N.J.) Board of Education*
Protection from Wrongful Discharge
    Hentzel vs. *The Singer Company*
    Gibson vs. *Starkist*
Reasonable Accommodation Due to Handicap
    Vickers vs. *Veterans Administration*
    Pletten vs. *U.S. Army*

These six approaches have all yielded successful results for nonsmokers (Eriksen 1985b). The only legal action that has not proven successful is an employee's appeal based on a "constitutional right" for a smoke-free environment.

Concurrent to the rise in litigation regarding smoking, there also has been an increase in the number of state and local ordinances regarding workplace and public smoking control. As of 1984, 38 states and the District of Columbia have passed smoking legislation or administrative regulation designed to reduce nonsmokers' exposure to secondhand smoke. Twenty-five states have "clean indoor air acts" (Walsh 1985). Many states that do not have state legislation have passed local ordinances (for example, California, Colorado, and New York). These legislative efforts have sought to regulate smoking, in many cases by actually requiring a written policy at the workplace.

Mounting legal and legislative action has increased pressure on industries to formulate formal smoking policies. Past history has shown a steady reluctance to develop such policies except in cases where clear occupational safety or health hazards existed or where traditional compromises for large public gathering places, such as employee cafeterias and lounges, have been in place. Many corporations have preferred not to put general policies in writing but have handled employee relations problems on a case by case basis.

There are very compelling reasons why many companies have chosen not to implement formal policies:

Ignorance of the health and social issues involved in smoking control.
Belief that smoking policies are not enforceable.
Belief that a formal smoking policy will stimulate legislation, employee relations problems, and/or potential labor relations problems.
Company business may be dependent upon a relationship with tobacco and/or tobacco-related companies.
Executive and/or key managers are smokers.

Whatever the reason for corporate reluctance to develop smoking polices, corporations must begin to react to impending local and state legislative endeavors by demonstrating their internal capacity to deal with the issue and by developing effective smoking control policies. What was once solely the responsibility of employers is increasingly being influenced by legal and legislative action.

Programmatic Issues

The increased concern over the health effects of smoking and the identification of this problem as a preventable lifestyle have led to the development of numerous smoking cessation methodologies. Programmatic interventions using behavior modification, social learning theory, hypnotism, acupuncture, social support, and nicotine substitutes have been blended to offer smokers extensive opportunities to change their smoking behavior.

But underlying the provision of cessation programs is an unresolved research question. How does one match the varied interventions to the needs of smokers? Although the research evidence citing smoking as an addiction is growing, the ability to clearly separate the addictive quality from the behavioral, social, and habituative patterns still remains unresolved. For some, smoking is a physiological and/or psychological addiction, as evidenced by the recent classification of certain smoking patterns by the American Psychiatric Association. For others, it is a complex behavioral pattern associated with, and reinforced by, personal and social cues over many years of habituation. For others, it is both an addiction and a lifestyle habit.

The research states that 95 percent of those individuals who quit smoking permanently quit on their own (USDHEW 1978). However, it is difficult to know how many of these individuals have previously participated in some formal intervention program and are using the associated skills to quit or which individuals are quitting cold turkey without the previous benefit of formal programs.

Additionally, the behavioral and epidemiological research data have yet to successfully predict the type of intervention(s) best suited for the wide variety of individuals who want to quit. For most individuals the choice of programs becomes "trial by error" until a program finally matches personality needs with timing and the skills needed to permanently remove the addiction and control the behavioral patterns.

A significant part of this programmatic dilemma is due to the lack of data on the relative effectiveness of various cessation interventions. Reasons for the absence of credible evaluative data are twofold. First and foremost, is the time lag in getting evaluative research from cessation programs into the literature or into practical usage channels. Evaluative studies are often completed by health promotion managers who do not have time to compile the results or who have not built in a formal evaluative process to control for variables that may confound the results. Second, lack of standard data collection mechanisms make intergroup comparisons among published research results difficult. Finally, cessation data are often viewed suspiciously when used for publicity and promotion of programs.

The last issue facing a programmatic solution to the smoking control problem involves the difficulty in determining actual quit rates. The smoking literature continues to demonstrate quit rates for addictive behaviors between 20 percent to 25 percent one year postcessation (Hunt and Bespalec 1974; Leventhal and Cleary 1980; and Lichtenstein and Brown 1980). Additionally, most companies are only able to get about 10 percent of their smoking population to participate voluntarily in cessation programs. Therefore, if only 30 percent to 35 percent of the working population smokes, 10 percent are interested in quitting and 25 percent of these quit permanently, only a small number of individuals in any one year will benefit from a program that may have involved a fair degree of managerial and organizational effort. Despite these issues, the seriousness of the health problem attributable to workplace smoking demands that smoking cessation programs receive serious consideration.

STRATEGIES FOR SMOKING CONTROL

Four major actions constitute the most coherent business strategy for controlling workplace smoking: corporate smoking policies, smoking cessation programs, incentives for nonsmoking, and environmental control measures.

Smoking Policies

The relative reluctance of industries to develop formal corporate policies on smoking has not diminished the need for such policies. Positive benefit can be derived from these efforts. In addition to the traditional approach of protecting equipment and, thereby, safeguarding an economic investment, industries also can safeguard the return on their human resource investment.

If one takes a look at why industries develop formal smoking policies, the following positive aspects are revealed. Smoking policies protect the health of workers, especially where environmental hazards exist; clarify the company's position on smoking and nonsmoking; provide clear guidelines for handling disputes among employees regarding smoking and nonsmoking areas; provide a consistent statement of the company's beliefs regarding employee welfare; assist in the company's strategy to manage health care costs; serve as a basis for responding to local and state legislative efforts; provide social support and reinforcement for health promotion programs that encourage nonsmoking and healthier lifestyles; and present a corporate image that demonstrates a culture that is concerned about the health of its employees (Eriksen 1985a; Walsh 1984).

A smoking policy cannot do several things. Survey research indicates that even smokers are supportive of smoking policies and may smoke less or try to quit if a policy is implemented, but there is little data proving a causal relationship between a smoking policy and an actual decrease in the amount of cigarette smoking (Eriksen 1985a). In addition, a smoking policy does not totally protect the company from future personnel problems arising out of conflicts between smokers and nonsmokers or from future legal claims from nonsmokers.

There is considerable debate regarding the adoption of workplace smoking policies. Shipley and Orleans (1985) estimate that at least 50 percent of all U.S. companies have adopted some type of restrictive smoking policy. Even research sponsored by the Tobacco Institute (Solomon 1985) indicates that nearly 40 percent of leading U.S. corporations have formal smoking policies. Because both local and state smoking legislation usually requires employers to develop and post a smoking policy, it can be anticipated that the prevalence of nonsmoking policies will increase in the future.

In an early attempt to publish a set of policy guidelines, "A Model Policy for Smoking in the Workplace" was developed out of recommendations from the National Conference on Smoking and Health held in the United States in 1981. While now somewhat out-dated, it is still available through local offices of the American Cancer Society. Another publication, "A Smoke-free Workplace," from the California Nonsmokers Rights Foundation, reprints model policies as does the American Lung Association's publication, "Creating Your Company Policy." Local voluntary organizations concerned with heart, cancer, and lung diseases, as well as major industries, also are sound resources for policy development and sample policies.

Employee Attitudes toward Smoking Policies

A 1983 Gallup poll in the United States revealed the following attitudes toward smoking. Ninety-two percent of all the respondents (smokers and nonsmokers) agreed with smoking's harmful effect. Workplace restrictions designating smoking areas or a total prohibition on smoking were favored by 87 percent of the nonsmokers and 75 percent of the smokers (American Lung Assoc. 1983).

In 1982, Pacific Bell (Eriksen 1985a) conducted an employee survey regarding workplace smoking. Survey results indicated that 60 percent of surveyed nonsmokers were either always or frequently bothered by smoking at work and that nearly 75 percent of all employees felt that the company should do something about the problem of workplace smoking. Interestingly, 51 percent of the smokers said they would either try to quit or cut down the amount smoked if the company adopted a smoking policy.

Policy Format

The components of a smoking policy follow a fairly standard format. Most common polices include the following elements:

statement of background or purpose
statement of policy
public work areas: cafeterias, lounges, libraries, cashier waiting lines, restrooms, and hallways
existing nonsmoking areas: elevators and areas with sensitive technical equipment or where fire hazards exist such as storage areas
private work spaces: shared work areas and private offices
educational programs for awareness and cessation: type of programs, the costs, availability, and other details.

Many smoking policies have traditionally regulated large public work areas by using signs to separate sections of smokers and nonsmokers. In the recent past, shared work spaces usually have been given to the smokers with barriers or ventilating devices being used. It is only recently that smoking policies have begun to reflect a change, giving the preference to the nonsmoker and completely banning smoking in those areas when an irreconcilable dispute arises. Private offices have traditionally been the province of the occupant. Prohibition for safety and occupational health guidelines have been the rule where technical or sensitive materials are present (McIntosh 1985). Companies such as Pacific Northwest Bell have chosen to ban smoking altogether in the workplace. Other companies, such as Manville, have instituted preemployment practices that do not allow the hiring of smokers because of the interrelationship between occupational exposures (for example, asbestos) and smoking.

Smoking Cessation Programs

The major goal of a workplace smoking control program is to reduce the prevalence of smoking among employees, thereby avoiding economic costs and improving the health of employees. In addition to the previously mentioned economic savings, it is estimated that most people who have quit smoking for 15 or more years have mortality risks very similar to their peers who have never smoked (USDHEW 1979). Thus, cessation programs are an integral part of making smoking policies acceptable and practical in the workplace.

Smoking cessation courses are an integral part of many health promotion programs. The National Interagency Council on Smoking and Health (1980) recently estimated that 15 percent of a sample of U.S. corporations offer cessation programs and another 33 percent would like to expand their programs to include such programs. A California survey of industries found smoking cessation programs to be offered by approximately 11 percent of the companies, with larger companies more likely to provide such programs (Fielding and Breslow 1983).

In reviewing workplace smoking cessation programs, Orleans and Shipley (1982) characterized six different types of workplace smoking cessation activities: educational or information campaigns, workplace smoking restrictions, self-help programs, physician advice, incentive programs, and actual smoking cessation programs.

Most programs involve different combinations of three levels of intervention: information and awareness, behavioral change skills, and social support. Most programs offer the traditional range of information regarding smoking hazards and self-awareness or monitoring techniques for identifying the amount and cues for smoking. Behavior modification principles often are used to break the network of social, personal, and behavioral cues that trigger the smoking response. New behavior patterns then are substituted. Social learning theory attempts to bolster participants' perceived self-efficiency in their ability to stop smoking. Some programs suggest that participants sign behavioral contracts that are monitored periodically. Rewards are given for compliance, similar to hypertension and diabetes control programs. Many programs offer a limited form of social support and reinforcement over time to help maintain the ex-smoker status.

Different approaches such as acupuncture, hypnotism, aversive techniques, and Nicorette gum may be used singly or in conjunction with the behavioral techniques. There is also a diverse range in the timing and intensity of interventions. Some programs last six to eight weeks; others are five days; still others are five consecutive days with two additional days for orientation and reinforcement. Most behavioral programs meet for one to two hours. Varying degrees of intensity and monitoring are required in the participants' homework assignments.

The success rates of these programs differ considerably. Hunt and Bespalec (1974) estimate the average quit rate after nine to eighteen months is 20 percent to 30 percent; some programs with intensive clinical and educational assistance have reported results of 33 percent to 80 percent. Some programs can maintain cessation at 40 percent to 60 percent after one year (Fielding 1982; Parkinson 1985). Those programs offering primarily information, instruction, and encouragement achieve only 15 percent to 27 percent quit rates (Fielding 1982). It is difficult to readily determine which of these various programs are the most cost-effective without separating out other environmental, social, and programmatic supports.

Numerous public and private voluntary health agencies, such as the American Lung Association, American Cancer Society, and American Heart Association, offer smoking cessation programs. In addition, private organizations, consultants, and hospital employee health promotion programs offer cessation programs to companies. Identifying smoking cessation program resources usually is not the problem. Rather, the difficulty lies in choosing which programs best meet the company's needs. Some companies have set internal guidelines to assist managers in this choice. Also, a recent review of smoking cessation program effectiveness can be found in Loeb et al. (1984).

Incentives

Recent investigations into the effectiveness of smoking cessation programs have revealed significant controversy with regard to the use of incentives to encourage quitting. A similar question is raised in conjunction with other health promotion programs. Frederiksen (1985) reviewed the use of incentives in such programs but did not reach any definitive conclusion of efficacy. Industries have used financial incentives to promote quitting either by requiring an initial or partial payment (thus increasing personal commitment) or by returning payment after successful quitting in the form of cash, credit toward other lifestyle programs, and/or credit toward raffles and other material incentives (T-shirts, mugs, pens, company products).

Health promotion programs, smoking or otherwise, have not sufficiently proven that incentives are a necessary part of programing. However, the anecdotal evidence cited by health promotion managers continues to support the use of incentives. Part of the problem in obtaining "proof" for incentives is the need to create a controlled environment in which some employees are denied incentives while others are recipients of such rewards. This type of discriminatory behavior, even within a research design, is difficult to conduct in a business setting.

Environmental Control

In addition to the policy and programmatic strategies promulgated by companies, specific environmental actions can be used to complement other smoking control tactics. The rationale for such control lies with employers with worksites that cannot ban smoking but want to protect their nonsmoking workforce from the irritation, annoyance, and possible hazard of side-stream smoke. Environmental controls simply provide a mechanism to limit the ambient smoke from the air. These controls include: ventilation, air purification (smokeless ashtrays and air filters or purifiers), and physical barriers or separations between smokers and nonsmokers. However, even the best researchers raise questions about the effectiveness of these techniques because of the uncontrollable factors such as the concentration of smoke in the air, control over air flow patterns, and inefficient ventilation devices.

FUTURE IMPLICATIONS AND CONCLUSIONS

This chapter identifies and discusses the reasons businesses are becoming involved in the control of workplace smoking. Health, economic, and legal reasons compel today's corporations to manage workplace smoking similarly to the management of other employee health problems.

What can be expected in the future? As previously discussed, companies are increasingly likely to offer smoking cessation programs and to implement restrictive workplace smoking policies. Simultaneously, local jurisdictions and states are proposing and adopting comprehensive smoking control ordinances with restrictive provisions for the workplace.

An increasing corporate concern is developing for future liability for smoking-related disorders among employed nonsmokers. Given the increasing evidence supporting the adverse health effects associated with exposure to secondhand smoke, it is not unlikely to assume that nonsmokers who contract smoking-related diseases (lung cancer and respiratory disorders) may seek financial compensation from the employer who allowed such smoking to occur. Corporate lawyers, human resource officials, and risk managers are increasingly looking for ways to limit potential liability from smoking-related problems.

While businesses are attempting to manage and control workplace smoking, tobacco-related concerns are actively launching countermeasures. The tobacco industries are aggressively promoting the social acceptability of smoking and attempting to refute the burgeoning nonsmoker's rights movement, particularly as it applies to the workplace. In addition, the Tobacco Institute has introduced a free magazine for smokers and those supportive of the tobacco industry and continues to fund and disseminate research supportive of their prosmoking perspective.

Despite the efforts of the tobacco industry, it is anticipated that businesses will continue to successfully manage and control workplace smoking. By developing a workplace smoking control program that includes a restrictive smoking policy, smoking cessation programs, and incentives for nonsmoking, corporations will continue to protect the nonsmoker and assist smokers who would like to stop smoking.

REFERENCES

Cancer Facts and Figures. New York: American Cancer Society, 1983.

Collishaw, N. E., J. Kirbridge, and D. T. Wigle. "Tobacco Smoke in the Workplace: An Occupational Health Hazard." *Canada Medical Association Journal* 131 (1984), 1199–1204.

Correa, P., L. W. Pickle, E. Fontham, Y. Lin, and W. Haenszel. "Passive Smoking and Lung Cancer." *Lancet* (September 1983), 595–97.

Doll, R., and R. Peto. "Mortality in Relation to Smoking: 20 Years Observation on Male British Doctors." *British Medical Journal* 2 (1976), 1525.

Epstein, N. "The Effects of Tobacco Smoke to the Eyes of the Allergic Non-Smoker." *Pro*

Eriksen, M. P. "Smoking Policies at Pacific Bell." *Corporate Commentary* 1:4 (1985a), 24–34.

____. "Workplace Smoking Control: Rationale and Approaches." *Advances in Health Education and Promotion* 1 (1985b).

Fielding, J. E. "Effectiveness of Employee Health Improvement Programs." *Journal of Occupational Medicine* 24 (1982).

____. "Smoking: Health Effects and Controls, Part 1." *New England Journal of Medicine* 313:8 (1985a), 491–97.

____. "Smoking: Health Effects and Control, Part 2." *New England Journal of Medicine* 313:9 (1985b), 555–61.

____. "Practical Solutions to Smoking Controls." *Corporate Commentary* 1:4 (1985c), 46–49.

Fielding, J. E., and L. Breslow. "Health Promotion Programs Sponsored by California Employers." *American Journal of Public Health* 73 (1983), 538–42.

Frederiksen, L. "Using Incentives in Worksite Wellness." *Corporate Commentary* 1 (November 1985), 51–57.

Friedman, G. D., D. B. Pettitti, and R. D. Bawol. "Prevalence and Correlates of Passive Smoking." *American Journal of Epidemiology* 121:5 (1985), 645–50.

Garland, C., E. Barrett-Connor, L. Suarez, M. H. Criqui, and D. L. Wingard. "Effects of Passive Smoking on Ischemic Heart Disease Mortality of Nonsmokers." *American Journal of Epidemiology* 121:5 (1985), 645–50.

Hammond, E. C., and I. J. Selikoff. "Passive Smoking and Lung Cancer with Comments on Two New Papers." *Environmental Research* 24 (1981), 444–52.

Hirayama, T. "Non-Smoking Wives of Heavy Smokers Have Higher Risk of Lung Cancer: A Study from Japan." *British Medical Journal* 282 (1981), 183–85.

Hunt, W. A., and D. A. Bespalec. "An Evaluation of Current Methods of Modifying Smoking Behavior." *Journal of Clinical Psychology* 30 (1974), 431–38.

Jackson, F. N., and R. H. O. Holle. "Smoking: Perspectives 1985." *Primary Care* 12:2 (1985), 197–216.

Jarvis, M. J., M. A. Russell, and C. Feyerabend. "Absorption of Nicotine and Carbon Monoxide from Passive Smoking under Natural Conditions of Exposure." *Thorax* 38 (1983), 829–33.

Kauffmann, F., J. F. Tessier, and F. Oriol. "Adult Passive Smoking in the Home Environment: A Risk Factor for Chronic Airflow Limitation." *American Journal of Epidemiology* 117:3 (1983), 269–80.

Kristein, M. M. "Wanted: Smoking Policies for the Work Place." *Business and Health* (November 1984), 14–18.

_____. "How Much Can Business Expect to Profit from Smoking Cessation?" *Preventive Medicine* 12 (1983), 358–81.

Leventhal, H., and P. D. Cleary. "The Smoking Problem: A Review of the Research and Theory in Behavioral Risk Modification." *Psychological Bulletin* 88:2 (1980), 370–405.

Lichtenstein, D., and R. A. Brown. "Smoking Cessation Methods: Review and Recommendations." In *The Addictive Behaviors: Treatment of Alcoholism, Drug Abuse, Smoking and Obesity,* edited by W. R. Miller, pp. 189–206. New York: Pergamon Press, 1980.

Loeb, L. A., V. L. Ernster, K. E. Walker, J. Abbots, and J. Laszlo. "Smoking and Lung Cancer: An Overview." *Cancer Research* 44 (1984), 5940–58.

Luce, B. R., and S. O. Schweitzer. "Smoking and Alcohol Abuse: A Comparison of Their Economic Consequences." *New England Journal of Medicine* 298 (1978), 569–70.

McIntosh, I. D. "An Employee Office Smoking Policy." *Canadian Journal of Public Health* 76 (1985), 61–62.

Miller, G. H. "Cancer, Passive Smoking, and Non-Employed and Employed Wives." *The Western Journal of Medicine* 140 (1984), 632–35.

National Institutes of Health. "Cardiovascular Primer for the Workplace." DHHS-NIH Publication No. NIH 81-2210, 1980.

NICSH. "Smoking and Health: Smoking and the Workplace." Final report (1980) of a national survey, available from the National Interagency Council on Smoking and Health, 291 Broadway, Room 1005, New York, NY 10007.

National Research Council, Committee on Indoor Pollutants. *Indoor Pollutants.* Washington, D.C.: National Academy Press, 1981.

Office of the Assistant Secretary for Health. *Healthy People* (USDHHS Publication No. 79-55071). Washington, D.C.: U.S. Government Printing Office, 1979.

____. "Promoting Health and Preventing Disease." USDHHS Publication, Fall 1980.

Office on Smoking Health. "Smoking, Tobacco, and Health: A Fact Book." USDHHS-PHS Publication No. PHS 80-50150, 1981.

Orleans, C. T., and R. H. Shipley. "Worksite Smoking Cessation Initiatives: Review and Recommendations." *Addictive Behaviors* 7 (1982), 1–16.

Parkinson, R. S. Unpublished smoking cessation results of AT&T programs (1985).

Remington, P. L., M. R. Forman, E. M. Gentry, J. S. Marks, G. E. Hogelin, and F. L. Trowbridge. "Current Smoking Trends in the United States: The 1981–1983 Behavioral Risk Factor Surveys." *Journal of the American Medical Association* 253:20 (1985), 2975–78.

Sandler, D. P., A. J. Wilcox, and R. B. Everson. "Cumulative Effects of Lifetime Passive Smoking on Cancer Risk." *Lancet* 3 (February 1985), 312–15.

Shipley, R. H., and C. T. Orleans. "Evaluating Smoking Control Programs at the Worksite." *Corporate Commentary* 1:4 (1985), 35–45.

Solomon, L. C. "Smoking Policies in Large Corporations." 1985. Available from the Human Resources Policy Corporation, 1729 Casiano Road, Los Angeles, CA 90049.

Survey of Attitude toward Smoking. New York: American Lung Association, 1983 (April).

Suta, B. E., and C. R. Thompson. "Smoking Patterns of Motor Vehicle Industry Workers and Their Impact on Lung Cancer Mortality Rates." *Journal of Occupational Medicine* 25:9 (1983), 661–67.

Trichopoulos, D., A. Kalandidi, L. Sparros, and B. Macmahon. "Lung Cancer and Passive Smoking." *International Journal of Cancer* 177 (1981), 1–4.

U.S. Department of Health and Human Services. "The Health Consequences of Smoking — Cancer: A Report of the Surgeon General." Public Health Service, Office on Smoking and Health, DHHS Publication No. PHS 82-50179, 1982.

____. "The Health Consequences of Smoking: Cardiovascular Disease — A Report of the Surgeon General." USDHHS, 1983.

____. "The Health Consequences of Smoking — Chronic Obstructure Lung Disease." Public Health Service, Office on Smoking and Health, 1984.

U.S. Department of Health, Education, and Welfare. "Smoking and Health: A Report of the U.S. Surgeon General." USDHEW Public Health Service Office for the Assistant Secretary for Health, Office on Smoking and Health, DHEW Publication No. PHS 79-5006, 1979b.

_____. "The Smoking Digest: Progress Report on a Nation Kicking the Habit." Public Health Service, 1978.

_____. "Adverse Health Effects of Smoking and the Occupational Environment." Current Intelligence Bulletin No. 31, National Institute of Occupational Safety and Health, DHEW Publication No. PHS 79-50066, 1979a.

Vogt, T. M. "Effects of Parental Smoking on Medical Care Utilization by Children." *American Journal of Public Health* 74 (1984), 30–34.

Walsh, D. C. "Corporate Smoking Policies: A Review and an Analysis." *Journal of Occupational Medicine* 26 (1984), 17–22.

Walsh, D. C., and N. P. Gordon. "Legal Approaches to Smoking Deterrence." *Annual Review of Public Health* 7 (1985), in press.

Warner, K. E. "The Effects of Publicity and Policy on Smoking and Health." *Business and Health* 2:1 (1984), 7–14.

Weis, W. L. "No Ifs, Ands or Buts — Why Workplace Smoking Should Be Banned." *Management World* (September 1981), 39–44.

Weiss, S. T., J. B. Tager, M. Schenker, and F. E. Speizer. "The Health Effects of Involuntary Smoking." *American Review of Respiratory Disease* 128 (1983), 933–42.

White, J. R., and H. F. Froeb. "Small Airway Dysfunction in Non-Smokers Chronically Exposed to Tobacco Smoke." *New England Journal of Medicine* 302 (1980), 720–23.

27 Training the Practitioner to Provide Comprehensive Health Promotion Programs

Richard Rotondo

Several movements in recent years have influenced U.S. business and industry to implement on-site health promotion programs. One major influence was the trend for U.S. business to pay the lion's share of health care costs. In 1981, U.S. businesses paid about $61 billion in medical insurance payments. These costs are rising at a rate of almost 15 percent a year. Indirect costs such as sick leave, disability payment, federal Medicare and disability insurance, and employee replacement was estimated to be another $52–$64 billion. This $113–$125 billion employee health bill amounted to 10 percent of the total U.S. payroll costs in 1981 (Oliver and Kirkpatrick 1982). U.S. businesses have strong economic incentives to keep their employees healthy. Most of these costs are experience rated, which means the actual cost of next year's premium is based on this year's actual payouts by the company. Any decreased use of benefits because of healthier employees saves the company money.

Another movement in society that has influenced the decision of U.S. business to implement health promotion programs is the increased interest in health and fitness. There has been a marked change in the consumption habits of Americans since 1963. The per capita consumption of milk declined from 12 percent to 33 percent. Cigarette tobacco has declined 27 percent. Jogging and physical activity have become a national pastime (Atherosclerosis Study Group 1984). Many of the top executives who make the decisions to implement health promotion programs are already living a healthy lifestyle. They believe in wellness and want to make it available to their employees.

U.S. businesses have employed a variety of different health professionals to provide services in a corporate health promotion program. In a majority of companies, the administration of a corporate health promotion program falls under the Human Resources/Personnel Department. The managers and providers of health promotion programs come from many different health disciplines. They may be physicians, nurses, health educators, exercise physiologists, psychologists, nutritionists, public health educators, or physical therapists. All of these professionals have completed a traditional curriculum and training to develop the skills necessary to become a competent practitioner.

As more companies become involved in health promotion programs, many practitioners from these various professions will be competing for primary positions of responsibility. The corporate environment is an attractive setting to do the work of health promotion and disease prevention. Many corporations are able to provide wages, benefits, prestige, and sophisticated support that is not available in schools, hospitals, clinics, and other settings where health care services have been traditionally offered.

Because many of the graduates of schools from these various professions are seeking jobs in corporate health promotion programs, universities are beginning to offer additional course work and internships in corporate settings. There is a growing effort in some schools to prepare a certain number of their students to manage health promotion programs in companies. The educational training institutions are beginning to recognize that managing a comprehensive health promotion program in a corporate setting demands a much broader range of knowledge and skills than the traditional curriculum currently provides.

The need for training competent practitioners to manage corporate health promotion programs is essential if the program is comprehensive. A comprehensive program is one that is on-going, is offered to a large number of the total employee population, and includes many of the following components:

Assessment of risk
Risk reduction classes and counseling in the areas of exercise, smoking cessation, weight control, nutrition education, stress management, early cancer detection, accident prevention, substance abuse control, and blood pressure control
Environmental and social support changes in the corporate culture
Evaluation of program (Parkinson 1982).

The health promotion manager is the person charged with the responsibility of coordinating, implementing, and evaluating all the components of a comprehensive health promotion program. Specific skills are required to manage an effective health promotion program. The following outline could be viewed as a general job description for a health promotion manager and as the basis for a training program.

SKILLS REQUIRED OF A HEALTH PROMOTION MANAGER

Coordination and Administration

Organize and lead an effective employee health task force.
Organize and schedule health promotion activities: open house, orientation sessions, health screenings, results counseling sessions, classes.
Organize an efficient data collection, management, and reporting system.
Track program members' attendance and progress.
Develop a budget and administer program income and expenditures.

Promotion and Marketing

Make the health promotion program visible and attractive to all employees.
Develop fresh and creative ideas to reach all segments of the employee population.
Develop attractive brochures, flyers, and other materials that advertise the program.

Clinical and Program Delivery

Teach, instruct, motivate, and counsel individuals on how to reduce risk factors and improve health and fitness.
Lead several levels of group exercise classes.
Take blood pressure.
Teach CPR training.

Teach smoking cessation, basic nutrition, stress management, back care programs.

Test individuals for physical fitness and write exercise prescriptions.

Organization Skills to Make the Corporate Environment Supportive of Healthy Lifestyle Habits

Influence the development and implementation of a smoking policy.

Influence the food selections of the cafeteria and vending machines.

Influence the reduction of unnecessary stress in the corporate environment.

Develop employee leadership and support groups to sustain positive health habits.

Evaluation and Reporting

Collect and organize program results data to determine if program objectives were met.

Analyze evaluation data and write reports to site management.

Selection and Supervision of Program Staff, Interns, Volunteers, and Outside Vendors

Teach the mission, objectives, and methods used in the health promotion program to all staff providing services to the programs.

Observe services provided to assess the quality of providers.

Interpersonal Relating Skills Working within Other Company Departments Charged with Some Aspect of the Health and Safety of the Employee

Develop a cooperative relationship with medical department, safety committee, EAP program, and recreation league.

Volunteer to serve as a resource person to these other departments.

Influence the improvement of the integration of projects and services of these various departments.

Recruit leaders of those various departments to participate in an employee health task force.

PROFILE OF THE HEALTH PROMOTION MANAGER

Given the job responsibilities and skills necessary to successfully manage a comprehensive program, it becomes obvious that the health promotion manager must possess a whole set of qualities. The manager should be enthusiastic, energetic, competent, knowledgeable, friendly, outgoing, caring, creative, a problem solver, highly organized, easy to relate to, and easy to work with. No one person will possess all the skills, qualities, training, and experience suggested in the job description of the health promotion manager. The company will have to decide what set of skills and qualities best matches its specific program emphasis and corporate culture. Other program staff or services can be recruited to complement the skills of the program manager.

Given that all health promotion managers will have significant gaps in their skills and experience, specific training for health promotion in the corporate setting is essential. The specific contents of any training program will be based on the model that the company adopts.

REFERENCES

"Atherosclerosis Study Group: Optimal Resources for Primary Prevention of Atherosclerotic Diseases." *Circulation* 70 (1984): 161A.

Oliver, P., and M. Kirkpatrick. *Employee Health Enhancement: A New Corporate Challenge*. Boston: Arthur D. Little, 1982.

Parkinson, R. S. *Managing Health Promotion in the Workplace*. Palo Alto, California: Mayfield Publishing Company, 1982.

28 Selecting a Health Promotion Program

Don R. Powell

Hospitals and corporations have varied reasons for offering health promotion programs. Hospitals conduct the programs to generate revenue, increase visibility, attract new patients, and prevent, as well as treat, illness. The programs are offered to their own employees, people in the community, and local businesses. Corporations are generally interested solely in their employees and, sometimes, their immediate families. They hope to reduce absenteeism, turnover, and health care insurance costs while increasing productivity and morale.

Regardless of the reasons for deciding to conduct health promotion programs, many hospitals and corporations are faced with another decision. It concerns the source of the programs. There are two basic choices. The hospital or company can develop its own programs, or it can contract with an outside organization that already provides the particular service either with its own staff or with others it trains.

The advantages of developing one's own programs include the ability to make use of already existing staff expertise and possible lower costs in the long term. The advantages of contracting with an outside organization include the ability to offer an established program that has a proven track record, elimination of program development costs that can range from $25,000 to $225,000, freeing staff time that would have gone into developing the program, being able to utilize attractive program materials, and the ability to begin offering the program sooner. Although their reasons for offering health promotion programs may differ, most hospitals and just about all corporations choose to contract with an outside organization that offers these programs. This is due to the numerous advantages cited above including time, money, and a philosophy of not wanting to "reinvent the wheel."

It is extremely important for those hospitals and companies that contract with health promotion providers to select high-quality programs. This chapter highlights what areas should be scrutinized, what questions should be asked, and what criteria should be employed when evaluating health promotion programs. The areas are presented in the general order of importance given them by hospital and corporation administrators and educators.

Program Content

The primary concern about a health promotion program is its content. Although most programs incorporate behavior modification to some degree or another, and may look similar on paper, they can still be significantly different. One needs to decide whether behavior modification should be an integral part of the program or whether it should be treated superficially. Behavior modification techniques can be presented in an interesting manner, and the participants can be motivated to utilize them. The state of the art in behavior change programs is what is called a multiple treatment program. Since no one method works for all people, it is better to present a variety of treatment procedures that allow participants to pick and choose from among them. In this manner, participants individualize the program to meet their particular needs.

How the techniques and procedures are presented is also extremely important. Difficulties in the area of behavior change do not always stem from inadequate treatment techniques, but rather from a failure to motivate participants to use them. Thus participant compliance must be addressed in the program. The program also needs to be entertaining for the participants. If they are enjoying the class meetings they are more likely to attend all of them, more likely to do what is asked of them, and thus more likely to be successful.

Finally, the program should have a strong maintenance component. It is one issue to get a participant to quit smoking or lose weight, but another thing to produce permanent behavior change in these areas. Here, too, a multiple component of maintenance procedures must be presented.

PROGRAM EFFECTIVENESS

Obviously, administrators want to choose health promotion programs that are effective in producing the desired behavior change. They want a smoking cessation program that enables participants to quit smoking, a weight control program that enables participants to lose weight, and a stress management program that enables participants to cope with stress. The difficulty they encounter is in determining whether the program being considered achieves its goals for a significant number of participants.

The key questions that should be asked include:

What percentage of program participants are successful?

How was success determined: by number of pounds lost, decrease in blood pressure, better food choices, no longer smoking?

When was the evaluation done: at the end of treatment, 3 months after treatment, 6 months after treatment, 1 year later?

Who was included in the evaluation: all participants who began the program, only participants who completed the whole program, only participants who sent back a questionnaire?

How was success verified: by self-report, reported by a spouse or co-worker, chemical verification (used to determine smoking status), test given by researcher?

Who conducted the evaluation: the organization promoting the program or an independent outside organization?

Has the success been replicated in other evaluation studies?

Programs must be compared using the same reference points. Otherwise, one may be comparing apples to oranges. For example, at the end of a one-year stop smoking program, "A" may claim a 75 percent success rate while program "B" claims only a 50 percent success rate. If program A's success is based only on those participants who sent back a survey form and program B's success rate is based upon all participants, with the ones who didn't return the surveys being counted as smokers, then program B is probably more effective. This is because research has shown that the nonresponders are more likely to be smokers (Powell and Arnold 1982).

PROGRAM COST

Make sure that you are aware of all costs (including hidden ones) from the start. Some programs may sound inexpensive, but by the time everything is paid for, they have become high priced. Organizations being trained need to inquire about the training fee, the licensing fee and whether it is a one-time or annual fee, prices for audiovisual aids that are used to conduct the program, the cost of participant materials, the price of marketing materials, and other purchases needed to conduct the program. Ask whether there are discounts for purchasing the participant materials in bulk and for training more than one employee.

Remember, too, that the most expensive health promotion programs are not necessarily the best programs. If you were interested only in an outside organization coming into your company or hospital to conduct an on-site program, you would be concerned with the cost for each participant, whether this is a discounted fee, what materials are included, if you receive a percentage of the revenue generated, and what you are required to provide (that is, room, equipment, registrar, advertising).

PROGRAM MATERIALS

The content and appearance of the program materials that are given to participants is important. The packaging of the program and its maintaining a professional appearance is a consideration, but do not judge the materials by appearance alone. Read through the handouts yourself to determine if they are well written, clear, concise, and of appropriate content.

If you are marketing your health programs to business and industry as well as to people in the community, attractive materials will certainly enhance your presentations. When people are purchasing a service like a physical fitness or stress management program, they like to see something concrete associated with it. Attractive materials can meet this need. Do not, however, expect fancy packages to mean an effective program. Research conducted at the American Institute for Preventive Medicine has shown that participants in health promotion programs do no better when the same content is presented in an attractive booklet format or in photocopied 8 1/2" x 11" handouts (Powell and McCann 1981). The attractive booklets, however, do increase enrollment percentages and the marektability of the program to other organizations.

MARKETING MATERIALS

There are numerous advantages to purchasing a program that comes with its own marketing materials and plan. This could save a great deal of time and money if the alternative meant having to go out and develop them yourself. You should find out if the organization selling the program provides the following promotional pieces: flyers, newspaper advertisements, posters, descriptive brochures, videotape presentations, slide shows and scripts, and press releases. The marketing expertise that you would also want includes how best to promote the program to both the general community and local corporations, how to attract mass media attention for the program, ways to encourage referrals from health professionals, how to maximize employee attendance, best times of the year to conduct the program, and best times of the day to conduct the program.

The following criteria apply only to hospitals and corporations that want their own employees, not representatives of the health promotion vendor, to instruct the programs. This training of trainers can be extremely cost-effective for organizations with 500 or more employees.

PROGRAM TRAINING

Many decision makers overlook the training program itself when evaluating wellness programs. Here the most important consideration involves who is actually conducting the training. Ideally you would want a person who was involved with the development of the program, rather than a second, third, or even fourth generation trainer. The developer is thoroughly knowledgeable with the program, can explain the rationales for all aspects of the program, and can translate the intricacies of the program extremely well. It is also reinforcing for the trainees to receive the information from the developer. When the trainer has learned the program from "a trainee of a trainee of the program's developer," a good deal can get lost in the translation.

In addition, look at the content of the training program to see what topics will be discussed and how they will be presented. It is an asset if the training does more than just teach how to conduct the specific health program and provides general background information about the topic so that the trainees develop an expertise in the field. For instance, a smoking cessation training might include information about why people smoke, the role of the tobacco industry, and the epidemiology of cigarette smoking. A weight control program could present material on the causes of obesity, proper nutrition, and various treatment approaches to obesity.

Finally, look at the length of time the training takes. A longer training program doesn't mean a better one. You must consider that each day your employees are away from your organization, there is a cost to you. Yet a training should not be so brief that the program material cannot be presented effectively.

QUALITY CONTROL

Consideration should be given to your trainees' evaluation to make sure they are presenting the program in the prescribed manner. A trainee who deviates from the program's protocols can adversely affect participants' perceptions of the program and success rates. With the hospital's and company's credibility and reputation on the line, this is the last thing that you want.

If there is quality control, find out how it is done. The more common ways include on-site observation of the trainee, evaluating audio or video cassette tapes of the trainee conducting the program, reviewing participants' evaluations of the program and the instructor, and evaluating ongoing success data. Also, ask if there is an additional charge for the quality control and who in the organization does it.

PROGRAM UPDATES

No health promotion program should ever be sealed in cement. Research is being conducted continually to devise new methods and procedures to facilitate behavior change (Powell and Arnold 1982). You should find out if there is anyone within the organization who follows the literature and conducts ongoing research to improve the program. If so, inquire about methods to disseminate these program updates to an existing trainee. Your organization always wants to be offering a program that is state-of-the-art.

The field of health promotion is growing quickly and is becoming a big business. Due to the "self-health" movement and people's desire to prevent rather than treat illness, wellness programs are proliferating at a rapid rate. Some of these programs are very good and are well grounded in scientific research; others leave much to be desired. It thus becomes even more important for the decision makers in a hospital or corporation to use special care when evaluating and selecting health promotion programs for their respective organizations.

REFERENCES

Powell, D. R., and C. B. Arnold. "Antismoking Program for Coronary Prone Men." *New York State Journal of Medicine* 82 (1982): 1435–38.

Powell, D. R., and B. S. McCann. "The Effects of a Multiple Treatment Program and Maintenance Procedures on Smoking Cessation." *Preventive Medicine* 10 (1981): 94–104.

Conclusion:
Will Heath Education and Fitness in the Workplace Remain Healthy and Fit for the Future?

Samuel H. Klarreich

If it continues to grow in a professional manner, if its activities continue to be audited carefully, if it continues to attract the high caliber of people which it is attracting today, and if it continues to be innovative in its approach to workplace programs, there is no doubt that health education and fitness will continue to remain healthy and fit well into the future.

In society, we are already seeing the tremendous influence of health education and fitness programs. People today, more than ever before, are paying attention to the foods they eat. People today, more than ever before, are taking pride in and gaining personal respect from smoking cessation. People today, more than ever before, are taking greater care of their bodies. Aerobics, jogging, dancercise, weight training, rowing, biking, and walking are just a few of the activities people are engaged in. More than ever before, people are purchasing health-related texts. These texts are heightening people's awareness to such problems as stress, burnout, cancer, heart disease, marital relationships, and communication. The public of today is probably more aware of health-related matters than ever before. The public of tomorrow will probably possess even greater awareness and knowledge because with the advent of technology, health awareness and health education opportunities will abound.

In the workplace, we are already seeing increased budgets for health education and fitness programs. Management, more than ever before, is truly recognizing the benefits of extensive health education and fitness programs both to the employees and to the organization. This trend can only grow.

In government circles, certain legislators are already beginning to set aside tax incentives and tax credits for those proactive corporations that are establishing health education and fitness programs. Certain governments recognize that with a healthier work force, there will be less of a strain on a health care system with limited health care funds. In the future, more local governments will become actively involved in establishing incentive programs for those corporations that seek to institute a health education or fitness curriculum.

In the professional arena more specialists from divergent backgrounds such as social work, education, employee assistance, psychology, public health, medicine, nursing, occupational therapy, physiotherapy, recreation, physical education, and rehabilitation are increasingly entering the field. They bring with them their own areas of expertise, ideas, plans, and innovations that will further professionalize and strengthen the field.

Within the sphere of health education and fitness, professional conferences occur with greater regularity. Wellness conferences, unknown in the past, are now standard annual events. These conventions provide an opportunity for health educators and fitness specialists from around the world to come together to share their ideas and to discuss their programs. It is an enriching opportunity for all, and it will certainly fortify the health education and fitness movement.

When considering all of the above trends, I can state, without fear of contradiction, that the future for health education and fitness indeed looks exceedingly bright. Further evidence of this statement is illustrated by the contributors to this textbook. If these practitioners, researchers, academics, and others like these, continue as leaders, the movement assuredly will remain healthy and fit.

Peters and Waterman (1982), in *In Search of Excellence,* stated that excellent corporations have a number of principles in common; these include: attention to people, treating people decently, commitment to people, satisfying people, and treating people as natural resources. What better way to provide all the above than to offer a health education and fitness program!

REFERENCE

Peters, T. J., and R. H. Waterman. *In Search of Excellence*. New York: Harper and Row, 1982.

Bibliography

BOOKS

Ardell, D. B. *High Level Wellness: An Alternative to Doctors, Drugs, and Disease.* Emmaus, Pennsylvania: Rodale Press, 1977.

Cataldo, M. F., and T. J. Coates. *Health Promotion in Industry: A Behavioral Medicine Perspective.* New York: Wiley, 1986.

Dunn, H. B. *High Level Wellness.* Arlington, Virginia: R. W. Beatty, 1961.

Fielding, J. E. *Corporate Health Management.* Reading, Massachusetts: Addison-Wesley, 1984.

Hockey, R. V. *Physical Fitness: The Pathway to Healthful Living.* St. Louis: Times Mirror/Mosby College Publishing, 1985.

Matarazzo, J. D., et al. *Behavioral Health: A Handbook of Health Enhancement and Disease Prevention.* New York: Wiley, 1984.

O'Donnell, M. P., and T. Ainsworth. *Health Promotion in the Workplace.* New York: Wiley, 1984.

Oliver, P., and M. Kirkpatrick. *Employee Health Enhancement: A New Corporate Challenge.* Boston: Arthur D. Little, 1982.

Parkinson, R. S., et al. *Managing Health Promotion in the Workplace.* Palo Alto, California: Mayfield, 1982.

Pelletier, K. *Healthy People in Unhealthy Places.* New York: Dell, 1984.

Steiglitz, E. J. *The Second Forty Years.* Philadelphia: J. B. Lippincott, 1952.

Windsor, R. A., et al. *Evaluation of Health Promotion and Education Programs.* Palo Alto, California: Mayfield, 1984.

ARTICLES

Brennan, A. J. J. "How to Set up a Corporate Wellness Program." *Management Review* 72 (May 1983): 41–47.

_____. "Wellness Comes to Work." *Management World,* February 1985, pp. 12–15.

Bryson, D. D. "Health and Productivity." *Ergonomics* 13 (1970): 561–68.

Cohen, C., and E. Cohen. "Health Education: Panacea, Pernicious, or Pointless." *New England Journal of Medicine,* 1978, pp. 718–20.

Cohen, W. S. "Health Promotion in the Workplace: A Prescription for Good Health." *American Psychologist* 40 (1985): 213–16.

Cox, M. H., R. J. Shephard, and P. Corey. "The Influence of an Employee Fitness Program upon Fitness, Productivity, and Absenteeism." *Ergonomics* 24 (1981): 795–806.

_____. "Corporate Investment in Human Resources: A New Twist." *The Canadian Business Review* 9 (1982): 9–14.

Davis, M. F. "Worksite health Promotion. An Overview of Programs and Practices." *Personnel Administrator* 29 (December 1984): 45–50.

Dedmon, R. E., J. W. Gander, M. P. O'Connor, and A. C. Paschke. "An Industry Health Management Program." *Physician Sports Medicine* 7 (1979): 56–67.

Dickerson, O. B., and C. Mandelblit. "A New Model for Employer Provided Health Education Programs." *Journal of Occupational Medicine* 25 (1983): 471–74.

Feuer, D. "Wellness Programs: How Do They Shape Up?" *Training,* April 1982, pp. 25–34.

Fielding, J. E. "Preventive Medicine and The Bottom Line." *Journal of Occupational Medicine* 21 (1979): 79–88.

_____. "Effectiveness of Employee Health Improvement Programs." *Journal of Occupational Medicine* 24 (1982): 907–16.

_____. "Evaluation of Worksite Health Promotion: Some Unresovled Issues and Opportunities." *Corporate Commentary* 1 (1984): 9–15.

Fielding, J. E., and L. Breslow. "Health Promotion Programs Sponsored by California Employers." *American Journal of Public Health* 73 (1983): 538–42.

Finney, C. "Recreation: Its Effect on Productivity. A Recent Study and Its Unexpected Results." *Recreation Management* 21 (1979): 10.

Foote, A., and J. Erfurt. "Hypertension Control at the Work Site." *New England Journal of Medicine* 308 (1983): 809–13.

Forouzesh, M. R., and L. E. Ratzker. "Health Promotion and Wellness Programs: An Insight into the Fortune 500." *Health Education,* December 1984/January 1985, pp. 18–22.

Frankenhaeuser, J. "Job Demands, Health, and Well-Being." *Journal of Psychosomatic Research* 21 (1977): 313–21.

Frederiksen, L. "Using Incentives in Worksite Wellness." *Corporate Commentary* 1 (November 1984): 51–57.

Green, L. W. "Toward Cost-Benefit Evaluations of Health Education: Some Concepts, Methods, and Examples." *Health Education Monographs,* 1974 (Supplement No. 1), pp. 34–60.

——. "How to Evaluate Health Promotion." *Hospitals,* October 1, 1979, pp. 106–8.

Grove, D., et al. "A Health Promotion Program in a Corporate Setting." *Journal of Family Practice* 9 (1979): 83–88.

Haggerty, R. J. "Changing Lifestyles to Improve Health." *Preventive Medicine* 6 (1977): 276–89.

Heinzelman, F., and R. W. Bagley. "Response to Physical Activity Programs with Their Effects on Health Behavior." *Public Health Report,* 1970, pp. 905–11.

Howard, J., and A. Mikalachki. "Fitness and Employee Productivity." *Canadian Journal of Applied Sports Sciences* 4 (1979): 191–98.

Lauzon, R. "The Bottom Line — Employee Fitness." *The Canadian Business Review* 9 (1982): 6–8.

Linden, V. "Absence from Work and Physical Fitness." *British Journal of Industrial Medicine* 26 (1969): 47–54.

Marcotte, B., and J. H. Price. "The Status of Health Promotion Programs at the Worksite — A Review." *Health Education,* July/August 1983, pp. 4–9.

Martin, J. "Corporate Health: A Result of Employee Fitness." *The Physician and Sports Medicine,* 1978, pp. 135–37.

McLeroy, K., L. Green, K. Mullen, and V. Foshee. "Assessing the Effects of Health Promotion in Worksites: A Review of Stress Program Evaluations." *Health Education Quarterly* 11 (1984): 379–401.

Megalli, B. "Employee Fitness Programs: Philanthropic Venture or Shrewd Investment." *The Labour Gazette.* 1978, pp. 174–82.

Phillips, R. M., and J. P. Hughes. "Cost-Benefit Analysis of the Occupational Health Program: A Generic Model." *Journal of Occupational Medicine* 16 (1974): 158–61.

Pyle, R. L. "Performance Measures of a Corporate Fitness Program." *Human Resources Management*, Fall 1979, pp. 26–30.

_____. "Corporate Fitness Program — How Do They Shape Up?" *Personnel*, 1979, pp. 58–67.

Ryan, A. "Employee Fitness Program: A Round Table." *Physcians Sports Medicine* 8 (1980): 64–72.

Saxl. L. R. "How to Create a Healthy Health Promotion Program." *Pension World* 20 (December 1984): 44–45.

Seidman, L. S., and G. G. Sevelius. "A Cost Effective Weight-Loss Program at the Worksite." *Journal of Occupational Medicine* 26 (1984): 725.

Shephard, R. J., P. Corey, and M. H. Cox. "Health Hazard Appraisal — The Influence of an Employee Fitness Program." *Canadian Journal of Public Health* 73 (1983): 183–87.

Shephard, R. J., P. Corey, P. Rengland, and M. H. Cox. "The Impact of Changes in Fitness and Lifestyle upon Health Care Utilization." *Canadian Journal of Public Health* 74 (1983): 51–54.

Index

absenteeism: cost of, 164, 235, 277, 346–47, 358; and creativity, 327; and fitness programs, 314, 339, 341; reasons for, 165, 345, 356; in the StayWell program, 118, 122; and stress management programs, 274. *See also* cost-containment

accessibility, 62, 64, 166, 310, 311, 316

addiction to smoking, 361

advisory committees. *See* health education committees

aerobic exercise, 158, 236, 277, 311

Agriculture, U.S. Department of, 86

Ainsworth, T., 119

Ajzen, I., 243

Alcoholics Anonymous, 192

alcoholism and the media, 307

alcoholism programs, 37, 38, 45, 46, 56, 94–97, 167, 277, 331–32

Allen, Robert F., 306

American Association of Certified Public Accountants, 101

American Association of University Affiliated Programs for Persons with Developmental Disabilities, 99

American Cancer Society, 363, 366

American Heart Association, 366

American Institute for Preventive Medicine, 381

American Lung Association, 363, 366

American Psychiatric Association, 361

Anderson, David R., 214, 284–98

Andrew, G. M., 248, 249

Ardell, Donald, 9, 10, 11

assertiveness, 207–8

AT&T (American Telephone & Telegraph), 277

atemporal technology, 96

athletes, 275

Ayoub, M. S., 154, 155

Azar, N., 19–20

Backer, Thomas E., 301–2, 325–37

back injuries, costs of, 271

back injury control programs, 110, 148–62, 277

Bagley, R. W., 243, 249

Bandura, A., 238, 239–40

Barrett, T. C., 245

Bawol, R. D., 357

Beatty, B. D., 243

behaviorism, 237–38, 239

behavior modification: approaches to studying, 236–51; and burn-out programs, 196; and the corporate culture, 35–38, 41; and EAPs, 47, 57; and evaluation, 218, 259; and fitness/health promotion/wellness programs, 310, 311, 379; and health education committees, 52–53; and health risk appraisals, 66–67, 311–12; and smoking control, 365; and the StayWell program, 285–87, 293-95. *See also* lifstyle change

Belloc, N. B., 86, 114

benefits: of back injury control programs, 153, 161; and the corporate culture, 36, 39–40, 42–43; of cost-containment, 373; of creativity, 325–27, 334–35, of evaluation, 258; of fitness programs, 309–10, 314, 338–45, 347–49, 385–86, and health education committees, 54–57; of the Health Plus program, 126; of health promotion programs, 5, 10, 67, 68, 167–68, 319, 378; of health and safety training programs, 25–26, 259–60, 268; of physical activity programs, 251; of planning, 85–92; of rehabilitation programs, 170; of smoking control, 362–63, 365; of the StayWell program, 115, 117–18, 121–22; of stress management programs, 172–73, 180, 273–74; of the Tel-Med program, 146; of wellness programs, 85–92, 321, 322

Benson, H., 329

Berkanovic, Emil, 213–14, 258–69

Bespalec, D. A., 366

biology, 7, 245, 334

Birch, D., 239

Blanchard Training and Development, 323

Bono, Edward de, 203

Bower, Marion, 61

Brawley, L. R., 250

Breslow, L., 86, 114

Brown Bag lunch hour, 84

Brownell, K. D., 238

buddy influence, 249–50

budgets: communications, 75; for evaluation, 218; for fitness programs, 311; for health education committees, 50–51; and implementation of programs, 67–68; and planning, 67–68

Bulka, R. P., 201

bulletin boards, computer, 96–97, 98, 104

Bureau of Labor Statistics, U.S., 151

burn-out, 55–56, 111, 178–79, 183–97, 202, 326, 328–29

Burns, David, 201

Burns, Frank, 98–99

Burton, T. L., 243

Buscaglia, Leo, 55, 56, 77

California Back School, 153

California Nonsmokers Rights Foundation, 363

California State Compensation Insurance Fund, 153

Calty Design Research, Inc., 333

Cameron, Carl, 99

Campbell, D., 328

Canada Life Assurance Company, 164, 247

Canadian Cancer Society, 55

Canadian Employee Fitness and Lifestyle project, 245

cancer, 55, 142, 271, 308, 355, 356, 357

Can-Dial program, 142

Cantlon, Angelica T., 31–32, 59–70

Cape Breton, Nova Scotia. See Tel-Med program

Capitol Wire Corporation, 277

Carter, Betty J., 31–32, 59–70

Center for Creative Leadership (North Carolina), 325, 331

Chapman, Larry S., 213, 215–31

characteristics of successful programs: and back injury control program, 155–56; and the corporate culture, 31, 32, 35–43; and EAPs, 59–60, 69–70, 166–67; and health risks, 315–16

choice and physical activity programs, 243–44

Chubb, H. R., 235

Chubb, M., 235

Clark, Alan D., 98, 103

Clear, Stephen E., 168

clinical settings, 274–75

Cohen, A., 19–20

Collishaw, N. E., 357

communications: and back injury control programs, 160–61; budgets, 75; and burn-out programs, 196; and the corporate culture, 75, 305–6; and creativity, 77–78; and culture, 306–7; delivery of, 140–46; and differences among programs, 305–18; and evaluation, 79–80; guidelines for, 73–75; and the Health Plus program, 132; and health risk behavior, 315–16; and the implementation of programs, 32, 71–80; and the media, 78; objectives, 73, 75–76; and personal excellence programs, 206–8; and physical activity programs, 246–47; and the Tel-Med program, 140–46; and wellness programs, 84. See also networking

competition, 240–41

CompuServe Information Service, 96–97, 103

computer networking, 32–33, 94–105

Computer Phone Book, 98

computers: and bulletin boards, 96–97, 98, 104; conferencing by, 98, 101, 104; future use of, 100–102;

hardware/software for, 95, 104, 105; and networking, 32–33, 94–102; and the StayWell program, 115–16, 293

confidentiality, 64, 119, 166

constructive medicine (Steiglitz), 6–7, 7–8

Control Data Corporation, 270–71, 272. *See also* StayWell program

Corey, P., 346

corporate backlash, 41

corporate culture: and communications, 305–6; and cost-containment, 301; definition of, 61–64; and downsizing, 176–78; and health risk behavior, 316; human factor in, 163–64; and implementation of health promotion program, 31, 40–43; and motivation, 307; overview of, 31, 35–43; and people orientation, 31, 35, 38–40, 41, 42; and personal responsibility for health, 35–36; and planning a health promotion program, 61–64; and staff, 376; and the StayWell program, 288; and values, 39, 41

corporate policies for smoking control, 359–60, 362–64

corporate profiles, 311

Correa, P., 357

cost-containment: and back injury control programs, 152–53, 277; benefits of, 373; and the corporate culture, 31, 36, 38, 39–40, 301; and EAPs, 277; and eavluation, 229; and fitness/health promotion/wellness programs, 301, 321–24, 339, 345–47; goals of, 301; and the Health Plus program, 139; and health risk profiles, 270–71, 275–78, 280, 284, 294; and health and safety training programs, 213–14; and physical activity programs, 235–36; and smoking, 313; and the StayWell program, 115, 122, 284, 294

costs: of absenteeism, 164, 235, 277, 346–47, 358; of back injuries, 271; of evaluations, 267; of health care in United States, 10–11; of health

promotion/wellness programs, 323, 378, 381; of a heart attack, 276, 346–47; of hypertension, 312; insurance, 153, 170; legal, 151, 213–14; of program operation, 92, 115, 260, 284, 285, 313; of smoking, 270–71, 358; social, 148, 170; for weight loss, 313

Cox, Michael H., 302, 338–54

Cox, S. G., 22, 24

Crandall, R., 241, 245

creativity, 77–78, 301–2, 325–37, 328

Crosstalk software, 95

Csikszentmihalyi, M., 244

culture, 37–38, 305–7, 310–11, 315–16, 348. *See also* corporate culture

Danielson, R. R., 242, 247, 249, 250

data bases, 104, 218, 219, 296

Davis, M., 175

Deal, T. E., 61

Deci, E. L., 239

delivery of health promotion programs, 115–16, 122, 155, 375–76

Derogatis, L. R., 175

Derr, W. Dennis, 301, 305–18

design, evaluation, 290–91, 296

Development Disability Councils, 99–100

Digital Equipment Corporation, 102

Directors Guild of America, 332

disability. *See* rehabilitation programs; workers compensation

diseases, lifestyle, 36

Diseher, R., 142

Dodge, D. L., 173

downsizing of corporations, 176–78

Drucker, Peter F., 200

drug abuse programs, 37, 38, 56, 277, 278–79, 331–32

Dunn, Halbert, 8–9, 10

EAP (Employee Assistance Program), 45–48, 51, 57, 110, 136, 139, 163–68, 170, 277. *See also* fitness programs; health promotion

programs; physical activity programs; wellness programs
Edington, D. W., 301, 310, 319–24
effectiveness. *See* benefits
elderly, 6, 340
Electronic Information Exchange System (EIES), 103
electronic mail, 98, 104
Ellis, Albert, 176, 205
emotional fitness, 55, 56, 77
Employee Fitness and Lifestyle Project (Canada), 246–47, 248
employee health survey, 222–23. *See also* health risk appraisals/profiles
employees: morale of, 279, 314; needs of, 60–61, 122, 292–93, 315, 321; and planning, 60–61, 64, 69; screening and placement of, 154–55; smoking control attitudes of, 363–64; training task group of, 155–56; turn-offs of, 64. *See also* participation
Endler, N. S., 237, 238
Entertainment Industry Referral and Assistance Center, 331–32
environment: and constructive medicine, 7; and creativity, 326, 333, 334; and evaluation, 218; and health promotion/wellness programs, 8–10, 65; and lifestyle change, 341; and planning, 32; and smoking control, 356–57, 360, 367; and study of behavior, 237–39
Equal Employment Opportunity, 155
ergonomics, 154
Ericksen, Michael P., 302, 355–72
Eshelman, E., 175
evaluation: analysis of, 291–95; and behavior modification, 218, 259; budgets for, 218; and communications, 79–80; constraints, 218–19, 230; and cost containment, 228–29; and cost of programs, 260; and data bases, 218, 219; definition of, 259; design, 260–63, 290–91, 296; of EAPs/fitness/health promotion programs, 167, 303, 340–48, 378–84;

elements, 259–63; and employee health surveys, 222–23; and the environment, 218; evaluating the, 295–96; followup, 84–85, 138, 167, 218, 228; formative/summative, 289–90; forms, 222–29; and health education committees, 54–56; and the Health Plus program, 134, 138; and health risk profiles, 288; of health and safety training programs, 25, 213–14, 258–69; and implementing programs, 259, 267–68; and lifestyle change, 86–92; and management, 218–19; modular approach to, 220–31; objectives, 290; and participation, 227, 292–93, 296; and personal excellence programs, 203; planning/strategy for an, 219–20, 266–68; purposes of, 116–17, 213, 215–17, 258, 268, 284–85; and reliability, 216–17, 219, 230, 263; and smoking control, 220–31, 361; and staff, 376; and the StayWell program, 116–22, 284–96; of stress management programs, 273–74; and the Tel-Med program, 142–44; timing of, 221, 230; tools for, 213, 220–31; uses of, 266–68; and validity, 215–17, 219, 230
evaluators, qualifications of, 268
Everson, R. B., 357
exercise management programs, 37, 136–37, 238
Exxon Corporation, 101

Farquhar, J. W., 175
Faulkner, R. A., 247
feedback, 17, 19, 20, 240–41, 250, 285, 311. *See also* evaluation
Ferris, Richard J., 165–66
Feyerabend, C., 357
Fielding, Jonathan E., 214, 270–83, 356, 357
Finney, C., 346
Fishbein, M., 243
fitness, definition of, 236, 316
fitness programs, 55, 277–79, 302,

309–11, 314, 319–20, 338–54, 385–86. *See also* EAPs; health promotion programs; physical activity programs; wellness programs
Fitzgibbons, D., 241
Fixx, Jim, 305
Fleming, Phyllis L., 32, 81–92
format, 172–73, 242
Franklin, B. A., 249
Frederiksen, L., 366
Friedman, G. D., 357
Friedman, M., 175
Froeb, H. F., 357
Frudenberger, H., 328
Fuller, Buckminster, 327
fun, 64, 244
future: of computer networking, 100–2; of fitness/wellness programs, 323–24, 385–86; of Health Plus program, 139; of smoking control, 367–68

General Motors, 165–66, 167, 277
Ghiselin, B., 329
Gmelch, W. H., 175, 178
goals: and the corporate culture, 36, 39–40, 42–43; of cost-containment, 301; and health promotion/wellness programs, 67, 68, 82, 83, 322, 324, 326; and health risk behavior, 316, and participation, 310; of personal excellence programs, 203, 204–5, 207, 208; of physical activity programs, 242–43, 249; and planning, 65–66; of stress management programs, 172–73; of the Tel-Med program, 140–41, 142–44
Goldston, S. E., 141–42
Green, Laurence, 164
Green, L. W., 290
Griffin, Georgia, 98
Grossberg, J. M., 238
groups, 20, 22, 131, 243, 245, 250

Haggerty, R. J., 339
Hallmark Cards, 333
Hammon, E. C., 357
hardiness and burn-out, 197

hardware, computer, 95, 104
Harper, Robert, 176, 205
health, definition of, 6, 8
health care costs: and back injury control programs, 151, 152–53, 159; and evaluations, 228–29; and stress management programs, 181; in the United States, 10–11, 113, 373. *See also* costs
health diaries, 296
health education committees, 48–57, 149–51
Health Education Electronic Forum, 103
Health and Human Services, U.S. Department of, 86
Health Interview Survey, 312–13
Health-Link (computer system), 98, 103
Health Plus Fitness program, 124, 125, 132–36, 137
Health Plus Learning Center, 124, 125, 132–33, 135, 136–38
Health Plus program, 109, 124–39
Health Promotion Planning Team approach, 60–70
health promotion programs: components of, 115, 319, 374; definition of, 308; dynamic aspects of, 91–92, 136, 383–84; growth of, 5, 113, 234–35, 278–80, 284, 319–20, 383–84; history of, 6–13; length of, 66, 383; models, 38; purpose of, 5, 7, 10, 11, 81, 124, 128, 165–66, 183–84, 270–72; and quality control, 383; selection of, 378–84. *See also* EAPs; fitness programs; physical activity programs; wellness programs; *specific type of program*
health risk appraisals/profiles: and behavior modification, 66–67, 311–12; and characteristics of successful programs, 315–16; and communications, 315–16; and cost-containment, 270–71, 275–78, 280, 284, 294; and the culture/corporate culture, 315–16; and evaluation, 289; and fitness programs, 339; and goals, 316; and health problems, 271–72, 274–75;

and implementation of programs, 66–67; and lifestyle change, 311–12; and participation, 275; and the StayWell program, 114, 288

health risks. *See name of specific behavior, e.g.* smoking

health and safety training programs, 13–26, 37, 213–14, 258–69

heart disease, 56, 202, 271, 275, 276, 342, 346–47, 355

Heath, E. D., 22

Heide, F. J., 329

Heinzelmann, F., 243, 249

Hippocrates, 3, 6

Hirsh, T., 154–55

Hockey, R. V., 236

Hoffman, W., 241–42

Holle, R. H. O., 356

Howard, J., 340, 342, 345

Hoyt, M. F., 244

human resource programs, 323, 324, 340

Hunt, W. A., 366

hypertension, 214, 271, 273, 274, 278–79, 312

IBM, 38, 279–80

imagination, 204–5

implementation: and an action plan, 59–70; and budgets, 67–68; and communications, 32, 71–80; and computer networking, 94–105; and the corporate culture, 31, 40–43; and evaluation, 259, 267–68; and health education committees, 45–57; and health risk appraisals, 66–67; of health and safety training programs, 14, 22–25; and management, 68; and marketing, 32, 68–70, 81–92; and personal excellence programs, 200–1; in a phased approach, 117, 161, 287; and planning, 31–32, 59–70; of the Staywell program, 115–16, 287; and stress management programs, 172–80

incentives, 69, 122, 131, 313–14, 315, 365, 366–67

information, 97–99, 266, 325. *See also* Tel-Med program

injuries, 246

insurance, 118, 166, 170, 270–71, 274, 294, 295, 314, 341, 346, 358

interactionist approach, 238–39

interpersonal relations, 37

intervention: and creativity, 332–33, 334; and EAPs, 45–47; and smoking control, 360–61, 365–66

Iso-Ahola, S. E., 240, 241

Ivancevick, J. M., 173

Jackson, F. N., 356

Jacobson, Jeannette M., 110, 148–62

Janis, I. L., 244

Jarvis, D. C., 9

Jarvis, M. J., 357

Johns Hopkins University, 99–100

Johnson and Johnson, 38, 272, 277, 279

Jones, C. R., 109, 113–23, 296

Jose, WIlliam S. III, 214, 284–98

Kanter, Rosabeth Moss, 57

Kar, S., 22, 24

Kass, R. A., 245

Kaufmann, F., 357

Keil, J. M., 335

Kemper Insurance Company, 166

Kennecott Copper Company, 167

Kennedy, A. E., 61

Kennedy Institute for Handicapped Children, 99–100, 102

Kimberley-Clark, 167

Kirbridge, J., 357

Klarreich, Penny R., 3, 5–12

Klarreich, Samuel H., 31, 45–57, 111, 183–99

Kodak Research laboratories, 333

Kofodimis, Joan, 331

Koskela, A., 247

Kranzler, J., 175

Kristein, Marvin, 358

Lakein, A., 175

Leavitt, S. S., 159

legal aspects of smoking control, 358–60, 363, 368

legislation, 41, 385–86
Lewis, Deborah J., 109, 124–39
Lifegain Health Practices Indicator, 306
lifestyle: definition of, 316; diseases, 10, 11, 36
lifestyle change: and communications, 74–75; course in, 115; and culture/ corporate culture, 31, 35, 37–38, 305–6; and the environment, 341; evaluation of, 86–92; and fitness programs, 341; and the Health Plus program, 125, 128–39, 137; health risk appraisals, 311–12; and health and safety training programs, 26; and management, 376; and medical identification programs, 312; and motivation, 37, 309; and participation, 89–90; and personal responsibility for health, 307; and program objectives, 307–8; and self perception, 305–6; and smoking control, 308, 313; and the StayWell program, 118–19, 122. *See also* behavior modification
litigation, 152, 157
Live for Life program. *See* Johnson and Johnson
Lockheed Corporaton, 248
Loeb, L. A., 366
Lombardi, Vince, 201
London, M., 241
Luce, B. R., 356

McCormack, Kevin, 109–10, 140–47
McGehee, Lockie Jayne, 110–11, 172–82
McGill, C. M., 159
McGrath, J. E., 173
McKay, M., 175
MacKeigan, A. L., 109–10, 140–47
Madara, Ed, 97, 102
Magnusson, D., 237, 238
management: and accessibility to programs, 310, 311; and creativity, 329, 330, 332, 335; and EAPs, 166; and evaluation, 218–19; and fitness/ health promotion/wellness programs, 53, 65–66, 68, 82, 314–15, 348,

385–86; and health education committees, 50; and implementation of programs, 68; and lifestyle change, 376; and physical activity programs, 248; and smoking, 307; and stress management programs, 179–80; and weight management programs, 307, 313–14
Manville Corporation, 364
marketing: and the corporate culture, 40, 42; definition of, 82; and EAPs, 166–67; and the Health Plus program, 131–32; and implementation of programs, 32, 68–70, 81–92; and media, 242; and motvation, 69; and physical activity programs, 243–44; and planning, 81–92; and selecting health promotion programs, 381–82; and staff, 375; and the StayWell program, 285, 288; and the Tel-Med program, 141
Martindale, C., 329
Martin, J. E., 238
Martin, R. A., 159
Martin, T. W., 173
Massachusetts Mutual Life Insurance Company, 273
Mattel Corporation, 38
Matteson, M. T., 173
media, 78, 174–75, 242, 307, 311, 315
medical identification programs, 312
mental health counseling, 45–46, 278–79, 332
Meta Network (computer system), 98–99
methodology, 66, 67, 131, 155
Mikalachki, A., 340, 342, 345
Miller, G. H., 357
models of health promotion programs, 38
morale, 279, 314
Morgan, W. P., 235, 237, 245
motivaton: and back injury control programs, 158, 160; and burn-out programs, 195; and the corporate culture, 307; and fitness programs, 342; and the Health Plus program, 137–38; and incentives, 69; and lifestyle change, 37, 309; and

marketing, 69; and personal excellence programs, 203–4; and physical activity programs, 213, 239–51; and stress management programs, 173; and the Tel-Med program, 146
Mutual Aid Self-Help groups (MASH), 97

National Conference on Smoking and Health (1981), 363
National Institute for Occupational Safety and Health, 19, 356
National Interagency Council on Smoking and Health, 365
Navy Lifeline studies, 157
Neale, Bette, 110, 163–70
networking, 51, 62, 65, 94–102, 248–50. *See also* communications
New Jersey Institute of Technology, 103
New Jersey Self-Help Clearinghouse, 97
New York Institute of Technology, 100–1
Nordby, E. J., 158
norms. *See* culture
nutrition programs, 37, 38, 56, 77, 84, 120, 137, 271

obesity, 271, 275, 342. *See also* weight loss programs
objectives: communictions, 73, 75–76; and constructive medicine, 7; evaluation, 290; and fitness programs, 349; and the Health Plus program, 125; health risk behavior and program, 316; and health and safety training programs, 16–17, 24–25; and lifestyle change, 307–8; and planning, 65–66
Occupational Safety and Health Act (1970), 13, 14, 25, 263
O'Donnell, M. P., 119
Oja, P., 247
Oldridge, N. B., 241, 245
Olson, J. M., 243
Ontario Health Insurance Plan, 342
Ontario Ministry of Culture and Recreation, 243

Ontario Ministry of Tourism and Recreation, 234, 235, 246, 249
Opper, Susanna, 32–33, 94–105
organizational structure, 301, 321–22, 324, 333, 374
Oriol, F., 357
Orleans, C. T., 363, 365
Orlich, Terry D., 205, 242

Pacific Bell, 364
Pacific Northwest Bell, 364
Pareto's Law, 152
Parker, J. D., 248, 249
Parkinson, Rebecca S., 302, 355–72
Partenen, T., 247
Participate Systems, Inc., 98
participation: and back injury control programs, 160; and EAPs/fitness/health promotion programs, 166, 314, 347–48, 379; and evaluation, 227, 292–93, 296; and goals, 310; and the Health Plus program, 125; and health risk profiles, 275; and lifestyle change, 89–90; and marketing, 83–84, 86, 87–90, 92; and physical activity programs, 242–50; and rehabilitation programs, 169; and smoking control programs, 275, 362; and the StayWell program, 119; and weight management programs, 275
Participation Network, 242
Paul, Bill, 101–2
PC-Talk software, 95
Peepre, M., 245
Pejsach, Michael, 96, 103
Pelletier, K., 326
people orientation, 31, 35, 38–40, 41, 42, 167, 323, 324, 386
perfectionism, 194, 201–4
personal counseling programs, 115, 167
personal energy, 325–26, 327, 342
personal excellence, 111, 200–8
personal responsibility for health, 9, 35–36, 46, 131, 307
personnel counseling movement, 45
Peters, T. J., 334, 386

Pettitti, D. B., 357

physical activity programs, 213, 234–51. *See also* EAPs; fitness programs; health promotion programs; wellness programs

physical fitness programs. *See* fitness programs; physical activity programs

planning, 31–32, 59–70, 72, 81–92, 114–15, 128–31, 133–36, 266–68

PLATO system, 115–16, 293

Powell, Don R., 303, 378–84

preventive strategies: and back injury control programs, 149, 150–58, 160; and constructive medicine, 7; and the corporate culture, 36; definition of, 47; and EAPs/fitness programs, 46–48, 165, 339; and the Health Plus program, 125, 126; and personal responsibility for health, 46; and the StayWell program, 114

psychotherapy, 45–48

Pulvermacher, Gerald D., 111, 200–8

Pyle, R. L., 346–47

quit rate, 361–62, 366

Radford Ammunition Plant, 273

Rawson, Anne, 32, 71–80

Red Ryder software, 95

rehabilitation programs, 110, 164, 168–70

reinforcements, 19, 21, 238, 240–41, 365. *See also* rewards

reliability, 216–17, 219, 230, 263

research. *See* evaluation; *name of specific researcher*

results. *See* benefits

rewards, 137–38, 240–41, 315, 365. *See also* incentives; reinforcement

Rhodes, S. R., 345

Riddle, P. K., 243

risk profiles. *See* health risk appraisals/profiles

risk-taking, 328

Robbins, L. C., 114

role models, 332

Romsa, G., 241–42

Rosenfeld, R., 333

Rosenman, R., 175

Rotondo, Richard, 302, 373–77

Russell, M. A., 357

rust-out, 178–79

Salk, Jonas, 333

Sandler, D. P., 357

Santa-Barbara, Jack, 31, 35–43

satisfaction and physical activity programs, 244–45

Schunk, D. A., 238, 239–40

Schweitzer, S. O., 356

scope: of EAPs/fitness/health promotion/wellness programs, 166, 277, 307–9, 314–15, 379–80; of the Health Plus program, 125, 128; of health and safety training programs, 16–25; of physical activity programs, 245; of smoking control, 360–62; of the StayWell program, 288; of stress management programs, 173–76; of the Tel-Med program, 141–42, 144–46

Seamonds, B., 277

seat belts, 214, 273, 306–7

selection of a health promotion program, 303, 378–84

self appraisal and burn-out programs, 191–92, 194–95

self concept, 37, 39, 57, 206–8, 240–41, 305–6, 342

self-study programs, 115–16, 120–21, 122, 293

Selikoff, I. J., 357

Selye, H., 173

Servo, J., 333

sexual practices program, 37

Shephard, R. J., 346

Shipley, R. H., 363, 365

situationist approach, 237–39

sleep, 89

Smartcom software, 95

smoking: addiction, 361; costs of, 358; and health risks, 214, 270–71, 274, 312–13, 355–58, 368; prevalence of, 356; and stress, 274 smoking control: benefits of, 362–63, 365; and corporate policies, 359–60, 362–64; and cost-containment, 313; employees attitudes about, 363–64; and the environment, 356–57, 360, 367; future of, 367–68; growth of, 278–79, 280; legal aspects of, 358–60, 363, 368; and management, 307; overview of, 302, 355–72; and quit rates, 361–62, 366; strategies for, 362–67, 368

smoking control programs: and behavior modification, 365; costs of, 313; evaluation of, 213, 220–31, 272, 361; growth of, 365–66; and the Health Plus program, 125, 137; and incentives, 366–67; and intervention, 360–61; and lifestyle change, 36, 37, 89, 220–31, 308, 313; and participation, 245, 275, 362; scope of, 360–62; and the StayWell program, 119–20; and timing, 365–66

Snook, S. H., 151, 154

social class, 310–11

software, computer, 95, 105

Source Telecomputing Corporation, 103

Southern Pacific Transportation Company, 153

staff: and back injury control programs, 159; demand for, 26, 374; and EAPs, 48, 51, 166, 168–69; and evaluation, 376; and the Health Plus program, 128, 139; and health and safety training, 22–23, 24, 26; and marketing of programs, 84, 375–76; and physical activity programs, 247–48, 250; and planning of programs, 63–64; and rehabilitation programs, 169; training/professionalization of, 23, 26, 51, 302, 373–77, 382–83, 386

StayWell program, 38, 113–22, 214, 284–96

Steers, R. M., 345

Steiglitz, Edward, 6–7

Steiglitz, Herbert, 11

Stevens, H. Chandler, 98

Stewart, G. W., 247

stress: and creativity, 325–26, 328–29, 331; and fitness/physical activity programs, 248–49, 342; and health problems, 214, 271; and norms, 38; and risk-taking, 328; sources of, 328; and substance abuse, 331–32. See also back injury

stress management programs, 110–11, 172–82; absenteeism, 277; benefits, 273–74; and creativity, 332; EAP, 163–64, 168; evaluation of, 273–74; growth of, 278–79; and health education committee, 54–55; and health education programs, 37; overview of, 172–81; the Health Plus program, 137; and wellness, 314

success and burn-out, 183–97

surveillance, 240–41

Suta, B. E., 357

systems approach, 95, 131, 160–61

task groups, 150–51

technology. See computers

Teletype Corporation, 273

Tellep, Dan, 248

Tel-Med program, 109–10, 140–47

Tenneco Co., 309–10

Teraslinna, P. T., 247

Tessier, J. F., 357

themes, 77, 128–29, 200

The Source (non-profit venture), 96–97

Thompson, C. R., 357

timing, 221, 230, 242, 247, 331, 365–66

Tinsley, H. E., 245

Tobacco Institute, 363, 368

Toyota Motors, 333

trait approach, 237

Travis, John, 9, 10

Trichopoulos, D., 357

turn-offs, 64

type A behavior, 202

Union Carbide Corporation, 109, 124–39

unions, 62, 155, 166

United Airlines, 166

United Cerebral Palsy Association,

99–100
University of Michigan, 322, 323
University of Pennsylvania, 201–2
University of Western Ontario, 165

validity, 215–17, 219, 230
values, 39, 41, 185–87, 295, 334, 339
Veatch, William, 99–100
Veroff, J., 239
Vojtecky, Michael A., 3, 13–28, 213–14, 258–69

Wankel, L. M., 235, 238, 241, 242, 243, 244, 247
Wanzel, R. S., 242, 247, 249, 250
Ward, B., 333
Warner, K. E., 355
Waterman, R. H., 334, 386
weight loss, costs of, 313
weight management programs, 120, 275, 307, 313–14
Weis, William, 358
Wellman, B., 248
wellness: books about, 323; continuum, 9; definition of, 8, 164, 317; model, 48; movement, 8–10, 373; overview of, 311–16; and self concept, 37
wellness programs: and behavior modification, 311; benefits of, 71, 321, 322; and cost-containment, 321–24; cost of, 323; dynamic aspects of, 7, 8; future of, 323–24; and management, 314–15; and organiza-tional structure, 321–22, 324; scope of, 311, 314–15. *See also* EAPs; fitness programs; health promotion programs; physical activity programs
Western Behavioral Institute, 101
White, J. R., 357
Wigle, D. T., 357
Wilcox, A. J., 357
Wolff, H. G., 173
Woodbridge Technology Center (Scottsdale, Arizona), 333
worker education. *See* health promotion programs
workers compensation, 159, 161, 277

Xerox Corporation, 242

Yardley, John K., 213, 234–51
Young Men's Christian Association, 6

Zanna, M. P., 243
Zohar, D., 19–20

About the Contributors

Since coming to Control Data in 1979, **David R. Anderson** in the position of manager of information services, healthcare services, has designed and implemented evaluations of numerous corporate human resource programs. He has been involved in the StayWell evaluation since its inception. His current responsibilities are to direct the evaluation and cost analysis of StayWell, health care claims, and related health benefit and service programs. He also provides consulting expertise to organizations concerned with health care cost-containment issues and has addressed this topic at several national conferences.

Before joining Control Data, he was assistant professor of psychology at the University of Wisconsin in Stevens Point. He earned his Ph.D. in psychology from the University of South Dakota. Since earning his Ph.D., Anderson participated in an experimental program in business at New York University.

Thomas E. Backer, Ph.D., is assistant research professor, School of Medicine, University of California at Los Angeles. His major areas of interest are the behavioral and environmental correlates of creativity, organizational change, and use of mass media to solve human problems. He is also senior research scientist, Human Interaction Research Institute, Los Angeles; is on the faculty of the Department of Management at California State University, Northridge; and is a management consultant and psychologist in private practice. He is a fellow of the American Psychological Association and the American Institute of Stress; and chair, advisory board, Entertainment Industry Referral and Assistance Center. Author of more than 200 books and articles, Dr. Backer also is an award-winning writer-producer of films and television programs.

Emil Berkanovic is professor of public health and head, division of behavioral sciences and health education, School of Public Health, University of California, Los Angeles. His research and teaching activities center on the evaluation of health education programs and the study of sociocultural aspects of health and illness. He holds a bachelor's and master's degree from the University of California, Berkeley, and a Ph.D. in sociology from the University of California, Los Angeles.

Angelica T. Cantlon is the manager of health care cost management for Avon Products, Inc., New York. Previous experience includes a number of senior positions in the field of health promotion, such as manager of health promotion/health cost control for Southern New England Telephone, New Haven, Connecticut. She has taught at the School of Nursing, Fairfield University, Fairfield Connecticut. She is a member of a number of professional associations and is active as a member of a professional peer review committee, as a contributing editor to *Self* magazine, as a guest on TV and radio programs and as a co-founder of Health Promotion Action Association in Connecticut. She has written chapters for textbooks and articles for journals and has had her own manuals and books published.

She holds a B.S. degree from Marymount College, Tarrytown, New York, an M.S. degree from New York University, New York, and has completed additional study at Columbia University, New York.

Betty J. Carter is a professional health educator with a B.S. in nursing and an M.S. in community health education. Multifaceted worksite experience includes teaching and curriculum development, program planning, and community clinical practice. She is the author of numerous publications specifically concerned with positive health behaviors necessary to prevent cancer and cardiovascular disease. She has been instrumental in the planning, developing, and implementation of various school and community worksite health promotion programs.

Larry S. Chapman is president of Corporate Health Design. His occupational background over the last 15 years includes executive director of a regional ambulatory health care center; university instructor in health care planning, evaluation, economics, and human resources; senior consultant on health care administration, health promotion, wellness, health planning, and cost containment for the U.S. Public Health Service. He presently serves as the civilian national consultant for health promotion to the Surgeon General of the U.S. Air Force. Over the last five years, he has developed more than 120 health promotion programs for business and industry and has given more than 300 presentations and workshops. His firm provides corporate health management services to many private and public sector organizations in such areas as health cost management, design of health cost management plans, employee health-related training, and employee health-related communications.

He obtained a B.S. in environmental health from U.C.L.A., an M.T. in medical technology from St. Johns Hospital, and an M.P.H. in medical care organization from the University of Michigan.

Dr. Michael H. Cox is a native of Chicago. He completed undergraduate and graduate degrees in physical education (B.S.) and exercise physiology (M.X.) at Southern Illinois University. In the early 1970s he received a research fellowship from the University of Toronto and the Ontario Heart Foundation. As a doctoral student he directed the noninvasive hemodynamic laboratory at the Toronto Rehabilitation Centre under the direction of Dr. Terry Kavanagh. In 1977 he joined the faculty of medicine, department of preventive medicine and biostatistics at the University of Toronto as a research associate. During this period he coordinated the research for the now highly referenced "Canada Life Study." Dr. Cox has published several scientific and lay articles on the effects of employee fitness programs and has made more than 100 major presentations on this subject since 1978. Currently, he is the coordinator for Canada's largest fitness section at the University of Toronto. He also is cross-appointed as an assistant professor in the School of Physical and Health Education, the department of preventive medicine, and the School of Graduate Studies.

W. Dennis Derr is currently corporate wellness coordinator and associate director of employee counseling for Michigan Bell Telephone Company. Before joining Michigan Bell nine years ago, he was instrumental in creating employee assistance programs for Detroit area industry as the occupational program consultant for Macomb County. Dennis Derr is a very active member of the Association of Labor-Management Administrators and Consultants on Alcoholism (ALMACA) both in Detroit and in the national organization. Previous publications have appeared in *EAP Digest, The Almacan,* and *National Institute of Drug Abuse Monographs*. He is a frequent presenter at both regional and national professional conferences on EAPs and wellness. Dennis Derr holds a B.A. in psychology from The University of Michigan and an M.A. in counseling from Wayne State University in Detroit.

D. W. Edington is professor and director of the division of physical education at the University of Michigan. He also is director of the Fitness Research Center at the university and a research scientist in the School of Public Health. He received his B.S. (mathematics) and Ph.D. (physical education) degrees from Michigan State University. He was trained as a biochemist and completed postdoctoral work at The University of Toronto and taught at The University of Massachusetts before coming to Michigan in 1976.

Dr. Edington is the author and co-author of numerous articles and books, including *Biology of Physical Activity, Biological Awareness, Frontiers of Exercise Biology,* and *The One Minute Manager Gets Fit.* His work with the Health Risk Appraisal and Lifestyle Analysis Questionnaire is considered to be the model for corporate development plans in health and lifestyle promotion. His specific interests are in the use of health and lifestyle promotion activities as strategies for health care cost containment, productivity, and human resource development.

Dr. Edington has served as a health and lifestyle consultant or speaker for numerous organizations and through his leadership the Fitness Research Center consults, implements, evaluates, and conducts lifestyle promotion programs for several of those organizations.

Michael P. Eriksen is the director of preventive medicine and health education for Pacific Bell. He established the disease prevention and health promotion programs for the largest corporation in California. His previous positions included community health educator, department of health and mental hygiene, state of Maryland, and health education, University of Pennsylvania, School of Dental Medicine. He has served as chairman for a number of health promotion committees and is on the editorial boards of *Health Education Quarterly* and *Advances in Health Education and Promotion.* He has received numerous honors and awards from such organizations as American Cancer Society, California Division; Society for Public Health Education; and National Institute of Occupational Safety and Health. He has published articles in a wide variety of journals on a number of health-related topics and co-authored the first major text for health promotion. Also he has been invited to deliver presentations on health promotion across North America.

He obtained a B.A. from Johns Hopkins University and M.S. and doctor of science degrees from Johns Hopkins University, division of health education, School of Hygiene and Public Health.

Jonathan E. Fielding is a physician, consultant, and educator who is a nationally recognized expert in health care cost management, utilization control, and preventive medicine. In addition to his position with U.S. Corporate Health Management, he is professor in the UCLA Schools of Medicine and Public Health where he concentrates on the organization and evaluation of employer-sponsored health programs. Dr. Fielding holds graduate degrees in medicine (Harvard), business administration (Wharton), and public health (Harvard).

By both education and experience, Dr. Fielding is particularly qualified to work with employers concerned about their rising health benefit costs. He has worked with many employers and business coalitions on health care cost-control programs, health data systems and data analysis, health promotion and employee assistance programs, assessment of health maintenance organizations, and the development of preferred arrangements with hospitals and physicians. He is a consultant to the Washington Business Group on Health and other prominent companies.

In 1975, Dr. Fielding was appointed commissioner of public health for Massachusetts, the youngest person ever to assume such a post in the United States. While holding this position, Dr. Fielding was responsible for developing state policy for health care cost control and for initiating a statewide comprehensive disease prevention initiative. Before taking this position in Massachusetts, he was director of the division of peer review, Department of Health, Education, and Welfare, which established the national utilization review program to reduce unnecessary hospital utilization.

Dr. Fielding has given more than 300 presentations to employer groups on various aspects of health cost management and health improvement programs. He has also written more than 50 articles on various aspects of health program development, preventive medicine, and health care regulation. He recently completed *Corporate Health Management* (Addison-Wesley). Dr. Fielding is a member of the editorial advisory boards of *Business and Health* and *Employee Health and Fitness*.

Phyllis L. Fleming has a Ph.D. in sociology and an M.S. in foods and nutrition from The Pennsylvania State University. She has served on university faculties in public health and sociology. She has been an evaluator for the Minnesota heart program and Control Data Corporation's StayWell program and has assisted many corporations with the planning, development, implementation, and evaluation of wellness programs. In addition, as president of Fleming and Associates, she assists hospitals, health maintenance organizations, and other health care delivery organizations in strategic thinking, the development of marketing plans, market research, and analysis.

Jeannette M. Jacobson is an occupational health consultant, a principal in J&J Resources, Seattle, Washington, and has completed a B.S. in psychology, an M.S. in health education, and a graduate business administration program from the University of Washington. She has specialized in developing safety and health programs for business, government, and community organizations for more than ten years and has personal background and experience in general business management. Her expertise in back injury control has been gained through training and consultation for numerous public agencies and private organizations. She is author of the book and audiovisual, *You Bet Your Sweet Back,* developed for employee education and clinical use, and has written a comprehensive manual, *Hands-On Backs,* to facilitate development of a team approach to worksite back injury control.

C. R. Jones is currently director of internal StayWell programs at Control Data, Minneapolis, Minnesota. Mr. Jones has worked in personnel since 1962, with experience in staffing, compensation and benefits, employee relations, employee assistance programs, and employee wellness. He has a B.A. in business administration from Macalester College, St. Paul, Minnesota; an M.A. in industrial relations from the University of Minnesota, and has completed additional postgraduate work in counseling psychology.

William S. Jose II joined Control Data in 1981. He was a project manager in the PLATO education business before joining the StayWell program. His current responsibilities include managing the ongoing StayWell evaluation and planning corporate incentive strategies for health promotion. He also provides consulting expertise to clients, distributors of the StayWell program, and other organizations concerning health promotion and evaluation programs.

Before joining Control Data he was a postdoctoral scholar at the Hershey Medical Center of The Pennsylvania State University, where he taught practical applications of sociological and social psychological theory to medical students, and contributed as a family therapist to a multidisciplinary weight control clinic. Dr. Jose has also served on the faculty of the University of South Carolina as an assistant professor. He earned a Ph.D. in sociology from

Stanford University specializing in social psychology and small group processes.

Penny R. Klarreich is the employee assistance program coordinator for a major government corporation. She received her Honors B.A. degree at York University in Toronto and her M.S.W. degree at the University of Toronto.

Ms. Klarreich coordinated a lifestyle change program for the Canadian Mental Health Association/Scarborough Branch, and published *Project Cope: A Demonstration Program to Teach Interpersonal Coping Skills*. She was employed by the Canadian Mental Health Association/Peel Branch as a group home supervisor for ex-psychiatric adults.

Ms. Klarreich did graduate work at the Clarke Institute of Psychiatry in Toronto in several units which included rehabilitation services, general psychiatry and the forensic service.

Samuel H. Klarreich is employee assistance program director and co-chairman of the health education committee for Imperial Oil Limited, Toronto Regional Health Centre. Previously, he was chief psychologist for a major Toronto hospital for six years. He has advanced training in hypnosis, biofeedback, and a variety of psychotherapies including rational-emotive therapy. He was an instructor at the University of Toronto, School of Continuing Studies; the Ontario Society of Clinical Hypnosis; the Y.M.C.A. Counseling and Human Relations Center; and is presently a lecturer at the Institute for Rational-Emotive Therapy in New York. He has conducted more than 500 lectures and workshops on a variety of topics in health education and EAPs. He is a member of more than 15 professional associations and has received a number of professional awards including diplomate in the International Association of Professional Counseling and Psychotherapy, fellow in the American Orthopsychiatric Association, and inclusion in the International Directory of Distinguished Psychotherapists. Also, he was awarded inclusion in the *Who's Who of Frontier Science and Technology*. He has written a number of journal articles on a variety of health-related topics and recently co-edited *The Human Resources Management Handbook: Principles and Practice of Employee Assistance Programs* (Praeger).

He obtained a B.A. in experimental psychology, an M.A. in applied psychology-special education, and a Ph.D. in counseling/clinical psychology from the University of Toronto.

Deborah J. Lewis is the manager of HEALTH PLUS, the health promotion and fitness program of Union Carbide Corporation. She has held this position for six years and was responsible for designing and implementing the program.

A member of various professional associations, she has numerous publications and has delivered presentations to many organizations on the topic of linking lifestyle to health care cost containment. She has an undergraduate degree from Tufts University and holds a master's degree in physical education from New York University. Also she obtained certification as an exercise test technologist from the American College of Sports Medicine.

A. L. MacKeigan, M.H.A. (University of Ottawa), was appointed executive director of the Cape Breton Hospital in 1977. He was a consultant and coordinator of health care services for the Nova Scotia Health Services and Insurance Commission from 1974–1977. Since taking reins at the Cape Breton Hospital, he has been credited with changing a chronic care psychiatric hospital into one of the most progressive facilities in the region. Some of the programs developed under his leadership include Tel-Med, Psychiatric Children's Services, Day Hospital, and an Active Treatment Unit. He is responsible for establishing the Cape Breton Hospital's Charitable Foundation. Mr. MacKeigan is also a part-time faculty member in business administration at the University College of Cape Breton.

Kevin McCormack, M.M.T. (Southern Methodist University, Dallas, Texas), has been the director of music therapy at the Cape Breton Hospital since 1979. He was involved with the original proposal to develop Tel-Med in Cape Breton and has coordinated the program from the beginning. He started the first music therapy program at any health facility in the Atlantic region. He frequently speaks to groups about both Tel-Med and music therapy. Mr. McCormack is a former Fulbright scholar.

Lockie Jayne McGehee is assistant professor of business and psychology at Rutgers University. She is the EAP consultant for General Electric Credit Corporation in Stanford, Connecticut. She maintains a private practice both in New York City, and Westport, Connecticut. She is a prolific speaker and writer and provides stress management programs to Fortune 500 companies.

She obtained an M.S. from the University of Chicago and a Ph.D. from Duke University.

Bette Neale is currently employed by Human Affairs, Inc., as their marketing director for Canada. With a background in nursing, Bette has gained experience in developing and managing a rehabilitation program for a large company and also in developing an EAP product. Her particular area of expertise is cost containment and health promotion through such services as employee assistance programs, health risk appraisals, fitness, and rehabilitation.

Susanna Opper is a New York City telecommunications consultant who designs and implements communication systems for organizations. Exxon, Coca-Cola, Avon, and the American Institute of Certified Public Accountants (AICPA) are on her list of clients. In 1985 she co-sponsored the first national intersystem Electronic Networking Symposium and continues to be active in the Electronic Networking Association, which was an outgrowth of that meeting. Ms. Opper is an award-winning writer and speaker who has spent much of her career communicating about technology to nontechnical audiences. Before starting her own business in 1983, she was a communications specialist with Exxon. She holds an M.B.A. in management and marketing from New York University and is a Phi Beta Kappa graduate in philosophy from Brown University.

Rebecca S. Parkinson is the program manager of employee health promotion for AT&T. She has established AT&T as a national leader in health promotion. Previously, she held senior managerial positions with the University of Medicine and Dentistry of New Jersey, the Office of Consumer Health Education, and the Compensive Health Planning Council of Northern New Jersey. She has been a chairperson or task force leader to a number of health promotion committees and consulted widely to business and industry, universities, the naval department, American Cancer Society, and the American Occupational Medical Association. She has taught in the schools of public health at Boston University, the University of North Carolina, and Montclair State College. She is affiliated with a dozen professional associations and organizations. She has given major presentations nationwide on topics related to health promotion and health education and has published many articles. She is the co-author of the first major text for health promotion.

She obtained a B.A. from Drew University, Madison, New Jersey, and an M.S.P.H. from the University of North Carolina, School of Public Health.

Dr. **Don R. Powell** is presently the executive director of the American Institute for Preventive Medicine in Southfield, Michigan. He is considered one of North America's foremost authorities on the development, implementation, and marketing of smoking cessation, weight control, stress management, and health education programs to corporations, hospitals, and the U.S. government.

Dr. Powell has received numerous and prestigious awards for his work in health promotion. He has also appeared on hundreds of television and radio talk shows. Dr. Powell played a major role in the development of the risk reduction intervention for two nationwide heart attack prevention programs: The Multiple Risk Factor Intervention Trial sponsored by the National Heart, Lung, and Blood Institute and the U.S. Air Force H.E.A.R.T. project.

Dr. Powell has also been a pioneer in the use of the mass media to deliver health promotion information. He originated and was the commentator of "For Your Health" on Channel 4 in Detroit and is presently a regular health expert on Channel 7. He developed a made-for-television stop smoking series that was broadcast in several cities. He also writes a column on cigarette smoking called the "Tobacco Tattler" for *Primary Care and Cancer* and was a free-lance health writer for the Detroit *News,* Michigan's largest daily newspaper.

Dr. **Gerald D. Pulvermacher** has been a practicing clinical and consulting psychologist in Ottawa, Canada, since 1973. His clinical work has focused on the treatment of anxiety states, psychosomatic disorders, depression, and phobic disorders. In the corporate arena, his firm conducts training and consulting services as well as employee assistance programs. His organizational clients include numerous Fortune 500 companies. He is a lecturer in the family development program at Queen's University. His research studies have focused on the computer-based assessment of coronary-prone behavior patterns and the identification of individuals who are at high risk to drive while impaired.

He obtained an M.A. from the University of Windsor in 1970 and a Ph.D. in clinical psychology also from the University of Windsor in 1973.

Anne Rawson is a senior consultant with the Martland Group, specializing in employee communications. She has held senior positions with several large Canadian corporations in marketing and advertising and is a member of the Employee Assistance Program Association of Toronto, Canada.

Richard Rotondo, M.A., is currently director of health promotion services for Medical Care Affiliates/Health Promotion Affiliates in Boston, Massachusetts. His responsibilities include administering comprehensive health promotion programs on a contract basis with corporate clients. Mr. Rotondo has written a training manual and conducts training for health promotion managers. He has also written a *Health Risk Appraisal Results* booklet which has been well received by users of the Centers for Disease Control Health Risk Appraisal. Mr. Rotondo has spoken at health promotion workshops and conferences on a variety of health promotion issues. He was director of intervention for the Boston University Multiple Risk Factor Intervention Trial (MRFIT), a federally funded study that investigated the potential for preventing coronary heart disease through risk factor modification.

Jack Santa-Barbara, Ph.D., clinical psychology, is president of Corporate Health Consultants, Ltd., a Canadian firm specializing in the provision of mental health services to business and industry. Dr. Santa-Barbara is director of Corporate Health's employee assistance program services. He currently administers both counseling and health promotion programs for more than 35,000 employees and their families. He is also operating a drug and alcohol prevention program for the Canadian Armed Forces.

Dr. Santa-Barbara has been on the faculty of health sciences at both McMaster University and the University of Toronto, where he developed an extensive background in human services program development and evaluation. He was also the founding president of the Canadian Evaluation Society.

Dr. Santa-Barbara has published widely in the areas of psychotherapy research, family assessment, employee assistance programs, and mental health promotion in the workplace. Most recently, he contributed a chapter to *The Human Resource Management Handbook* (Praeger 1985).

Dr. Santa-Barbara's current interest is in applying social marketing techniques to mental health and lifestyle issues in the workplace.

Michael A. Vojtecky is assistant professor of public health at the University of California, Los Angeles. He is a member of the faculty of the division of behavioral sciences and health education and is associated with the University of California's Southern Occupational Health Center. His research, teaching, and service activities center on the design and conduct of worker health education programs. He holds a bachelor's degree in economics from The Pennsylvania State University, a master's degree in economics from The Pennsylvania State University, a master's degree in public health from the University of Pittsburgh, and a Ph.D. in health education from the University of Pittsburgh.

John K. Yardley was born in New Zealand and received a B.S. (psychology) and B.A. (education) from the University of Otago in Dunedin, New Zealand. He also received a Trained Teachers Certificate from the Department of Education, New Zealand. After teaching in New Zealand and Australia, he moved to Edmonton, Alberta, Canada, received an M.A. (recreation administration), and carried out research into motivation for physical activity with special emphasis on adherence. He is employed as a lecturer at Brock University, St. Catharines, Ontario, Canada, in the bachelor of recreation and leisure studies program. Ph.D. studies (psychology) are currently being undertaken at the State University of New York at Buffalo. Research interests center on lifestyle change and employee recreation fitness and assistance programing.